D1636832

About this book

The pressing need to [illegible] consensual sex among young people – an issue shrouded by denial, under-reporting and stigma – is self-evident. Despite the growing body of research regarding young people's sexual behaviours, the study of coercive sexual experiences has generally been overlooked by both researchers and national programmes. Available evidence has been scattered and unrepresentative and despite this evidence, non-consensual sex among young people is perceived to be a rare occurrence. This volume dispels any such misconception. It presents a disturbing picture of non-consensual sex among girls as well as boys, and among married as well as unmarried young women in a variety of settings. This volume documents, moreover, the expanse of non-consensual experiences that young people face – from unwanted touch to forced penetrative sex and gang rape. Although the focus is on young females, the volume also sheds light on the experience of young males as both victims and perpetrators.

This pioneering volume highlights key factors placing young people at risk, whilst outlining the significant distinctive health and social implications they face. *Sex Without Consent* also documents the unsupportive – and sometimes abusive or negligent – roles of families, teachers, health care providers and law enforcement agents, outlines promising efforts intended to prevent non-consensual sex or support survivors, and argues for profound changes in norms and values that tolerate or encourage non-consensual sex. The editors, based at the Population Council (New Delhi), the World Health Organization (Geneva), and Family Health International (Virginia) argue compellingly for a radical review and reform of existing programmes designed to prevent this kind of abuse and to support young survivors of sexual trauma in the developing world. Addressing the magnitude, determinants and consequences of sex without consent, this volume provides evidence-based directions for programming.

SHIREEN J. JEJEEBHOY, IQBAL SHAH
AND SHYAM THAPA | editors

Sex without consent

Young people in developing countries

Zed Books
LONDON | NEW YORK

Property of WLU
Social Work Library
DISCARD

Sex without consent: Young people in developing countries was first published by Zed Books Ltd, 7 Cynthia Street, London N1 9JF, UK and Room 400, 175 Fifth Avenue, New York, NY 10010, USA in 2005

www.zedbooks.co.uk

Editorial copyright © Shireen J. Jejeebhoy and the Population Council, Inc., Iqbal Shah and the World Health Organization, and Shyam Thapa and Family Health International, 2005, and individual chapters © individual contributors

The rights of the editor and contributors to be identified as the authors of this work have been asserted by them in accordance with the Copyright, Designs and Patents Act, 1988.

Cover designed by Andrew Corbett
Set in Arnhem and Futura Bold by Ewan Smith, London
Index: ed.emery@britishlibrary.net
Printed and bound in Malta by Gutenberg Press

Distributed in the USA exclusively by Palgrave Macmillan, a division of St Martin's Press, LLC, 175 Fifth Avenue, New York, NY 10010.

A catalogue record for this book is available from the British Library.
US CIP data are available from the Library of Congress.

All rights reserved

ISBN 1 84277 680 0 hb
ISBN 1 84277 681 9 pb

ISBN 978 1 84277 680 3 hb
ISBN 978 1 84277 681 0 pb

The publishers express grateful thanks to Family Health International/YouthNet Project, the Population Council and the World Health Organization/Department of Reproductive Health and Research for their generous support of this book.

Contents

Figures and tables

Figures

Tables

Preface

The need to assemble and synthesize what we know about non-consensual sex among young people in developing countries is evident. Despite the considerable interest in research and programmes relating to young people's sexual behaviours, non-consensual sex among them has been relatively overlooked in both research and programmes. In order better to understand the situation and needs of young people in this regard, a consultative meeting, co-organized by the Population Council (New Delhi, India), the Department of Reproductive Health and Research, World Health Organization (Geneva, Switzerland) and Family Health International/YouthNet Project (Arlington, Virginia), was held in September 2003 in New Delhi, India. The meeting brought together researchers, programme implementers, legal scholars and public health specialists, and provided an opportunity to assemble insights into and evidence on the topic from a variety of perspectives and a range of developing-country settings. This volume comprises a collection of peer-reviewed papers presented at this meeting.

Thus far, available evidence has been scattered and unrepresentative and has often given the impression that non-consensual sex among young people is a rare occurrence. This volume dispels any such misconception. Its chapters present a disturbing picture of non-consensual sex among girls as well as boys, and among married as well as unmarried young women, in a variety of settings. They document, moreover, the expanse of non-consensual experiences that young people face – from unwanted touch to forced penetrative sex through favours, deception, threats and physical force, to gang rape. They shed light on the experience of young males as both victims and perpetrators. And they highlight key factors placing young people at risk of experiencing non-consensual sex and the significant health and social implications for the lives of those who have had such an experience. And finally, they document the unsupportive – and sometimes perpetrative – roles of families, teachers, healthcare providers and law enforcement agents. Conclusions argue compellingly for a radical review of programmes to incorporate squarely the prevention, screening and treatment of non-consensual sex experienced by young people.

This multi-disciplinary effort would have been impossible without the insights, cooperation and support of many.

Saroj Pachauri (Regional Director, South and East Asia, Population Council), Paul Van Look (Director, Department of Reproductive Health and Research, World Health Organization) and Nancy Williamson (Family Health International/YouthNet Project) have been pivotal in this endeavour. They responded enthusiastically to the idea of organizing a consultative meeting on the topic and publishing a volume of peer-reviewed papers presented at this meeting. We owe them a special debt of gratitude for this and for their valuable guidance and support, both for the consultative meeting and for the preparation of this volume.

We are also grateful to a team of peer reviewers who provided valuable comments and suggestions that authors acknowledge improved the overall quality and rigour of the articles assembled here. Many colleagues and friends, all over the world, have given of their time peer-reviewing and discussing various chapters of this volume. Their insights and comments, incorporated in the text, have helped shape the focus of the book and have enriched the comprehensiveness of many chapters. We gratefully acknowledge the valuable comments and suggestions of Sarah Bott, Deborah Billings, John Cleland, Rebecca Cook, Bernard Dickens, Alex Ezeh, Philip Guest, Sarah Harbison, Rachel Jewkes, Nancy Luke, Poonam Muttreja, Edith Pantelides, Roberto Rivera, K. G. Santhya, Larry Severy, John Townsend and Ina Warriner.

Turning any collection of papers into a volume with twenty-three chapters and forty-two contributors is not a simple task and required attention from many. The assistance of Komal Saxena, Asha Matta and Nicky Sabatini-Fox in managing the administrative requirements attached to the production of this book is gratefully acknowledged. Komal Saxena not only ably managed the meeting at which these articles were first presented, but also ably coordinated the project, responding to concerns raised by editors, authors and management, and preparing many versions of the manuscript.

Deepika Ganju, our consulting editor, has been the backbone of the volume. As authors, we would like to record our appreciation of her rigorous technical review and substantive suggestions for modifications, her constructive comments and her painstaking attention to detail. Deepika's involvement in the project has certainly made the volume more readable and precise and we are hugely indebted to her for this. We are also indebted to Anna Hardman and to the publication team at Zed Books who so ably, constructively and efficiently guided and expedited the publication of the volume.

This project could not have happened without generous financial support from many. We gratefully acknowledge support from the MacArthur Foundation, the United Nations Population Fund, the Ford Foundation (Brazil and Indonesia), the Rockefeller Foundation (Thailand), the South and East Asia Regional Office of the World Health Organization and the US Agency for International Development (USAID), which contributed generously to making the meeting and this volume a reality. Our own organizations, the Population Council, the UNDP/UNFPA/WHO/World Bank Special Programme of Research, Development and Research Training in Human Reproduction (HRP), Department of Reproductive Health and Research, World Health Organization and Family Health International have also made significant contributions. We are particularly grateful to Sarah Harbison and Shanti Conly, USAID (Washington, DC), Poonam Muttreja and Dipa Nag Chowdhury, MacArthur Foundation, Meiwitta Buddhiharsana and Ondina Fachel Leal, Ford Foundation, and François Farah and Ena Singh, United Nations Population Fund, for their support, insights and recommendations.

We are grateful to the authors themselves for agreeing to take on this ambitious project, and for responding so amiably to a host of requests, from incorporating suggestions from peer reviewers on their own contributions to providing peer reviews of those of colleagues. We would like to record our appreciation to them for their contributions, their collegiality and their commitment to this project.

We would like to end by expressing, on behalf of all authors, our appreciation to our three organizations and many of the staff members of these organizations, who helped in small and big ways in making this volume possible.

We hope that the evidence and recommendations contained in this volume will raise awareness about the prevalence and consequences of non-consensual sex among young people in developing countries, highlight major programmatic challenges and, at the same time, inform the design and content of policy-relevant empirical research on non-consensual sexual experiences of young people in developing countries.

Shireen J. Jejeebhoy, Iqbal H. Shah, Shyam Thapa
March 2005

ONE | Introduction

1 | Non-consensual sexual experiences of young people in developing countries: an overview

SHIREEN J. JEJEEBHOY AND SARAH BOTT

Although researchers have paid increasing attention to risky *consensual* sex among young people in developing countries, less attention has been paid to *non-consensual* sexual experiences, and much reproductive health programming for young people assumes that sexual activity is voluntary (Mensch et al. 1998). Indeed, few interventions have been specifically designed to prevent the perpetration of non-consensual sex or protect young people from the physical and psychological risks of such experiences. At the same time, anecdotal evidence, crime data and findings from a number of small case studies present a disturbing picture of a broad range of non-consensual sexual experiences among significant numbers of young people, particularly girls and young women but also boys and young men. While experiences of non-consensual sex may occur at any age, the circumstances of young people's lives and the resources at their disposal are quite different from those of adults, requiring a special focus on their experiences and needs. In particular, young people may be less equipped than adults to avoid incidents of non-consensual sex and in reality may have fewer choices available to them when they do experience such incidents.

Moreover, the implications of non-consensual sexual experiences for young people's rights, their health and development and the risks they pose in the transition to adulthood are often severe and multi-faceted. Such experiences are traumatic for young victims and compromise their right to exercise informed choice. Non-consensual sexual experiences adversely affect subsequent behaviours and relationships and may lead, for example, to risky consequent consensual sex. They have, in addition, such mental health consequences as depression, anxiety and even thoughts of suicide; as well as physical health consequences, such as the risk of unintended pregnancy, unsafe abortion and sexually transmitted infections including HIV/AIDS. Indeed, growing evidence indicates that the perpetration of non-consensual sex against young people plays a significant role in the spread of the HIV/AIDS pandemic (see Krug et al. 2002; UNICEF/UNAIDS/WHO 2002).

The issue of non-consensual sexual experiences among young people in developing countries is clearly an important yet under-researched subject with considerable gender and public health implications (see, for example, National Research Council and Institute of Medicine 2005). While there is a fairly well-developed literature in the developed world, particularly North America, it is difficult to draw lessons from this literature for developing countries with wide differences in the sociocultural context, notably the gender and poverty scenarios. Indeed, the subject is of concern in multiple sectors, including for those working in the areas of violence, adolescent health and development, sexual and reproductive health and HIV/AIDS, as well as gender relations and human rights. In September 2003, the Population Council, India, in coordination with the UNDP/UNFPA/WHO/World Bank Special Programme of Research, Development and Research Training in Human Reproduction, Geneva, and the YouthNet Project (Family Health International, Washington, DC), held a consultative meeting in New Delhi that brought together leading researchers and programme implementers to deliberate on the situation and needs of young people largely in the age group ten to twenty-four with regard to non-consensual sex in a variety of developing countries.

This volume brings together the rich insights reported at this meeting. Chapters in this volume present evidence and perspectives on the non-consensual sexual experiences of young people in developing countries, synthesize a profile of the magnitude and correlates of such experiences, describe some promising avenues for prevention and programming, and draw lessons for the formulation of appropriate strategies and policies to address these issues. The volume adopts the World Health Organization definition of young people to encompass in general those aged ten to twenty-four. It includes the contributions of over thirty researchers currently working on this subject in different parts of the developing world. Articles address a broad spectrum of non-consensual sexual experiences: gang rape and rape; coerced sex through threats and deception; sex in exchange for gifts and money; and unwanted touch and molestation. Trafficking, forced prostitution and forced sex in situations of conflict are important examples of non-consensual sexual experiences among young people; we have opted to exclude them in this volume, however, in order to focus on those forms that are experienced more generally by young people in developing countries.

In this chapter, our aim is to provide an overview and synthesize what is known about the non-consensual sexual experiences of young people in developing countries. The chapter presents an extensive sweep of the available literature and complements this with the fresh insights and evidence presented in this volume. We begin by defining and operationalizing the concept of non-consensual sex and then explore the context, levels, correlates, outcomes and underlying risk factors of such experiences among young people as gleaned from the available evidence. We also draw lessons from the few available programmatic innovations for future directions.

Defining and operationalizing non-consensual sex

In recent years, researchers have defined and operationalized non-consensual sex, sexual violence and sexual coercion in diverse, heterogeneous and often ambiguous ways, making it difficult to produce comparable estimates of magnitude from different settings. These terms have often been used interchangeably, as the following definitions suggest, but in general, definitions acknowledge a continuum of behaviours, from threats and intimidation to physical force, and from verbal harassment to unwanted touch to rape. For example, the World Health Organization has defined sexual violence as 'any sexual act, attempt to obtain a sexual act, unwanted sexual comments or advances, or acts to traffic, or otherwise directed against a person's sexuality using coercion, by any person regardless of their relationship to the victim' (Krug et al. 2002: 149).

In their definition of sexual coercion, Heise, Moore and Toubia have outlined a range of coercive situations and underscore the absence of any choice available to the victim that does not involve severe physical or social consequences. Specifically, they define sexual coercion as follows:

> [the] act of forcing (or attempting to force) another individual through violence, threats, verbal insistence, deception, cultural expectations or economic circumstances to engage in sexual behaviour against her/his will. As such, it includes a wide range of behaviours from violent forcible rape to more contested areas that require young women to marry and sexually service men not of their choosing. The touchstone of coercion is an individual woman's lack of choice to pursue other options without severe social and physical consequence. (Heise et al. 1995: 8)

Some researchers have broadly operationalized non-consensual sex to include sex obtained through threats of abandonment or other pressure from peers or partners, and lack of choice without severe social consequences. As such, some researchers consider young men who report that they engaged in unwanted sex in response to pressure to prove their masculinity as having experienced non-consensual sex (see Ajuwon, this volume; Cáceres, this volume; Njue, Askew and Chege, this volume; Marston, this volume). In the literature, the terms sexual coercion, sexual violence and non-consensual sex are variously used by many authors, including those whose articles appear in this volume, in their discussions of young people's experiences.

Studies have also used different methods to measure the prevalence of non-consensual sex, and as mentioned earlier there is often ambiguity in definitions and interpretation. Most surveys that report on this subject ask a fairly general question, usually on the lines of 'Have you ever been forced to engage in sex?' Others have measured prevalence by asking questions concerning respondents' motives for engaging in sexual relations, and estimating the number who responded that the experience was 'forced'. Increasingly, research has begun to look at the circumstances of sexual initiation. Typically the question is posed as follows: 'Your first sexual experience, was it something that you wanted at that time, something that you agreed to but did not want, or something that you were forced to do against your will?'

Several significant limitations of these operational definitions have been noted. First, such definitions do not reflect the variety of non-consensual experiences that young people may face. For example, adolescents' narratives often suggest the experience of a continuum of force from male 'pleading' and 'persuading' to physical assault (Hulton et al. 2000).

Second, such definitions may not encompass the dynamic nature of young people's interpretations of non-consensual sexual experiences. For example, young people who submit under pressure to a partner's demands for sex as an expression of commitment may not respond in the affirmative to a general question on 'forced' sex. There is a tendency, for example, as observed in a case study in Mexico, to identify a sexual experience as non-consensual only if the perpetrator was someone with whom the respondent was not romantically involved; with boyfriends, irrespective of the apparent degree of pressure, adolescent girls did not report the experience as one of coercion (Marston, this volume). Likewise, in a facility-based study in South Africa, girls tended to associate the concept of rape only with the actions of strangers or groups of men rather than those of a peer or boyfriend (Jewkes et al. 2002; Wood and Jewkes 2001; Wood et al. 1996, 1998). Many women construe coercion as 'rape' only if the man behaves 'disrespectfully' afterwards (for example, does not sustain the relationship); as long as the subsequent relationship is perceived to be in the context of a loving partnership, prior situations in which a substantial degree of coercion was used are sometimes perceived as consensual (Jewkes, this volume; Wood 2003).

Third, young people engaging in transactional sexual relations may not respond in the affirmative to general questions enquiring about whether the respondent had ever engaged in sex in return for gifts or money (see, for example, Luke, this volume). As these questions do not specifically make a link between commodity exchange and sex, responses tend to be restricted to relationships that are clearly transactional (for example, those with a sex worker) and not others, such as perhaps some 'sugar daddy' relationships or relationships in which an exchange of gifts is perceived to entitle the male partner to sex; what is therefore required is a series of questions that cover a range of transfers within all non-marital partnerships (Luke, this volume).

Fourth, young males' definitions of non-consensual sex vary considerably depending on the sex of the perpetrator. For example, case studies in Kenya and Peru report that young males rarely considered sexual advances by women on men as coercive; in fact, such advances were regarded as harmless and potentially pleasant. If the perpetrator was male, however, the incident was more likely to be perceived as rape and the victim perceived to be at risk of losing his masculinity and becoming a homosexual (Cáceres, this volume; Njue, Askew and Chege, this volume).

Indeed, while there is a large body of research in the United States on views of 'dating violence' and sexual abuse among adolescents and child abuse survivors, few studies in developing countries have explored young people's own terminologies and definitions of non-consensual sexual relations. A rare qualitative study in Nigeria (Ajuwon, this volume; Ajuwon et al. 2001a) of young people's perceptions of non-consensual relations reports considerable diversity in responses, which highlights the ambiguities in the definitions mentioned above. In this study, young people drew up lists of coercive behaviours, which included the use of force (from threats to unwanted touch to rape) as well as actions that occurred before or after the sexual event and those that left the victim with little choice. For example, boys and young men listed actions that they recognized as an integral part of preparing for or plotting the coercive act, such as forcing girls to watch pornographic films or drugging them, while girls and young women focused on lack of choice, such as, for example, forced abortion, forced pregnancy and the non-use of condoms or contraception, as coercive behaviour. Despite these broad definitions, however, when asked to narrate and role-play coercive incidents, young people overwhelmingly depicted scenes of rape. Youths recognize, however, the power differentials manifested in many non-consensual experiences. For example, young people in case studies in Kenya describe situations at work, school or even within the family in which more powerful individuals abuse their authority and pressure or force the less powerful to engage in sexual relations, often to avoid harm (see for example, Njue, Askew and Chege, this volume).

Finally, we must acknowledge the great diversity that exists across developing countries in terms of the sociocultural context and legal framework within which adolescent partnerships occur more generally, which may influence the risk of non-consensual sex among young people in different ways. For example, there are differences in terms of the age at which young females and males marry, the extent to which society allows adolescent girls and boys to interact socially, and attitudes towards sexual activity and pregnancy among the unwed. In some settings, pregnancy precedes formal marriage among significant proportions of young women; in others, it rarely does. So also there is diversity in the autonomy, legal rights and social status of girls and young women compared to their male counterparts. In many settings women have fewer rights than men, and even within marriage they may have limited rights either as a matter of law or practice (see Human Rights Watch 2002b). For example, not all countries have legislation that gives women the right to refuse a forced marriage, recognizes (and penalizes) marital rape, or gives women the same rights to divorce as men (CRLP 2002). In some countries, marital rape may not be recognized as an offence if the woman is older than fifteen. In many settings rape in general is not recognized if penile penetration has not occurred (see, for example, Jaising, this volume).

In this overview, we adopt the over-arching term 'non-consensual sex'. While this term is roughly similar to the terms 'sexual violence' and 'sexual coercion' discussed in the above definitions, there are some subtle differences. Specifically

TABLE 1.1 Examples of contexts, perpetrators and forms of non-consensual sex as experienced by young people in developing countries

Context	Perpetrator	Form
Forced sex within marriage/formal union	Husband/formal partner	Physical force; threats and intimidation, including threats of physical violence, abandonment, withholding economic support
Forced penetrative pre- or extramarital sex (can include oral, anal or vaginal penetration)	Peer; partner; family member; figure of authority, including teacher, boss; acquaintance; stranger	Physical force; threats and intimidation; emotional manipulation/abuse; deception; blackmail; taunts about masculinity, fears of compromised masculinity
Attempted rape; unwanted touch or fondling/molestation; non-contact forms of abuse such as verbal harassment, forced viewing of pornography, flashing, etc.	Partner; peer; family member; figure of authority, including teacher, boss; acquaintance; stranger	Physical force; threats and intimidation; deception; blackmail
Exchange or transactional sex	Substantially older partners ('sugar daddy', 'aunty', 'sugar mummy'); peer	Material and non-material incentives, particularly in the context of extreme poverty
Trafficking, forced prostitution	Third party	Organized movement of people, usually women, between countries and within countries for sex work (sometimes promising economic opportunity) Physical force, threats and intimidation
Rape in conflict situations	Combatant	Physical force and threats of violence

we define non-consensual sex to encompass a range of behaviours including unwanted penetrative sex, attempted rape, unwanted touch, non-contact forms of abuse such as, for example, verbal harassment or forced viewing of pornography, as well as exchange or transactional sex. These acts may be experienced in many forms, for example through physical force as well as through threats, intimidation, emotional manipulation, deception, blackmail and material and non-material incentives. They may take place before or after marriage or in extramarital relations. Above all, our definition underscores the fundamental lack of realistic choices available to the victim to prevent or redress the situation without facing severe physical or social consequences. Thus, non-consensual sex embraces a broad range of experiences that may include physical violence, threats, intimidation or other pressures to engage in sex. It may or may not include penetrative sex. Our definition is applicable to the experiences of both young females and young males, and includes the behaviours identified by young people themselves. Table 1.1 presents the range of experiences encompassed in our definition of non-consensual sexual experiences among young people in developing countries. This classification is illustrative and these categories are not always mutually exclusive.

Data sources and limitations

Although there is a growing body of research on non-consensual sexual experiences among young people in developed countries (see NCIPC 2000a, 2000b, 2003; RAINN n.d.), few representative or large-scale studies on this issue have been carried out in developing countries. Evidence in this volume generally comes from three kinds of studies: school- or community-based surveys, facility-based surveys (typically among survivors of non-consensual sex who have sought healthcare) and qualitative studies.

The existing data have several limitations. First, non-consensual sex is a sensitive subject, which often remains undisclosed because of shame, blame, fear of additional violence or trauma and other factors (Krug et al. 2002). In many settings, the only information on non-consensual sex comes from police reports, which are notorious for underestimating even the most severe forms of such behaviours (Jewkes, this volume). In other settings, researchers have begun to investigate the prevalence and patterns of non-consensual sex among young people, but large, community-based, comparable surveys on the subject are rare. Finally, measuring the prevalence and patterns of non-consensual sex among young people presents a host of methodological and ethical challenges that few large-scale studies have been able to address.

Until recently, most evidence of non-consensual sexual experiences has come from small-scale, heterogeneous studies that use widely diverse definitions and methods, and whose findings are thus difficult to generalize or compare across settings. Often, samples have been drawn from special sub-groups such as school/college-based populations, apprentices and factory workers from selected work places, or girls and women attending health facilities for antenatal care or reproductive health problems. The age range of samples also varies considerably. Some studies have focused on young people aged ten to twenty-four, or a sub-set of these, while others have drawn from the retrospective responses of adult samples (see, for example, Gupta and Ailawadi, this volume). Many studies have focused on the more extreme forms of non-consensual sexual experiences, such as rape or forced sex, while other have explored experiences involving non-penetrative abuse, deception, pressure or exchange, as well as other forms of harassment.

The available evidence is, moreover, unevenly distributed. For example, most research has explored non-consensual sexual experiences among unmarried rather than married young people, and the experiences of girls rather than boys; while this focus reflects the greater vulnerability of girls to non-consensual sex, it also obscures the fact that significant minorities of young boys also experience various forms of non-consensual sex. In addition, data tend to come from a limited number of countries in each region – indeed, the largest number of studies from any one country is from South Africa – and may well distort the picture of non-consensual sexual experiences among youth more generally. There is moreover a dearth of research evidence on the nature and patterns of non-consensual sexual relations in the context of trafficking, forced prostitution and situations of conflict.

Only recently has there been an attempt to incorporate questions on the 'wantedness' of sexual initiation in large-scale studies of young people's sexual and reproductive health. For example, the Demographic and Health Survey (DHS) has incorporated questions on the circumstances of first sex; this issue has also been addressed in surveys on adolescent sexual and reproductive health in some settings and among women of reproductive age in others (INEC 2001). In addition, several Demographic and Health Surveys have incorporated modules on violence against women, which include questions about sexual violence by intimate partners and sometimes include questions about forced sex by any perpetrator. While these surveys are carried out among women of reproductive age, they generally include a substantial proportion of adolescent respondents, and a recent comparative analysis of nine surveys presented data on non-consensual sexual experiences by age (Kishor and Johnson 2004). Nevertheless, because this research has not primarily focused on either non-consensual sex or on adolescents and young people, it can give only a limited view of the situation, both in terms of the issues explored and the sample characteristics.

Another important potential source of information on non-consensual sex among adolescent girls and young women in developing countries is the World Health Organization multi-country study on women's health and domestic violence (García-Moreno et al. 2003). This study gathered data on physical and sexual violence by intimate partners in Bangladesh, Brazil, Chile, China, Ethiopia, Indonesia, Japan, Namibia, New Zealand, Peru, Samoa, Serbia, Tanzania and Thailand. Nearly one-third of the approximately one thousand respondents in each country were between the ages of fifteen and twenty-four, and the sample was not restricted by marital status. Again, however, this database has some limitations; for example, the primary focus of the research was violence by intimate partners rather than by any perpetrator; studies were limited to female respondents; and since the focus was not on youth, instruments did not contain the range of non-consensual situations to which young people are exposed and did not include insights into factors potentially underlying vulnerability to such experiences. Nevertheless, both the Demographic and Health Survey and the World Health Organization multi-country study represent a major step forward in making available comparable multi-country data on sexual violence against girls and young women by intimate partners.

A serious limitation of much existing data is the reliability of young people's responses on a subject as sensitive as non-consensual sex. Many young people do not disclose such experiences to anyone, much less to interviewers who may have limited time to build adequate rapport with respondents (Mulugeta et al. 1998; Guest, this volume). As mentioned earlier, stigma, shame and fear may all contribute to under-reporting, both by young females and young males. Moreover, in some settings young people may believe that violence, coercion and lack of consent are normal, and they may not, therefore, describe their experiences as 'forced' or non-consensual. On the other hand, some adolescent girls and young women may report consensual premarital encounters as unwanted because of gender double standards that condemn premarital sex. The effect of these influences on reported experiences of non-consensual sex may vary from culture to culture, and between young men and women, making comparisons difficult.

Given the sensitivity of the subject, research involves a host of methodological challenges. Researchers have only recently begun to document what methods appear to produce more and less reliable data, and consider ways of framing questions to elicit a range of behaviours that might not ordinarily be perceived as non-consensual. For example, the World Health Organization multi-country study framed questions to elicit such behaviours, and structured the questionnaire to encourage respondents to remember abuse in different contexts (Ellsberg, this volume). Other researchers have used computer-assisted self-interviewing techniques (ACASI) that offer young respondents complete confidentiality as a way to enhance the reliability of responses. In a study comparing responses on identical questions using face-to-face and computer-assisted self-interviewing techniques among youth in Kenya, reports of non-consensual sex increased dramatically among those responding in the self-interview arm of the study (Mensch et al. 2003). Similarly, a study comparing responses on self-administered questionnaires and computer-assisted self-interviewing techniques among students in Thailand found that reporting of non-consensual sex was significantly higher among girls in computer-assisted interviews compared to traditional self-administered questionnaires; however, no differences were observed for male respondents (Rumakom et al., this volume). Likewise, studies in Latin America and the Caribbean have noted that women reporting in self-administered questionnaires were considerably more likely to admit a non-consensual sexual experience than were those reporting in face-to-face interviews (Ellsberg, this volume). Despite the availability of these new approaches, many studies continue to have methodological flaws, and more work is needed to understand the best approaches for studying such a sensitive topic in developing countries (see Guest, this volume; Rumakom et al., this volume).

Finally, the ethical challenges of this type of research are formidable (see Townsend, this volume). Studies among younger adolescents must grapple with the issue of how to obtain informed consent from minors and how to handle requirements for parental consent in certain settings for a subject as sensitive as non-consensual sex. Moreover, researchers may identify young respondents experiencing or even perpetrating ongoing abuse, and some respondents may be in danger of additional violence perpetrated by partners, family members or persons in the community should it become known that they have disclosed their experiences to an interviewer. Researchers studying non-consensual sex may thus face difficult questions about how to respond to young people in distress, how to protect respondents' safety and how to handle the discovery of coercive behaviour. These issues can be further complicated in settings in which services for young and adult victims of non-consensual sex are inadequate, and law enforcement systems remain insensitive and ineffective.

The context of non-consensual sexual experiences

This section explores the context, magnitude and circumstances of non-consensual experiences among young people in developing countries. As mentioned earlier, much of this evidence comes from qualitative small-scale studies that cannot be generalized across the entire region, much less the whole developing world. Given the diversity noted above, there are large differences in young people's experiences from setting to setting. Nevertheless, the literature also points to many similarities and patterns, and we will try to draw out those findings that appear to reflect common themes and experiences.

Non-consensual penetrative sex among young women Studies reiterate that while non-consensual penetrative sex – that is, sex obtained through physical force, threats, deception or by drugging an unwilling victim – is experienced by young women (up to twenty-four years) in a host of settings, wide variations are observed in the proportions reporting such experiences over the course of their lifetime, ranging from under 5 per cent to over 20 per cent (see Figure 1.1).

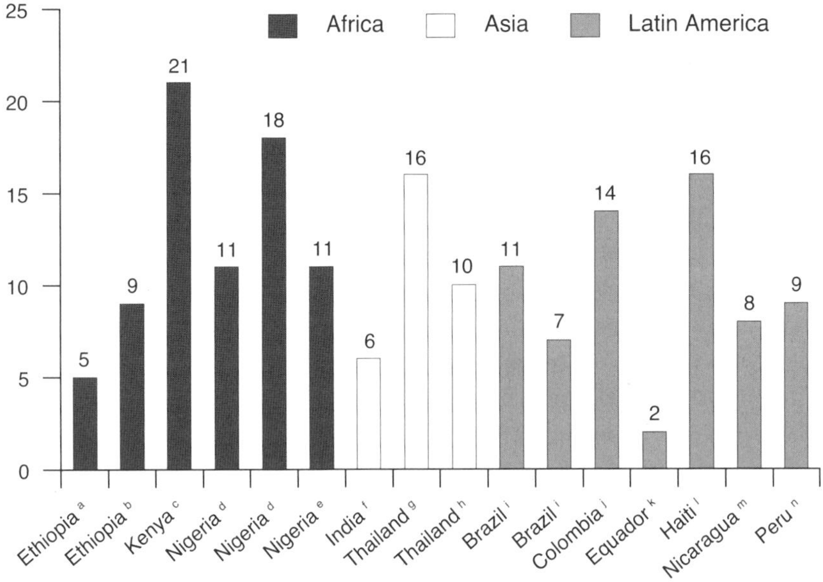

Note: Study site, type of sample and age of respondents reported above are listed by source: [a]Addis Ababa, Western Shoa; 14 high schools; ages 12–23 (Mulugeta et al. 1998) [b] Debark Town, north-west; students in Classes 9–11; ages 12–21 (Worku and Addisie 2002) [c] Njeri district, Central Province; population-based survey; ages 10–24 (Erulkar 2004) [d] Ibadan; students and apprentices (11% and 18% respectively); ages 15–19 (Ajuwon et al. 2001a) [e] Plateau State; secondary school; ages 12–21 (Slap et al. 2003) [f] Goa; school-going; age 16 (Patel and Andrew 2001) [g] Province approximately one hour from Bangkok; second-year college students; mean age 20 (Rumakom et al., this volume) [h] Bangkok and Nakornsawan Province; population-based survey; ages 15–24 (Im-em et al., this volume) [i] Pernambucco and São Paolo (11% and 7% respectively); population-based survey; ages 15–19 (Schraiber and d'Oliveira 2002) [j] Nationally representative (DHS); ages 15–19 (PROFAMILIA 2000) [k] Nationally representative (Reproductive Health Survey); ages 15–19 (CDC/CEPAR 1995) [l] Nationally representative (DHS); ages 15–19 (Cayemittes et al. 2001) [m] Nationally representative (DHS); ages 15–19 (Rosales et al. 1999) [n] Lima; young adults requesting issue of mandatory police certificates; ages 16–17 (Cáceres et al. 1997)

Figure 1.1 Magnitude of lifetime experience of non-consensual penetrative sex among young females aged less than twenty-five: findings from various surveys

Evidence from South Africa (not reported in Figure 1.1) suggests generally higher rates: while 3 per cent of women aged fifteen to nineteen reported that they had been raped before they were aged fifteen (Jewkes et al. 2002), in a case study in and around Cape Town, 72 and 60 per cent of sexually experienced currently pregnant and non-pregnant adolescents reported respectively having engaged in sex against their wishes and 11 and 9 per cent reported respectively that they had been raped (Jewkes et al. 2001).

Evidence on non-consensual first sex among girls and young women aged under twenty-five who have ever engaged in premarital sexual relations comes largely from Africa; studies suggest that by and large between one-tenth and one-quarter reported that their first premarital sex was non-consensual (Awusabo-Asare and Anarfi 1999; Buga et al. 1996; Chapko et al. 1999; Erulkar 2004; Jewkes et al. 2001; Koenig et al., this volume; Njue, Askew and Chege, this volume).

For large proportions, initiation occurred as a result of 'deception' or 'pressure' from a partner (for example, see Isarabhakdi 1995; Kim 1998; Njue, Askew and Chege, this volume; Youri 1994). In a case study from Dar es Salaam, Tanzania, young males described many scenarios through which they obtained sex from an unwilling female partner, including force, money and false declarations of love. As one male explained, 'There are many ways of force. Some use body power to rape, some use money' (Lary et al. 2004).

Findings reported above are intended to be suggestive. They come from a diverse set of studies and are clearly not comparable. Study populations differ, as do the inclusiveness of the definition of non-consensual sex (some studies focus, for example, only on rape), the ways in which the questions were framed and the approach adopted in implementing the study.

Findings from several studies in developing countries indicate that the earlier the sexual initiation among girls, the more likely the experience was to have been non-consensual (see, for example, Bohmer and Kirumira 1997; Heise et al. 1999). Also evident is that the circumstances surrounding non-consensual sex tend to vary by age. For example, a qualitative study of adolescent girls in Kenya (Balmer et al. 1997) found that while the youngest respondents (aged twelve to fourteen) reported random incidents in which, typically, they were waylaid on their way home and forced into sex, by age sixteen, girls reported more deliberately planned rapes by young men whose advances they were perceived to have rejected.

As discussed earlier, evidence suggests that young women are likely to under-report experiences of non-consensual sex. First, there is a reluctance to disclose sensitive and traumatic events to an interviewer. A case study of college-going young females in Thailand observed, for example, that reports of non-consensual sex increased from 9 per cent among those asked in a face-to-face interview to 16 per cent among those who responded in an anonymous computer-assisted self-administered questionnaire (Rumakom et al., this volume). Second, in reporting a non-consensual incident adolescents may well define what appears to be non-consensual as consensual, especially if within the context of a long-term relationship. For example, a qualitative study of low-income youth in Mexico observed that many girls described clearly non-consensual encounters as consensual; one respondent described an incident in which she reports she said 'No, no, I don't want to, and he didn't want to let go of me at that point' as a willing encounter; another describes a situation that occurred when she was fifteen, in which a twenty-eight-year-old male tricked her into sex as consensual (Marston, this volume).

Non-consensual penetrative sex within marriage or formal unions Evidence suggests that a substantial number of women experience non-consensual penetrative sex within marriage or formal unions and that this is often accompanied by physical violence. An analysis of over fifty population-based surveys found that approximately 10–50 per cent of adult women around the world reported having been physically assaulted by an intimate male partner (including their husbands) at some point in their lives, and one-third to one-half also reported sexual abuse (Heise et al. 1999). A chapter in this volume reviews nine studies from various settings in Latin America and the Caribbean, and notes that between 4 and 47 per cent of women aged fifteen to forty-nine had ever experienced intimate partner sexual violence at some time and between 3 and 23 per cent reported such an experience in the last twelve months (Ellsberg, this volume).

According to some studies, married adolescent girls appear to be at particular risk of non-consensual penetrative sex within marriage, compared to older women and sexually active unmarried women. For example, evidence from Nicaragua suggests that young ever-partnered women aged fifteen to nineteen were about as likely to report such an experience as were older women, despite the shorter duration of exposure; they were, moreover, more likely to report severe acts of violence. Likewise, younger women not only reported more recent incidents (in the last year) than older women but they also reported more severe acts of violence during this period (ibid.). Similarly, in Thailand, more ever-partnered (married or in formal unions) young women aged fifteen to twenty-four reported a sexually coercive experience in the twelve months preceding the survey than did older women (23 per cent compared to 16 per cent among women in general; Im-em, Kanchanachitra and Archvanitkul, this volume). A study in Nyeri, Kenya, among young people (aged ten to twenty-four) suggests that married young women may even be at higher risk of experiencing sexual coercion compared to their unmarried sexually active counterparts (Erulkar 2004).

A number of qualitative studies from South Asia have explored young women's experiences of forced sexual debut within marriage. These narratives uniformly describe pain, terror, force, tears and spousal indifference; and many women report submission to sex for fear of abandonment (Santhya and Jejeebhoy, this volume; see also George and Jaswal 1995; Khan et al. 1996). The narratives of young men in these settings corroborate a sense of male entitlement to force sex (see Sodhi and Verma 2003). In other settings, such as Zimbabwe and Brazil, researchers have documented how young girls similarly recalled that early sexual relations with their husbands were violent, terrifying and painful (Goldstein 1994; Hof and Richters 1999).

Some studies have explored older women's recollections about the extent to which experiences of non-consensual sex persisted over the course of married life. Women who experienced forced early sex by their partners reported a variety of experiences in later married life, including continued passive acceptance ('I allow him to have sex whenever he wants ... I am helpless'; Joshi et al. 2001), avoiding sexual relations (feigning menstruation, using children as buffers, threatening to scream or commit suicide), or building intimacy with their husbands over time ('then my fear went away ... there is some pleasure'; George 2002).

Non-consensual penetrative sex with boys and young men Evidence on the experience of boys and young men as victims of non-consensual penetrative sex is far more limited than what is available for girls and young women. What is available confirms that boys and young men do report forced sexual relations, though at much lower levels (usually less than 10 per cent) compared to young women (see Figure 1.2). Again, disparities in levels of reporting may reflect not only contextual differences but also differences in study populations, framing of questions and inclusiveness of definitions.

Several chapters in this volume provide evidence about young males as victims of non-consensual penetrative sex. A case study of young persons (aged sixteen to seventeen and nineteen to thirty) in Lima, Peru, observes that of the young men reporting a heterosexual experience, 11 per cent reported a non-consensual experience at first sex; among those reporting a homosexual experience, as many as 45 per cent reported non-consensual initiation (Cáceres, this volume). A case study of adolescents aged ten to nineteen in Kenya reports that 4 per cent of boys were forced into first sex and another 6 per cent were 'persuaded' against their will to engage in sex; similar percentages (4 per cent, 4 per cent) reported that last sex was forced or 'persuaded' (Njue, Askew and Chege, this volume).

These studies support findings reported elsewhere. For example, the study of young people aged ten to twenty-four in Nyeri, Kenya, found that 11 per cent of young sexually experienced males reported experiencing non-consensual sex: while 1 per cent reported rape and 1 per cent reported physical force, 6 per cent reported that they were 'deceived' or 'tricked' into sex (Erulkar 2004). Qualitative studies in other settings (India and South Africa, for example) have also found evidence of non-consensual sex among young males (see, for example, Barker 1993; Raffaelli et al. 1993; Ramakrishna et al. 2003; Sodhi and Verma 2003). As in the case of girls, evidence seems to suggest that the younger the age at first sex, the more likely that the experience would have been non-consensual (see, for example, Cáceres, this volume).

It is evident from these studies that the descriptions of non-consensual sex varied according to the sex of the perpetrator. Where the perpetrator was male, descriptions of the experience consistently reflected force and violence. In addition, respondents reported that victims of male perpetrators were stigmatized and perceived to be at risk of losing their masculinity: for example, in the case study in Peru young males labelled male victims as 'queers' (ibid.). Those reporting that the perpetrator was female, however, generally described the experience as 'pressure' and almost never in terms of violence; for example,

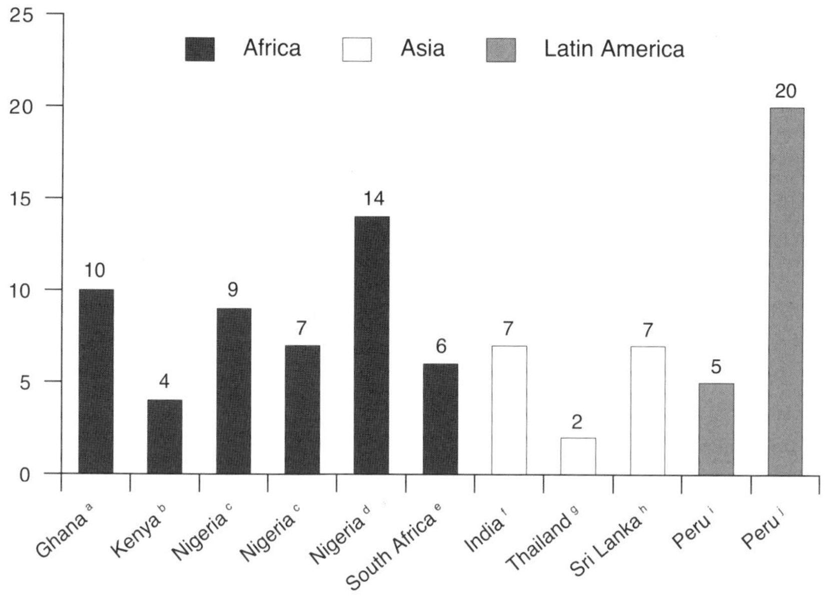

**Note*: In the case of Sri Lanka, the sample covers young males up to age 28. Study site, type and age of sample are listed by source: [a] 6 districts; community-based, reporting retrospectively; ages 15+ (Awusabo-Asare and Anarfi 1999) [b] Vihiga and Busia districts; Western Province; population-based; ages 10–19 (Njue et al., this volume) [c] Ibadan; students and apprentices (9% and 7% respectively); ages 15–19 (Ajuwon et al. 2001a) [d] Plateau State; secondary school, sexually experienced; ages 12–21 (Slap et al. 2003) [e] Transkei; school-going; Classes 5–7; sexually experienced; ages 14–18 (Buga et al. 1996) [f] Goa; school-going; age 16 (Patel and Andrew 2001) [g] Province approximately one hour from Bangkok; second-year college students; mean age 21 (Rumakom et al., this volume) [h] In and around Kandy; sexually experienced community youth and university students; ages 17–28; first sex was male-to-male intimacy by age 13 (Silva et al. 1997) [i] Lima, Cusco, Iquitos; secondary school students; ages 13–19 (Alarcon and Gonzales 1996) [j] Lima; young adults requesting issue of mandatory police certificates; ages 16–17 (Cáceres et al. 1997)

Figure 1.2 Magnitude of experience of non-consensual penetrative sex (lifetime or at initiation) among young males aged less than twenty-five:* findings from various surveys

they described peer pressure by male peers to engage in sex – often with sex workers – or pressure by male peers, female partners or older, married women to prove their masculinity and have sex (Ajuwon et al. 2001b; Cáceres, this volume; Marston, this volume). Similarly, young males in Mexico City reported that girls put pressure on them to have sex through such actions as undressing, touching and commenting on their penis, or taunting them for their lack of virility. Even so, in their narratives of such experiences, young males underscored their adherence to traditional norms of masculinity, for example by describing the significant decision-making role they played in these events (Marston, this volume).

Attempted rape, unwanted touch or fondling/molestation Few studies have explored non-penetrative non-consensual sexual experiences of young people, such as unwanted touch or fondling, molestation and attempted rape. Findings from small studies in different settings in Africa and South Asia demonstrate the extent to which focusing solely on forced sexual intercourse can obscure the full picture of non-consensual sexual experiences among young people (see, for example, Ajayi et al. 1997; Ajuwon, this volume; Patel and Andrew 2001; Stewart et al. 1996). Evidence suggests that compared to the numbers of victims of non-consensual penetrative sex, considerably larger proportions of male and female adolescents or youth have experienced unwanted sexual touch, verbal intimidation, harassment or threats, and 'unsuccessful' attempts at forced penetrative sex. In a case study from Nigeria, for example, while 15 per cent of young females and 8 per cent of young males reported a forced penetrative sexual experience, 27 per cent and 10 per cent, respectively, reported attempted rape, assault and other attempts at forcing sex; and 44 per cent and 23 per cent reported the experience of unwanted sexual touch (Ajuwon, this volume).

Gang rape Some researchers have documented incidents of gang rape in studies from diverse settings such as Cambodia (Wilkinson, Bearup and Soprach, this volume), Kenya (Balmer et al. 1997), Nigeria (Ajuwon, this volume), Peru (Cáceres, this volume) and South Africa (Jewkes, this volume).

Some 14–15 per cent of young males in case studies in the Eastern Cape (N = 1,374) and Winterveldt, north of Pretoria (N = 75), reported having participated in gang rape, known as 'streamlining' in South Africa. In both Nigeria and South Africa, gang rape was perceived as an expression of power, and a means of teaching a lesson to girls who consider themselves 'superior' or who have spurned a young man's advances (Ajuwon, this volume; Ajuwon et al. 2001a; Jewkes, this volume).

Bauk, as gang rape is known in Cambodia, is generally perpetrated on sex workers and other women perceived to be 'loose'. *Bauk* literally means 'plus' and denotes the additional 'value' derived for perpetrators. A case study in which waitresses and university students interviewed their peers found that students would arrange to have sex with a woman, often a mobile sex worker, and then force the woman to engage in sex with four to ten of their peers. *Bauk* was perceived as a group bonding exercise and was usually accompanied by verbal abuse, threats and violence against the victim. In this study, students reported engaging in *bauk* at least once a month. A survey of young people found that some 34 per cent of school-going males, 50 per cent of out-of-school males and 60 per cent of university students reported that they knew someone involved in *bauk*; among females, corresponding percentages were 19, 15 and 5. Indeed, the only concern that young people raised about *bauk* was the fear of acquiring an infection. Moreover, only 14 per cent of both females and males equated *bauk* with rape. According to the narratives of both young men and women in the Cambodian study, *bauk* was justified because it was perpetrated only on 'bad' girls and girls who were not 'virgins', and since the girls 'are not virgins, nobody would believe they were forced' (Wilkinson, Bearup and Soprach, this volume).

Exchange or transactional sex In recent years, a growing body of literature has explored 'exchange' or 'transactional' sex. Transactional sex is generally understood to involve an exchange of material goods in return for sex. One theme from the literature on exchange or transactional sex is the extent to which it straddles definitions of non-consensual sex, notably because the victim is perceived to lack any 'choice to pursue other options without severe social and physical consequences' (Heise et al. 1995). Using these criteria, transactional sex becomes non-consensual when it involves the exchange of sex for material gain, as a means of economic or social survival, or when acceptance of material goods or favours leads men to expect sex in return. At the same time, researchers acknowledge that young people who exchange sex for material gain often perceive the incident as consensual. This is a grey area which depends on both the exact definitions used and descriptions of the nature of the sexual relationship.

A central characteristic of relations of transactional sex is a power differential between the partners, whereby the more powerful partner has greater access to financial resources, is older or in a position of authority. In situations of extreme poverty, for example, where girls and young women lack sources of economic livelihood, they become vulnerable to the advances of men who are financially better off.

The most obvious form of exchange is the purchase of sex from commercial sex workers. Indeed, studies suggest that significant proportions of boys and young men visit sex workers in many developing countries (see, for example, Brown et al. 2001). A growing body of literature, however, primarily from sub-Saharan Africa, explores a broad variety of forms of exchange for sex, including more ambiguous transfers such as food, material necessities in situations of conflict, monetary support in situations of poverty and other kinds of material gifts, promotions in the workplace and other favours (Luke and Kurz 2002). Typically, the transfer of goods is from older men to girls or young women, though studies have documented many examples of boys and young men receiving material goods in exchange for sex, either as sex workers or under more ambiguous circumstances (see, for example, Bohmer and Kirumira 1997 for Uganda; Kim 1998 for Korea; Meekers and Calves 1997 for Cameroon).

Luke (this volume) reviews findings from ten Demographic and Health Surveys conducted in sub-Saharan Africa and notes that between 7 and 38 per cent of currently unmarried girls aged fifteen to nineteen had either given or received money, gifts or favours for sexual relations in the twelve months preceding the interview, compared to between 1 and 9 per cent among married girls aged fifteen to nineteen and between 2 and 50 per cent among unmarried boys aged fifteen to nineteen. In more in-depth studies in Ondo Town, Nigeria, and Kisumu, Kenya, however, almost three-quarters of the men engaged in a premarital or extramarital relationship reported making material transfers to their partner; moreover, the value of these transfers was significant (ibid.).

The economic motivation for a partnership is especially obvious in relationships with substantially older partners, frequently observed among adolescent girls (Balmer et al. 1997 for sub-Saharan Africa; Brown et al. 2001 for Kenya; Meekers and Calves 1997 for Cameroon; Fraser 2000 for Trinidad and Tobago; Kgosidintsi 1997 for Botswana). In some settings engaging in sexual relations with older partners has even become the *norm* among adolescent girls (Luke 2003; Luke and Kurz 2002). As noted in a case study from Dar es Salaam, Tanzania, girls described transactional relationships with substantially older partners, saying they 'wanted to get it over with as quickly as possible but he is my major source of income'; and that 'I love him because he gives me money' (Silberschmidt and Rausch 2001). One of the serious implications of this phenomenon is that it appears to contribute to the spread of the HIV/AIDS pandemic, as it may produce a vicious cycle whereby older men increasingly seek younger girls with whom to engage in sexual relations for fear of infection from older women (Human Rights Watch 2002a; Njue, Askew and Chege, this volume).

Not all transactional sex involves an age difference between partners, however. Material transactions may also characterize relationships in which both partners are young, ranging from paying for a girl's drinks and food to an explicit exchange of money for sexual favours (Bohmer and Kirumira 1997; Meekers and Calves 1997; Njue, Askew and Chege, this volume). The link between material transfers and sex is well recognized among youth, although with distinct gender disparities. Qualitative research in diverse settings suggests, for example, that young women often perceive gifts and money as a signal of their partner's affection, commitment and intent to engage in what they perceive as a loving relationship; men, in contrast, are more likely to perceive gifts and money as entitlement to sex (see, for example, Kaufman and Stavrou 2002; Nnko and Pool 1997; Nnko et al. 2001). Studies also suggest, however, that young women and men often associate material transfers with sexual leverage and the subsequent right to sex. In some settings, material gifts are even seen as a necessary precursor to a sexual relationship. As one young man from Uganda explained, 'If a girl realizes that you don't have money, she abandons you' (Bohmer and Kirumira 1997). Indeed, lack of resources is perceived as a major impediment to sex, and young men explained that in some settings rape is perceived as one option for those who cannot afford to make material transfers (UNAIDS 1999). In some cases young people also spoke of the 'detoothing' of boys, which involved the deliberate acceptance of gifts or money by girls who then evaded the sexual payback (Bohmer and Kirumira 1997).

Perpetrators of non-consensual sex

Most of the literature on the circumstances of non-consensual sex among young people is based on the reports of young female and, less frequently, male victims of sexual coercion. In a few cases, studies have explored the perspectives of perpetrators. Data from the perspectives of both female and male victims can be difficult to interpret, however, as young people are less likely to report forced encounters perpetrated by persons with whom they are close to than others (Jewkes, this volume). Even so, what is clear is that, contrary to popular belief, strangers represent no more than a minority of all reported perpetrators. Incidents of non-consensual sex are more likely to occur in familiar settings (such as the neighbourhood, home or school), and in the course of routine activities (see, for example, Ajuwon et al. 2001a; 2001b; Anonymous 2000; Brown et al. 2001; Gupta and Ailawadi, this volume; Patel and Andrew 2001, this volume; Stewart et al. 1996).

Peers and intimate partners Many studies, including those in this volume, concur that even among unmarried young people, peers and intimate partners are among the leading perpetrators of non-consensual sex. For example, a pilot study of 150 female volunteers participating in an HIV prevention trial in the Eastern Cape province of South Africa found that 15 per cent reported having been sexually coerced by a boyfriend and 12 per cent by an acquaintance or someone with whom the victim did not perceive an intimate relationship (Jewkes, this volume). In a small study in Lima, Peru, 38 per cent of young females who reported a steady partner at first sex indicated that initiation was non-consensual (Cáceres, this volume).

A case study of youth in two districts of Western Province, Kenya, reports that among young women whose first sex occurred with a boyfriend or fiancé, 19 and 12 per cent respectively reported being persuaded or forced; these proportions increased to 27 and 14 per cent, respectively, among those whose first sex occurred with a friend or acquaintance; in contrast, under 7 per cent of young males reported any of these experiences (Njue, Askew and Chege, this volume). In a second study in Nyeri province, Kenya, some 51 per cent of girls and young women aged ten to twenty-four who disclosed the experience of non-consensual sex reported that the perpetrator was a boyfriend, while 28 per cent reported that it was the husband and another 22 per cent reported that it was a friend, neighbour or classmate (Erulkar 2004). In a case study in India, among unmarried school-going adolescents, the most common perpetrators of non-consensual sex reported by both female and male victims were older students or friends (Patel and Andrew 2001).

In a number of studies among young males, significant proportions reported experiencing a non-consensual experience perpetrated by a girlfriend or female peer. For example, in the case study in Peru, 13 per cent of young males reported being coerced by a steady female partner (Cáceres, this volume). As mentioned earlier, in the case study in Mexico too, young men reported being persuaded, taunted or pressured into having sex by a girl (Marston, this volume). In a study from Kenya (Nyeri province), twenty-three of the thirty-seven males who reported being victims of non-consensual sex declared that the perpetrator was a girlfriend and thirteen said that the perpetrator was a classmate, neighbour or friend (Erulkar 2004). As discussed earlier, however, young males who reported non-consensual heterosexual sex tended to perceive the incident casually or to say that they were unaffected by it, in contrast to those young men who reported coercion by male perpetrators (see, for example, Cáceres, this volume; Marston, this volume).

Studies that have directly investigated reports of young males as perpetrators of non-consensual sex are rare. In one such study in Peru, a large proportion of unmarried young men confirmed that they had coerced their partners into sex (Cáceres et al. 1997). Likewise, a study in Kenya reports that some 21 per cent of sexually experienced unmarried young males aged ten to nineteen had at some time 'persuaded' or forced a girl to engage in sex (Njue, Askew and Chege, this volume).

Studies reporting on the perspectives of husbands as perpetrators of non-consensual sexual relations are also rare. Three such studies, located in India and Kenya, conclude that significant proportions of young men admitted perpetrating forced sex on their wives. In one study in India, one-third of husbands aged thirty or younger compared to one-quarter of older husbands reported having forced sex on their wives at some point in their married lives (Martin et al. 1999). In a second study, also in India, two-thirds of husbands aged fifteen to twenty-four, compared to two-fifths of older husbands, reported perpetrating violence on their wives in the twelve months preceding the interview (Duvvury et al. 2002). A third study of young people in Nyeri, Kenya, reports that among young married women who were forced to engage in sex, two-thirds (67 per cent) named the husband as a perpetrator (Erulkar 2004).

Authority figures Studies of young people and adults recalling their early sexual experiences suggest that sexual abuse occurring in childhood and adolescence is typically perpetrated by those who enjoy positions of power and authority, including religious leaders, employers and teachers (Ajuwon et al. 2001b for Nigeria; Ganatra and Hirve 2002 for India; Human Rights Watch 2002a for Zambia; Kwon Tai-Hwan et al. 1994 for South Korea; Mirsky 2003 global; Silva et al. 1997 for Sri Lanka). Studies suggest that younger adolescents are more likely to have experienced incidents of non-consensual sex perpetrated by an authority figure (Ajuwon et al. 2001b; Balmer et al. 1997; Jewkes et al. 2002).

In the education sector, there is growing evidence from sub-Saharan Africa and other selected settings that experiences of non-consensual sex, including sexual violence and harassment, within schools are widespread. In many settings, teachers frequently demand sex from students in return for grades, or simply use their power to force sex on students (Ajayi et al. 1997; Mirsky, this volume). For many young women, the most common place where incidents of non-consensual sex are experienced is in school settings (Krug et al. 2002). In the South African DHS, for example, one-third of women who disclosed having been raped by the time they were fifteen reported that the perpetrator was a school teacher (Jewkes et al. 2002). In a study of young people in Nyeri, Kenya, 5 per cent of females reporting non-consensual sex named a teacher as the perpetrator; in contrast, not a single young male reporting a non-consensual experience did so (Erulkar 2004). In another study, girls report being told that they would fail if they did not have sex with their teacher (see, for example, Jewkes, this volume).

Many studies have also documented incidents of non-consensual sex perpetrated against young women in the work place. In South Africa, for example, a three-province study found that 3 per cent of female employment seekers and 2 per cent of employed young women reported having to engage in sex with an employer in order to secure employment (ibid.).

Family members Data on the perpetration of non-consensual sex by family members are limited, given the extreme sensitivity of the topic, the hidden nature of the crime and the young age of most victims. Nevertheless, studies have increasingly documented family members as perpetrators of non-consensual sex in developing countries, especially among younger adolescent girls. These studies reveal that the proportion of young female victims of sexual abuse reporting a family member as the perpetrator appears to vary widely by setting and age of the victim, from under 10 per cent to almost half of all those who had ever experienced non-consensual sex (Singh et al. 1996; Fraser 2000; Hulton et al. 2000; Jewkes et al. 2002; Patel and Andrew 2001). In a multi-site study in India, 36 per cent of 561 young and adult women who reported non-consensual sexual experiences in childhood or adolescence disclosed that the perpetrator was a family member, from fathers and brothers to, more typically, uncles and cousins (Gupta and Ailawadi, this volume).

Case studies from other settings, including Latin America and sub-Saharan Africa, corroborate these conclusions. For example, a case study of literate, urban men and women aged twenty-five to forty-four in Nicaragua found that 33 per cent of males and 66 per cent of females who reported sexual abuse in adolescence declared that the perpetrator was a family member (Ellsberg, this volume). Similarly, one-quarter of women in the 1998 South Africa Demographic and Health Survey who acknowledged being raped by age fifteen reported that the perpetrator was a family member (Jewkes, this volume; Jewkes et al. 2002). Likewise, a case study of adolescents in Western Province, Kenya, found that 5 per cent of adolescent girls and 17 per cent of adolescent boys who reported non-consensual sex named a relative as the perpetrator. It is noteworthy that in their narratives young males described heterosexual incestuous relationships as a means to learn about sex, even if 'forced'; as one young man explained, 'if you want to learn to cycle ... you train yourself in the home, meaning that if you want a lady for friendship you begin with your relative' (Njue, Askew and Chege, this volume).

Outcomes of non-consensual sex

The experience of non-consensual sex in childhood and adolescence has adverse short- and long-term health, behavioural, emotional, psychological and social consequences (see Heise et al. 1999).

Serious health consequences of non-consensual sex include unwanted pregnancy and consequent abortion, and gynaecological and sexually transmitted infections (STIs), including HIV/AIDS (Cáceres, this volume; Cáceres et al. 1997; Gupta and Ailawadi, this volume; Hof and Richters 1999; Koenig et al., this volume; Mpangile et al. 1999; Mulugeta et al. 1998; Silberschmidt and Rausch 2001; Worku and Addisie 2002; Zierler et al. 1991; see Erulkar 2004 for the consequences of unsafe abortion). A recent study of women in Rakai, Uganda, provides evidence of the extent to which non-consensual experiences compromise young people's reproductive health (Koenig et al., this volume). This study found that a significantly higher percentage of women whose first intercourse was coercive reported having ever being pregnant; of those who had ever experienced pregnancy, a significantly higher percentage of those whose first intercourse was non-consensual indicated that they had experienced at least one unintended (either mistimed or unwanted) pregnancy. The study also found a systematic and significant difference in the likelihood of reporting one or more genital tract symptoms, with rates more than twice as high among women reporting non-consensual first intercourse than among other women, both married and unmarried. Likewise, a study of school-going adolescents in Goa, India, reports that boys and girls who reported a non-consensual penetrative sexual experience were significantly more likely than others to experience one particular symptom of infection, that is, discharge (odds ratios: 3.32 for boys, 2.81 for girls) (Patel and Andrew, this volume).

Non-consensual sexual experiences in childhood and adolescence are also associated with subsequent risky behaviours, such as unprotected sex, multiple partners, early consensual sex, drug and alcohol abuse and, in extreme cases, prostitution (Boyer and Fine 1992; Ellsberg, this volume; Gupta and Ailawadi, this volume; Handwerker 1993; Heise et al. 1995; Somse et al. 1993; Stewart et al. 1996). Relationships involving material transfers have also been associated with a higher likelihood of unsafe sexual behaviour (Luke, this volume). Several studies note a close association between non-consensual first intercourse and early consensual sexual activity in settings as diverse as Barbados (Handwerker

1993), India (Gupta and Ailawadi, this volume; Patel and Andrew 2001), Nicaragua (Ellsberg, this volume) and Soweto, South Africa (Jewkes, this volume). Evidence from several settings suggests, moreover, that women who experienced attempted or completed rape were likely to have a larger number of subsequent sexual partners (Ellsberg, this volume for Nicaragua; Koenig et al., this volume for Uganda; Erulkar 2004 for Kenya). Finally, research among women in Rakai, Uganda, supports various findings that unmarried women whose first intercourse was coercive were significantly less likely to have used a condom consistently, or at last intercourse, or used a condom consistently with their current partner during the preceding six months (Koenig et al., this volume).

Moreover, early non-consensual sexual experiences appear to be associated with the risk of experiencing or perpetrating non-consensual sex subsequently in intimate partnerships (for example, see Stewart et al. 1996). A study in Thailand reports a significant association between early non-consensual penetrative sex and subsequent experience of non-consensual penetrative sexual experiences within intimate partnerships; likewise, women who reported physical violence by their partner were significantly more likely than others to also report sexual violence (Im-em, Kanchanachitra and Archvanitkul, this volume). A case study of school-going adolescents in Goa, India, found that adolescents who had experienced non-consensual penetrative sex were more likely than their peers to have experienced other forms of violence and abuse in the previous twelve months (Patel and Andrew 2001). A case study in Kenya found that young males aged ten to nineteen who reported being victims of non-consensual first sex were significantly more likely than others to admit that they had ever perpetrated non-consensual sex in subsequent sexual encounters (Njue, Askew and Chege, this volume).

Research has also documented the emotional and mental health outcomes of early experiences of non-consensual sex. Victims of such incidents are more likely than other young people to report feelings of worthlessness and powerlessness and to experience inability to distinguish sexual from affectionate behaviour; difficulty in maintaining appropriate personal boundaries; inability to refuse unwanted sexual advances; difficulty trusting people; and feelings of shame, self-blame, fear and guilt about sex. They are also more likely to experience emotional consequences such as post-traumatic stress disorder, depression and suicidal thoughts (Gupta and Ailawadi, this volume; Heise et al. 1995; Luster and Small 1997; Mulugeta et al. 1998; Stewart et al. 1996; Stock et al. 1997; United Nations ESCAP et al. 2001; Worku and Addisie 2002). School-going adolescent girls and boys in Goa, India, for example, who reported experiences of non-consensual sex, were significantly more likely than others to experience depression or anxiety and to feel that life was not worth living; in addition, adolescent boys were significantly more likely than others to report alcohol consumption (Patel and Andrew, this volume).

One chapter in this volume presents a case study of women from India abused in childhood or adolescence, and explores the mental health consequences of such experiences at length. Women reported a sense of betrayal by not only their abusers but also their parents or other close family members for denying them protection. Some articulated difficulty in forming trusting relationships, others reported indiscriminate trust in others. Women described feelings of isolation and confusion. Several women recalled seeking love and care on the one hand and thwarting or rejecting other people's attempts to develop relationships with them on the other. Many believed that they had no rights over their own body and reported compulsive behaviours, substance abuse and eating disorders as well as self-inflicted injuries and suicide attempts (Gupta and Ailawadi, this volume).

The social consequences of non-consensual sexual experiences can also be enormous, ranging from poor educational achievement to withdrawal from school, inability to build adult partnerships to poor marriage prospects, as well as rejection by family or friends, who react negatively to disclosure of the incident (Mulugeta et al. 1998; Patel and Andrew 2001; Worku and Addisie 2002). In cases where non-consensual sex results in premarital pregnancy, similar social consequences may occur (Wood and Jewkes 2001; Wood et al. 1998). The context of schooling itself can be dangerous, and in several settings fear of sexual harassment and rape, often on the way to and from school, is a reason that parents cite for withdrawing adolescent daughters from school (Mensch and Lloyd 1998; Sathar and Lloyd 1993). Moreover, in extreme cases, particularly in traditional societies of South Asia and the Middle East, disclosing experiences of non-consensual sex may put young women at risk of being killed by their own families in so-called 'honour killings' (see, for example, Graitcer and Youssef 1993; Human Rights Watch 1999; Palestinian Human Rights Monitor 2002; Shalhoub-Kevorkian 2000).

Underlying risk factors

Understanding the risk factors of non-consensual sex is complicated by the multiple forms and contexts in which it occurs, as well as the different factors associated with experiences of victimization and perpetration (Krug et al. 2002). Risk factors also exist at different levels, from the individual to the community and societal levels (see, for example, Flisher, this volume).

For example, evidence suggests that a number of risk factors at the individual level may increase the vulnerability of young people to non-consensual sex, including age, alcohol and drug consumption, previous experiences of non-consensual sex and multiple partner relations. Some studies suggest, moreover, that young people who experience non-consensual sex are more likely than others to report migrant status, residence away from parents and in some settings, low educational attainment (see, for example, Bohmer and Kirumira 1997; Cheng Yimin et al. 2001; Krug et al. 2002). Studies also suggest that among young males, important correlates of the perpetration of non-consensual sex are, similarly, alcohol and drug use (Wilkinson, Bearup and Soprach, this volume), non-attendance at school and living with only one parent (Njue, Askew and Chege, this volume).

Structural and environmental factors that may put young people at greater risk of experiencing non-consensual sex include poverty, patriarchal norms that justify sexual violence and encourage gender double standards and inequity, traditions that encourage early marriage, and a general lack of awareness of women's rights. Other risk factors include inadequate education and health systems and lack of communication about sexual health matters within families and communities. Ineffective laws and policies, and the poor institutional response of health services, the legal system and social service agencies compound the risk of experiencing non-consensual sex. An important and pervasive factor contributing to the persistence of non-consensual sex is the failure on the part of legal institutions to recognize the problem of non-consensual sex among young people and punish the perpetrator rather than the victim. Some of these structural and environmental factors are discussed in the following sections.

Gender norms that condone male violence As suggested above, gender double standards appear to be a consistent factor underlying non-consensual sexual experiences of young people. Violence against women – both physical and sexual – appears to be more common in settings where gender roles are rigidly enforced and where masculinity is associated with toughness and dominance and femininity with submissiveness (see, for example, Heise et al. 1999; UNAIDS 1999). Norms that condone premarital and extramarital sexual relations for men but stigmatize sexually active women often make it difficult for young women to communicate about, seek help for or avoid non-consensual sexual advances. Closely tied with these double standards is a lack of awareness among youth about their rights.

Unequal gender norms and power imbalances often perpetuate a sense of entitlement among young men to force sex and a widespread perception that men's sexual needs are beyond their control and require immediate satisfaction. In many settings, little social pressure is applied on men and boys to discourage them from perpetuating rape; in South Africa, for example, the use of a certain amount of violence and even rape by young men is regarded as part of 'normal' boyish behaviour and often tolerated or ignored by adults (Wood and Jewkes 2001). A study from Kenya found that in Luhya culture, force was tolerated in the belief that males were inherently predatory; not surprisingly, young males who admitted perpetrating forced sex were significantly more likely than others to justify male violence against female partners (Njue, Askew and Chege, this volume). In a case study in Nigeria, about half of all young female and male respondents agreed that 'men are usually unable to control their sexual desires and that's why they coerce girls'; 62 and 77 per cent of male students and apprentices, compared to 45 and 34 per cent of young female students and apprentices, agreed, similarly, that 'girls are usually the ones who provoke boys to coerce them'. In many settings, this sense of entitlement appears to be fuelled by the belief that young women who resist sexual advances are conforming to traditional role expectations and in fact enjoy the coercive incident, a belief reported by 40–50 per cent of young female respondents and 60–75 per cent of young male respondents in one case study of students and apprentices from Ibadan, Nigeria (Ajuwon, this volume). In another study, young male focus group discussion participants from Kenya explained, 'Girls want sex as much as boys but they have to say "no" to maintain their reputation' (Njue, Askew and Chege, this volume). In Cambodia, young males said that although they realized that rape might be wrong, their 'passion' was too 'strong' to control (Wilkinson, Bearup and Soprach, this volume).

At the same time, there is a tendency in most societies to hold the victim responsible. Studies from many settings have documented a widespread belief among both young men and women that female victims often 'invite' or 'provoke' the coercive incident (for example, see Jewkes, this volume). In a study conducted in and around Johannesburg, more than half of young women believed that women who had been raped were at least partially responsible for the incident, and over 10 per cent argued that they had no right to avoid sexual abuse; 30 per cent of young men thought that women who were raped 'asked for it' (Anonymous 2000; Wood et al. 1996). Provocation may be reflected, for example, in perceptions about inappropriate dress or speech or refusal to engage in sex after the perpetrator has spent money on the victim (Bohmer and Kirumira 1997; Hulton et al. 2000). In qualitative narratives in a case study in Ibadan, Nigeria, youths reported that rape was 'inevitable' in their setting; that it was an acceptable or 'normal' way to 'teach a haughty/unwilling girl a lesson' (Ajuwon et al. 2001a); that 'arrogant' and 'rude' girls should be 'punished'; that 'once a girl agrees to be a girlfriend she should be available for sex'; and that a man is entitled to have sex with a girl on whom he has spent a lot of money, even if by force (Ajuwon, this volume). A case study in Cambodia reports that, even while condemning rape, female respondents blamed the victim for provoking the incident. In contrast, male respondents typically justified violence when women were being 'difficult' or if they 'unfairly' denied sex to them (Wilkinson, Bearup and Soprach, this volume).

In a case study in Kenya, young males distinguish between 'soft' or justifiable rape of girls and young women who are perceived to deserve it for flaunting themselves or challenging men and unjustifiable coercion (Balmer et al. 1997). In Peru, similarly, young men perceive that they are entitled to force sex because they are responding to the urges of their body; girls labelled as 'easy' were perceived as fair play to be drugged, duped or forced to engage in sex (Cáceres, this volume).

Young male respondents often cite a need to 'prove' their masculinity as a factor underlying forced sex. For example, in a case study in Kenya some boys argued that using force is an integral part of the seduction process (Njue, Askew and Chege, this volume). Several studies describe how male peers collude in plotting the timing and circumstances of a forced sexual encounter, and even help to waylay or hold down the female victim (see Ajuwon et al. 2001a; Sodhi and Verma 2003; Varga 2001). And in Cambodia young males argued that 'He wouldn't be a man if he was unable to rape her' (Wilkinson, Bearup and Soprach, this volume). Gang rape is viewed as an extreme manifestation of masculinity, entitlement and the exercise of male power as described in several chapters in this volume from diverse geographical and cultural settings (Jewkes for South Africa; Ajuwon for Nigeria; Njue, Askew and Chege for Kenya; Wilkinson, Bearup and Soprach for Cambodia; Cáceres for Peru). Wilkinson et al. (this volume) associate two factors with the phenomenon of gang rape, or *bauk*, observed in Cambodia: traditional gender-stratified roles and women's subordinate social status on the one hand, and young men's desire for male bonding on the other. Jewkes (this volume) likewise describes gang rape, or 'streamlining', as an expression of male strength and a way of gaining deference from peers as well as women. In all these settings, many young respondents described gang rape as justifiable when perpetrated on young females deemed to 'deserve' it (sex workers, 'easy' women or those who have spurned the advances of a young male).

In many settings, these norms translate into fear, expectation or even acceptance that men will pressure women to have sex and/or use force. In several studies, girls reported continuing to comply with male sexual demands for fear that if sex were refused, the partner would lose interest or abandon them (see Sodhi and Verma 2003, India; Wood and Jewkes 2001; Wood et al. 1996, South Africa). Case studies in diverse settings report that girls tolerate non-consensual sex in premarital relationships as a mark of commitment in a relationship or an expression of love from the partner (Sodhi and Verma 2003; Wood and Jewkes 1997).

Unequal gender norms also condone the perpetration of non-consensual sex within marriage. In many settings, double standards keep many young women totally unaware of and unprepared for sexual life prior to their marriage – a combination likely to constrain young women's ability to communicate and negotiate with their husbands on sexual matters (Santhya and Jejeebhoy, this volume). According to research from various settings (notably South Asia and sub-Saharan Africa), young women and girls are socialized to believe that it is their duty to accept the sexual advances of their husbands, even when forced, as part of their marital duties (Amado 2004; Khan et al. 1996; Santhya and Jejeebhoy, this volume). Narratives report the extent to which young women submit to forced marital relations ('I had to accept my husband's wishes'; Santhya et al. 2001; and 'If you don't give [in to] him then he would force [you] and you will have pain';

George 2003). They also highlight young men's sense of entitlement to forced marital sex ('She refused ... started crying. I made her keep quiet and after that ... I did my work'; Sodhi and Verma 2003). A case study in Dar es Salaam, Tanzania, notes that young people were more likely to justify the use of force to have sex within marital relationships than in non-marital ones; they argued that, when married, men (a few also indicated women) have a right to sex with their partners and if a partner refuses, force is justified (Lary et al. 2004).

In some settings, research has documented a positive change in awareness of young women's right to refuse unwanted sexual advances. For example, the case study in Nigeria found that the large majority of young respondents – particularly young females – supported a girl's right to refuse sex, believed that girls should be able to choose their own husbands, and disagreed with the statement that there is nothing wrong with males sexually coercing girls (Ajuwon, this volume). Likewise, a case study in Dar es Salaam, Tanzania, found that some young men recognized women's sexual rights and argued that forced sex could not be justified under any circumstance (Lary et al. 2004). Similarly, Santhya and Jejeebhoy (this volume) cite evidence that the attitude of young married women justifying forced sex within marriage appears to be changing in some settings. Likewise, Ellsberg (this volume) notes that young women in Nicaragua appear to have more options than in the past, and are more likely to leave a violent relationship than are older women.

On the other hand, there is substantial evidence of a non-linear relationship between women's empowerment and the risk of sexual violence. In fact, male violence against women (whether physical or sexual) has sometimes been observed as a backlash in settings where gender roles are in transition. Research from settings as diverse as Bangladesh, South Africa, Zimbabwe and the United States suggest that women may experience greater levels of sexual and/or physical violence as they begin to attain higher levels of education or earning (Jewkes et al. 2002; Krug et al. 2002).

Power dynamics and the inability to negotiate on sexual matters Lack of communication between partners on sexual issues and of the skills to negotiate sexual matters are obvious risk factors of non-consensual sex which researchers have explored directly through young people's own narratives or through indirect means, such as measuring age and power differentials between partners (Im-em, Kanchanachitra and Archvanitkul, this volume; Lary et al. 2004; Santhya and Jejeebhoy, this volume; Wood and Jewkes 2001; Wood et al. 1998).

In many studies, female and male respondents cite an inability to communicate or negotiate as a factor underlying non-consensual sex. For example, in a case study in Kenya boys cited this factor and the consequent inability to approach girls as reasons for committing rape, and even gang rape (Balmer et al. 1997). As noted earlier, a review of studies from several sub-Saharan African settings found that girls often perceived that they had no right to insist on condom use when they had accepted gifts or money from a man, particularly when the value of the gift was substantial (Luke and Kurz 2002). In a study in South Africa, many girls reported that if they agreed to accompany a man home in order to talk, drink or do his ironing, they would be unable to negotiate themselves out of having sex afterwards and would face threats and assault if they resisted (Wood et al. 1996). Young women in Mexico City reported that previous sexual experience compromised their ability to negotiate; once they had engaged in sex with a boyfriend, they were expected to continue to do so. At the same time, female respondents reported difficulty refusing sex with a new partner if the partner knew that they were not virgins (Marston, this volume).

It is obvious that lack of autonomy will severely compromise young women's ability to negotiate sex in intimate partnerships. Evidence from Nicaragua and Haiti suggests, for example, that young women reported with greater frequency than older women that their partners controlled their contact with family and friends, their mobility and their studies; they were correspondingly more likely to believe that women do not have the right to refuse sex and that men were entitled to beat their wives (Ellsberg, this volume). In a case study in Mumbai, India, young women with little access to resources reported being advised, as they were about to be married, that their economic security was closely tied to succumbing to their husband's demands for sex, even if unwanted (George and Jaswal 1995).

Less direct evidence suggesting inability to negotiate comes from studies that explore the links between non-consensual sex and the age of the younger partner, the age difference between partners and preparedness for sex. Evidence from India and other South Asian settings, for example, suggests that women who marry early and are considerably younger than their husbands are less able to assert themselves or build egalitarian relationships than are those who marry later or are married to men who are of approximately the same age (see also Jensen and Thornton 2003; Nurse 2003). Evidence from settings in India, Bangladesh and Nepal also confirm that those married in early adolescence were especially vulnerable to non-consensual sexual experiences in marriage (Joshi et al. 2001; Khan et al. 2002; Outtara et al. 1998; Puri et al. 2003). A surprisingly similar finding is noted among young men in a case study in Kenya, where young males who were five or more years younger than their first sexual partner were significantly more likely to report a non-consensual experience than those whose partner was closer in age (Erulkar 2004). Aside from age, lack of familiarity with the husband prior to marriage may also inhibit negotiation. For example, a study in West Bengal, India, found that women whose marriages were arranged were significantly more likely to report non-consensual sex than were those who had prior acquaintance with their husbands (Santhya and Jejeebhoy, this volume).

Lack of supportive family and peer environments Studies from many developing-country settings suggest that young people (especially girls and young women) often feel that their parents, families and communities are unsupportive and judgemental with regard to their sexuality, making it difficult for them to navigate healthy and wanted sexual outcomes. Evidence indicates that non-consensual sexual experiences are common events even in settings in which parents strictly limit girls' interaction with the opposite sex (see, for example, Mehra et al. 2002a, 2002b for India). Moreover, a restrictive and judgemental environment with regard to girls' socialization, mobility and sexuality may actually compound risk factors rather than provide protection (Ajuwon, this volume; Gupta and Ailawadi, this volume). In many settings the taboo against discussing sexual issues with parents makes it unlikely that girls will turn to parents for help when they feel threatened or need assistance in dealing with ongoing harassment or abuse. In some cases, girls expect that their parents would even accuse them of having incited the coercive incident (Bohmer and Kirumira 1997). Indeed, a recent study from Kenya found that only 23 per cent of young females and 22 per cent of young males who reported experiences of non-consensual sex had previously shared the experience with anyone (Erulkar 2004).

A study in Kenya found, for example, that young girls believed that the extent of support they would receive from their parents and other adults would vary according to their relationship to the perpetrator. They explained that unless the perpetrator was a stranger, it would not be prudent for them to seek help from their parents or the police if they were raped for fear that their parents would accuse them of colluding with the perpetrator; or parade them in the community complaining that they were raped and that the police would accuse them of prostitution (Balmer et al. 1997).

Lack of family support has also been cited as a factor underlying sexual coercion of young married women (Santhya and Jejeebhoy, this volume). In studies from India, women articulated the extent to which they perceived this lack of family support ('one does feel like running away ... But where does one go? ... the only place is the parental home but parents will always try and send you back'; Visaria 2000). Indeed, women generally perceived that the only option available to them was to remain in the marriage and tolerate the abuse (for example, see George 2003).

Many studies suggest that parents may collude in hiding incidents where their daughters have been sexually abused. Girls, for example, have described being silenced and warned not to bring shame upon the family; some have described being threatened with physical violence if they revealed the incident (for example, see Human Rights Watch 2002a for Zambia). Shame and stigma are pervasive in societies throughout the world, and often the girl herself is blamed for inciting the incident (United Nations ESCAP et al. 2001). In a case study in India, victims of abuse by trusted adults reported the extent to which they were denied support when they disclosed the incident to a parent; the mother of one respondent called her 'a dirty girl who had a vivid imagination'; a father accused another respondent of 'lying to conceal [her] madness'; a third reflected that she had not disclosed the event because she 'would be reprimanded or held responsible for being within reach of the abuser. Silence would be demanded' (Gupta and Ailawadi, this volume).

Few studies have explored the protective influence of close relationships with parents. While cause and effect remain unclear, several studies have found a consistent positive relationship between closeness to parents and lower risk of forced sex (see Patel and Andrew, this volume; see also Cheng Yimin et al. 2001 for China; Human Rights Watch 2002a for Zambia). Patel and Andrew's study (this volume) in Goa, India, suggests that a supportive family could reduce the negative mental health consequences of non-consensual sexual experiences such as depression and the feeling that life is not worth living among both boys and girls. Other research illustrates how supportive parents can enable prompt action, including seeking healthcare and reporting coercive incidents to the authorities (Ajuwon, this volume).

Peers may not necessarily be any more supportive of young victims than are parents (for example, see Ajuwon et al. 2001b). A study of Xhosa adolescent girls in South Africa found that even peers advocated silence (Jewkes, this volume; Wood et al. 1996).

Given the pervasiveness of attitudes that blame the victim, it is not surprising that many young people who experience non-consensual sex do not seek help, even from friends or the family; the typical response of a victim is inaction and silence (Stewart et al. 1996; United Nations ESCAP et al. 2001).

The response of health services, the legal system and the educational sector

Ideally, young people who experience non-consensual sex should be able to turn to healthcare providers and social service and law enforcement agencies for help that their friends and family cannot provide. Often, they need compassionate counselling, emergency contraception, treatment for STIs and care for other health problems. Victims who want to bring a perpetrator to justice through the courts need access to a competent and sensitized police force and judicial system. They may also need access to forensic examinations by someone authorized to collect legally valid evidence (in many countries a medical doctor is not necessarily considered qualified to document legal evidence of rape). Unfortunately, throughout the developing world (and many parts of the developed world) the institutional response to young people who experience non-consensual sex is woefully lacking. Moreover, the experience of seeking help from healthcare providers, and even more so from law enforcement agencies, is in itself traumatizing, given that the negative attitudes towards victims of non-consensual sex that permeate the larger society are also often pervasive among staff of healthcare institutions, and even more so of police and judicial systems (Heise et al. 1999; Human Rights Watch 1999).

Furthermore, legislation and the enforcement of laws against rape and other forms of non-consensual sex remain limited in many settings. Laws often fail to criminalize certain forms of non-consensual sex, such as marital rape, forced penetration other than penile–vaginal sex (oral sex, penetration with fingers or objects), non-penetrative assault such as unwanted touch and molestation, and forced sex through non-physical forms of threats and intimidation. The law in some countries has assumed that rape occurs only to females, and therefore does not recognize boys as victims of rape. In some cases, the law does criminalize sexual assault that is not strictly penile–vaginal (see, for example, Jaising, this volume; Ngwena, this volume); actual sentences imposed in these cases tend, however, to be modest.

Some developing countries have begun to reform their legislation and law enforcement systems. For example, South Africa publicly acknowledged that the country's laws had failed to respond effectively to sexual exploitation, particularly among women and children (Ngwena, this volume), and in recent years has introduced new legislation, revised many policies regulating the police and judiciary, and carried out extensive training among law enforcement personnel.

Regardless of the law, the proportion of young victims who seek redress from the courts in most developing countries continues to be small; and few reported rape cases result in convictions (Gangrade et al. 1995; Omorodion and Olusanya 1998). In developing-country settings where researchers have explored the issue, young people appear to be aware of the weakness of their legal systems. In Uganda and Ethiopia, for example, young people were aware that the majority of rapes were not prosecuted, and they felt that more stringent punishment was needed (Bohmer and Kirumira 1997; Heise et al. 1999; Worku and Addisie 2002).

The health sector response to non-consensual sexual experiences is also inadequate in many settings, and many healthcare facilities are inadequately prepared to care for young victims of non-consensual sex (Bott, Guedes and Guezmes, this volume). Providers often fail to recognize the signs and consequences of non-consensual sexual experiences. Many health professionals share the beliefs of the broader society, for example that violence against women is normal or that victims are responsible for the sexual violence that they suffer (see, for example, Bott, Guedes and Guezmes, this volume; Heise et al. 1999). In baseline studies of provider attitudes in three Latin American settings (the Dominican Republic, Peru and Venezuela), 40 per cent of health providers stated that adolescents often provoke sexual abuse through their inappropriate behaviour; 35 per cent blamed mothers for sexual abuse committed by males against their daughters; 20 per cent believed that men 'cannot control their sexual behaviour'; and 23 per cent believed that women stayed in violent partnerships because they liked being treated that way (Bott, Guedes and Guezmes, this volume). The baseline study also found that providers generally felt unprepared to address issues of non-consensual sex with their clients: only 40 per cent believed they could identify such cases and only 19 per cent reported that they felt comfortable talking with clients about non-consensual sex. Physicians in particular reported a host of barriers inhibiting such discussion.

A limited but growing collection of studies has examined the response of schools and universities to non-consensual sex, including sexual abuse and harassment (Human Rights Watch 2001; Leach et al. 2003; Mirsky 2003). This research suggests that sexual abuse and harassment, primarily against girls, by teachers, administrators and male students, is widespread in many settings. Teachers and administrators, however, often ignore the abuse, fail to condemn perpetrators and often respond to disclosures of sexual abuse by blaming the victim. As described above in relation to healthcare providers, a number of studies have also documented attitudes among teachers and administrators which blame the victim and fail to condemn sexual harassment. For example, a study of teachers in a South African setting found that one-quarter believed that women provoke their partners into violence; fewer than one in three teachers perceived that schools could play a role in addressing sexual violence; and only one-quarter said that they would know how to address an incident of gender-based violence in a school setting (Mirsky, this volume). These attitudes are not confined to Africa or even to developing countries more generally. For example, even in the UK a study has shown that some 22 per cent of teachers agreed that girls can provoke violence and abuse by the way they dress or behave (ibid.).

Promising directions

Non-consensual sex among young people falls at the nexus of many sectors and disciplines, including justice, health, education, development and human rights. It falls within the mandates of programmes addressing young people, reproductive and sexual health and gender-based violence. Ideally, all these sectors need to evolve common strategies for prevention and response. Unfortunately, few interventions have explicitly tried to prevent or improve the response to non-consensual sex. Even fewer have been well documented, much less rigorously evaluated. As a result, the existing evidence provides programme implementers and policy-makers with little information about what approaches may be effective; the most we can say is that some approaches appear to hold promise (see, for example, Flisher, this volume).

Some initiatives have aimed to prevent non-consensual sex at the individual level through school or community-based life or livelihood skills programmes. These vary from setting to setting but in general they focus largely on girls rather than boys and aim to expose girls to the world around them and build agency among them in all spheres, including the sexual. These initiatives, and sexuality education programmes, often work to enable young people to communicate and negotiate with their partners, understand their own sexual and reproductive health and rights, recognize the role of gender norms that justify the perpetration of non-consensual sex, and in some cases improve their ability to seek help. One well-evaluated intervention in Zimbabwe that aimed to promote sexual responsibility and improve young people's access to health services more generally observed that girls who were exposed to the intervention were indeed more likely than others to say no to unwanted sex and to avoid 'sugar daddies', and were better able to resist pressures to engage in sex (Guest, this volume; Kim et al. 2001).

Research from settings in developed countries (notably the United States), however, has found that programmes aimed at preventing non-consensual sex by equipping young people with skills to avoid unwanted sex have almost always failed to prevent it in the long run (for example, see reviews by Chalk and King 1998; Finkelhor and Strapko 1992; Meyer and Stein 2000). These experiences suggest that while life skills and sexuality education programmes may be necessary, they are not sufficient. Equally necessary are approaches to prevention that aim to improve the norms, values and behaviours of young men who may be potential perpetrators. To meet this end, numerous programmes aimed at promoting gender equity and non-violence among boys and young men have been launched in developing-country settings (Barker et al. 2004; EngenderHealth 2003; Guedes et al. 2002; Levack 2001; White et al. 2003). With evaluations of these programmes planned for the near future, the next few years should bring a better understanding of what is effective in this area.

In the education sector, several promising strategies have been implemented to overcome the systemic limitations described earlier. Student-oriented interventions have included changes in the sexuality education or life skills curriculum to include wider issues of gender violence and sexual coercion. Unfortunately, life skills and sexuality education are not themselves widely incorporated in school curricula in developing-country settings. Mirsky (this volume) describes the efforts of NGOs in Nigeria, South Africa and Zimbabwe to fill this gap through theatre and other communication methods, as well as providing mentoring schemes and safe spaces for discussion of topics relating to violence for both females and males, and promoting peer education techniques. At the same time, school- and teacher-level interventions have also been implemented. These include in-service teacher training that enables teachers to change traditional misconceptions and build awareness of young people's rights: for example, an in-service training programme in South Africa succeeded in changing teachers' attitudes justifying gender-based violence and in enhancing teachers' confidence in their ability to address gender-based violence in the school setting. Other interventions have ranged from efforts to modify institutional policies on sexual violence and provide support to the wider school environment on the one hand, to challenging gender norms more generally on the other (Mirsky, this volume).

In recent years, efforts have been launched within the health sector to improve the health service response to young women who experience violence. Many of these initiatives have focused on physical violence against adult women, however, rather than sexual violence against adolescents. Moreover, many have not been well documented, evaluated or evidence-based. A promising intervention is presented by Bott et al. in this volume. This chapter describes a regional initiative to improve the health sector response to gender-based violence in three Latin American member associations of the International Planned Parenthood Federation (PROFAMILIA in the Dominican Republic, PLAFAM in Venezuela and INPPARES in Peru). The initiative focused on (a) addressing limitations of clinic facilities and resources, including providing printed materials, equipment and supplies, and ensuring that the clinic infrastructure allowed private consulting spaces; (b) improving provider knowledge, attitudes and practices, including their ability to detect and respond to cases of violence; (c) improving provider skills, including their ability to counsel women; and (d) most importantly, increasing provider awareness about non-consensual sex and changing their attitudes. Follow-up evaluation studies indicated that the intervention succeeded in improving the quality of care provided to young victims of non-consensual sex, in large part by changing provider attitudes and skills.

On the legal and human rights front, efforts are under way in settings as diverse as South Africa and India to modify rape laws and ensure a more comprehensive response to victims. For example, South Africa amended its rape law (the Criminal Law Amendment Bill of 2003) to broaden its scope in three significant ways: it now encompasses non-consensual behaviours that are not strictly penile–vaginal; it recognizes that non-consensual sex can be perpetrated by means other than the use of actual force, for example by threats and abuse of authority; and it clarifies that both males and females can be victims of rape (Ngwena, this volume). In India, too, the Law Commission has recommended replacing the uni-focal definition of rape to include other forms of penetration; unlike the reforms in South Africa, however, the definition recommended would continue to exclude many offences, including unwanted touch, non-penetrative sexual abuse and marital rape (Jaising, this volume). Clearly, the kinds of lacunae within the law reflect the lack of sensitivity and responsiveness of the wider society to the specific circumstances and needs of young victims. Both articles conclude that legal responses to non-consensual sexual experiences of young people must recognize their basic human right to sexual health and sexuality, and that national constitutions and domestic laws must expand their scope to enable young people to engage in sexual relations without force or coercion. The extent to which these laws can be enforced, however, remains to be seen.

Finally, significant efforts are currently under way to reverse the dearth of data and evidence on the prevalence of non-consensual sexual experiences of young people and the context in which they occur (Guest, this volume). Guest notes that the topic is both extremely sensitive and poorly researched, but a growing number of studies have managed to explore these issues using comparable community-based investigations and operationalizing definitions, and by using innovative methods to increase reliability and protect the safety and well-being of young respondents.

Conclusions

This overview suggests that non-consensual sex among young people in developing countries is a relatively common occurrence that has been seriously overlooked in sexual and reproductive health promotion activities. Evidence presented here challenges the commonly held assumption that all sexual activity among young people is consensual. Indeed, it draws attention to the fact that substantial proportions of young people – females as well as males, the married (females) as well as the unmarried – have experienced non-consensual sex, and that experiences are diverse and range from unwanted touch to forced penetrative sex and even gang rape. It identifies a host of factors that place young females and, to a lesser extent, males at risk, ranging from unbalanced gender norms to unequal power relationships and inability to negotiate or communicate on sexual matters, unsupportive family relationships, inadequate health and education sector responsiveness and inappropriate law enforcement. Outcomes of non-consensual sex are significant and consistently documented: they range from unintended pregnancy and infection to severe feelings of worthlessness and anxiety, suicidal tendencies and compromised subsequent consensual sexual experiences. Evidence presented in this chapter also challenges unbalanced programme attention that currently focuses on ensuring safe sex while ignoring the fact that unwanted or non-consensual sex may be a key factor underlying the compromised sexual and reproductive health of adolescents and youth in many developing countries.

References

Ajayi, A., W. Clark, A. Erulkar et al. (1997) *Schooling and the Experience of Adolescents in Kenya*, Nairobi: The Population Council

Ajuwon, A. J., I. Akin-Jimoh, B. O. Olley et al. (2001a) 'Sexual coercion: learning from the perspectives of adolescents in Ibadan, Nigeria', *Reproductive Health Matters*, 9(17): 128–36

Ajuwon, A. J., B. O. Olley, I. Akin-Jimoh et al. (2001b) 'Experience of sexual coercion among adolescents in Ibadan, Nigeria', *African Journal of Reproductive Health*, 5(3): 120–31

Alarcon, I. and G. F. Gonzales (1996) 'Attitudes towards sexuality, sexual knowledge and behaviour in adolescents in the cities of Lima, Cusco and Iquitos', Lima: Peru, Cayetano Heredia Peruvian University, Unpublished final report submitted to the UNDP/UNFPA/WHO/World Bank Special Programme of Research, Development and Research Training in Human Reproduction, Geneva

Amado, L. E. (2004) 'Sexual and bodily rights as human rights in the Middle East and North Africa', *Reproductive Health Matters*, 12(23): 125–8

Anonymous (2000) 'Rape in South Africa, Uganda and Zambia', *Reproductive Health Matters*, 8(16): 180

Awusabo-Asare, K. and J. K. Anarfi (1999) 'Rethinking the circumstances surrounding the first sexual experience in the era of AIDS in Ghana', *The Continuing HIV/AIDS Epidemic, Health Transition Review*, supplement to vol. 9: 9–18

Balmer, D. H., E. Gikundi, M. C. Billingsley et al. (1997) 'Adolescent knowledge, values, and coping strategies: implications for health in sub-Saharan Africa', *Journal of Adolescent Health*, 21: 33–8

Barker, G. (1993) 'Research on AIDS: knowledge, attitudes and practices among street youth', *Children Worldwide*, 20(2–3): 41–2

Barker, G., M. Nascimiento, M. Segundo and J. Pulerwitz (2004) 'How do we know if men have changed? Promoting and measuring attitude change with young men: lessons from Program H in Latin America', in S. Ruxton (ed.), *Gender Equality and Men: Learning from Practice*, Oxfam, pp. 147–61

Bohmer, L. and E. Kirumira (1997) 'Access to reproductive health services: participatory research with Ugandan adolescents', Final report and working paper, Makerere University, Child Health and Development Centre and Pacific Institute for Women's Health

Boyer, D. and D. Fine (1992) 'Sexual abuse as a factor in adolescent pregnancy and child maltreatment', *Family Planning Perspectives*, 24(1): 4–11, 19

Brown, A. D., S. J. Jejeebhoy, I. Shah et al. (2001) 'Sexual relations among young people in developing countries: evidence from WHO case studies', Occasional Paper no. 4, Geneva: World Health Organization, Department of Reproductive Health and Research, WHO/RHR/01.8

Buga, G., D. Amoko and D. Nacyiyana (1996) 'Sexual behaviour, contraceptive practice and reproductive health among school adolescents in rural Transkei', *South African Medical Journal*, 86: 523–52

Cáceres, C. F., B. V. Marin, E. S. Hudes et al. (1997) 'Young people and the structure of sexual risks in Lima', *AIDS*, 11 (suppl. 1): S67–77

Cayemittes, M., M. F. Placide, B. Barrere et al. (2001) *Enquête Mortalité, Morbidité et Ulilisation des Services EMMUS-III Haiti 2000*, Petionville: Institut Haitien de l'Enfance, ORC Macro: 489

Center for Reproductive Law and Policy (CRLP) (2002) *Bringing Rights to Bear. An Analysis of the Work of UN Treaty Monitoring Bodies on Reproductive and Sexual Rights*, New York: Centre for Reproductive Law and Policy

Centers for Disease Control (CDC) and Centro de Estudios de Población y Desarrollo Social (CEPAR) (1995) *ENDEMAIN-94: Encuesta Demográfica y de Salud Materna e Infantil: Informe General*, Atlanta, GA: Centers for Disease Control

Chalk, R. and P. A. King (eds) (1998) *Violence in Families: Assessing Prevention and Treatment Programs*, Washington, DC: National Academy Press

Chapko, M. K., P. Somse, A. M. Kimball et al. (1999) 'Predictors of rape in the Central African Republic', *Health Care for Women International*, 20: 71–9

Cheng Yimin, Kang Baohua, Wang Tieyan et al. (2001) 'Case-controlled study on relevant factors of adolescent sexual coercion in China', *Contraception*, 64: 77–80

Duvvury, N., M. Nayak and K. Allendorf (2002) 'Links between masculinity and violence: aggregate analysis', in *Domestic Violence in India: Exploring Strategies, Promoting*

Dialogue – Men, Masculinity and Domestic Violence in India: Summary Report of Four Studies, Washington, DC: International Center for Research on Women

EngenderHealth (2003) *MAP Evaluation Report*, New York: EngenderHealth

Erulkar, A. S. (2004) 'The experience of sexual coercion among young people in Kenya', *International Family Planning Perspectives*, 30(4): 182–9

Finkelhor, D. and N. Strapko (1992) 'Sexual abuse prevention education', in D. J. Willis, E. W. Holden and M. Rosenberg (eds), *Prevention of Child Maltreatment: Developmental and Ecological Perspectives*, New York: John Wiley and Sons

Fraser, T. (2000) *Early Sexual Activity Raises HIV Risk for Trinidad and Tobago Girls. Findings of Teenage Survey Spur Calls for Key Policy Changes in Light of HIV/AIDS*, Washington, DC: Population Reference Bureau

Ganatra, B. and S. Hirve (2002) 'Induced abortions among adolescent women in rural Maharashtra, India', *Reproductive Health Matters*, 10(19): 76–85

Gangrade, K. D., R. Sooryamoorthy and D. Renjini (1995) 'Child rape: facets of a heinous crime', *Social Change: Issues and Perspectives*, 25(2–3): 161–76

García-Moreno, C., C. Watts, H. Jansen et al. (2003) 'Responding to violence against women: WHO's multi-country study on women's health and domestic violence', *Health and Human Rights*, 6(2): 113–27

George, A. (2002) 'Embodying identity through heterosexual sexuality – newly married adolescent women in India', *Culture, Health and Sexuality*, 4(2): 207–22

— (2003) 'Newly married adolescent women: experiences from case studies in urban India', in S. Bott et al. (eds), *Towards Adulthood: Exploring the Sexual and Reproductive Health of Adolescents in South Asia*, Geneva: World Health Organization, pp. 67–72

George, A. and S. Jaswal (1995) 'Understanding sexuality: an ethnographic study of poor women in Bombay, India', Women and AIDS Research Program Report Series no. 12, Washington, DC: International Center for Research on Women

Goldstein, D. M. (1994) 'AIDS and women in Brazil: the emerging problem', *Social Science and Medicine*, 39(7): 919–29

Graitcer, P. and Z. Youssef (1993) *Injury in Egypt: An Analysis of Injuries as a Health Problem*, Washington, DC and Cairo: US Agency for International Development and Ministry of Health

Guedes, A., S. Bott, A. Guezmes et al. (2002) 'Gender-based violence, human rights, and the health sector: lessons from Latin America', *Health and Human Rights*, 2(1): 177–93

Handwerker, W. P. (1993) 'Gender power differences between parents and high-risk sexual behaviour by their children: AIDS/STD risk factors extend to a prior generation', *Journal of Women's Health*, 2–3: 301–16

Heise, L., M. Ellsberg and M. Gottemoeller (1999) 'Ending violence against women', Population Reports Series L, *Issues in World Health*, 11: 1–43

Heise, L. L., K. Moore and N. Toubia (1995) *Sexual Coercion and Reproductive Health: A Focus on Research*, New York: Population Council

Hof, C. and A. Richters (1999) 'Exploring intersections between teenage pregnancy and gender violence: lessons from Zimbabwe', *African Journal of Reproductive Health*, 3(1): 51–65

Hulton, L. A., R. Cullen and S. W. Khalokho (2000) 'Perceptions of the risks of sexual activity and their consequences among Ugandan adolescents', *Studies in Family Planning*, 31(1): 35–46

Human Rights Watch (1999) *Crime or Custom? Violence against Women in Pakistan*, New York: Human Rights Watch

— (2001) *Scared at School: Sexual Violence against Girls in South African Schools*, New York: Human Rights Watch

— (2002a) *Suffering in Silence: The Links between Human Rights Abuses and HIV Transmission to Girls in Zambia*, New York: Human Rights Watch

— (2002b) *World Report 2002*, New York: Human Rights Watch

INEC (Instituto Nacional de Estadisticas y Censos) Ministerio de Salud (MINSA) (2001) *Encuesta Nicaraguaense de Demografia y Salud*, Managua: Ministerio de Salud

Isarabhakdi, P. (1995) 'Determinants of sexual behaviour that influence the risk of pregnancy and disease among rural Thai young adults', Nakorn Pathom, Thailand: Institute for Population and Social Research, Unpublished final report submitted to the UNDP/UNFPA/WHO/World Bank Special Programme of Research, Development and Research Training in Human Reproduction, Geneva

Jensen, R. and R. Thornton (2003) 'Early female marriage in the developing world', *Gender and Development*, 11(2): 9–19

Jewkes, R. (2002) 'Intimate partner violence: causes and prevention', *Lancet*, 359: 1423–9

Jewkes, R., C. Vundule, F. Maforah et al. (2001) 'Relationship dynamics and adolescent pregnancy in South Africa', *Social Science and Medicine*, 52: 733–44

Jewkes, R., J. Levin, N. Mbananga et al. (2002) 'Rape of girls in South Africa', *Lancet*, 359: 319–20, 26 January

Joshi, A., M. Dhapola, E. Kurian et al. (2001) 'Experiences and perceptions of marital sexual relationships among rural women in Gujarat, India', *Asia-Pacific Population Journal*, 16(2): 177–94

Kaufman, C. E. and S. E. Stavrou (2002) '"Bus fare, please": the economics of sex and gifts among adolescents in urban South Africa', *Population Council Policy Research Division Working Paper* no. 166, New York

Kgosidintsi, N. (1997) 'Sexual behaviour and risk of HIV infection among adolescent females in Botswana', Gaborone, Botswana, National Institute of Development, Research and Documentation, Unpublished final report submitted to the UNDP/UNFPA/WHO/World Bank Special Programme of Research, Development and Research Training in Human Reproduction, Geneva

Khan, M. E., J. W. Townsend, R. Sinha et al. (1996) 'Sexual violence within marriage', *Seminar*, 447: 32–5

Khan, M. E., J. W. Townsend and S. D'Costa (2002) 'Behind closed doors: a qualitative study on sexual behaviour of married women in Bangladesh', *Culture, Health and Sexuality*, 4(2): 237–56

Kim, S. R. (1998) 'High school girls' knowledge and behaviour on sex', *People and Development Challenges*, 5(9): 17–18

Kim, Y., A. Kols, R. Nyakauru et al. (2001) 'Promoting sexual responsibility among young people in Zimbabwe', *International Family Planning Perspectives*, 27(1): 11–19

Kishor, S. and K. Johnson (2004) *Profiling Domestic Violence – a Multi-country Study*, Calverton, MD: ORC Macro

Krug, E. G., L. L. Dahlberg, J. A. Mercy et al. (2002) *World Report on Violence and Health*, Geneva: WHO

Kwon Tai-Hwan, Jun Kwang and Cho Sung-nam (1994) 'Sexuality, contraception and abortion among unmarried adolescents and young adults: the case of Korea', Seoul: College of Social Sciences, Seoul National University, Unpublished final report submitted to the UNDP/UNFPA/WHO/World Bank Special Programme of Research, Development and Research Training in Human Reproduction, Geneva

Lary, H., S. Maman, M. Katebalila et al. (2004) 'Exploring the association between HIV and violence: young people's experiences with infidelity, violence and forced sex in Dar es Salaam, Tanzania', *International Family Planning Perspectives*, 30(4): 200–206

Leach, F., V. Fiscian, E. Kadzamira et al. (2003) *An Investigative Study of the Abuse of Girls in African Schools*, London: Policy Division, Department for International Development

Levack, A. (2001) 'Educating men in South Africa on gender issues', *SIECUS Report*, 29(5): 13–15

Luke, N. (2003) 'Age and economic asymmetries in the sexual relationships of adolescent girls in sub-Saharan Africa', *Studies in Family Planning*, 34(2): 67–86

Luke, N. and K. Kurz (2002) *Cross-generational and Transactional Sexual Relations in Sub-Saharan Africa: Prevalence of Behaviour and Implications for Negotiating Safer Sexual Practices*, Washington, DC: ICRW and PSI

Luster, T. and S. Small (1997) 'Sexual abuse and sexual risk-taking among sexually abused girls', *Family Planning Perspectives*, 29(5): 204–11

Martin, S. L., B. Kilgallen, A. Ong Tsui et al. (1999) 'Sexual behaviour and reproductive health outcomes: associations with wife abuse in India', *Journal of the American Medical Association*, 282(20): 1967–72

Meekers, D. and A. Calves (1997) '"Main" girlfriends, girlfriends, marriage, and money: the social context of HIV risk behaviour in sub-Saharan Africa', *Health Transition Review*, suppl. to vol. 7: 361–75

Mehra, S., R. Savithri and L. Coutinho (2002a) 'Gender double standards and power imbalances: adolescent partnerships in Delhi, India', Paper presented at the Asia-Pacific Social Science and Medicine Conference, Kunming, China, October

— (2002b) 'Sexual behaviour among unmarried adolescents in Delhi, India: opportunities despite parental controls', Paper presented at the IUSSP Regional Population Conference, Bangkok, June

Mensch, B. and C. Lloyd (1998) 'Gender differences in the schooling experiences of adolescents in low-income countries: the case of Kenya', *Studies in Family Planning*, 29(2): 167–84

Mensch, B. S., J. Bruce and M. E. Greene (1998) *The Uncharted Passage: Girls' Adolescence in the Developing World*, New York: Population Council

Mensch, B., P. Hewett and A. Erulkar (2003) 'The reporting of sensitive behaviors by adolescents', *Demography*, 40(2): 247–68

Meyer, H. and N. Stein (2000) *Review of Teen Dating Violence Prevention* (electronic publication), National Violence against Women Prevention Research Center, Wellesley Centers for Women, Wellesley College, <www.musc.edu/vawprevention/research/teendating.shtml>

Mirsky, J. (2003) *Beyond Victims and Villains: Addressing Sexual Violence in the Education Sector*, Panos Report no. 47, London: Panos Institute

Mpangile G. S., M. T. Leshabari and D. J. Kihwele (1999) 'Induced abortion in Dar es Salaam, Tanzania: the plight of adolescents', in A. I. Mundigo and C. Indriso (eds), *Abortion in the Developing World*, New Delhi: Vistaar Publications, pp. 387–403

Mulugeta, E., M. Kassaye and Y. Berhane (1998) 'Prevalence and outcomes of sexual violence among high school students', *Ethiopian Medical Journal*, 36: 167–74

National Research Council and Institute of Medicine (2005) *Growing Up Global: The Changing Transitions to Adulthood in Developing Countries*, Panel on Transitions to Adulthood in Developing Countries (C. B. Lloyd, ed.), Committee on Population and

Board on Children, Youth and Families. Division of Behavioral and Social Sciences and Education, Washington, DC: National Academies Press

NCIPC (National Center for Injury Prevention and Control) (2000a) Dating Violence Fact Sheet, Atlanta, GA, National Center for Injury Prevention and Control, Centers for Disease Control and Prevention, <www.cdc.gov/ncipc/factsheets/datviol.htm>

— (2000b) Rape Fact Sheet, Atlanta, GA: National Center for Injury Prevention and Control, Centers for Disease Control and Prevention, <www.cdc.gov/ncipc/factsheets/rape.htm>

— (2003) Sexual Violence Facts, Atlanta, GA: National Center for Injury Prevention and Control, Centers for Disease Control and Prevention, <www.cdc.gov/ncipc/factsheets/svfacts.htm>

Nnko, S. and R. Pool (1997) 'Sexual discourse in the context of AIDS: dominant themes on adolescent sexuality among primary school pupils in Magu District, Tanzania', *Health Transition Review*, suppl. 3(7): 85–90

Nnko, S., B. Chiduo, G. Mwaluko et al. (2001) 'Pre-marital sexual behaviour among out-of-school adolescents: motives, patterns and meaning attributed to sexual partnership in rural Tanzania,' *African Journal of Reproductive Health*, 5(3): 162–74

Nurse, J. (2003) 'Gender based violence in married or partnered adolescents', Background paper presented at WHO meeting on Married Adolescents, Geneva, December

Omorodion, F. I. and O. Olusanya (1998) 'The social context of reported rape in Benin City, Nigeria', *African Journal of Reproductive Health*, 2(2): 37–43

Outtara, M., P. Sen and M. Thomson (1998) 'Forced marriage, forced sex: the perils of childhood for girls', *Gender and Development*, 6(3): 27–33

Palestinian Human Rights Monitor (2002) 'Honor killing: the killing of women on the basis of family', *Palestinian Human Rights Monitor*, 6(4), August

Patel, V. and G. Andrew (2001) 'Gender, sexual abuse and risk behaviours in adolescents: a cross-sectional survey in schools in Goa', *National Medical Journal of India*, 14(5): 263–7

PROFAMILIA (2000) *Salud Sexual y Reproductiva: Resultados Encuesta Nacional de Demografía y Salud 2000*, Bogotá: Asociación Probienestar de la Familia Colombiana

Puri, M., J. Cleland and Z. Matthews (2003) 'Extent of sexual coercion among young female migrant workers and their sexual health problems in Nepal', Paper presented at the Annual Meetings of the Population Association of America, Minneapolis, April

Raffaelli, M., R. Campos, A. P. Merritt et al. (1993) 'Sexual practices and attitudes of street youth in Belo Horizonte, Brazil', *Social Science and Medicine*, 37(5): 661–70

RAINN (Rape, Abuse and Incest National Network) (n.d.) Statistical database and bibliography, <www.rainn.org/statistics.html>

Ramakrishna, J., M. Karott and R. S. Murthy (2003) 'Experiences of sexual coercion among street boys in Bangalore, India', in S. Bott, S. Jejeebhoy, I. Shah et al. (eds), *Towards Adulthood: Exploring the Sexual and Reproductive Health of Adolescents in South Asia*, Geneva: World Health Organization, pp. 95–8

Rosales, J., E. Loaiza, D. Primante et al. (1999) *Encuesta Nicaraguense de Demografia y Salud, 1998*, Managua: Instituto Nacional de Estadisticas y Censos

Santhya, K. G., E. McGrory and N. Haberland (2001) First Time Parents Project, Supplemental Diagnostic Report, Kolkata, unpublished

Sathar, Z. and C. Lloyd (1993) 'Who gets primary schooling in Pakistan: inequalities among and within families', *Research Division Working Papers* no. 52, New York: Population Council

Schraiber, L. B. and A. F. d'Oliveira (2002) *WHO Multi-country Study on Women's Health and Domestic Violence, Brazil*, São Paolo: World Health Organization

Shalhoub-Kevorkian, N. (2000) *Mapping and Analysing the Landscape of Femicide in Palestinian Society*, Unpublished report submitted to UNIFEM

Silberschmidt, M. and V. Rausch (2001) 'Adolescent girls, illegal abortions and "sugar-daddies" in Dar-es-Salaam: vulnerable victims and active social agents', *Social Science and Medicine*, 52: 1815–26

Silva, T. K., S. L. Schensul, J. Schensul et al. (1997) 'Youth and sexual risk in Sri Lanka', Women and AIDS Program Research Report Series, Phase II, no. 3, Washington, DC: International Center for Research on Women

Singh, H. S. S. A., W. Y. Wong and N. K. N. Hjh (1996) 'Prevalence of childhood sexual abuse among Malaysian paramedical students', *Child Abuse and Neglect*, 20(6): 487–92

Slap, G. B., L. Lot, Bin Huang et al. (2003) 'Sexual behaviour of adolescents in Nigeria: cross sectional survey of secondary school students', *British Medical Journal*, 326: 15–18

Sodhi, G. and M. Verma (2003) 'Sexual coercion amongst unmarried adolescents of an urban slum in India', in S. Bott, S. Jejeebhoy, I. Shah et al. (eds), *Towards Adulthood: Exploring the Sexual and Reproductive Health of Adolescents in South Asia*, Geneva: World Health Organization, pp. 91–4

Somse, P., M. K. Chapko and R. V. Hawkins (1993) 'Multiple sexual partners: results of a national HIV/AIDS survey in the Central African Republic', *AIDS*, 7(4): 579–83

Stewart, L., A. Sebastini, G. Delgado et al. (1996) 'Consequences of sexual abuse of adolescents', *Reproductive Health Matters*, 7: 129–34

Stock, J. L., M. A. Bell, D. K. Boyer et al. (1997) 'Adolescent pregnancy and sexual risk-taking among sexually abused girls', *Family Planning Perspectives*, 29(5): 200–203, 227

UNAIDS (1999) *Sex and Youth: Contextual Factors Affecting Risk for HIV/AIDS*, Geneva: UNAIDS

UNICEF/UNAIDS/WHO (2002) *Young People and HIV/AIDS: Opportunity in Crisis*, Geneva: UNAIDS

United Nations ESCAP, Government of Japan, National Commission for Child Welfare and Development, Pakistan (2001) *Sexually Abused and Sexually Exploited Children and Youth in Pakistan: A Qualitative Assessment of their Health Needs and Available Services in Selected Provinces*, Bangkok: UNESCAP

Varga, C. (2001) 'The forgotten fifty per cent: a review of sexual and reproductive health research and programs focused on boys and young men in sub-Saharan Africa', *African Journal of Reproductive Health*, 5(3): 175–95

Visaria, L. (2000) 'Violence against women: a field study', *Economic and Political Weekly*, 13 May, pp. 1742–51

White, V., M. Greene and E. Murphy (2003) *Men and Reproductive Health Programs: Changing Gender Norms*, Washington, DC: The Synergy Project/Social and Scientific Systems, Inc.

Wood, K. M. (2003) 'An ethnography of sexual health and violence among township youth in South Africa', PhD thesis, University of London

Wood, K. and R. Jewkes (1997) 'Violence, rape, and sexual coercion: everyday love in a South African township', *Gender and Development*, 5(2): 41–6

— (2001) '"Dangerous" love: reflections on violence among Xhosa township youth', in R. Morrell (ed.), *Changing Men in Southern Africa*, Pietermaritzburg: University of Natal Press, pp. 317–36

Wood, K., F. Maforah and R. Jewkes (1996) 'Sex, violence and constructions of love among Xhosa adolescents: putting violence on the sexuality education agenda', Unpublished paper, Pretoria: CERSA – Women's Health, Medical Research Council

— (1998) '"He forced me to love him": putting violence on adolescent sexual health agendas', *Social Science and Medicine*, 47(2): 233–42

Worku, A. and M. Addisie (2002) 'Sexual violence among female high school students in Debark, north west Ethiopia', *East African Medical Journal*, 79(2): 96–9

Youri, P. (ed.) (1994) 'Female adolescent health and sexuality in Kenyan secondary schools: a survey report', AMREF unpublished report, Nairobi

Zierler, S., L. Feingold, D. Laufer et al. (1991) 'Adult survivors of childhood sexual abuse and subsequent risk of HIV infection', *American Journal of Public Health*, 81(5): 572–5

TWO | Non-consensual sexual experiences and underlying gender norms

2 | Sexual violence against women and girls: recent findings from Latin America and the Caribbean

MARY C. ELLSBERG

In recent years, international research has begun to focus on the links between sexual violence and women's reproductive health. Although population-based surveys on this subject are limited, available evidence indicates that the majority of incidents of sexual violence against women occur in the context of marriage or dating relationships. In the case of child sexual abuse and sexual assault by non-partners, recent studies in Latin America, Asia and Africa indicate that women and girls are most likely to be abused by someone known to them, often a member of their family. These studies also show that young women are at greater risk of suffering sexual assault, either by an intimate partner or others, than older women (Heise et al. 1999).

Sexual violence has been associated with subsequent high-risk sexual behaviour among women, such as early sexual debut, multiple sexual partners and non-use of condoms, which in turn increases the risks of early pregnancy and sexually transmitted infections, including HIV/AIDS (Carballo-Dieguez and Dolezal 1995; Ferguson 1997; Luster and Small 1997; Stock et al. 1997; Widom and Kuhns 1996; Wingood and DiClemente 1997). Nevertheless, information regarding the occurrence, characteristics and consequences of child and adolescent sexual abuse outside the industrialized world is still insufficient. Data from population-based studies and research that include men are particularly rare (Leventhal 1998).

This chapter describes the major findings of research conducted in Latin America and the Caribbean on sexual violence among adolescents and young people, as well as underlying methodological and ethical challenges for researchers in this area. Many of the studies described are large-scale population-based surveys such as the Demographic and Health Surveys (DHS) and Reproductive Health Surveys. The article also discusses the findings of recent epidemiological research carried out in Nicaragua, which highlight some of the health effects associated with sexual violence.

Prevalence of sexual violence against women by an intimate partner

Table 2.1 presents findings from seven recent surveys carried out in six countries in Latin America and the Caribbean which included questions on violence against women. The findings were not comparable, however, due to discrepancies with regard to how violence was defined and measured. Four of

TABLE 2.1 Recent survey data on sexual violence in marriage from Latin America and the Caribbean, women aged fifteen to forty-nine

Country	Intimate partner sexual violence (%)* Ever	Intimate partner sexual violence (%)* Last 12 months	Sexual violence by non-partners (%)** Ever
Brazil, Pernambuco (2002) (Schraiber and d'Oliveira 2002)	14	6	9
Brazil, São Paolo (2002) (Schraiber and d'Oliveira 2002)	10	3	13
Colombia (2000) (PROFAMILIA 2000)	14	11***	7
Ecuador (CDC/CEPAR 1995)	4	4****	na+
Haiti (2000) (Cayemittes et al. 2001)	17	15	–
Nicaragua (1995) (Ellsberg et al. 1999)	22	–	–
Nicaragua (1998–99) (Rosales et al. 1999)	10	4	8
Peru, Cusco (2002) (Guezmes et al. 2002)	47	23	17
Peru, Lima (2002) (Guezmes et al. 2002)	23	7	26

Notes: *Ever-partnered women aged 15–49 who have experienced sexual violence by an intimate partner ** Women aged 15–49 who have experienced rape or sexual violence by a non-partner ***Refers to ongoing violence (Does he usually ...?) **** Refers to currently married women + Not available. However, 4% reported that they had at some time experienced sexual violence perpetrated by a non-partner or partner

these studies are nationally representative surveys (Colombia 2000; Ecuador 1995; Haiti 2000; Nicaragua 1998–99) designed primarily to measure reproductive health outcomes among women (DHS conducted by MACRO International, and Reproductive Health Surveys conducted by Centers for Disease Control [CDC], Atlanta). Three of the studies, in Brazil, Nicaragua (1995) and Peru, focused specifically on different forms of violence against women, and were conducted in one or two regions in these countries. The Brazil and Peru studies were each conducted in two sites, as part of a WHO multi-country study on domestic violence and women's health. All the studies included at least one question on sexual violence (Table 2.1). Six studies (Brazil 2002; Ecuador 1999; Haiti 2000; Nicaragua 1995; Nicaragua 1998–99; Peru 2002) addressed sexual violence by intimate partners, and four studies included questions on sexual violence by non-partners (Brazil 2002; Colombia 2000; Nicaragua 1998–99; Peru 2002).

The inconsistencies in the methodology employed include differences in the reference period used (lifetime prevalence, twelve-month prevalence or ongoing violence), the number of questions asked on violence, and the age cut-off for abuse (before and after twelve years, before and after fifteen). Another important difference is related to the framing of the questions. Some surveys ask questions such as 'Have you ever been raped?' while others use behaviourally specific questions such as 'Have you ever been forced to have sex against your will?' and include other types of sexual act and types of coercion ('being forced to do something sexual against your will' and 'having sex when you didn't want to because you were afraid of what he might do') (WHO 1997).

While one must be cautious in making generalizations because of the differences in framing questions and the study population, these findings indicate that between 10 and 47 per cent of ever-married women have experienced sexual violence by an intimate partner and between 8 and 26 per cent of women have suffered sexual violence by a non-partner either as a child or adult. In all cases these figures are likely to be underestimates of the actual prevalence of sexual abuse, as many women are reluctant to disclose violence owing to shame and fear of reprisals (Koss 1993). There is some evidence that large-scale surveys that are not primarily designed to assess violence, such as the DHS, are more likely to underestimate the prevalence of violence than studies that focus specifically on violence (Ellsberg et al. 2001a). In particular, specialized training of interviewers, greater emphasis on the privacy and safety of respondents, and measures such as providing multiple opportunities for disclosure have been found to have a positive effect on women's reporting of violence (Ellsberg and Heise 2002; Ellsberg et al. 2001a; García-Moreno et al. 2003).

Considerable overlap has been found in Latin America between sexual violence and physical violence. For example, in the León, Nicaragua, study, all but four ever-partnered women who reported sexual violence had also experienced physical violence (Ellsberg et al. 2000). In this study, sexual coercion was associated with the most severe forms of physical violence, including violence during pregnancy and violence resulting in injuries. Similar findings were reported in Peru and Brazil (Guezmes et al. 2002; Schraiber and d'Oliveira 2002). In contrast, studies in Indonesia found that sexual violence among ever-partnered women often occurred outside the context of physical violence, and was in fact more common than physical partner violence (Hakimi et al. 2002). This underscores the importance of examining the patterns of violence cross-culturally, and viewing sexual violence within intimate partnerships in the context of other forms of violence.

Sexual violence against adolescent women by intimate partners

Studies show that younger women (fifteen to nineteen years) are only slightly less likely than all women aged fifteen to forty-nine to have experienced sexual violence by an intimate partner (Figure 2.1). This is in itself an important finding, as young women presumably have been exposed to the risk of partner violence for a much shorter period of time than older women, and it might therefore be expected that lifetime prevalence of violence would be considerably higher in older women. A more appropriate indicator for age comparison may be the

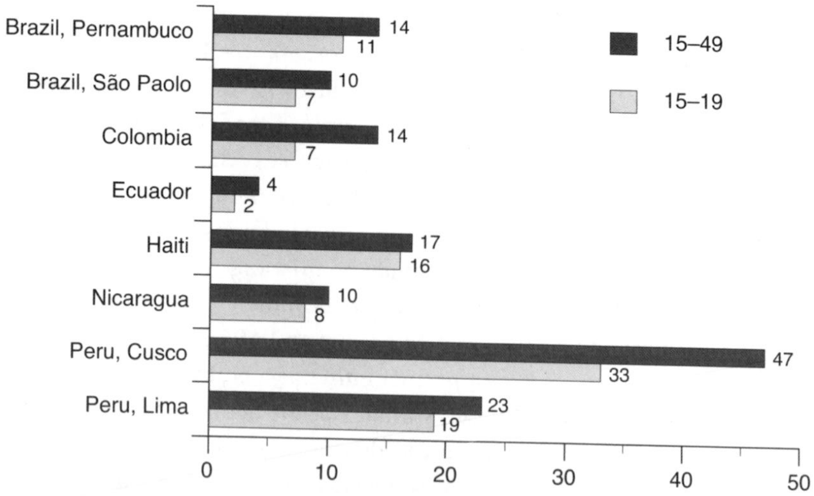

Figure 2.1 Percentage of ever-partnered women (fifteen to forty-nine) and women aged fifteen to nineteen who have at some time experienced sexual violence by an intimate partner (*Source*: Brazil, Pernambuco and São Paolo, Schraiber and d'Oliveira 2002; Colombia: PROFAMILIA 2000; Ecuador: CDC, CEPAR 1995; Haiti: Cayemittes et al. 2001; Nicaragua: Rosales et al. 1999; Peru, Cusco: Guezmes et al. 2002; Peru, Lima: Guezmes et al. 2002)

prevalence of violence in the twelve months before the study (referred to here as current violence) and violence that occurred prior to the previous twelve months (Figure 2.2). According to the 1998 DHS for Nicaragua, younger ever-married women were much more likely to report sexual violence in the last twelve months than older women (Rosales et al. 1999). This indicates that sexual violence starts early in a relationship, and may become less frequent over time. Similar findings have been reported with regard to physical partner violence in Nicaragua (Ellsberg et al. 2000). In this study of 488 women aged between fifteen and forty-nine, it was found that 50 per cent of physical partner violence started within the first two years of marriage, and that 80 per cent of violence started within four years of marriage.

Available research indicates that young women in partnerships have generally less autonomy and are at greater risk of both physical and sexual violence than older women. In Nicaragua, for example, not only did ever-partnered women between fifteen and nineteen years report more physical and sexual violence within the last twelve months than older women, but they also experienced more severe acts of violence (Rosales et al. 1999). In both Nicaragua and Haiti, young women reported with greater frequency than older women that their partners controlled their daily activities, such as contact with friends and family, studies and leaving the house (Cayemittes et al. 2001; Rosales et al. 1999). Surprisingly, younger women in these countries had more traditional attitudes towards gender relations, for example the belief that women do not have the right to refuse sex

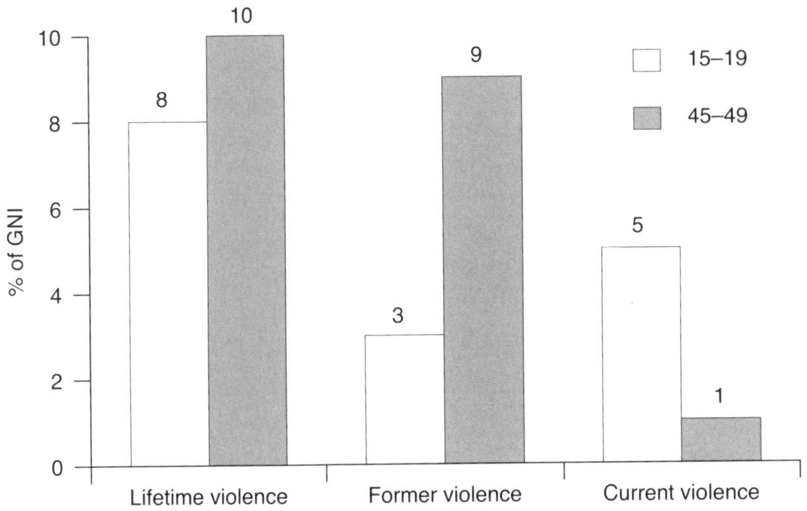

Figure 2.2 Percentage of women aged fifteen to nineteen and forty to forty-nine who have experienced lifetime, former and current and sexual violence by an intimate partner, Nicaragua (*Source*: Rosales et al. 1999)

when they do not feel like it, and that men are justified in beating their wives under certain circumstances.

Paradoxically, younger women seem to be more likely to leave an abusive relationship than older women, as can be seen from the León, Nicaragua, study (Figure 2.3) (Ellsberg et al. 2001b). This may be the result of a cohort effect, indicating that cultural norms have changed in the last twenty years, making it more acceptable for women to leave violent relationships, which would primarily be manifested among younger women.

Forced sex on women and girls by non-partners

Research on sexual violence against women by non-partners, either in childhood or as adults, is even more rare than research on intimate partner violence, and is fraught with methodological difficulties. According to a review by Finkelhor (1994), between 7 and 36 per cent of women and 3 and 29 per cent of men reported the experience of child sexual abuse in different countries. The reasons for the wide variation in figures may be because different definitions of abuse were used, different study groups and study design selected, and different data collection methods employed (Ferguson 1997).

Research on sexual abuse of girls and adolescents is further hampered by a number of methodological and ethical challenges. For example, the first incident of sexual abuse may be difficult to distinguish from sexual debut. Some women may consider their sexual debut to be the first time they had intercourse, regardless of the circumstances, whereas other women may include only con-

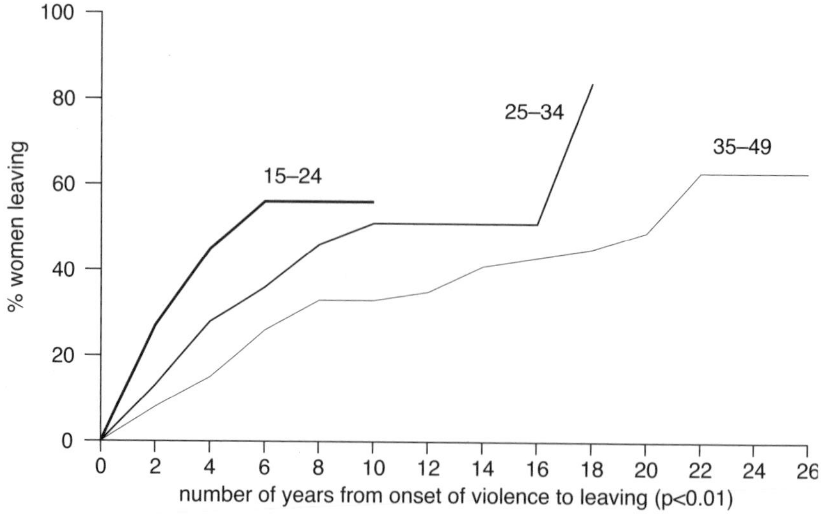

Figure 2.3 Number of years that women stay in a violent relationship, using Kaplan Meier Life Table Analysis, according to age groups, Nicaragua (*Source*: Ellsberg et al. 2001b)

sensual acts. Most questions on sexual debut simply refer to the first time a woman has sexual intercourse. In some surveys, such as the WHO study on domestic violence and women's health, follow-up questions are asked on the circumstances of the sexual encounter, such as 'Was your first sexual intercourse something you wanted at the time, something you didn't want but went along with, or something you were forced into?' (WHO 1997). These questions allow for a more nuanced understanding of the different elements of coercion, including social or economic pressure, beyond physical force.

A further difficulty is that women are typically more reluctant to discuss sexual abuse by non-partners than by partners, and therefore special methods are needed to encourage disclosure (Ellsberg et al. 2001a). For example, two studies conducted in León, Nicaragua, by the same researchers among similar populations found strikingly different results depending on the methodology used. In face-to-face interviews, only 8 per cent of women reported having been sexually abused at some point in their life by a non-partner, whereas an anonymous survey using self-completed questionnaires and a behaviourally specific definition of abuse (both contact and non-contact abuse) found that 27 per cent of women had been abused (Olsson et al. 2000).

Similar findings were obtained in the WHO multi-country study. The WHO questionnaire attempts to enhance disclosure by suggesting several different questions and formats to answer. Women are asked, 'Since the age of fifteen has anyone other than your partner ever forced you to have sex or to perform a sexual act when you did not want to?' and 'Before the age of fifteen, do you remember if anyone in your family ever touched you sexually, or made you do something sexual that you didn't want to?'. For each type of abuse, additional probing questions are asked to encourage respondents to remember possible abuse in different contexts, such as in school or at work. Finally, after the face-to-face interview, women are given the opportunity to indicate anonymously on a card whether they have experienced sexual abuse before the age of fifteen. In all cases but one (Lima, Peru), disclosure of sexual abuse has been considerably higher using the anonymous questions than in the face-to-face interviews (García-Moreno et al. 2003).

Sexual coercion and high-risk sexual behaviour

A study conducted in León, Nicaragua, in 1996 as a reproductive and child health research collaboration between León University and Umeå University in Sweden provides insights into the health effects of sexual coercion on adolescent women and men. The study sought to determine the prevalence of sexual abuse during childhood and adolescence among both men and women, and to examine whether these experiences were associated with subsequent increased sexual risk-taking behaviour (Olsson et al. 2000).

A sub-sample of literate urban men and women aged twenty-five to forty-four years was selected from a representative sample of households in León, and was invited to a public health event. Of these, 154 men and 213 women (53 and 66 per cent respectively of the men and women invited) participated in providing written answers in an anonymous questionnaire. Respondents were asked about experiences of sexual abuse before and after the age of twelve, including both contact and non-contact abuse.

Twenty per cent of men and 26 per cent of women reported that they had experienced sexual abuse. Women had been victims of attempted or completed rape twice as often as men (15 per cent as compared to 7 per cent respectively). Thirty-three per cent of men and 66 per cent of women who had ever experienced violence reported that the abuse was committed by a family member. Women who had experienced attempted or completed rape were more likely to have subsequently had a higher number of sexual partners compared to non-abused or moderately abused women.

The median age at first incident of abuse was ten for both men and women. Among those reporting abuse, 68 per cent of men and 74 per cent of women reported that the first episode of abuse had occurred by the age of twelve. Around one-third of men and 16 per cent of women who had experienced severe abuse before the age of thirteen stated that they had subsequently experienced severe abuse in adolescence.

The median age of sexual debut (defined as the first time they had sex, thus potentially referring to heterosexual or homosexual sexual debut) was 13.6 years among men who reported experiences of moderate or severe sexual abuse and

15.0 years among non-abused men ($p = 0.01$). There was no significant difference in age at sexual debut when comparing only the severely abused with the rest. When comparing men who had experienced sexual abuse and those who had not been abused, no significant differences were observed with regard to the number of lifetime partners and the number of sexual partners during the last five years or the last year, or in terms of use of condoms.

Women who had experienced severe abuse (including forced penetration) initiated their sexual life at 15.8 years (median) while women who had experienced either non-contact abuse or no abuse made their sexual debut more than two years later ($p = 0.02$). Moreover, severely abused women reported a higher number of sexual partners compared to the rest, in their lifetime, during the last five years as well as during the last year. Condom use was low in both groups (80 per cent of non-abused women and 77 per cent of abused women had never used a condom), and no significant differences were found between the groups with regard to condom use.

Conclusions

Research from Latin America and the Caribbean suggests that sexual violence against girls and young women is a serious threat to their sexual and reproductive health. Although violence against adolescent girls and young women occurs most often in the context of marriage or dating relationships, sexual violence by non-partners, particularly family members and acquaintances, is also common in many settings. These findings are particularly disturbing because they indicate that girls and young women are at greatest risk of sexual violence in their homes.

The results of the studies reviewed suggest the need to address sexual coercion in all programmes designed to improve the sexual and reproductive health of young men and women. Health services need to incorporate identification and care for abused women and girls within primary health services, in particular within youth-friendly services. Because sexual violence is stigmatized in most cultures, it is difficult for women to disclose abuse and obtain the help they need. Preventive measures are also needed, such as communications/information, education and communication (IEC) projects that draw attention to the harmful effects of sexual abuse, and challenge traditional gender norms that give men and boys control over women's bodies.

Additional research is needed to identify the prevalence of different types of sexual violence as well as their health effects. One of the most important challenges facing researchers is the need for increased consistency in the way sexual coercion is measured and reported. The use of measures to enhance disclosure and ensure the safety of respondents is also required (Ellsberg and Heise 2002; WHO 1999).

References

Carballo-Dieguez, A. and C. Dolezal (1995) 'Association between history of childhood sexual abuse and adult HIV-risk sexual behaviour in Puerto Rican men who have sex with men', *Child Abuse and Neglect*, 19: 595–605

Cayemittes, M., M. F. Placide, B. Barrere et al. (2001) *Enquête Mortalité, Morbidité et Utilisation des Services EMMUS-III Haiti 2000*, Petionville: Institut Haitien de L'Enfance, ORC Macro: 489

CDC/CEPAR (Centers for Disease Control and Centro de Estudios de Población y Desarrollo Social) (1995) *ENDEMAIN-94: Encuesta Demográfica y de Salud Materna e Infantil: Informe General*, Atlanta, GA: Centers for Disease Control

Ellsberg, M. and L. Heise (2002) 'Bearing witness: ethics in domestic violence research', *Lancet*, 359(9317): 1599–604

Ellsberg, M. C., R. Peña, A. Herrera et al. (1999) 'Wife abuse among women of childbearing age in Nicaragua', *American Journal of Public Health*, 89(2): 241–4

— (2000) 'Candies in hell: women's experiences of violence in Nicaragua', *Social Science and Medicine*, 51(11): 1595–610

Ellsberg, M., L. Heise, R. Peña et al. (2001a) 'Researching domestic violence against women: methodological and ethical considerations', *Studies in Family Planning*, 32(1): 1–16

Ellsberg, M., A. Winkvist, R. Peña et al. (2001b) 'Women's strategic responses to violence in Nicaragua', *Journal of Epidemiology and Community Health*, 55(8): 547–55

Ferguson, A. G. (1997) 'How good is the evidence relating to the frequency of childhood sexual abuse and the impact such abuse has on the lives of adult survivors?', *Public Health*, 111: 387–91

Finkelhor, D. (1994) 'The international epidemiology of child sexual abuse', *Child Abuse and Neglect*, 18: 409–17

García-Moreno, C., C. Watts, H. Jansen et al. (2003) 'Responding to violence against women: WHO's multicountry study on women's health and domestic violence', *Health and Human Rights*, 6(2): 112–27

Guezmes, A., N. Palomino and M. Ramos (2002) *Violencia Sexual y Física contra las Mujeres en el Perú*, Lima: Flora Tristan, Organización Mundial de la Salud, Universidad Peruana Cayetano Heredia, p. 119

Hakimi, M., E. Nur Hayati, M. Ellsberg et al. (2002) 'Silence for the sake of harmony: domestic violence and health in Central Java, Indonesia', Yogyakarta, Indonesia: Gadjah Mada University

Heise, L., M. Ellsberg and M. Gottemoeller (1999) 'Ending violence against women', *Population Reports*, 27, Baltimore, MD: Johns Hopkins University

Koss, M. P. (1993) 'Detecting the scope of rape: a review of prevalence research methods', *Journal of Interpersonal Violence*, 8(2): 198–222

Leventhal, J. M. (1998) 'Epidemiology of sexual abuse of children: old problems, new directions', *Child Abuse and Neglect*, 22: 481–91

Luster, T. and S. A. Small (1997) 'Sexual abuse history and number of sex partners among female adolescents', *Family Planning Perspectives*, 29: 204–11

Olsson, A., M. Ellsberg, S. Berglund et al. (2000) 'Sexual abuse during childhood and adolescence among Nicaraguan men and women: a population-based anonymous survey', *Child Abuse and Neglect*, 24(12): 1579–89

PROFAMILIA (2000) *Salud Sexual y Reproductiva: Resultados Encuesta Nacional de Demografía y Salud 2000*, Bogotá: Asociación Probienestar de la Familia Colombiana

Rosales, J., E. Loaiza, D. Primante et al. (1999) *Encuesta Nicaraguense de Demografia y Salud, 1998*, Managua: INEC

Schraiber, L. B. and A. F. d'Oliveira (2002) *WHO Multi-country Study on Women's Health and Domestic Violence, Brazil*, São Paolo: World Health Organization

Stock, J. L., M. A. Bell, D. K. Boyer et al. (1997) 'Adolescent pregnancy and sexual risk-taking among sexually abused girls', *Family Planning Perspectives*, 29(5): 200–203, 227

WHO (World Health Organization) (1997) *Protocol for WHO Multi-country Study on Women's Health and Domestic Violence*, Geneva: WHO

— (1999) 'Putting women's safety first: ethical and safety recommendations for research on domestic violence against women', Geneva: Global Programme on Evidence for Health Policy, World Health Organization, p. 13.

Widom, C. S. and J. B. Kuhns (1996) 'Childhood victimization and subsequent risk of promiscuity, prostitution and teenage pregnancy: a prospective study', *American Journal of Public Health*, 86: 1607–12

Wingood, G. M. and R. J. DiClemente (1997) 'Child sexual abuse, HIV sexual risk, and gender relations of African-American women', *American Journal of Preventive Medicine*, 13: 380–84.

3 | Young women's experiences of forced sex within marriage: evidence from India

K. G. SANTHYA AND SHIREEN J. JEJEEBHOY[1]

Experiences of forced sexual relations, often perpetrated by an intimate partner, have been increasingly documented over the last decade. An analysis of over fifty population-based surveys revealed, for example, that between 10 and 50 per cent of adult women globally reported having been physically assaulted by an intimate male partner, including husbands, at some point in their lives, and in more than one-third of these cases sexual abuse was also experienced (Heise et al. 1999). A recent review of non-consensual sexual experiences of young people, largely those aged thirteen to twenty-four, also suggests that between 2 and 20 per cent of adolescent and young women have experienced non-consensual sexual relations (Jejeebhoy and Bott, this volume). Although significant proportions of sexually active adolescent and young women (fifteen to twenty-four-year-olds) in developing-country settings are married, the literature is surprisingly silent on the sexual experiences of these young women and the extent to which these experiences are wanted or consensual. This chapter seeks to synthesize the limited evidence available from India on the magnitude of forced sex among married young women and the factors that may precipitate such experiences.

The *World Report on Violence and Health* has defined sexual violence as 'any sexual act, attempt to obtain a sexual act, unwanted sexual comments or advances, or acts to traffic, or otherwise directed against a person's sexuality using coercion, by any person regardless of their relationship to the victim' (Krug et al. 2002). Others have defined coerced sex to include 'more contested areas that require young women to marry and sexually service men not of their choosing' (Heise et al. 1995). Clearly, any sexual act in which the woman herself is unwilling and which she cannot refuse without suffering adverse social and physical consequences is coercive, even if the perpetrator is the victim's husband. It is this definition which has guided our review of the literature and selection of materials synthesized below.

This chapter has focused on India because among developing countries characterized by a high prevalence of early marriage among girls, forced sex among married adolescents appears to have been most widely studied in this country. In this overview, we have gathered evidence from several types of studies, including both qualitative and quantitative, published and unpublished. These include the few – largely small-scale – studies that were specifically designed to explore the nature of both young and adult women's sexual lives and report, in that context,

TABLE 3.1 Forced sex within marriage: women's reports of early marital sexual experiences

Sites	Sample, methodology	Women's reports/narratives/testimonies	Source
Kolkata	Young women married in adolescence, in-depth interviews (N = not available)	'I used to be scared when he came to get me and carry me to his bed ... I used to cry ... but he'd ... come and get me' (38-year-old woman, married at 14)	Ouattara et al. 1998
Delhi, low-income setting	Adolescents, in-depth interviews (N = 71)	'She did not want to celebrate the first night but her husband was annoyed ... he didn't agree and did it forcefully. She was having a lot of pain so her *bhabhi* [sister-in-law] took her to the dispensary the next morning' (18-year-old girl describing her sister's wedding night)	Sodhi and Verma 2003
Rural Uttar Pradesh	115 abortion seekers various ages; in-depth interviews	'It was a terrifying experience; when I tried to resist, he pinned my arms above my head. It must have been so painful and suffocating that I fainted' (32-year-old woman, married at 13)	Khan et al. 1996
One village, Kheda district, Gujarat	Survey, 109 married women 15–50 years (of whom 53 were <25)	34 women reported that the first sex was performed under pressure	Sharma et al. 1998
8 villages, Gujarat, Vadodara district	Repeated in-depth interviews, 69 women	'When it happened the first time ... I felt as though something had hurt me. After that I had problems while urinating; it used to burn a lot. Yet my husband insisted on doing it every day ... I would cry and tell him that it was painful ... still he would continue ...' (adult woman recalling early marital experiences)	Joshi et al. 2001

Mumbai, mixed ethnic community	Migrant women and men from Uttar Pradesh, aged 20–50; in-depth interviews with 26 women and 19 men	14 of 26 women reported at least one coercive experience, most on the wedding night. 'That night I was very sad and was not in a mood for anything. When he came near me I felt like crying ... I tried running out of the house but he caught hold me of me and gave me a slap. He didn't care about my feelings ... he seemed interested only in my body' (adult woman, recalling early marital experiences)	Maitra and Schensul 2004
Mumbai slums	Working-class women (20–40 years), repeated focus group discussions (35) and in-depth interviews (65)	'When he did it the first time, it was painful. I cried for days. I would tell my mother-in-law that I wished the night never came because at night her son used to come inside to sleep. She used to laugh at this and say I should go to him, I am no longer a child' (adult woman recalling early marital experiences)	George and Jaswal 1995; George 2002
Rural Tamil Nadu	66 ever-married women aged < 35 ('younger' women, mean age 26) and >35 ('older women', mean age 40), some with abortion experience, in-depth interviews	21 of 32 younger women and 19 of 34 older women reported forced sex. 'If I object strongly he shouts: "Are you sleeping with someone else?" After my first delivery, he called me for sex within a month. When I objected he beat me. This is a regular happening in my life' (woman in the younger age group, with experience of abortion, recalling early marital experiences)	Ravindran and Balasubramanian 2004

on experiences of forced sex in the early stages of marriage and/or at the time of interview. They also include studies of married men reporting perpetration of forced sex on their wives. Where appropriate and available, we have also included insights from other countries, including national-level estimates of the experience of forced sex within marriage from Demographic and Health Surveys (DHS).

We start with a few words of caution. As is well known, given the culture of silence around the subject of domestic violence, many women – especially the recently married – may not report or may under-report such experiences. There could be differential under-reporting by women in different sub-groups of the population; there are differences in the framing of questions used in studies to measure forced sex within marriage or intimate partnerships in different settings; and the findings from small-scale studies may be unrepresentative, coming largely from qualitative studies and from the retrospective experiences of adult women. These differences call for caution in making cross-study comparisons.

Forced sexual experience

Evidence on forced sexual experiences within marriage among adolescents and young women in India comes largely from qualitative studies. Quantitative data are also available, however, from three small-scale surveys that highlight the prevalence of such experiences. These surveys, conducted in the states of Gujarat and West Bengal, observe that between 6 and 13 per cent of young married women reported forced sexual experiences perpetrated by their husband (IIPS and Population Council 2004;[2] Visaria 2000). These rates roughly coincide with those reported in recent DHS in a variety of settings: Cambodia (3 per cent), Zambia (6 per cent), Colombia (8 per cent) and Nicaragua (8 per cent) (see <www.measuredhs.com>). Significantly higher rates are reported in two studies, however – DHS data from Haiti (22 per cent) (see <www.measuredhs.com>) and a case study of migrant carpet and garment factory workers in the Kathmandu valley of Nepal (23 per cent; Puri et al. 2003).

Findings from qualitative studies also reflect a consistent picture of forced early sexual experiences and highlight the sexual vulnerability of newly married – usually adolescent – women irrespective of whether data are derived from retrospective information from older women on their experiences as newly married adolescents or from young women themselves. Table 3.1 presents excerpts from a number of qualitative studies in India that focus on the nature of first or early sexual relations within marriage. Typically, these experiences with husbands are described as coercive, traumatic, distasteful and painful, and often involving the use of physical force. Sexual coercion described in these studies ranges from force and violence to submission to sex as a result of threats of abandonment or fear of abuse.

Findings from qualitative studies in Bangladesh, Nepal, Zimbabwe and Brazil underscore the fact that forced sexual experiences are common early in marriage in other settings as well (see also Ellsberg et al. 2000). The testimonies of young women in Bangladesh are illustrative: 'When I was sent to the bedroom of my husband, he asked me to come close to him and take off his watch. But when I went to him, he caught me and forced me on the bed. He had repeated intercourse on the same night forcefully, without any consideration to my pain, or my crying, and begging that he should not do it again' (twenty-five-year-old urban woman, secondary school education, Bangladesh; Khan et al. 2002). Similarly, in Nepal, Zimbabwe and Brazil young women reported: 'I did not sleep with him for two or three nights ... After a few days he did it to me by force ... I had no other way ... I could not make any sound or cry out' (eighteen-year-old uneducated woman, Nepal; Puri et al. 2003); 'I told my sisters-in-law that my husband had forced me into sex, but they told me that this is part of life' (pregnant adolescent, Zimbabwe; Hof and Richters 1999); and 'I screamed. He said, "You have to do it." It was a sad bloodbath, the next day I couldn't even walk' (low-income factory worker married in adolescence, Brazil; Goldstein 1994).

Indeed, authors suggest that the reactions of young brides often echo those experienced by sexually abused children and those suffering post-traumatic stress, and are associated with feelings of hopelessness, helplessness and depression (Finkelhor 1988; Khan and Lynch 1997; Terr 1994).

Surveys conducted among men in India that shed light on men's reports of forced sex perpetrated on their wives underscore the likelihood that women under-report such experiences. A study of 6,600 married men aged fifteen to sixty-five in Uttar Pradesh, India, enquired from men whether they had ever had sex with their wives 'even if she was not willing' and whether they had ever 'physically forced' their wives to have sex. Findings suggest that one-third (33 per cent) of younger men (aged thirty or younger) and one-quarter (26 per cent) of older men (over thirty-one) reported having non-consensual sex (with or without physical force) with their wives at some time in their married life (Martin et al. 1999). From a study in three states, Punjab, Rajasthan and Tamil Nadu, while the exact wording/framing/phrasing of questions was not available, as many as 67 per cent of young men (aged fifteen to twenty-four) compared to 43 per cent of older men (aged thirty-six to fifty) reported forcing sex on their wives in the twelve months preceding investigation (Duvvury et al. 2002).

Threats of abandonment and seeking sexual gratification elsewhere also characterize the coercive experiences of young brides. For example, in qualitative explorations with first-time pregnant and recently delivered young women in India, a few young women in Kolkata narrated instances where the exercise of sexual choice was met with threats of remarriage and arguments. For example:

> I decided to stop it since I used to feel uneasy while having sex with a big abdomen. But my husband used to get angry if I told him that I did not want to have

sex. He used to tell me that he would remarry if I refused to have sex with him. I tried to explain to him, but he did not want to listen. He used to get angry if I refused and we had some tiffs on this issue. I had to give in to his demands after a few days and our tiffs were resolved. We continued in this manner till my ninth month. (eighteen-year-old, recently delivered mother; Santhya et al. 2001)

Still other studies note a sense of submission among women, and their helplessness is articulated, for example, in a study of adult women in low-income settings in Mumbai, who recalled their early marital lives: 'I was scared. I felt he would beat me if I refused. I did not like sleeping with him, right under my mother-in-law's cot. I felt he was using force on me. There was no need to sleep so soon in front of everyone. But he never experienced any shame' (George 2002). Similarly, 'Many women explained to me that if you do this, a woman has a life or else he [your husband] will move away from you. They would all say this' (George 2003).

Underlying risk factors

As with the evidence on the dimensions of forced sex within marriage among young women, reliable data on the factors underlying such experiences are also sparse. The limited evidence available from India, however, points to several factors that appear to be associated with such experiences among newly married young women, and are described below.

Early age at marriage Despite rising age at marriage and laws prohibiting early marriage in India, half of women continue to marry as adolescents (IIPS and ORC-Macro 2000). Women who marry in adolescence may be more likely to experience forced sex than women who marry in adulthood for a number of reasons. First, because of their young age and the associated psychological, physical and emotional immaturity, women who marry in adolescence may not be capable of giving consent to a sexual relationship. Studies worldwide suggest that the earlier the sexual initiation among girls, the more likely it is to have been forced (Jejeebhoy and Bott 2003). In a study in Uttar Pradesh, for example, women argued, 'How could a twelve-and-a-half-year-old child enjoy that [sex]?' (twenty-six-year-old married at twelve; Khan et al. 1996); and in Gujarat women observed: 'I married at the tender age of twelve. What would a girl know about it [sex] at that age?' (recollection of adult woman; Joshi et al. 2001).

Second, women who marry in adolescence are more likely to marry considerably older men. In India, for example, women who married at ages fifteen or below have an average spousal age gap of 7.3 compared to a gap of 4.7 for women who married at ages between twenty-one and twenty-five (Jensen and Thornton 2003). Women who marry considerably older men may be less capable of asserting themselves and power differentials between partners may be greater in such marriages than in marriages between partners of similar age, which may increase the risk of forced sex (ibid.; Nurse 2003).

These arguments are substantiated by the limited evidence available from India and other countries in South Asia on young women's perceptions and experiences of gender-based violence, including sexual violence. In India, data from the National Family Health Survey show that 62 per cent of women who married at ages fifteen or below, compared to 44 per cent of women who married at the ages of twenty-one and twenty-five, believed that a husband is justified in beating his wife for certain reasons (Jensen and Thornton 2003). A study in West Bengal reports that girls married at or below the age of fifteen were found to be especially vulnerable to forced sex in marriage (Ouattara et al. 1998). Likewise, a study of women in rural Gujarat notes that women who married in adolescence were significantly less likely than those who married in adulthood to report that marital sexual experiences were 'positive' (Joshi et al. 2001). Similar conclusions about the link of early marriage with the inability to negotiate sex and vulnerability to forced sex are drawn in studies in Bangladesh and Nepal (Khan et al. 2002; Puri et al. 2003).

Lack of familiarity with the husband-to-be Although patterns of marriage are in transition in several societies, including India – notably in terms of increased exercise of choice in timing of marriage and partner among younger generations – many young people, particularly girls, continue to be married and consummate marriage at a young age in the absence of informed consent (UNICEF 2001). For example, a recent study exploring female autonomy in selected sites in Pakistan, and north and south India, concludes that fewer than one-fifth of married women aged up to thirty-nine years reported any say in choice of husband in rural Uttar Pradesh, in north India and Punjab, Pakistan, and only about one-third participated in this decision in rural Tamil Nadu, south India (Jejeebhoy and Sathar 2001). Further analysis of data from Tamil Nadu and Uttar Pradesh, India, reveals moreover that for the overwhelming majority in both settings, irrespective of religion, marriages were arranged either by parents alone or with relatives and matchmakers (Jejeebhoy and Halli 2005). Qualitative evidence from other settings in India reiterates this lack of involvement in decision-making (Santhya et al. 2001).

Lack of involvement in the choice of husband is closely linked with a lack of familiarity with the husband prior to marriage, and indeed, many meet for the first time on the wedding day (IIPS and Population Council 2004). Lack of familiarity with the husband can exacerbate the non-consensual nature of early sex. For example, in a study in West Bengal young women who had an arranged marriage were twice as likely to report a non-consensual sexual experience compared to those who had a 'love' marriage (ibid.).

Lack of preparedness for sexual life Several studies in India (George 2002; George and Jaswal 1995; Haberland et al. 2001; Jejeebhoy 2000; Khan et al. 1996; Ouattara et al. 1998) and other developing countries have documented that young girls are often kept uninformed about sexual matters until they are married (Goldstein 1994; Khan et al. 2002; Puri et al. 2003). This lack of awareness compounds a young bride's lack of preparedness for sex. In studies in rural Gujarat and West Bengal, for example, women argued: 'What would a girl know about it [sexual relations] at that age? I used to think that after marriage a boy and a girl stay together and the girl has to cook – nothing beyond that' (adult woman, recalling early married life, Gujarat; Joshi et al. 2001); and 'I was scared and I did not know anything. I had not seen it or/and I had not talked about it [sexual relations] to anyone' (twenty-year-old woman who learned about sex from her husband, West Bengal; Haberland et al. 2001).

Indeed, parental attitudes ensure that young females remain poorly informed about sexual matters; parents typically (mis)perceive that deliberate withholding or obfuscating of information is a protective strategy (Mehra et al. 2002). As mothers observed, for example, 'Why give them so much information at this stage? They will learn when they need to ... [after marriage]' (Delhi slum; ibid.).

In contrast, young husbands are more likely to be informed about sex, and in many cases are sexually experienced before marriage.

Though sound evidence is limited, it is likely that lack of information about and preparedness for sexual life may instil fear about sexual intercourse in many young women, and contribute to the trauma or unwantedness that many associate with first or early sexual experiences. Lack of preparedness may likewise constrain young women's ability to communicate and negotiate with their husbands on sexual matters.

Unbalanced gender norms and power relations The perpetration of forced sex against women by their husbands or intimate partners is reinforced by unbalanced gender norms that associate masculinity with toughness and dominance, and femininity with submissiveness, and the notion that it is a woman's duty to submit to sex with her husband. Evidence suggests that traditional gender norms are indeed deeply entrenched and offer newly married women little room to express their sexual rights. The importance of submission is typically conveyed to about-to-be-married girls, as corroborated by excerpts from a number of studies: 'If you won't give him [sex] then he would force and you will have pain' (adult woman, Mumbai, recalling early marital experiences; George 2003); 'I had feelings of discomfort but I had to accept my husband's wishes' (eighteen-year-old, recently delivered mother; Santhya et al. 2001); and 'My friends and family told me [just before her first sexual experience], "Don't make a noise, you must bear the touch of a man. This man has married and brought you here for this"' (adult woman, Mumbai, recalling early marital experiences; George 2003).

At the same time, norms that expect women not to display an interest in sex and even resist 'wanted' sexual advances offer husbands a justification for ignoring their wives' preferences. As can be seen in the following narratives, in some studies in Mumbai men who forced sex on their wives on their wedding night justified their actions: 'I think she was doing *nakharas* [playing hard to get]. All women say "no" but actually they want it. So I did it. She cried a lot, it was very painful for her and she kept abusing me through the night. She said this was not love, only *hawas* [lust]' (adult male, recalling early marital experiences; Maitra and Schensul 2004). Similarly:

> Friends also told me that on the first night, of course, the bride would feel shy and hesitate ... forcefully I had sex twice. But on the second night she completely refused to have intercourse and told me she was getting a severe pain in the vagina due to forceful sex on the first night. I shared the experience with my friends ... they told me nothing was wrong in this, every woman searches for an excuse to avoid sex ... when women have pain, they enjoy it more. (adult male, recalling early marital experiences; Verma and Schensul 2004)

Moreover, unbalanced gender norms socialize men with a sense of entitlement to sex, even if forced, with their wives. The narratives of young males in a number of studies corroborate this sense of entitlement. For example, 'At night, I asked her to take off her clothes. She refused. When I asked her two–three times, she started crying. I made her keep quiet, and after that I took her clothes off and did my work' (nineteen-year-old painter, Delhi, referring to his wedding night; Sodhi and Verma 2003). Similarly: 'If she objects when she is not well or when she is menstruating, I accept it. But if she objects for other reasons I don't accept it and will have it [sexual relations] by compulsion without her desire. I beat her in two types of situations. One is when I am drunk and the other is when she says no to sex' (young man whose wife has had experience of induced abortion, rural Tamil Nadu; Ravindran and Balasubramanian 2004).

Lack of social and legal support The social and economic dependence of married women, especially young married women, on men and the lack of alternative support systems may compromise their ability to negotiate sex, to prevent forced sex or to take recourse in such situations. As mentioned above, young women are told prior to or early in marriage that only if they comply and provide sex whenever the man wants will they have security. In the absence of alternative support systems, women may passively accept non-consensual or unwanted sexual relations as a strategy for survival, as is evident from the following narratives of women: 'A woman needs some support. How long will her parents support her? So, a woman like me will say, "If I've got to have clothes to wear and food to eat, then you do whatever you want [with my body] but keep me as a wife should be kept." If women do not live up to the expectations of a wife, including being sexually available, then husbands can shift their attention to other women who may be more willing. So, to have a "life", status, esteem and honour, married women have to submit to the demands of their husbands' (adult low-income migrant woman, recalling early married life, Mumbai; George 2003).

The narratives of women in rural Gujarat were similar: 'One does sometimes feel like running away from it all. But where does one go? There should be a place where women can go. The only place is the parental home but parents will always try and send you back' (adult woman in an abusive marriage; Visaria 2000).

The absence of perceived alternatives may inhibit women from even reporting forced sexual experiences. In a study in Kolkata, for example, a woman noted that the investigation enabled her, for the first time in twenty-four years, to reveal her experiences of forced sexual relations perpetrated by her husband (Ouattara et al. 1998).

Access to legal support is also denied to women suffering forced sex within marriage. Indeed, women who suffer such experiences are also denied state protection. The Indian Penal Code does not recognize marital rape as an offence unless the woman is aged fifteen or less, or is separated from her husband (Jaising, this volume; Sen and Karnya 2000).

Divergent sexual experiences later in marriage

The most consistent finding of this review is that force and submission mark sexual initiation within marriage for significant numbers of newly married young women. In contrast to the consistency of reports of forced early sexual relations, however, several patterns emerge from profiles of sexual experiences later in marriage, as highlighted below.

Passive acceptance One pattern that emerges is that for a significant number of women subsequent sexual experiences continued to be marked by unwantedness; however, passive acceptance had replaced fear and trauma. In several studies, women said that their fear vanished as sex became a 'habit' (George 2002; Joshi et al. 2001). Similar experiences were reported in a study of abortion seekers in rural Uttar Pradesh: 'He gets angry when I refuse – but in the end I always agree. No, it doesn't reach the degree of violence' (twenty-five-year-old, uneducated woman; Khan et al. 1996). In a study of rural women in Gujarat, women did not perceive any options: 'To keep him at home, I allow him to have sex whenever he desires, otherwise he will go to a prostitute ... I am helpless' (adult woman, recalling early marital experiences; Joshi et al. 2001).

Avoidance strategies A second pattern suggested by some women was that familiarity with the husband and a better understanding of sexual issues enabled them to develop strategies to avoid unwanted sex with their husbands. These included threats of screaming, endangering the husband's prestige, threats of suicide, waking young children and feigning menstruation (George 2002; Khan et al. 1996). Similar findings are also evident in studies in neighbouring Bangladesh and Nepal (Khan et al. 2002; Puri et al. 2003).

Greater intimacy with the husband A third pattern was that women reported greater intimacy with their husbands in the course of married life. Indeed, while women acknowledged that early experiences were likely to have been forced, several reported pleasurable sexual experiences and even that *habit* enabled them to gain the confidence to express their sexual desire to their husbands (see, for example, Joshi et al. 2001; for Bangladesh, see Khan et al. 2002). In the study in rural Gujarat, while only nineteen of sixty-nine women reported that first or early sexual encounters with their husbands were pleasant, as many as fifty-three reported that current sexual relations with their husbands were pleasant and that they had a better understanding with their husbands; indeed, twenty-eight described ways in which they communicated their desire for sex to their husbands (Joshi et al. 2001). Likewise, in the study of low-income women in Mumbai, women reported that the feeling of fear had receded and had been replaced by pleasure: 'For a year, year and a half I had fear ... [then] my fear went away. I did not dislike it [sexual relations]. If a man touches you, then something happens to the woman too. If something happens from both sides, then there is some pleasure in it' (adult woman, recalling early marital experiences; George 2002).

In the study of abortion seekers in Uttar Pradesh, young married women reported, for example, 'We have an understanding' (Khan et al. 1996). And in a study of young married women in Kolkata and Vadodara, women suggested that as their marriage progressed, they were increasingly able to assert themselves (Haberland et al. 2001). Similarly, among low-income migrants in Mumbai, while almost all women perceived sexual access by their husbands as a male right, at least half reported that they were able to refuse sex when they did not want it (Maitra and Schensul 2002).

Conclusions

This review synthesizes what is known about forced sexual experiences perpetrated by husbands among married adolescents and young women in India, and the factors that may precipitate such experiences. Although based on a few studies that highlight this issue, findings suggest that forced sex within marriage among adolescents and young women is not uncommon. Yet it remains a taboo subject that is deeply mired in an unquestioning acceptance of gender inequalities.

The single most consistent finding that emerges is the pervasiveness of forced sexual relations early in marriage, specifically at sexual initiation. Indeed, it would appear that large proportions of marriages initiated in adolescence are consummated with force and without the consent of the young bride. It is notable that fear, threats and pain typically characterize the narratives of women recalling their early marital experiences; equally notable is the absence of such terms as pleasure or understanding.

A number of factors are hypothesized to underlie these experiences in the Indian context. Early and arranged marriages in which the young bride scarcely knows her husband-to-be and has had little say in marriage-related decisions clearly condition the extent to which she can exercise choice in sexual – or any other – matter in her marital home. The lack of information on sexual matters or on what to expect of sexual relations compounds the anxiety and fear that young women so frequently describe to characterize their early marital experiences and also compromises their ability to negotiate sex. The lack of alternative support systems also clearly compromises young married women's ability to refuse sex or to take recourse in a coercive situation. The most pervasive underlying factor, however, is deeply rooted gender inequality and traditional norms that justify female submissiveness and male entitlement to forced sex within marriage, and which reinforce the reality of limited familial or societal support.

Findings also suggest that while early marital experiences are fairly uniformly described as forced, subsequent experiences tend to be varied. Many women continue to submit to forced sexual relations with their husbands, replacing fear and pain with passive acceptance. Others exercise sexual choice in different ways. Women develop strategies successfully to avoid unwanted sex with their husbands, while some report the development of more sexually equitable relationships and pleasurable experiences based on a better understanding with their husbands and a growing ability to communicate on sexual matters.

These findings are clearly tentative, based on a few studies conducted among small populations. There is a need to further our understanding of the prevalence, forms and context of forced sexual relations among married young women and the factors that may heighten their vulnerability to such relationships within marriage and, conversely, those that equip them to negotiate wanted sexual relations within marriage. While restricted to India, these findings may well be similar to experiences in several other Asian, as well as African and Middle Eastern, settings in which marriage patterns are broadly similar but from where even fewer investigations of non-consensual sexual experiences of married young women are available.

The paucity of information makes it difficult to draw programme recommendations from this review. A few programmatic directions are suggested, however. Existing programmes implicitly assume that sexual relations within marriage are consensual and that women exercise choice in sexual and reproductive decisions – indeed, findings underscore the need for programmes to appreciate the non-consensual nature of marital sexual relations, especially among young women at the early stages of their married life. Findings also highlight the need for sexuality and life skills education that focuses on breaking down traditional gender stereotypes and attitudes that justify the perpetration of forced sex in marriage. Life skills education is also key to equipping young women with information on sexual matters, and the ability to communicate about sexual matters with family and future partners, as well as providing them with the skills to negotiate wanted sexual outcomes and to protect themselves from coercive sexual experiences, both within and outside of marriage.

Findings also argue for action at the level of parents, families and communities. It is important that adult gatekeepers are sensitized to the deleterious consequences of withholding information on sexual matters from their daughters and the need to equip them with such information. Gatekeepers also need to be sensitized to the reality of sexual coercion in marriage and the need to provide a supportive environment. Findings strongly endorse the need to persuade adult gatekeepers of the desirability of delayed marriage and of enabling young brides-to-be to play a more active role in decisions on the timing of marriage and the selection of husband, and to develop a better acquaintance with the husband-to-be prior to marriage. Finally, it is important that legal systems are sensitized about the particular needs and vulnerabilities of married young women and that legal recourse is available to those who suffer forced sexual relations. Equally important is that procedural barriers, gaps and biases that undermine the law's ability to deter violence in marriage and protect women from sexual harassment and forced sex from their partners and others are addressed.

Notes

1 We are grateful to Asha Matta and Komal Saxena for assistance.

2 These percentages may well under-report experience of sexual coercion as they reflect only the extent of coercion among those who reported conveying to their husbands their reluctance to have sex; the question was not asked of those who may not have wanted to have sex but were too intimidated to convey this to their husbands.

References

Duvvury, N., M. Nayak and K. Allendorf (2002) 'Links between masculinity and violence: aggregate analysis', in *Domestic Violence in India: Exploring Strategies, Promoting Dialogue – Men, Masculinity and Domestic Violence in India: Summary Report of Four Studies*, Washington, DC: International Center for Research on Women

Ellsberg, M., R. Pena, A. Herrera et al. (2000) 'Candies in hell: women's experiences of violence in Nicaragua', *Social Science and Medicine*, 51: 1595–610

Finkelhor, D. (1988) 'The trauma of child sexual abuse', in G. E. Wyatts and G. J. Powell (eds), *Lasting Effects of Child Sexual Abuse*, Beverly Hills, CA: Sage Publications, pp. 61–82

George, A. (2002) 'Embodying identity through heterosexual sexuality – newly married adolescent women in India', *Culture, Health and Sexuality*, 4(2): 207–22

— (2003) 'Newly married adolescent women: experiences from case studies in urban

India', in S. Bott et al. (eds), *Towards Adulthood: Exploring the Sexual and Reproductive Health of Adolescents in South Asia*, Geneva: World Health Organization, pp. 67–72

George, A. and S. Jaswal (1995) *Understanding Sexuality: Ethnographic Study of Poor Women in Bombay*, Women and AIDS Program Research Report Series no. 12, Washington, DC: International Center for Research on Women

Goldstein, D. M. (1994) 'AIDS and women in Brazil: the emerging problem', *Social Science and Medicine*, 39(7): 919–29

Haberland, N., E. McGrory and K. G. Santhya (2001) 'First time parents project, supplemental diagnostic report', Vadodara: unpublished

Heise, L., M. Ellsberg and M. Gottemoeller (1999) 'Ending violence against women', Population Reports Series L, *Issues in World Health*, 11:1–43

Heise, L. L., K. Moore and N. Toubia (1995) *Sexual Coercion and Reproductive Health: A Focus on Research*, New York: Population Council

Hof, C. and A. Richters (1999) 'Exploring intersections between teenage pregnancy and gender violence: lessons from Zimbabwe', *African Journal of Reproductive Health*, 3(1): 51–65

IIPS (International Institute for Population Sciences) and ORC Macro (2000) *National Family Health Survey (NFHS-2), 1998–99: India*, Mumbai: IIPS

IIPS (International Institute for Population Sciences) and Population Council (2004) 'Intervention research on pregnancy and postpartum programmes for first-time parents – baseline report', unpublished

Jejeebhoy, S. (2000) 'Adolescent sexual and reproductive behaviour: a review of the evidence from India', in R. Ramasubban and S. Jejeebhoy (eds), *Women's Reproductive Health in India*, Jaipur: Rawat Publications, pp. 40–101

Jejeebhoy, S. and S. Bott (2003) 'Non-consensual sexual experiences of young people: a review of the evidence from developing countries', *Population Council Regional Working Paper* no. 16, New Delhi: Population Council

Jejeebhoy, S. and S. S. Halli (2005) 'Marriage patterns in rural India: influence of sociocultural context', in J. Behrman, C. Lloyd, N. Stromquist et al. (eds), *Studies on the Transition to Adulthood in Developing Countries*, Washington, DC: National Academy of Sciences

Jejeebhoy, S. and Z. Sathar (2001) 'Women's autonomy in India and Pakistan: the influence of religion and region', *Population and Development Review*, 27(4): 687–712

Jensen, R. and R. Thornton (2003) 'Early female marriage in the developing world', *Gender and Development*, 11(2): 9–19

Joshi, A., M. Dhapola, E. Kurian et al. (2001) 'Experiences and perceptions of marital sexual relationships among rural women in Gujarat, India', *Asia-Pacific Population Journal*, 16(2): 177–94

Khan, M. E., J. W. Townsend and S. D'Costa (2002) 'Behind closed doors: a qualitative study on sexual behaviour of married women in Bangladesh', *Culture, Health and Sexuality*, 4(2): 237–56

Khan, M. E., J. W. Townsend, R. Sinha et al. (1996) 'Sexual violence within marriage', *Seminar*, 447 (November): 32–5

Khan, N. Z. and M. A. Lynch (1997) 'Recognising child maltreatment in Bangladesh', *Child Abuse and Neglect*, 21(8): 815–18

Krug, E. G., L. L. Dahlberg, J. A. Mercy et al. (2002) *World Report on Violence and Health*, Geneva: World Health Organization

Maitra, S. and S. Schensul (2002) 'Reflecting diversity and complexity in marital sexual relationships in a low-income community in Mumbai', *Culture, Health and Sexuality*, 4(2): 133–51

— (2004) 'The evolution of marital relationship and sexual risk in an urban slum community in Mumbai', in R. K. Verma et al. (eds), *Sexuality in the Time of AIDS: Contemporary Perspectives from Communities in India*, New Delhi: Sage Publications, pp. 129–55

Martin, S. L., B. Kilgallen, A. O. Tsui et al. (1999) 'Sexual behaviors and reproductive health outcomes: associations with wife abuse in India', *Journal of the American Medical Association*, 282(20): 1967–72

Mehra, S. R., R. Savithri and L. Coutinho (2002) 'Gender double standards and power imbalances: adolescent partnerships in Delhi, India', Paper presented at the Asia-Pacific Social Science and Medicine Conference, Kunming, China, October

Nurse, J. (2003) 'Gender based violence in married or partnered adolescents', Background paper presented at WHO meeting on Married Adolescents, Geneva, December

Ouattara, M., P. Sen and M. Thomson (1998) 'Forced marriage, forced sex: the perils of childhood for girls', *Gender and Development*, 6(3): 27–33

Puri, M., J. Cleland and Z. Matthews (2003) 'Extent of sexual coercion among young female migrant workers and their sexual health problems in Nepal', Paper presented at the Annual Meetings of the Population Association of America, Minneapolis

Ravindran, T. K. and P. Balasubramanian (2004) '"Yes" to abortion but "no" to sexual rights: the paradoxical reality of married women in rural Tamil Nadu, India', *Reproductive Health Matters*, 12(23): 88–99

Santhya, K. G., E. McGrory and N. Haberland (2001) 'First time parents project, supplemental diagnostic report', Kolkata: unpublished

Sen, P. and A. Karnya (2000) 'CHANGE: non-consensual sex in marriage', *The British Council: The Network Newsletter*, 20: 8–11

Sharma, V., S. Rachna and A. Sharma (1998) 'Can married women say no to sex? repercussions of the denial of the sexual act', *Journal of Family Welfare*, 44(1): 1–8

Sodhi, G. and M. Verma (2003) 'Sexual coercion among unmarried adolescents of an urban slum in India', in S. Bott et al. (eds), *Towards Adulthood: Exploring the Sexual and Reproductive Health of Adolescents in South Asia*, Geneva: World Health Organization, pp. 91–4

Terr, L. C. (1994) 'Childhood traumas: an outline and overview', *American Journal of Psychiatry*, 148: 10–20

UNICEF (2001) *Early Marriage: Child Spouses*, Florence: Innocenti Research Centre

Verma, R. K. and S. L. Schensul (2004) 'Male sexual health problems in Mumbai: cultural constructs that present opportunities for HIV/AIDS risk reduction', in R. K. Verma et al. (eds), *Sexuality in the Time of AIDS: Contemporary Perspectives from Communities in India*, New Delhi: Sage Publications, pp. 243–61

Visaria, L. (2000) 'Violence against women: a field study', *Economic and Political Weekly*, 13 May, pp. 1742–51

4 | Sexual coercion among ever-partnered women in Thailand

WASSANA IM-EM, CHURNRURTAI KANCHANACHITRA AND KRITAYA ARCHAVANITKUL

Although the experience of physical and sexual violence by women in intimate relationships is prevalent in Thailand, evidence remains sparse. Indeed, the majority of available studies that address violence in intimate partnerships are based on surveys of small samples of women (see Somswasdi and Corrigan 2004), making generalizations difficult. The findings of these studies, however, point to disturbing levels of violence. For example, in a survey of married women from 122 households in a suburban community of Bangkok, 21 per cent reported the experience of violence perpetrated at some time by their husbands (Achara 1998). Similarly, in a study in the urban area of Srakaew province, a total of 88 per cent of sampled women reported the experience of sexual, physical or psychological violence perpetrated by their husbands; with some one-third reporting the experience of physical and sexual violence respectively (Bussarin 1999). Another study of 221 married female staff members of Thammasat University reveals that 67 per cent had experienced psychological violence and 32 per cent had experienced physical violence (Panchalee 1998). Finally, in a study of 652 female students in secondary schools and colleges in one province (Nakornsawan), some 20 and 39 per cent of secondary school and college students, respectively, reported that they had been sexually abused at some point in their lives; 11 and 21 per cent respectively reported the experience of attempted rape; and 9 and 24 per cent, respectively, reported the experience of rape; perpetrators were predominantly boyfriends or lovers (Srinual and Archavanitkul 2004).

While these studies are pioneering, they have several limitations that render the findings unrepresentative of the country. For example, the findings are not comparable as studies have used a variety of definitions to measure violence experienced by women. In addition, few studies were community-based and representative samples were not used. Discussions of the quality of data have not been provided. All the available studies focus on lifetime experience of violence and do not give a picture of recent experience of violence; some did not distinguish between violence inflicted by partners and non-partners, and several studies that explore rape by non-partners draw their data from newspaper reports, statistics obtained from shelter homes for women or police records.

Similar limitations were noted in other studies on domestic violence, and the need for more solid and representative data has been widely acknowledged. In view of this need, the World Health Organization (WHO) initiated a multi-country research programme on domestic violence against women and implications for women's health. Eight countries from different parts of the world participated in the programme, including Thailand. The study in Thailand was conducted by the Institute of Population and Social Research, Mahidol University (IPSR) and the Foundation for Women (FFW).

The objectives of this chapter are to discuss the findings of this study and to shed light on non-consensual sexual experiences of young women in these two settings. It specifically discusses the prevalence of sexual coercion in intimate partnerships and the underlying factors that heighten risk or protect young women from such experiences.

The study

The study was conducted in Bangkok and Nakornsawan province and included a combination of qualitative and quantitative approaches. In a formative research phase, conducted in 1999, key informant interviews and focus group discussions with women and men (conducted separately) were held in order to gain insights into the experience of coercion among women and to inform the development of the survey questionnaire. This was followed, in 2000, by a population-based survey entitled 'Women's Health and Life Experiences' using a structured questionnaire and face-to-face interviews to investigate issues surrounding sexual coercion in intimate partnerships in Thailand. Finally, in a third phase, conducted in 2000/01, in-depth interviews were held with women and couples who reported the experience of sexual coercion in intimate partnerships, which were intended to shed light on the survey findings. This chapter will focus on findings of the survey only.

The study employed a multi-stage probability design. The sample was selected from villages and urban wards, and thereafter households and women were selected proportional to size. A total of 2,817 women aged fifteen to forty-nine from the two sites were interviewed. In each selected household, only one woman was randomly selected for the interview. If the selected woman was not at home when the interviewer arrived, the interviewer would make an appointment to revisit her; up to three such call-back visits were made and the substitution of other women from the same household was not permitted.

The survey questionnaire comprised a household schedule and a questionnaire for women. The household schedule was addressed to any adult member of the household who could provide information on the household, and the interview lasted approximately fifteen minutes. The questionnaire addressed to women contained twelve sections, and was administered to selected women regardless of whether or not they had experienced coercion in intimate partnerships. The questionnaire was designed, with appropriate skip patterns, to be relevant for both single and married women. Interviews typically lasted thirty to ninety minutes, depending on whether the respondent had ever cohabited with a partner, or experienced sexual coercion in intimate partnerships or violence during childhood.

The research team recognized that the issue of sexual coercion in intimate partnerships is highly sensitive. On the one hand, this issue is considered a private matter and inappropriate for discussion with non-family members; there is moreover a tendency to blame the woman for provoking a coercive incident. On the other hand, for women who suffer coercion the experience remains a traumatic one, and often women who have survived such incidents are ashamed to reveal their experiences. In view of the sensitivity of the topic, the research team gave primary importance to the research process. The study team accorded high priority to ensuring women's safety. The questionnaire was designed to minimize anxiety among respondents, and interviews were conducted only if privacy and confidentiality could be assured.

Moreover, the study team recruited interviewers carefully and all interviewers and supervisors underwent an intensive three-week training programme. The first week of training focused on gender, sexuality and reproductive health and rights as they relate to sexual coercion against women. In the following two weeks, interviewers were given a thorough orientation in the study, the questionnaire and its administration. They were prepared to probe intimate issues in a sensitive way. In addition, interviewers received training on how to cope with stressful events and how to create and maintain privacy and confidentiality during the interview; they were also given information on appropriate referral services for women in need, but were trained to resist from counselling respondents. A total of thirty-two women were employed as supervisors and interviewers, and undertook the survey over a period of five months.

Operationalizing sexual coercion

The study explored sexual coercion in two ways: sexual coercion perpetrated by an intimate partner and forced sexual initiation. Questions related to sexual coercion perpetrated by an intimate partner were addressed to ever-partnered women – that is, those who were, at the time of interview, currently married, currently unmarried but living with a man, those who currently had a regular sexual partner but were living apart, and those who were divorced, separated or widowed. The following questions explored sexual coercion perpetrated by an intimate partner: 'Has your current partner or any other partner ever physically forced you to have sexual intercourse when you did not want to? Did you ever have sexual intercourse you did not want because you were afraid of what he might do? Did he ever force you to do something sexual that you found degrading or humiliating?'

If the respondent reported the experience of sexual coercion in intimate partnerships, she was asked whether she had experienced an incident in the past twelve months, how often she had ever experienced coercion and how often she had had such experiences in the past twelve months. Thus, data are available on coercion perpetrated by an intimate partner experienced over the respondent's lifetime and within the past twelve months.

In order to assess coerced sexual initiation, likewise, a number of questions were asked. These questions were addressed to all women who reported any sexual experience, irrespective of their current marital status. For example: 'How would you describe the first time that you had sex? Would you say that you wanted to have sex, you did not want to have sex but it happened anyway, or were you forced to have sex?'

In addition, the following two questions were asked of all women to explore their experience of sexual coercion by non-intimate partners: 'Since the age of fifteen, has anyone [for women with current or past partner: other than your partner/husband] ever forced you to have sex or to perform a sexual act when you did not want to? If yes, who did this to you?' and: 'Before the age of fifteen, do you remember if anyone in your family ever touched you sexually, or made you do something sexual that you didn't want to? If yes, who did this to you?'

Results

The survey covered a total of 4,899 households, 2,800 in Bangkok and 2,099 in Nakornsawan province. Of these, some 95 per cent responded to the household schedule (91 per cent in Bangkok and 99 per cent in Nakornsawan province). Of a total of 3,173 women approached, 2,817 women agreed to the interview, that is a response rate of 89 per cent for the woman's schedule (85 per cent in Bangkok and 94 per cent in Nakornsawan province). A mere 11 per cent did not respond, either because they refused to be interviewed or because they could not be reached within three contacts; several of these women were either working outside their home, were travelling or were hospitalized. The non-response rate was higher in Bangkok than in Nakornsawan province (15 and 6 per cent, respectively). The high response rates obtained for both the household schedule and the women's schedule were largely attributable to the efficient coordination of the village health volunteers and provincial statistics officers in Nakornsawan province and postal service officers in Bangkok, who assisted study teams in locating selected households.

A comparison of the age distribution of survey respondents with that recorded in the 2000 census suggests that younger women, notably those aged fifteen to twenty-four, are somewhat under-represented (and correspondingly older women over-represented, particularly in Nakornsawan province) in the survey as compared to the census (National Statistical Office 2000). By and large, however, the age profiles obtained in the survey do reflect the age distributions obtained in the survey.

Socio-demographic profile Table 4.1 presents a socio-demographic profile of

TABLE 4.1 Socio-demographic characteristics of respondents by age group (fifteen to forty-nine years)

Socio-demographic characteristic	Age group 15–24	25–34	35–49	All women
Number	702	859	1,256	2,817
Partnership and marital status (%)				
Never partnered	66	16	11	26
Ever partnered	34	84	89	74
Currently married and living together	21	68	71	58
Currently living together, not married	8	9	7	8
Currently partnered or married, living apart	4	2	1	2
Separated, divorced, widowed	1	6	10	7
% reporting a single lifetime intimate partner/ husband	90	83	85	85
Current residence: (%) urban	71	70	59	65
Level of education (%)				
No education	0	2	4	3
Primary education	16	46	61	45
Secondary education	56	25	16	29
Higher than secondary education	28	27	19	24
Currently working for wages (% yes)	42	81	83	72
Relative living near by (% yes)	80	72	73	74
Frequency seeing/talking to a member of natal family (%)				
At least once a week	71	61	63	64
At least once a month	13	17	15	15
At least once a year	15	19	18	18
Never	1	3	4	3
Have a family member to turn to for help (% yes)	96	95	92	94
Median age at first sex (life table)	18.4	21.2	22.7	20.8
% who experienced first sex by age 18	29.3*	29.3	21.9	25.7

Note: *Excludes 203 who were aged 15–17 at the time of interview.

respondents. In terms of partnership status, three-quarters of all women reported that they had had at least one intimate partner over the course of their lives. The majority (58 per cent) were currently married and co-residing; fewer than 10 per cent were currently living together but not married, currently partnered or married but living apart, or separated, divorced or widowed. On average, ever-partnered women reported a single intimate partner; only 15 per cent reported more than one intimate partner or husband over the course of their lives. In terms of educational status, about half had attained a primary school education and about one-quarter had more than a secondary education. Almost three-quarters of the women worked and earned an income of their own. Although about one-quarter did not live near a member of their natal family, the majority (94 per cent) reported that they had a family member to turn to in times of need, and 97 per cent reported that they were in touch with natal family members. The median age at sexual initiation derived from life table analysis was 20.8 years; 26 per cent of the sample reported first sex by the time they were aged eighteen.

As can be seen from Table 4.1, young women, that is those aged fifteen to twenty-four, differed from older women in several ways. Fewer young women compared to older women had ever been partnered (34 as against over 80 per cent). Of the ever partnered, those aged fifteen to twenty-four appear to be somewhat less likely than others to be currently married and co-residing with the partner. In general, younger women were better educated than older women: over 80 per cent had attained a secondary or higher education compared to 52 per cent of women aged twenty-five to thirty-four and 35 per cent in the older group. Younger women were also less likely than older women to work for wages (42 per cent compared to over 80 per cent respectively). In terms of sexual debut, young women tended to initiate sex earlier than older women (median age 18.4 years and over 21 years respectively). Indeed, almost 30 per cent of women aged eighteen to twenty-four and twenty-five to thirty-four, compared to 22 per cent of older women, had initiated sex by the age of eighteen.

Experience of sexual coercion by an intimate partner As Table 4.2 shows, some 29 per cent of all women had experienced sexual coercion (were subject to forced sexual intercourse, or consented to sex out of fear of their partner, or were forced to engage in an unwanted sexual act) at some point in their lives, and 16 per cent had experienced coercion in the twelve months preceding the interview. In addition, 23 per cent reported that first sex was non-consensual: 4 per cent reported that it was forced and 19 per cent reported that they succumbed but did not want it. What is notable is that, compared to older women, young women are moderately more likely to report lifetime experiences of sexual coercion by an intimate partner and are considerably more likely to report recent experiences of coercion by an intimate partner.

Findings show that experiences of coercion are not isolated incidents. Indeed, the majority of women (88 per cent) who had experienced sexual coercion at some time reported that they had experienced it on more than one occasion, and more than one-third (36 per cent) reported that they had experienced sexual coercion more than five times in their lives (not reported in tabular form).

As can be seen from Table 4.2, the majority of women who had any sexual experience reported that they had consented to sex out of fear of their partner's reaction: 27 per cent at least once in their lives, and 15 per cent within the twelve

TABLE 4.2 Lifetime and recent experience of sexual coercion among ever-partnered women (aged fifteen to forty-nine), by type of coercion and age (% distribution)

Experience of sexual coercion	Age group 15–24	25–34	35–49	All women
Number	239	725	1,114	2,078
*Lifetime experience (%)**				
Never	67.4	70.3	71.6	70.7
Ever experienced (one or more of those listed below)	32.6	29.7	28.4	29.3
Forced sexual intercourse	10.2	8.7	6.6	7.8
Consent to sex out of fear	27.5	27.2	25.8	26.5
Forced to engage in unwanted sexual act	7.2	4.7	3.8	4.5
*Current experience (within last 12 months) (%)***				
Never	77.0	82.8	85.7	83.7
Experienced in the last 12 months (one or more of those listed below)	23.0	17.2	14.3	16.3
Forced sexual intercourse	7.5	3.3	2.9	3.6
Consent to sex out of fear	18.4	16.4	12.7	14.7
Forced to engage in unwanted sexual act	4.2	2.5	1.3	2.1
*First sexual experience (%)****				
Wanted	59.2	76.3	80.7	76.7
Did not want but happened anyway	32.8	18.8	15.9	18.9
Forced	8.0	4.8	3.4	4.4

Notes: *p value 0.516 **p value <.003 ***p value < 0.000

months preceding the survey. Age differences in reporting of submission out of fear are negligible with regard to lifetime experience; however, younger women are more likely to report a recent experience than are older women. Women's descriptions of fear of partner were further probed during the lengthy fieldwork period. Some women reported that they submitted to sex out of fear that refusal would encourage the partner to engage in extramarital sexual relationships; others feared that they or their children might be physically injured if they refused to have sex.

Fewer than 10 per cent reported a recent or lifetime experience of forced sexual intercourse or being forced to engage in an unwanted sexual act. In both cases, younger women were more likely to report the experience than older women, including over the twelve months preceding the survey. Notably, while about 8 per cent of young women had experienced forced sexual intercourse in the twelve months preceding the interview, fewer older women (about 3 per cent) reported such a coercive experience.

Similar differences are observed in reports of coerced first sex. Indeed, while

41 per cent of young women report that they were forced (8 per cent) or submitted despite being unwilling (33 per cent) to engage in sex the first time, fewer (5 and 19 per cent respectively) of those aged twenty-five to thirty-four reported these experiences. Older women (thirty-five to forty-nine) reported even lower levels, but we acknowledge that their responses may be subject to recall bias.

Factors associated with women's lifetime experience of sexual coercion In Table 4.3, we explore the bi-variate links between women's lifetime experience of sexual coercion and (a) the socio-demographic characteristics of the respondent and her partner; (b) the respondent's sexual experiences; and (c) the nature of the relationship with the partner and supportiveness of kin. As noted earlier, 85 per cent of women reported a single intimate partner and hence both reports of intimate partner sexual coercion and partner and relationship characteristics reported in Table 4.3 refer, for the large majority, to the current intimate partner. Findings are presented separately for younger (ages fifteen to twenty-four) and older (ages twenty-five to forty-nine) women. A look at bi-variate relationships suggests that while younger women are somewhat more likely to have experienced sexual coercion than older women, differences are insignificant.

Findings suggest that few socio-demographic factors are significant correlates of sexual coercion. Not only are educated women about as likely as others to have experienced intimate partner sexual coercion, but working women are somewhat more likely than those not earning wages to be victims of coercion. Women with working husbands appear, moreover, to be somewhat more protected from sexual coercion than those whose husbands are unemployed.

Findings confirm those of other studies suggesting an association between both early sexual initiation and early coercive sexual experiences and the experience of sexual coercion in intimate partnerships. Women whose first sex occurred in adolescence and those who had experienced sexual coercion at a young age by someone other than an intimate partner were more likely (significantly so among older women) than others to report intimate partner coercion.

Findings suggest, not unexpectedly, the importance of partner relations: women who report marital conflict or physical abuse by the partner are significantly more likely than others also to report the experience of sexual coercion; so also are women whose partners are reported to have multiple sexual relationships. Moreover, women whose partners are involved in substance abuse and perpetrate violence outside the home are also more likely to be at risk of experiencing sexual coercion within the partnership. Evidence also suggests that the availability of kin support is unrelated to the experience of intimate partner sexual coercion.

Conclusion

Findings of this study suggest that a significant number of ever-partnered women in Thailand have experienced sexual coercion perpetrated by an intimate

TABLE 4.3 Correlates of sexual coercion perpetrated by an intimate partner, among ever-partnered women (aged fifteen to forty-nine): % ever experienced sexual coercion perpetrated by an intimate partner

	All ages	< 25 years	25+ years
Total	29.3 (2,078)	32.6 (239)	29.0 (1,839)
SOCIO-DEMOGRAPHIC CHARACTERISTICS			
Place of residence			
Urban	29.5 (1,283)	33.1 (166)	29.0 (1,117)
Rural	28.9 (795)	31.5 (73)	28.7 (722)
Respondent's education level			
None	32.8 (67)	–	32.8 (67)
Primary school	30.0 (1,152)	33.3 (78)	29.8 (1,074)
Secondary school	28.8 (493)	32.0 (128)	27.7 (365)
Higher education	26.9 (364)	33.3 (33)	26.3 (331)
Respondent's economic activity status			
Not working for wages	25.2 (444)[1]	33.3 (144)	23.4 (350)[2]
Working for wages	30.5 (1,631)	31.9 (94)	30.2 (1,487)
Partner's age			
< 24	35.3 (116)	33.3 (102)	50.0 (14)[1]
25–34	29.4 (565)	37.2 (113)	27.4 (452)
35–49	30.8 (825)	11.1 (18)	31.2 (807)
50+	26.0 (566)	–	26.1 (563)
Partner's education level			
Primary school or none	28.2 (1,055)	29.5 (88)	28.0 (967)
Secondary school	31.7 (593)	33.3 (105)	31.4 (488)
Higher education	29.1 (426)	39.5 (43)	27.9 (383)
Partner's current work status:			
Unemployed/retired/student	36.5 (156)[1]	46.9 (32)[1]	33.9 (124)
Currently working	28.7 (1,922)	30.4 (207)	28.5 (1,715)
Number of times respondent was married or partnered			
Once	28.1 (1,761)[2]	32.2 (214)	27.5 (1,547)[2]
More than once	36.0 (317)	36.0 (25)	36.0 (292)
Duration of current marriage (years)			
< 5	33.6 (262)	32.4 (102)	34.4 (160)
5–10	27.7 (465)	32.0 (50)	27.2 (415)
11–15	28.8 (365)	–	28.8 (365)
16+	27.1 (657)	–	27.1 (657)
WOMEN'S SEXUAL EXPERIENCE			
Age at first intercourse (years)			
<20	32.7 (920)[2]	33.7 (199)	32.5 (721)[2]
20+	26.6 (1,152)	28.2 (39)	26.5 (1,113)
*Ever experienced sexual coercion by men other than husband or intimate partner after age 15***			
No	28.4 (1,991)[2]	31.7 (221)	28.0 (1,770)[2]
Yes	52.4 (84)	44.4 (18)	54.5 (66)

	All ages	< 25 years	25+ years
Ever experienced sexual coercion by men other than husband or intimate partner before age 15			
No	28.0 (1,959)[2]	31.3 (211)	27.6 (1,748)[2]
Yes	52.6 (116)	42.9 (28)	55.7 (88)
FAMILY AND PARTNER-LEVEL FACTORS			
Frequency of quarrels with spouse/partner			
Rarely	23.8 (1,311)[2]	23.9 (138)[2]	23.8 (1,173)[2]
Sometimes	31.9 (492)	47.1 (68)	29.5 (424)
Often	51.9 (268)	43.3 (30)	52.9 (238)
Respondent ever experienced physical coercion by intimate partner			
No	22.1 (1,492)[2]	24.7 (166)[2]	21.8 (1,326)[2]
Yes	47.6 (586)	50.7 (73)	47.2 (513)
*Partner ever had relationships with other women while living with respondent***			
No	38.6 (57)	(33.3) (6)	39.2 (51)
May have	33.5 (209)	27.8 (18)	34.0 (191)
Don't know	23.9 (1,369)	29.1 (179)	23.1 (1,190)
Yes	43.3 (439)[2]	57.6 (33)[2]	42.1 (406)[2]
Partner ever visited sex workers in last 12 months			
No	29.0 (1,994)[1]	33.2 (226)	28.5 (1,768)[1]
Yes	37.5 (80)	30.0 (10)	38.6 (70)
Partner's consumption of alcohol			
Never	24.5 (580)[2]	28.8 (66)	23.9 (514)[2]
Sometimes	26.8 (611)	34.5 (84)	25.6 (527)
Often (every day or every week)	34.5 (877)	34.9 (86)	34.5 (791)
Partner ever used drugs			
No	28.5 (1,981)[2]	31.3 (208)	28.1 (1,773)[2]
Yes	59.6 (52)	45.0 (20)	68.8 (32)
Partner ever fought with other men			
No	26.4 (1,759)[2]	31.0 (187)	25.9 (1,572)[2]
Yes	45.7 (315)	40.8 (49)	46.6 (266)
Respondent has relatives living near by			
No	30.8 (603)	34.4 (64)	30.4 (539)
Yes	28.7 (1,475)	32.0 (175)	28.2 (1,300)
Respondent has a family member to turn to for help			
No	36.6 (145)	37.5 (16)	36.4 (129)
Yes	28.7 (1,922)	32.0 (222)	28.3 (1,700)

Notes: 1. P< = 0.05. 2. P< = 0.01 (p values refer to odds ratios obtained from bi-variate logistic regression analyses). Total Ns for each category are in parentheses. Ns do not add up to total in case of non-response.

partner. Indeed, over one in four women reported the experience of sexual coercion in intimate partnerships at some time in their lives, and 16 per cent reported such an experience in the twelve months preceding the interview, a finding consistent with those reported in studies of other developing countries (Krug et al. 2002). The majority of women experiencing sexual coercion reported submission to non-consensual sex out of fear of partner; in addition, 8 per cent reported having experienced forced sexual intercourse at some time. Young women aged fifteen to twenty-four were about as likely to have experienced sexual coercion at some point in their lives as older women but were significantly more likely to have experienced sexual coercion in the recent past. And while equally likely to have submitted to sex out of fear at some time, they were more likely than older women to have experienced forced sexual intercourse, especially in the recent past.

Of interest too are findings relating to factors associated with coercive sexual experiences with an intimate partner. Among socio-demographic factors, it is notable that while women who control resources – that is, those who are engaged in wage-earning activities – are more vulnerable than others to sexual coercion, women whose husbands work appear to be less at risk than those whose husbands are unemployed. By and large, findings suggest that women who have experienced sex in adolescence and those who have had early coercive experiences are more likely than others to report intimate partner sexual coercion. So also, those who report disharmonious partner relations, as measured by frequent conflict and physical violence, and those who report substance abuse, general violence and multiple partner relations among partners, are more likely than others to report sexual coercion.

While further analysis is warranted, the findings of this study provide a strong argument for actions, programmes and legislation that address women's vulnerability within intimate partnerships and marriage. Actions are needed across the life cycle to protect adolescent girls from non-consensual first and early sex, to sensitize women and men to the rights of women, including the right to refuse sex, to enable women to negotiate safe and wanted sexual relations, and to provide women supportive alternatives to sexually coercive and violent partnerships.

References

Achara, S. (1998) 'Factors associating with violence in married couples', Unpublished MA thesis, Faculty of Nursing, Mahidol University, Bangkok

Bussarin, K. (1999) 'Family violence: the study of wife abuse in the provincial district of Sakaew province', Unpublished MA thesis, Faculty of Public Health, Mahidol University

Krug, E. G., L. L. Dahlberg, J. A. Mercy et al. (2002) *World Report on Violence and Health*, Geneva: World Health Organization

National Statistical Office (2000) *The 2000 Population and Housing Census*, Bangkok: Office of the Prime Minister

Panchalee, C. (1998) 'Violence against intimate partners', Unpublished MA thesis, Faculty of Sociology and Anthropology, Thammasat University

Somswasdi, V. and K. Corrigan (eds) (2004) *A Collection of Articles on Domestic Violence in Thailand*, Chiang Mai University, Foundation of Women, Law, and Rural Development and the Women's Studies Center, Faculty of Social Sciences

Srinual, R. and K. Archavanitkul (2004) 'Sexual violence against in-school female adolescents', in V. Somswasdi and K. Corrigan (eds), *A Collection of Articles on Domestic Violence in Thailand*, Chiang Mai University: Foundation of Women, Law, and Rural Development and the Women's Studies Center, Faculty of Social Sciences, pp. 13–36

5 | Non-consensual sex among South African youth: prevalence of coerced sex and discourses of control and desire

RACHEL JEWKES

The *World Report on Violence and Health* identifies coerced sex as both a human rights violation and a major public health problem (Krug et al. 2002). This is perhaps nowhere more sharply evident than in South Africa. In 2002, according to recently released police statistics, 52,107 rapes were reported to the police, which amounts to a rate of rape of approximately 230 per 100,000 women (Crime Information Analysis Centre 2004). In 1996 South Africa had the highest rate of rape of any Interpol country member (Interpol 2001); it seems likely that nine years later the situation is unchanged.

Rape in South Africa is also often associated with unusually high degrees of violence. Rape homicide, for example, is twelve times more common in South Africa than in the United States (Martin 1999). Of the rapes reported to the police in South Africa, 30 per cent have multiple perpetrators (ibid.), compared with 11 per cent in Canada (McGregor et al. 2002). While these figures are striking, they represent only a part of the spectrum of sexual coercion perpetrated in South Africa, as many incidents of coerced sex are never reported to the police (Jewkes and Abrahams 2002).

Sexual coercion in South Africa covers a broad range of behaviours and may take the form of verbal persuasion (coercive talking), begging, pleading, blackmail and trickery or more violent behaviours, including rape. The spectrum of sexual coercion includes acts directed against intimate and non-intimate partners. Coercion of intimate partners includes the use of force during first or subsequent episodes of intercourse between spouses or dating partners. Coercion of non-intimate partners includes stranger and (non-dating) acquaintance rape, incest and forced first intercourse where the perpetrator was not (and did not become) a boyfriend. It also includes sex that is coerced, often by threats rather than force, by people in positions of power, for example teachers, employers, landlords or policemen. A form of coercion in South Africa that spans these two categories is 'streamlining', which is a form of gang rape that is often organized by a woman's boyfriend as well as other men in the line-up (Wood 2001).

In trying to understand the magnitude of the problem, coerced sex may be viewed as an iceberg (as illustrated in Figure 5.1). The most visible part of coerced sex is that which is reported to the police as rape or attempted rape, and includes rape homicides. These cases represent just a small proportion of the problem, however, as, for reasons discussed elsewhere (Jewkes and Abrahams 2002), many women do not report rape to the police. Women's experiences may be captured through surveys conducted with appropriate methodology (see ibid.; Koss 1992). Such sensitively conducted research can make visible another set of experiences of coercion; however, it is likely that there are even more women who experience sexual coercion but will not reveal their experiences in these interviews.

The prevalence of rape in South Africa

A representative household survey of 1,306 women aged eighteen to forty-nine years was conducted in 1998 in three provinces of South Africa (Jewkes and Abrahams 2002). The study found that the one-year prevalence of coerced sex (defined as being 'forced to have sex against your wishes' or experiencing such an attempt) was 2,070 per 100,000. In other words, 2 per cent of women experienced rape or attempted rape in the year prior to the survey. Although only a rough comparison can be made, this figure is just under ten times higher than the rate of rape and attempted rape derived from police statistics for the same year, which was 244 per 100,000 women. In the survey, women revealed that perpetrators of coercion were strangers (50.0 per cent), acquaintances (26.6 per cent), landlords (8.5 per cent) and others (3.0 per cent). Intimate partners were only responsible for 7.5 per cent of these instances of rape (equivalent to a one-year prevalence of intimate partner coercion of 0.16 per cent).

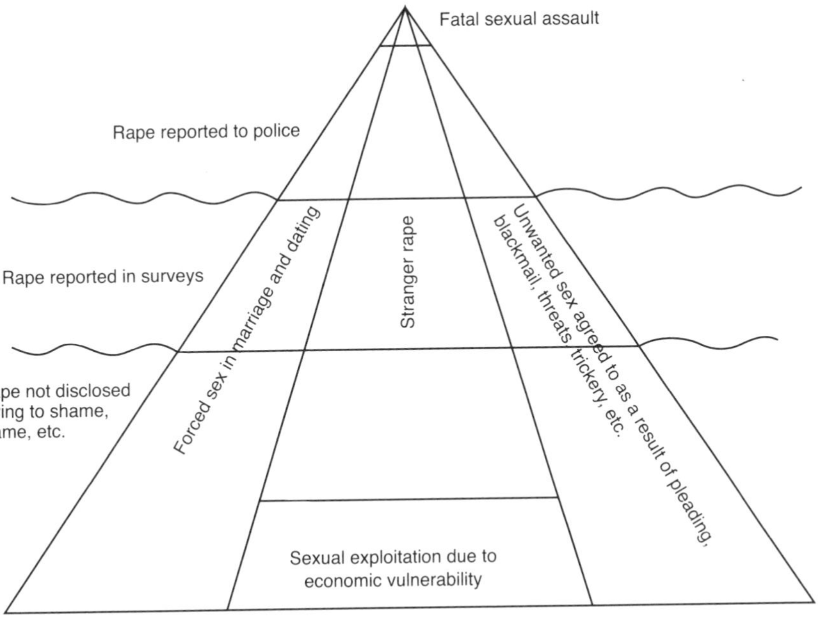

Figure 5.1 Iceberg of sexual coercion (*Source*: Jewkes and Abrahams 2002)

This surprisingly low prevalence of coercion by intimate partners may reflect the general nature of the questions posed and the lack of specific enquiry about, or probing of, experiences of coercion by intimate partners. Studies that have specifically asked about coercion by intimate partners found a much higher prevalence. For example, a study of antenatal clinic attendees in Soweto using the instrument of the WHO multi-country study on violence against women to ask about intimate partner sexual violence found that of a total of 1,395 pregnant women interviewed, 9.7 per cent had experienced sexual abuse by an intimate partner in the past year and 20.1 per cent had had such an experience during their lifetime (Dunkle et al. 2004). Although the data-sets are not directly comparable, the evidence suggests that intimate partner sexual violence may be substantially under-reported if specific questions are not asked.

Forced first intercourse is a particular form of sexual coercion that has been shown to have predictive value in terms of sexual and reproductive health outcomes (Jewkes et al. 2001). In the Soweto study, pregnant women were asked about their experiences of first intercourse and to describe its circumstances. The prevalence of forced first intercourse in this group was found to be 12.4 per cent. The median age of first intercourse in the sample was 17 years (range 5–29). A highly significant association was found between forced first intercourse and early age at first intercourse. For example, among women reporting first sex before the age of thirteen, 97.0 per cent described it as forced; in contrast, among women who reported first sex at ages thirteen to fourteen and fifteen and older, 26.7 and 8.9 per cent respectively reported that first sex was forced (Dunkle et al. 2004). This finding has important methodological implications as several studies have been conducted with youths in their mid-teens which reveal a much higher prevalence of forced first intercourse (e.g. Buga et al. 1996: Jewkes et al. 2001; Richter 1996). These figures are not as generalizable as had been earlier assumed, however, as youths with younger ages at first sex were over-represented in their samples compared with the general population.

Child sexual abuse is a major problem in South Africa. In the 1998 South Africa Demographic and Health Survey, which is a nationally representative sample of 11,375 women aged fifteen to forty-nine years, 1.6 per cent of women interviewed reported being raped before the age of fifteen. Perpetrators of rape were schoolteachers (33 per cent), strangers (20 per cent), relatives (25 per cent) and family friends (11 per cent) (Jewkes et al. 2002). Such large surveys are not well suited to measuring sensitive issues, however, and estimates are likely to be subject to substantial under-reporting. Research being conducted with a group of volunteers participating in an HIV prevention trial in the Eastern Cape province is enquiring into the experiences of sexual abuse in childhood of both men and women. A pilot study with 150 men and 150 women found that both experienced abuse – 10.2 per cent of men and 14.5 per cent of women reported unwanted sexual touch or being made to touch someone sexually before the age of eighteen; 28.9 per cent of women and 16.3 per cent of men had had sex with someone more than five years older than them before they were eighteen; 3.4 per cent of men reported being forced to have sex with a man; and 14.5 per cent of women had been sexually coerced by a boyfriend and 11.8 per cent by a non-intimate partner.

No representative sample survey data are available on the participation of men in gang rape or streamlining. In order to explore the possibility of getting men to talk about their experiences, questions were included in two questionnaires, which were administered to different groups of men in the course of HIV prevention trial research. These were non-random samples of young men who volunteered to help with the intervention research. The findings have been very similar in the two settings from diverse parts of the country. In both the Eastern Cape (N = 1,374) and in a small study undertaken in Winterveldt, north of Pretoria (N = 75), a similar proportion of men (13.9 as against 15 per cent) reported having ever been involved in streamlining (Jewkes et al. 2004; Wood et al. 2002).

Most forms of coercion involve a degree of physical force. Women in South Africa, however, recognize that although sometimes physical force is not used, they may end up having unwanted sex (soon a law on sexual offences will recognize this as well). The use of drugs is increasingly being reported in cities in South Africa and Namibia (Jewkes et al. 2005). In the three-province study, 3 per cent of female employment seekers had had to have sex with a man before getting a job. Of those who were working, 2 per cent had to have sex with their boss to keep their job, and 2 per cent of those who had been to school had been told they would fail if they did not have sex with their teacher (Jewkes and Abrahams 2002).

Why does South Africa have such a high prevalence of coerced sex?

Reasons for the high prevalence of coerced sex in South Africa have preoccupied researchers, and a tentative hypothesis is attempted in this section. It is difficult to contextualize the problem of rape as in its essence it does not readily lend itself to a rational analysis. The factors that have been described as associated with sexual violence are, however, for the most part, strongly rooted in the socio-economic and cultural aspects of society. They may also include individual psychopathology, the effects of which may be mediated through broader social processes (Krug et al. 2002).

In seeking to understand rape it is helpful to consider some aspects of the historical position of women and gendered codes (whether supported or resisted) that provide a social framework within which sexual relationships are enacted. The control of women by men has been central to the organization of gender relations in South Africa from pre-capitalist societies until the present day. It has been argued that not only was the control and appropriation of women's productive and reproductive capacities central to the structure of southern Africa's pre-capitalist societies, but 'it was *the* social feature on which society was based' (Guy 1990: 40). In these societies cattle were regarded as an indicator of wealth and were needed for *lobola* (bride price payment), which was (and still is) paid to the bride's father. A wife was (or wives were) essential for the maintenance of the homestead and lineage, with girls providing labour to the homestead until they themselves were married and *lobola* received, while boys would extend the lineage through marriage and tend the cattle. Marital arrangements were conditional on the wife remaining obedient to her husband (and being fertile). Men's power within the family was positional power, contingent on their maleness and position in the domestic unit. In some parts of South Africa, notably among the Xhosas, abduction and rape of the bride were enacted as part of traditional marriage practices, particularly if the woman would not agree to a marriage her parents favoured. In rural areas deep in the Eastern Cape, research shows that this practice is still followed (Jewkes, unpublished research findings).

While pre-capitalist society was premised on the control of women, South African women had the potential to exercise power within the system. If the land they were given on marriage by their husband was good, they had a significant degree of economic independence, as they could retain most of what was produced for their own use. Moreover, the fact that value was created by their fertility gave women a significant role in society. They had a degree of sexual independence as long as their behaviour was discreet, as marriage was more to ensure that children had a family than to ensure biological parentage. Since all children born to a woman in marriage were regarded as the offspring of the husband, it mattered less who the biological father was.

It would be incorrect to assume that this system of marriage was a rural idyll. Many married women experienced considerable hardship and brutality, or abandonment, and throughout the last century, most particularly in the early decades, ran away from oppressive homes to cities, where they made independent lives, often by brewing beer and sex work (Bonner 1990).

During this time unmarried mothers, divorcees and widows were in positions of being marginal to the 'ideal' of domestic units because they were located in their natal home (Delius and Glaser 2003). They had considerable freedom to control their own sexuality, however, including having lovers who were expected to give them presents or a certain amount of material support in return. Thus while control of women and prescribed male power was central to South African society, not insignificant numbers of women lived outside the formal structure of this framework and actively resisted it.

This parallel strand of resistance to male control is beautifully captured in the following extract from the autobiography of A. S. Mopeli-Paulus, a Witsieshoek chief's son, describing a scene he witnessed on the streets of Benoni on the East Rand (near Johannesburg) in the 1930s:

> I saw my Basutho women dressed in print skirts an inch below the knee, their blouses an inch above the navel, bracelets round their legs, running in the streets, swinging their coloured blankets in the air shouting, 'If you are a man, come let me tell you, keep away my boy! Go to the Christians! Here is Benoni-Twatwa. We rule ourselves!' (cited in Bonner 1990: 231).

Women living outside or on the margins of traditional domestic units have always been vulnerable to rape (Delius and Glaser 2003; Niehaus 2005). While this in part reflects the limited ability of men to provide support in the extended kinship structure, it probably more importantly reflects the fact that the number of women living on the margins of domestic units was mirrored by the number of men who were also outside formal domestic units. Such (usually single) men were denied access to a prescribed and uncontested source of power in the face of the decline of rural agricultural production, high unemployment and poverty. Yet these men continued to live in a context where they were expected to control women and exercise gender-based power over them, although they could offer them little. It is argued that it is in this context of a decline of prescribed masculine identities that acts of performed masculinity became crucial (Niehaus forthcoming). I want to suggest that the dialectic created between men's attempts to control women and women's resistance creates tensions, which some men seek to resolve by extreme acts of performed masculinity. Rape is thus both an ultimate symbol, however short lived, of male domination over women, as well as often rooted in feelings of powerlessness in the face of women.

Rape and performed masculinity

Evidence from extended ethnographic research with young men in the rural Eastern Cape province (Wood 2003) suggests that rape of women commonly occurs within the context of the performance of masculinity among male peers. It is of note that apart from the sexual aspects of relationships, South Africa is a largely gender-segregated society. There is little cross-gender companionship of a non-sexual nature, and for the most part companionship is sought from gender-segregated peer activities and association. The control of women is a key aspect of the 'successful' assertion of masculinity among young men, nowadays primarily defined in terms of their ability to have the right partner (i.e. the one most desirable to others), a greater number of partners and power over their girlfriends (Wood and Jewkes 2001). Masculinity is constructed and evaluated in ongoing acts of competition in relation to male peers.

For Xhosa men in South Africa, the teenage years, before circumcision and initiation into manhood, are a stage of exploring their (gendered) power within society, and exploring the boundaries that society sets for them as well as the boundaries they set for themselves. Young men are given considerable latitude by society, in part because of a belief that if they have not had a chance to act wildly as adolescents they will not be able to curtail their behaviours when they become men (ibid.). In the process of exploring boundaries, some men may perpetrate rape when the opportunity arises and when they think they will not get caught.

Men also perpetrate rape in groups in the course of exploration of comparative peer position (Niehaus forthcoming; Wood and Jewkes 2001). In this context, gang rape can be seen as an expression of superior strength and a way of achieving deference from peers as well as women. Streamlining of girlfriends can be seen in part as a way of demonstrating control over women, as well as creating bonds of support between peers. It may also be seen as an act of punishment of the woman (Wood 2001). Streamlining may also be practised by young men as a way of overcoming their anxiety about sex with women and displaying their heterosexual prowess to their peers (Niehaus 2005). This may explain why it is common for men in their early teenage years to participate in gang rape (Jewkes 2003).

Most groups of men involved in gang rape are just friends who 'hang out' together and not formal gangs, although formal gangs are found in townships. The criminal elements in townships, known as *tsotsis*, are an extreme form of male peer association. They are armed, dangerous and regard themselves as superior to everyone, both men and women (Wood 2003), and use gang rape to assert their position. Particular targets are women who reject their propositions or are perceived to be virgins, or who are seen as thinking of themselves as superior. They also target women of low social status, such as those who get drunk in public, because they can get away with humiliating them, or women who they perceive as challenging them, either by dressing in revealing clothes or standing up to them in other ways (e.g. nurses). It has been argued that women who are successful in the community are often targeted as an act of 'revenge of the unemployed' (Niehaus 2005).

The prevalence data presented earlier show that forced sex is often part of dating relationships. In trying to understand this, the observation of Wood and Jewkes (2001) regarding the centrality of relationships in the self-evaluation of men means that dating becomes a contest with high stakes. This is particularly a feature among men who live in circumstances of poverty where there are few other avenues through which to demonstrate 'success'. Scripts of everyday relationships place women in a vulnerable position (Nduna and Jama 2001; Wood 2003). The discourses of male control lead men to expect to determine the start and progress of relationships. Women have relatively little space to manoeuvre when propositioned by men: they risk slurs on their reputation (indicating that they are either cold or 'worn out' by too much sex) or even rape as a price of rejection. They must not immediately accept propositions, however, lest they are thought of as being loose or a 'bitch'. Men pride themselves on their ability to persuade women to accept proposals and often use physical violence.

In this context of men's ideas of their right to control women and secure acceptance of their propositions, and female-scripted responses of ambiguity and reticence, there is considerable scope for genuine miscommunication or abuse of power being perceived by men as part of the dating 'game'. Forced sex lies at one end of a spectrum of persuasive tactics for initiating relationships, which chiefly relies on verbal coercion, pleading and use of arguments, and often more naive girls are tricked into sex. It is important that women themselves are very lenient in what they regard as forced sex or rape. Many women construe coercion as 'rape' only if the man behaves 'disrespectfully' afterwards (e.g. does not sustain the relationship) (Wood 2003). This interpretation provides a degree of legitimacy for men's coercion, even of women whom they did not really know before the act or where a substantial degree of violence was used.

An important question that arises in the context of South Africa is how does society understand the high prevalence of coerced sex without challenging prevailing ideas of gender hierarchy? Two processes are important here. The first relates to the apportionment of blame. Parents, families and society put little social pressure on men and boys to discourage them from perpetrating rape. The onus of preventing rape is placed on women, and they are usually blamed for provoking the incident. This issue is starkly highlighted in the following extract from an interview with a young woman on rape and her perceptions of risk. She explained: 'It is not easy for me to wear tight trousers when there are men at home ... when my father, my uncle or my brother is there I don't wear them because if they rape me, I can't blame them' (eighteen-year-old girl; Jewkes et al. 2005).

Blaming women for rape allows society to deflect its focus from the men who perpetrate the rape and so avert scrutiny of the social institutions and processes that create tensions which are (momentarily at least) resolved through rape and legitimize it in the eyes of some men.

The second process relates to the construction of the 'criminal'. The use of a certain amount of violence and rape by young men is regarded as part of 'normal' boyish behaviour and ignored or gently derided by adults (Wood and Jewkes 2001). Questions are not asked about the sexual conduct of young men unless it is forced on the attention of adults, which is usually when the victim has a higher social status (e.g. is a respected adult) or the incident occurs in a 'respectable' public space, i.e. not in a bar. In other situations, young men are 'allowed' to do anything they can get away with.

When sexual violence is seen as particularly cruel or unacceptable, the perpetrator is branded as a 'criminal' (*tsotsi*) and a distinction is made between his actions and those related actions, perceived to be less extreme, that are condoned by society. Rape, in this manner, is perceived by society as the action of men who are bad, perhaps mad, or high on alcohol, and consequently the system of patriarchal social relations, which creates the space for the high prevalence of rape in the society, remains unchallenged.

Conclusion

South Africa is a country where rape and sexual coercion are particularly common occurrences. This chapter has drawn on a range of historical data and present-day ethnographic sources to argue that the roots of the problem currently experienced in the country lie in part in the dialectical relations between male expectation and attempts to control women and women's resistance to this. The tensions, thus created, may be resolved through rape as an extreme act of performed masculinity, which provokes momentary feelings of power. Rape may also occur in the spaces created by the social latitude given to young men, including in male peer bonding activities. It is enacted as an expression of power and superiority, which is sometimes linked to other 'criminal' behaviour. It may also be a by-product of miscommunication within the context of adolescent dating.

In seeking to understand how South African society makes sense of the high prevalence of coerced sex without challenging the position of men, I have argued that two key processes are involved: victim-blaming and the selective process of construction of the 'criminal'. This analysis suggests that an effective social or public health response to rape should have two closely linked foci. The first is the public's perception of blame in cases of rape, which needs to be decisively shifted on to the rapist. The second focus should be the current social tolerance of certain forms of coerced sex. An effective response must create a climate of intolerance to all forms of sexual coercion.

References

Bonner, P. L. (1990) '"Desirable and undesirable Basotho women?" Liquor, prostitution and the migration of Basotho women to the Rand, 1920–1945', in C. Walker (ed.), *Women and Gender in Southern Africa to 1945*, London: James Currey, pp. 221–50

Buga, G. A. B., D. H. A. Amoko and D. Ncayiyana (1996) 'Sexual behaviour, contraceptive practices and reproductive health among school adolescents in rural Transkei', *South African Medical Journal,* 86: 523–7

Crime Information Analysis Centre (2004) <http://www.saps.gov.za 8%5Fcrimeinfo/200309/index.htm>

Delius, P. and C. Glaser (2003) 'The myth of polygamy: a history of extra-marital and multi-partnership sex in South Africa', Paper presented at the Sex and Secrecy Conference, University of the Witwatersrand, Johannesburg, 23–25 June

Dunkle, K. L., R. K. Jewkes, H. C. Brown et al. (2004) 'Prevalence and patterns of gender-based violence and revictimization among women attending antenatal clinics in Soweto, South Africa', *American Journal of Epidemiology*, 160: 230–39

Guy, J. (1990) 'Gender oppression in Southern Africa's precapitalist societies', in C. Walker (ed), *Women and Gender in Southern Africa to 1945*, London: James Currey, pp. 33–47

Interpol (2001) *International Crime Statistics*, Lyons: Interpol

Jewkes, R. (2003) 'Child sexual abuse in the Eastern Cape', Paper presented at the Second South African Gender-based Violence and Health Initiative Conference, 7–9 May, Fourways, Johannesburg

Jewkes, R. and N. Abrahams (2002) 'The epidemiology of rape and sexual coercion in South Africa: an overview', *Social Science and Medicine*, 55: 153–66

Jewkes, R., C. Vundule, F. Maforah et al. (2001) 'Relationship dynamics and adolescent pregnancy in South Africa', *Social Science and Medicine*, 52(5): 733–44

Jewkes, R., J. Levin, D. Bradshaw et al. (2002) 'Rape of girls in South Africa', *Lancet*, 359: 319–20

Jewkes, R., M. Nduna, K. Dunkle et al. (2004) 'Rape of women who are not intimate partners: risk factors for raping and association with HIV risk behaviours', XV International AIDS Conference, 11–16 July, Bangkok (poster)

Jewkes, R., L. Penn-Kekana, H. Rose-Junius (2005) '"If they rape me, I can't blame them": reflections on gender in the social context of child rape in South Africa and Namibia', *Social Science and Medicine*, 61: 1809–20

Koss, M. P. (1992) 'The under-detection of rape: methodological choices influence incidence estimates', *Journal of Social Issues*, 48(1): 61–75

Krug, E. G., L. L. Dahlberg, J. A. Mercy et al. (2002) *World Report on Violence and Health*, Geneva: World Health Organization

McGregor, M., J. Du Mont and T. Myhr (2002) 'Sexual assault forensic medical examination: is evidence related to successful prosecution?' *Annals of Emergency Medicine*, 39: 639–47

Martin, L. (1999) 'Violence against women: an analysis of the epidemiology and patterns of injury in rape homicide in Cape Town and in rape in Johannesburg', Unpublished M.Med forensic pathology thesis, University of Cape Town

Nduna, M. and N. Jama (2001) 'Preliminary findings from stepping stones workshops', AIDS in Context conference, 25 April, Johannesburg

Niehaus, I. (2005) 'Masculine domination in sexual violence: interpreting accounts of three cases of rape in the South African Lowveld', in G. Reid G and L. Walker, *Men Behaving Differently*, Cape Town: Double Storey Books

Richter, L. (1996) 'A survey of reproductive health issues among urban black youth in South Africa', Final Grant Report, Medical Research Council, Pretoria

Wood, K. M. (2001) 'Defining "forced" sex, rape, "streamline" and gang rape: notes from a South African township', in Proceedings of the Fourth Meeting of the International Research Network on Violence against Women, Johannesburg, 22–24 January, Pretoria: Medical Research Council

— (2003) 'An ethnography of sexual health and violence among township youth in South Africa', PhD thesis, University of London

Wood, K. and R. Jewkes (2001) '"Dangerous" love: reflections on violence among Xhosa township youth', in R. Morrell (ed.), *Changing Men in Southern Africa*, Pietermaritzburg: University of Natal Press, and London: Zed Books, pp. 317–36

Wood, K. M., P. N. Jama, R. K. Jewkes et al. (2002) 'Gang rape in South Africa', XIVth International AIDS Conference, Barcelona, 7–12 July

6 | Attitudes, norms and experiences of sexual coercion among young people in Ibadan, Nigeria

ADEMOLA J. AJUWON[1]

According to the World Health Organization (WHO), sexual violence is 'any sexual act, attempt to obtain a sexual act, unwanted sexual comments or advances, or acts to traffic or otherwise directed against a person's sexuality using coercion, by any person regardless of their relationship with the victim, in any setting including but not limited to home and work' (Krug et al. 2002: 149). Coercive sex refers to a continuum of behaviours ranging from unwanted touch, verbal intimidation and rape to cultural expectations that require girls to marry and sexually service men against their will (Heise et al. 1995).

Sexual violence is a serious human rights and public health problem. Non-consensual sex is a concern because it violates the rights of victims and reinforces women's subordination to men (ibid.). The public health consequences of coercive sex are profound, and include chronic pelvic pain, sexually transmitted infections (STIs), unwanted pregnancy, adverse pregnancy outcomes such as miscarriage and low-birth-weight babies and depression (Ellsberg et al. 2001; Heise et al. 1995). Coercive sex is also increasingly observed to be associated with HIV/AIDS infection (Cáceres et al. 2000; Maman et al. 2001; Van der Straten et al. 1998). Although there is growing evidence that boys are also victims of coercion, girls are disproportionately affected. Unequal gender norms and role expectations exacerbate young women's vulnerability to forced sex. The use of violence or the threat of violence in sexual relationships also undermine a woman's ability to negotiate safe sex. Moreover, women who have been sexually abused in childhood have a greater propensity to participate in risky consensual sexual activities as adolescents or adults than women who have not been abused.

This chapter presents the findings of a large study conducted in Nigeria. The study aimed to explore young people's attitudes, norms and experiences of sexual coercion, understand the context in which non-consensual sexual activities occur in this population and assess the consequences of coercion for victims.

Setting

The study was conducted in Ibadan North West local government area (LGA), one of the five administrative units of Ibadan, a metropolis of approximately 3 million persons. The population of the LGA is approximately 147,000 persons, who are mainly Yoruba, the major ethnic group in south-western Nigeria. The study covered young persons aged fifteen to twenty-five, who represent approximately a third of the population in the area. Only about one-third of these youths are enrolled in secondary schools (UNDP 2000), and approximately three-fifths are apprentices and hawkers.

In Nigeria, an apprentice is a young person with limited formal education who learns a vocation under the direct supervision of an instructor. Typically, apprenticeships are part of small and largely informal businesses. Apprenticeships are conducted in workshops, but the owners have no government recognition, registration or support. The workshops in the study area focused on five trades: sale of patent medicines, automobile repair, tailoring, shoemaking and hairdressing. Hawkers are young persons who typically sell snacks and beverages on major streets and in bus and truck stations in urban areas, and are also part of the informal sector (Ajuwon, Fawole and Osungbade 2001). As it is difficult to enumerate and access hawkers, the study covered only students and apprentices.

Study design

Qualitative and quantitative data for the study were drawn from narrative workshops, a survey of adolescents and in-depth interviews with victims of rape. In the first phase of the study, four narrative workshops were conducted, which were attended by seventy-seven male and female students and apprentices aged fifteen to twenty-one. Samples were drawn from school lists and lists of apprentice workshops. Participants were randomly recruited from two out of the seven secondary schools and twenty out of the approximately one hundred small businesses in the study area.

Narrative workshops are appropriate for the exploration of sensitive issues. Despite the sensitive nature of sexual coercion, this format enabled young persons to discuss the issue freely without needing to refer to personal experiences or feel fear of disclosure (WHO 1993). Indeed, participants not only identified behaviours that they perceived to be coercive but narrated the context in which each of these behaviours occurred.

The second component of the study was a survey of 1,025 secondary school students and apprentices (214 male and 265 female students, and 276 male and 270 female apprentices aged fifteen to nineteen). Students were randomly selected from the five schools that had not participated in the narrative workshops. Students from the two schools that had participated in the workshops were excluded from the survey in order not to over-sensitize them to the issues investigated in the survey. From each school, one arm each from junior and senior classes was selected and all the students found in each arm on the day of the visit were invited to participate in the study.

Apprentices were recruited from the remaining eighty businesses that had not been enlisted for the narrative workshops. The study team met the leaders of each group to enlist their support and cooperation; they also visited every workshop to seek permission from the instructors. All the apprentices who met the inclusion criteria were interviewed.

In-depth interviews were conducted with eight female victims of rape, identified through the survey, to explore the context in which the rape had occurred, their health-seeking behaviours and the consequences of the experience on their lives. We must acknowledge that while the study intended to interview twenty victims of rape in depth, only eight victims consented to be interviewed. Indeed, not a single male victim consented. The sensitive and painful nature of the coercive experience was clearly key in victims' unwillingness to participate in in-depth interviews. Even among willing participants, protecting the privacy of participants and conducting the in-depth interviews in an environment that ensured the safety and confidentiality of the respondent proved to be challenging. For these reasons, eventually only eight such interviews could be held, and the consequent selectivity of the sample must be acknowledged.

Informed consent was obtained from all the participants. The Ethical Review Committees of the World Health Organization, Geneva, and the College of Medicine, University of Ibadan, reviewed and approved the research design.

Findings

A socio-demographic profile drawn from the survey shows that the mean age of the respondents was seventeen years. About three-fifths of the sample were aged fifteen to seventeen years; however, the students were generally younger than the apprentices. For example, 67 per cent of the male apprentices and 51 per cent of the female apprentices were aged eighteen to nineteen, compared to 18 per cent and 16 per cent of the male and female students, respectively. The distribution by religion suggests that while the majority of students were Christian (about 75 per cent), the majority of apprentices were Muslim (about 55 per cent). A small proportion (13 per cent) of survey respondents had worked for money at some time; among female apprentices, however, some 22 per cent had worked for wages or salary. Non-sexual risk behaviours were also measured in terms of alcohol and tobacco use. About 13 per cent of adolescents reported alcohol consumption and a negligible 2 per cent reported tobacco use. A detailed demographic profile of the respondents is discussed elsewhere (Ajuwon et al. 2001b).

That non-consensual sexual behaviour takes many forms was clearly familiar to young study participants. In the course of narrative workshops, participants identified eleven behaviours that they perceived to be coercive, discussed the norms associated with each and narrated the context in which they occurred. These behaviours can be broadly grouped into three categories: (a) those that involved threatened and forced sex such as rape, unwanted touch, incest, assault, verbal abuse and unwanted kissing; (b) those that focused on deception and were perceived as setting the stage for non-consensual sex, such as forced exposure to pornographic films and the use of drugs for sedation; and (c) those that did not allow the partner any choice in determining the outcome of sex, such as insisting that the woman should have an abortion (Ajuwon et al. 2001a).

As Table 6.1 suggests, significant minorities of adolescents, especially girls, had experienced some form of non-consensual sex. Indeed, among girls, 15 per cent had experienced forced penetrative sex, over a quarter reported attempts to force sex and over two in five reported being touched sexually against their wishes (see Ajuwon et al. 2001b for details).

TABLE 6.1 Experience of various forms of non-consensual sex among adolescent students and apprentices, Ibadan, Nigeria (%)

	Girls (N = 535)	Boys (N = 490)
Experience of forced sex (includes rape and forced sex through deception or drugging)	15.1	7.8
Attempted forced sex (includes attempted rape, assault, other attempts to force)	27.3	10.2
Unwanted touch	44.1	22.9

Source: Ajuwon et al. 2001b

The study also sheds considerable light on factors underlying forced sex, notably with adolescent girls. Findings highlight the extent to which gender norms and attitudes condone sexual gratification, even forced perpetration, among adolescent boys, limit sexual negotiation among adolescent girls and force young female victims into inaction for fear of societal reprisal and lack of support.

Gender norms and attitudes as key factors underlying the sexual coercion of young women The survey instrument included a series of attitudinal questions that were developed from findings of the narrative workshops. As seen in Table 6.2, both adolescent girls and especially adolescent boys do indeed hold attitudes that condone forced sex in a variety of situations: for example, if a man has paid bride wealth for a woman (80–98 per cent) and to a lesser extent if he has spent a lot of money on her (37–74 per cent). Supporting these attitudes are findings from the narrative workshops in which both young men and women believed that 'once a girl agrees to be a girlfriend she should be available for sex'. In general females are less likely to hold these attitudes than males; nevertheless, significant percentages of young women do also report attitudes that condone forced sex.

Also evident is that young people – males in particular – continue to hold attitudes that justify forced sex on two grounds. First, about half of all respondents, irrespective of sex, agree that young men have uncontrollable sexual urges that compel them to seek gratification, even forced. Second, and conversely, respondents (60–75 per cent of males and 40–50 per cent of females) do hold attitudes that blame the female victim for inviting the forced incident. Indeed, findings from narrative workshops underscore the extent to which young men agreed that a girl who refuses to accede to their request for friendship or sex is 'arrogant and rude' and should therefore be 'punished'.

In the course of in-depth interviews held with eight female survey respondents who reported the experience of rape, the expression of these attitudes was abundantly clear. Indeed, the theme of rape as a weapon of punishment with which to teach an unwilling female a lesson was repeatedly voiced, as evident in the narratives of two victims, reproduced below:

> I was returning from school one day when I realized that two boys were following me ... One of the boys had earlier tried unsuccessfully to make me be his girlfriend. After some time they overtook and stopped me. The boy who had wanted to befriend me earlier said, 'What about the matter we discussed earlier.' I said I did not know what he was talking about. He then said, 'Today na today,' meaning today is a day of reckoning. I sensed what he was up to and said, 'I'm still a small girl.' He did not hear my plea. He got hold of me and tore off my clothes, threw me to the ground and forcefully had sex with me. Meanwhile, his friend forcibly held me down and kept watch for passers-by. I tried to free myself but could not because the boys were much stronger than I. (sixteen-year-old girl in junior secondary school, raped on the bush path; Ajuwon et al. 2004)

> The incident occurred when I was 14 years old in junior secondary school. One day during school hours, I checked on Sarah, one of my friends who was absent from school for some days. I met three boys in front of Sarah's house and asked if that was Sarah's house. One of them confirmed it ... when I got into the room, I did not see her. Before I realized what was happening one of the boys locked the door to the room. One of the boys said, 'Now that we have caught you, you will know what you have done.' Suddenly, I saw one boy who had 'toasted' me [attempted to befriend me] earlier ... He said if I had agreed to befriend him, this would not have happened to me. So I began to shout for help and they pushed me to the bed. I found it difficult to breathe. Two of them forcefully had sex with me before I could muster enough strength to push them off. (fourteen-year-old girl in secondary school; ibid.)

Findings from in-depth interviews confirmed that victims of rape tended to suffer in silence. Six of the eight victims who were interviewed in depth reported that they had not disclosed the incident to anyone, including their parents. Feelings of shame and the fear that they would be stigmatized or blamed for provoking the incident (including by their parents) were key factors inhibiting disclosure,

TABLE 6.2 Attitudes towards forced sex and exercise of choice among adolescent students and apprentices, Ibadan, Nigeria

Statements	Students		Apprentices	
	Boys (N=214)	Girls (N=265)	Boys (N=276)	Girls (N=270)
Attitudes on male right to force sex in selected situations:				
A man has the right to have sex with a girl on whom he has paid the bride wealth (dowry)	171 (80)	244 (92)	257 (93)	264 (97.8)
A man has a right to have sex with a woman if he has spent a lot of money on her	111 (56)	113 (43)	204 (74)	100 (37)
Justification for forcing sex:				
Men are usually unable to control their sexual desires and that is why they coerce girls	87 (41)	145 (55)	173 (63)	121 (45)
Girls often say no to the first sexual gestures but would yield if a man exerts enough pressure	132 (62)	131 (49)	213 (77)	116 (43)
Girls are usually the ones who provoke boys to coerce them	139 (65)	118 (45)	199 (72)	93 (34)

Note: Figures in brackets are percentages.

as evident from the following statement by one victim: 'I did not tell anybody about the incident because I fear that people I tell may tell other people and thus spread the news. I felt too ashamed to tell my parents or elder siblings' (sixteen-year-old girl student).

Indeed, of the eight rape victims who were interviewed in depth, only two had revealed the incident to anyone. Of them, only one confided in her parents and reported that, contrary to victims' fears, she was indeed encouraged by her parents to seek care from a health facility and to report the incident to the authorities.

Emerging indications of changing attitudes Despite this overwhelmingly negative scenario, findings suggest that not all young people justify or condone the use of force in sexual relations. Indeed, as survey findings suggest (see Table 6.3), over 90 per cent of young women and fewer young men – four in five apprentices and two in three students – acknowledge that sexual coercion of girls is unacceptable. Indeed, there are some – albeit weak and inconsistent – signs of a shift towards more gender-equal attitudes. Young women overwhelmingly agree on their right to choose their own husbands and to refuse sex if they do not want it; what is interesting is that young men by and large agree.

TABLE 6.3 Acceptability of exercise of choice among adolescent students and apprentices

Statements	Students		Apprentices	
	Male (N=214)	Female (N=264)	Male (N=276)	Female (N=270)
There is nothing wrong in a male sexually coercing a girl	68 (32)	21 (8)	51 (18)	11 (4)
It is all right for a girl to say no if she does not want to have sex	166 (78)	257 (97)	222 (80)	266 (99)
Girls should have the right to choose their own husbands	187 (87)	255 (96)	264 (96)	270 (100)

Note: Figures in brackets are percentages.

A shift towards more egalitarian attitudes was also noticed in the course of narrative workshops. An unanticipated positive outcome of these workshops was the consistency with which participants reported becoming sensitized to the unacceptability of all forms of coercive behaviours. Many young women stated that the workshop had changed their belief that victims of sexual coercion were to blame for provoking the incident, and that the workshop empowered them with skills to prevent coercive behaviours and to deal with perpetrators in the future. Young men too reported greater sensitivity; many made commitments to refrain from perpetrating forced sex (Ajuwon et al. 2001a).

Evidently, young people are in flux; many, including young men, appear to be questioning strongly held gender norms about girls' and young women's sexual rights and the acceptability of forcing sex upon them.

Summary and way forward

Several important lessons were learned from the study. First, attitudes that justify the perpetration of forced sex on girls and young women continue to be held by large proportions of young females and especially young males. Gender power differences and attitudes that justify sex as a male entitlement are apparent. Young people continue to agree, for example, that a man is entitled to have sex with a girl on whom he has spent a lot of money, that forced sex must be condoned because men have uncontrollable sexual urges and that it is women who provoke men to rape, whether by their attitude or by refusing the advances of their pursuers. These norms are deeply rooted in Nigerian culture, and their origin may be traced to the generally low socio-economic status of women in the country, where poverty is a major problem (Adekunle and Ladipo 1992; UNDP 2000).

Second, and related to wide gender disparities, is the prevalence of a culture of silence among young victims of rape or other forms of coerced sex. Young victims (female) seldom communicate the incident to anyone, and particularly not their parents, and few seek medical care or legal redress. By and large, victims fear that they will be blamed and stigmatized for provoking the incident, and many believe that it is their lot to endure such a violent act (Ajuwon et al. 2004; Fawole et al. 2002; Odujirin 1993). In these circumstances, the sense of male entitlement is further reinforced; few perpetrators are apprehended.

At the same time, and on a more positive note, there are indications that more egalitarian attitudes and a greater sensitivity to young women and their right to exercise choice are emerging. There was a consensus, for example, among young men and women that a girl has the right to choose her husband and to a lesser extent to refuse sex, and large proportions of young people agreed that it is wrong to force sex on a girl. In short, young people clearly displayed inconsistent attitudes towards sexual coercion, and there is a significant need for programmes to strengthen these somewhat latent egalitarian attitudes.

The findings of the study offer a strong argument for the need to provide life skills and gender-sensitive interventions for both young women and men which enable them to respect women's rights, to communicate on intimate matters, including sex, and to question prevailing gender norms. Multiple strategies are clearly required. Young men need to learn skills that would enable them to resolve conflicts peacefully. Young women and men need to develop a better understanding of women's rights; and young women clearly need to develop the negotiation skills that would build their self-esteem and enable them to avoid relationships that are potentially risky. In addition, public awareness programmes through the media are required to address the stigma associated with rape in Nigeria. Reducing the stigma would encourage greater disclosure of incidents of rape and lead to the prosecution of perpetrators, which would in turn deter those with a propensity for this type of behaviour. Finally, organizations that will respond to the specific needs of victims are urgently needed. Such agencies will help with advocacy, legal assistance and care and support for victims.

Young people's attitudes towards sexual coercion are shaped by community norms that assign women subordinate positions in Nigeria. Interventions, including training targeted at adolescent boys and girls and the entire community, are needed to influence negative norms that favour coercion. The public perception of sexual coercion also needs to be changed to encourage victims to seek care and redress.

Note

1 I would like to thank Oladapo Olley and Iwalola Akin-Jimoh, the co-investigators of the study; Olagoke Akintola for conducting the in-depth interviews; and Frederick Oshiname for reviewing a draft of the paper. This study was supported by the Special

Programme of Research, Development and Research Training in Human Reproduction of the World Health Organization.

References

Adekunle, A. O. and O. A. Ladipo (1992) 'Reproductive tract infections in Nigeria: challenges for a fragile health infrastructure', in K. K. Germain, P. Piot and R. Wasserhelt (eds), *Reproductive Tract Infections: Global Impact and Priorities for Women's Reproductive Health*, New York: Plenum Press, pp. 297–315

Ajuwon, A. J., O. I. Fawole and K. O. Osungbade (2001) 'Knowledge about AIDS and risky sexual behaviours for HIV among young female hawkers in motor-parks and bus stations in Ibadan, Nigeria', *International Quarterly of Community Health Education*, 20(2): 131–41

Ajuwon, A. J., I. Akin-Jimoh, B. O. Olley et al. (2001a) 'Sexual coercion: learning from the perspectives of young persons in Ibadan, Nigeria', *Reproductive Health Matters*, 9(17): 128–36

Ajuwon, A. J., B. O. Olley, I. Akin-Jimoh et al. (2001b) 'The experience of sexual coercion among young persons in Ibadan, Nigeria', *African Journal of Reproductive Health*, 5(1): 120–31

Ajuwon, A. J., B. O. Olley, O. Akintola et al. (2004) 'Sexual coercion in adolescents: exploring the experiences of rape victims in Ibadan, Nigeria', *Health Education*, 104(1): 8–17

Cáceres, C. F., M. B. Vanoss and E. S. Hudes (2000) 'Sexual coercion among youth and young adults in Lima, Peru', *Journal of Adolescent Health*, 27(5): 361–7

Ellsberg, M., L. Heise, R. Pena et al. (2001) 'Researching domestic violence against women: methodological and ethical issues', *Studies in Family Planning*, 32(1): 1–16

Fawole, O. I., A. J. Ajuwon, K. O. Osungbade et al. (2002) 'Prevalence of violence against young female hawkers in three cities in southwestern Nigeria', *Health Education*, 102(5): 230–38

Heise, L., K. Moore and N. Toubia (1995) *Sexual Coercion and Reproductive Health: A Focus on Research*, New York: Population Council

Krug, E. G., L. L. Dahlberg, J. A. Mercy et al. (2002) *World Report on Violence and Health*, Geneva: WHO

Maman, S., J. Mbwanbo, M. Hogan et al. (2001) *HIV and Partner Violence: Implications for HIV Voluntary Counseling and Testing Programmes in Dar es Salaam, Tanzania*, Washington, DC: Population Council, Horizons Project

Odujirin, O. (1993) 'Domestic violence among married women in Lagos', *International Journal of Gynecology and Obstetrics*, 34: 361–6

UNDP (United Nations Development Progamme) (2000) *Nigeria Country Report*, New York: UNDP

Van der Staten, A., R. King, O. Grinstead et al. (1998) 'Sexual coercion, physical violence and HIV infection among women in steady relationships in Kigali, Rwanda', *AIDS and Behavior*, 2(1): 61–72

WHO (World Health Organization) (1993) 'Adolescent sexual behaviour and reproductive health: from research to action: the narrative method', Report of a joint meeting, Geneva

7 | Investigating exchange in sexual relationships in sub-Saharan Africa using survey data

NANCY LUKE

There is increasing interest in the role of economic exchange between non-marital sexual partners in the context of the continuing HIV/AIDS epidemic in sub-Saharan Africa. Findings from a number of qualitative studies reveal that exchange, or the giving of money, gifts or other material assistance, is accompanied by pressure to engage in sexual intercourse and to accept unsafe sexual activity (see Luke 2003 for a review). The practice of exchange in sexual relationships is believed to be widespread, especially among adolescent girls, who are particularly vulnerable in non-marital partnerships. Available quantitative data on exchange are limited in concept and scope, however, which we argue stems from a lack of theoretical grounding in the meaning of exchange in sexual relationships.

This chapter examines the concept of exchange across various types of non-marital sexual partnerships.[1] We provide a theoretical framework for exchange and discuss methodological limitations of previous research in sub-Saharan Africa. We also describe our recent study in Kisumu, Kenya, which has several methodological advantages over available research on exchange. Finally, we review the findings of a number of studies and highlight the prevalence of exchange relationships in sub-Saharan Africa and the link to unsafe sexual behaviour and adverse reproductive health outcomes.

The theoretical framework of exchange in sexual relationships

Much of the recent literature on exchange relationships in the era of HIV/AIDS assumes that exchange has similar purposes in most non-marital relationships and that it is consistently associated with unsafe or unwanted sexual practices (Fuglesang 1997; Komba-Malekela and Liljestrom 1994; Silberschmidt and Rasch 2001; Ulin 1992). We recognize, however, that not all relationships involving exchange are homogeneous and exchange may have various meanings and connections with sexual behaviour in different types of partnerships (Kaufman and Stavrou 2004; Luke 2003). In order to take this variation into account, we follow a general definition of exchange as the offering of items or services by one partner in a relationship to the other. We use the term 'transfer' to refer to items or services given or received, including, but not limited to, money, gifts or other assistance. Our theoretical framework separates exchange relationships into two broad categories: gift and commodity exchange. We follow Carrier (1991), who uses a Maussian perspective to differentiate between gift and commodity exchange in social relationships, and we apply the concepts to non-marital sexual relationships in particular.

Carrier (ibid.) describes gift exchange as the *obligatory* transfer of *inalienable* objects or services between *related* transactors.[2] Relationships that reflect gift exchange occur between people who are tied together in a social relationship, and in this sense they are related. Gifts between parties signify that the relationship is reaffirmed and extended, and are thus obligatory for the relationship to continue. Nevertheless, gifts are not given on a one-to-one basis or because the giver expects an equivalent return gift. Therefore, gifts do not operate coercively, and gift exchange does not involve bargaining between individuals over reciprocal expectations. Gifts are not merely presents, but encompass a range of objects and services, such as cooking, job advice or sexual intercourse. The gifts exchanged are inalienable; in other words, they have meaning for the two partners but may not have utility or meaning for individuals outside the relationship. Numerous types of non-marital sexual relationships embody gift exchange. For example, gifting may be represented in dating or longer-term serious relationships, where transfers serve as symbols of interest and the giver expects nothing sexual in return. It is important to note that in gift exchange relationships the receiver of any type of transfer is not compelled to provide sexual favours directly in return for accepting the gift.

Commodity exchange involves the *inobligatory* transfer of *alienable* objects or services between *unrelated* transactors (ibid.), and thus the three main elements of gift exchange are reversed. Commodity exchange is evident in non-marital relationships when sexual activity is traded for a monetary equivalent on the sexual market. Formal prostitution is often considered best to embody the concept of commodity exchange. In its strictest form, the two people in a commercial sexual relationship do not know one another, the sexual activity could similarly be provided by any number of sex workers, and the parties separate after the exchange is completed. More informal means of commodity exchange also exist, where exchange activity is not part of an individual's profession, the items exchanged are not restricted to money, and the transfer may not be pre-determined or explicitly stated (Hunter 2002; Wojcicki 2002). Examples of informal commodity exchange are a woman who has sexual relations with her landlord in exchange for rent or a schoolgirl who receives school fees from her partner in exchange for sex. Notably, there is a direct association between the transfers and sexual activities performed in all these relationships.

In commodity exchange relationships, outcomes are determined by the bargaining power of the individuals in the partnership; the one with more power or resources can expend this power to ensure that his or her sexual demands are met. It is generally believed that the more powerful individual (usually male) prefers unsafe sexual activities, such as dry or unprotected sex, and that more risky sexual activities should be more highly compensated on the sexual market (see, for example, Campbell 2000; Leclerc-Madlala 2003; Varga 2001; Wojcicki and Malala 2001). Thus, we find that men will pay higher sums of money to commercial sex workers for sex without a condom (Campbell 2000; Leclerc-Madlala 2003; Varga 2001; Wojcicki and Malala 2001). In addition, larger transfers can be exchanged for unsafe sexual activities in informal exchange relationships as well. For example, a qualitative study in South Africa shows that adolescents associated certain sexual activities with higher-value transfers and reported that, while kissing was considered an appropriate response to small transfers like drinks, consenting to oral sex, full penetrative intercourse or unprotected sex was expected in return for more expensive items, such as gold jewellery (Kaufman and Stavrou 2004).

Gift and commodity exchange are not mutually exclusive categories but represent poles at either end of a continuum of relationships (Carrier 1991). The meaning of transfers and their connection with sexual expectation vary across relationships, as well as within partnerships or as the relationship progresses (Campbell 2000; Meekers and Calves 1997a; Orubuloye et al. 1992). For example, in a study of sex workers in South Africa, Varga (2001: 359) describes how some commodity relationships may be 'gradually transformed into more intimate personal attachments' where sex is no longer traded for money. Thus, there is a 'grey area' along the continuum which precludes the clear-cut labelling of relationships as either gift or commodity exchange and therefore makes it difficult to estimate the prevalence of either type.

In a strict sense, sexual coercion – or non-consensual sex in the form of physical or sexual violence perpetrated by one individual or another – should not play a role within either gift or commodity exchange relationships. Gifts cannot force the recipient to engage in sexual activities, and commodities are exchanged willingly, otherwise the transaction will break down. Some research has shown, however, that coercion and violence can be associated with transfers in specific cases, for example when there are differences in the interpretation of transfers by both partners. Several qualitative studies find that adolescent girls sometimes interpret transfers as gifts that symbolize commitment or affection, while male givers view them as inducements and expect sexual activities in return. As a result, some girls may be forced to have sex if they have accepted a transfer (Bohmer and Kirumira 1997; Jejeebhoy and Bott 2003; Nnko and Pool 1997).

A broader definition of sexual coercion acknowledges that, owing to poverty and the lack of alternative options for income, young girls and women may be compelled to engage in commodity exchange relationships (Jejeebhoy and Bott 2003; Outwater et al. 2000; Wojcicki and Malala 2001). In this sense, the perpetrator is not the individual sexual partner; the responsibility for this type of coercion rests in structural factors that constrain individual opportunities to resist unwanted actions (Jackman 2002).[3]

The theoretical framework for gift and commodity exchange helps operationalize the concept of exchange in non-marital sexual relationships and provides a structure for further descriptive and explanatory research. Several hypotheses arise out of the framework regarding the association between transfers and sexual activity which may be empirically tested using survey data. For example, we expect to find larger transfers from male to female partners to be associated with higher probabilities of risky sexual behaviour in commodity exchange relationships. Relationships that are purely gift exchange would display no association between transfers and sexual activity. Finally, transfers may be associated with sexual coercion if one partner is forced to engage in commodity exchange owing to poverty or if the couple does not agree on the interpretation of the transfer.

Vulnerability of adolescent girls in commodity exchange relationships

It is generally believed that non-marital sexual relationships in sub-Saharan Africa are highly commercialized, and formal prostitution has been studied for many years (Varga 2001; White 1990). With the advent of the HIV/AIDS epidemic, attention has shifted to informal commodity exchange relationships, where money, gifts or other assistance is traded for sexual relations between casual or longer-term sexual partners (Barker and Rich 1992; Bohmer and Kirumira 1997; Caldwell et al. 1993; Dunkle et al. 2004; Haram 1995; Komba-Malekela and Liljestrom 1994; Leclerc-Madlala 2003; Meekers and Calves 1997b; Nzyuko et al. 1997; Webb 1997; Wojcicki 2002). These relationships have been referred to as 'sex-for-money exchange' or more generally as 'transactional sex' in the literature. Informal commodity exchange relationships have gained wide acceptance in many African settings and are not stigmatized to the degree that formal prostitution is (Gage 1998; Görgen et al. 1993; Kaufman and Stavrou 2004; Komba-Malekela and Liljestrom 1994; Leclerc-Madlala 2003; Nyanzi et al. 2000; Rasch et al. 2000; Silberschmidt and Rasch 2001; Webb 1997; Wojcicki 2002). Although a range of motivations for involvement in informal commodity exchange relationships have been documented, including seeking love or a marriage partner, many such relationships in Africa are believed to arise from financial need (Fuglesang 1997; Leclerc-Madlala 2003; Luke 2003; Meekers and Calves 1997a; Wojcicki 2002).

Adolescent girls in sub-Saharan Africa are believed to be particularly vulnerable to unsafe sexual activities within commodity exchange relationships owing to their weaker bargaining position in relation to their male partners,[4] which may be due to a number of factors. First, the economic value of sexuality is pronounced for adolescent girls, who have fewer market opportunities than older women, and informal commodity exchange may be the only opportunity they have to meet their needs (Bohmer and Kirumira 1997; Calves and Meekers 1997; Nyanzi et al. 2000; Orubuloye et al. 1992; Webb 1997).

Second, population growth and deteriorating economic conditions have resulted in a partner squeeze in many African settings, where there is a shortage of economically secure men while poor young girls are in plentiful supply (Görgen et al. 1998; Leclerc-Madlala 2003; Vos 1994). Thus, girls may find it hard to negotiate the terms of sexual relationships with men because of the easy availability of substitute female partners.

Third, adolescent girls' lack of knowledge and experience in sexual negotiations weakens their bargaining power (Bohmer and Kirumira 1997; Nyanzi et al. 2000; Webb 1997). Finally, adolescent girls in sub-Saharan Africa are generally uninformed about their sexuality and safe sexual practices (Gage 1998; Silberschmidt and Rasch 2001). As a result, they are unaware of the risks associated with unsafe sex and are therefore likely to use their limited bargaining power to negotiate for higher economic gains rather than safe sexual practices.

Despite this common view that adolescent girls in sub-Saharan Africa have less bargaining power in sexual relationships than older women, several researchers support the opposing view. Adolescent girls could command more than adult women because they are men's preferred partners, as they are perceived to be free of HIV/AIDS and other sexually transmitted infections, or because younger partners boost male prestige among their peers (Haram 1995; Longfield et al. 2002; Silberschmidt and Rasch 2001). Furthermore, several studies reveal girls' understanding of the negotiating process with respect to commodity exchange. They indicate that most girls and young women understand that acceptance of a transfer must be reciprocated with sexual activity (Barker and Rich 1992; Bohmer and Kirumira 1997; Görgen et al. 1998; Leclerc-Madlala 2003; Wojcicki 2002) or that insistence on safe sex practices will jeopardize a lucrative relationship and ongoing financial reward (Preston-Whyte 1994; Rasch et al. 2000; Silberschmidt and Rasch 2001).

This contextual background on adolescent girls in sub-Saharan Africa leads to additional hypotheses regarding exchange that can be tested using survey data. We would expect to find a higher prevalence of commodity exchange relationships among adolescent girls, while adolescents would receive less in value of transfers compared to adult women. Taking the view that adolescent girls are more vulnerable in exchange relationships than adult women, the relationship between transfers and unsafe sexual activity should be *stronger* for adolescent girls than for older women.

Measuring exchange in sexual relationships using survey data

A number of Demographic and Health Surveys in sub-Saharan Africa, as well as smaller population-based surveys, have gathered data on the prevalence of exchange in women's and men's relationships, and have focused on money and gifts as the primary items of transfer (see Luke 2003 for a review). We argue, however, that the standard survey questions on exchange are problematic in terms of their validity and are limited scope, and these issues are discussed below.

Validity of questions on exchange Survey questions on exchange typically tend to focus on the end of the continuum where an overt connection between transfers and sexual activity is recognized. For example, the standard Demographic and Health Survey question reads, 'Have you ever given or received money, gifts, or favours for sexual relations in the past 12 months?' and is usually asked of both men and women who have ever been sexually active or sexually active in the past twelve months. Similarly, a survey in Soweto, South Africa, asks women if they have 'ever become involved with a [non-primary partner][5] because he provided you with or you expected that he would provide you with ... ' any of a list of commodities (Dunkle et al. 2004) (see Table 7.1 for a listing of survey questions on exchange).

This line of questioning fails to capture gift exchange on the whole. Furthermore, such survey questions can lead to under-reporting of commodity exchange relationships for several reasons. First, questions that enquire about money or gifts that have explicitly been 'exchanged for sex' or are motivated by material gain may imply formal prostitution, which is considered stigmatized behaviour, particularly for women. Interestingly, most Demographic and Health Survey reports refer to the questions on commodity exchange as 'payment for sexual activity', which suggests that these questions are meant to measure behaviours akin to prostitution.

Second, the 'grey area' between gift and commodity exchange relationships makes it difficult for respondents to define their relationships as either category. Individuals may not recognize the direct connection between transfers and the sexual outcomes of their relationships. This is especially problematic when there is a temporal lag between the transfer and sexual activity, although the transfer did indeed play a role in subsequent sexual behaviour.

Third, most past surveys have relied on standard question phrasing with respect to exchange, including the Demographic and Health Surveys, which allows for useful cross-setting comparisons. Nevertheless, such questions may be understood differently across settings depending on how they are translated into the local language. For example, a study of commodity exchange in South Africa reveals that some terms for exchange are associated with prostitution while others refer to more acceptable forms of informal commodity exchange (Wojcicki 2002; see also Hunter 2002). Thus, the translation of standard questions may not capture commodity exchange behaviour if translations are not sensitive to local nuances of stigmatized behaviour.

In short, past survey questions on exchange have limited validity as they tend to under-report relationships in the 'grey area' that do not represent overt commodity exchange but nevertheless display a direct connection between transfers and sexual activity. Such data can also bias the estimated statistical relationship between transfers and sexual activity, as data that are concentrated at the end of the spectrum where sexual activity is overtly related to transfers would

TABLE 7.1 Survey questions on exchange

Demographic and Health Surveys, various sub-Saharan African countries

1. Have you ever given or received money, gifts, or favours for sexual relations in the past 12 months?

Soweto, South Africa study

1. Have you ever become involved with a [non-primary partner] because he provided you with or you expected that he would provide you with ... ?:

Food — Cosmetics — Clothes
Transportation — Tickets or money for transport
Items for children or family such as clothes, food or school fees
Own school or residence fees — Somewhere to sleep
Cash

Ondo Town, Nigeria study

1. What kind of help or assistance do you give her/them [each non-marital partner]?

Money and other assistance
No money, but general material assistance (food, etc.)
Only help with studies — Only advice, moral support
None

2. Do you give her/them payment? [If YES] What is this for?

No — Yes — For assistance — For sexual service

3. Do your partners know that they are practising commercial sex? [If YES] What do they feel about it?

No — Yes — Enjoy the life
Feel fairly positive, no problems — Feel it is a necessity
Feel ashamed

Kisumu, Kenya study

1. It is common for men to give women gifts or other assistance when they are in a relationship. What have you given your [non-marital] partner(s) in the last month? [If YES, record value in Kenyan shillings for each category]

Money — Gifts — Rent
Meals/drinks — Other (specify)

Sources: Demographic and Health Surveys: <www.measuredhs.com/>; Soweto, South Africa: Dunkle et al. 2004; Ondo Town, Nigeria: Orubuloye et al. 1992; Kisumu, Kenya: Luke 2005

overestimate the average effect of transfers on sexual activity in the population of interest.

Scope of questions on exchange As mentioned earlier, there are many aspects of exchange relationships that can vary across partnerships, and questions on exchange behaviour in earlier surveys are limited in scope in two important respects. For one, past survey figures pertain only to the prevalence or incidence of commodity exchange behaviour, i.e. they report on *individuals* who have ever or recently been involved in exchange in any of their relationships, and there is limited information on specific *partnerships* that involve transfers (for exceptions see Konde-Lule et al. 1997; Orubuloye et al. 1992). Without data on multiple sexual partnerships for each respondent, including transfers given to/received from each partner and the sexual activities with each partner, we are unable to test for the association between the transfer from a particular man and risky behaviour within that partnership (Luke 2003).

Second, surveys generally have not collected information on the specific types of transfers or the value of items exchanged (exceptions are Dunkle et al. 2004; Orubuloye et al. 1992, discussed below). More detailed information on the nature of transfers could help determine whether the value or type of transfer has implications for the perpetration of unsafe sexual behaviour in different settings.

Given the limitations of past studies and the lack of a theoretical framework, it is suggested that survey questions be framed to elicit information on a broad range of exchange relationships. Questions should use wording that is context specific, that is not associated with stigmatized behaviour and which does not tie transfers temporally to specific sexual activities. In addition, more detailed information is needed on transfers across an individual's multiple partnerships.

The Kisumu study

Our interest in the study of exchange in non-marital sexual relationships in sub-Saharan Africa led to the inclusion of questions in a survey we conducted in Kisumu, Kenya, in 2001. We attempted to improve on some of the drawbacks of past survey work on exchange and gather data that would allow us to test some of the hypotheses that stem from our theoretical framework.

The Kisumu study examined the non-marital sexual behaviour of urban males of the Luo ethnic group. The survey covered 2,700 males aged twenty-one to forty-five (see Luke 2005; Luke and Munshi forthcoming for details). In addition to gathering demographic and socio-economic information on the respondents, specific questions were asked on their sexual behaviour, including the number of non-marital sexual partners in the past year and details of the five most recent partners.[6] Partner information included the ages and marital status of female partners, the duration of each relationship, when sexual intercourse had last occurred, whether a condom was used at last sexual intercourse, and transfers given to the partner in the month preceding the study.

The questions on material transfers were particularly framed to capture both gift and commodity exchange. The survey question read: 'It is common for men to give women gifts or other assistance when they are in a relationship. What have you given your partner(s) in the last month?' This wording ensured that the reported transfers were not stigmatized and occurred regardless of accompanying sexual activity. Respondents were asked whether they had given the major types of material assistance that were uncovered in the pre-testing phase of the project, including money, gifts, rent and meals or drinks. An open category was also included, where respondents could list other types of assistance provided. For each category of transfer, the amount of money or the value of the items given was recorded. In order to ensure accurate recall on the specific type of assistance given and its value, the question was limited to transfers that occurred in the last month.

The advantage of this method of questioning on exchange is that detailed data could be gathered on a range of transfers within all non-marital partnerships, thus overcoming many of the limitations of earlier surveys. This line of questioning does have several drawbacks, however. First, while the Kisumu study focused on material or tangible items whose value could be quantified, information was not collected on other kinds of transfers that could be associated with unsafe sexual activity, for example offering a lift to school or providing moral support.

Second, it is difficult for any study to accurately estimate the prevalence of either commodity or gift exchange owing to the 'grey area' along the exchange continuum. For example, if our questions on material transfers are used to estimate commodity exchange, they would tend to provide an overestimate, as responses would also include gift exchange. In addition, our analysis of the association between transfers and sexual activity would tend to provide a conservative estimate of the average effect, as our measure of transfers would also include gift exchange, or relationships that should not display an association between the transfer and risky sexual activity.

Third, an aspect we did not include in our study, which has also not been included in earlier surveys, is the measurement of sexual coercion within exchange relationships. As noted, coercion that is associated with exchange may occur owing to motivations of poverty or divergent interpretations of the meaning of the transfer between partners. To measure connections to poverty, surveys should enquire about the motivations of individuals to engage in exchange in each partnership, as well as assess the economic status of both partners. With respect to divergent interpretations of transfers, respondents could be asked about their understanding of the influence of the transfer on sexual activity, as well as their perceptions of coercion within the partnership more generally.

Prevalence of exchange relationships

A recent review of studies of commodity exchange relationships among adolescent girls finds that between 5 and 80 per cent of adolescent girls have engaged in sexual relations at some time in exchange for money or gifts in various settings in Africa (Luke 2003). This section reviews two additional sets of studies that measure the prevalence of exchange: the Demographic and Health Surveys conducted in sub-Saharan Africa which use standard questions on exchange, and three studies in Soweto, South Africa, Ondo Town, Nigeria, and Kisumu, Kenya, which use context-specific definitions of exchange (Table 7.1 lists the questions on exchange behaviour in these studies).

Table 7.2 shows the percentage of women who gave or received money, gifts or favours for sexual relations in the twelve months preceding the survey (the last four weeks in Zimbabwe and at last sexual encounter in Uganda) by marital status and age as reported in the Demographic and Health Surveys <www.measuredhs.com>. Although the question in the Demographic and Health Survey includes involvement as either giver or receiver, it is assumed that in most cases young women are the recipients of transfers. As can be seen from Table 7.2, the percentage of unmarried adolescent girls aged fifteen to nineteen who have engaged in commodity exchange in the twelve months preceding the survey ranges from 7.2 per cent in Côte d'Ivoire to 38.4 per cent in Zambia. The figures for married adolescents are much lower, which may reflect the support they receive from their husbands or their tendency to under-report exchange. Irrespective of marital status, adolescent girls are generally more likely to have given or received money or gifts for sex than older women.

The percentage of men who gave or received money, gifts or favours for sexual relations in the twelve months preceding the survey (the last four weeks in Zimbabwe 1994) is shown in Table 7.3. Among unmarried adolescents aged fifteen to nineteen, figures range from 2.1 per cent in Zimbabwe to 49.6 per cent in Chad. Most figures for married adolescent boys are suppressed owing to the limited number of cases. There is no consistent association between age and commodity exchange relationships. Among young men (younger than twenty-five years), however, the unmarried appear to have been more likely than the married to have engaged in recent commodity exchange relationships, perhaps because the latter have greater access to sexual relations through marriage.

We now compare the findings from the three studies that examine exchange behaviour in greater detail. The studies use different definitions and measurements of exchange, and we briefly describe the methodology of each. The Soweto study was conducted in 2001/02, and sampled 1,395 women aged sixteen to forty-four seeking antenatal care (Dunkle et al. 2004). Respondents were asked about their involvement with a non-primary sexual partner specifically for material gain, which the authors refer to as 'transactional sex'. The study in Ondo Town, Ekiti District, Nigeria, was undertaken in the early 1990s, and sampled 488 men aged fifteen to fifty (Orubuloye et al. 1992). Respondents were asked about their non-marital sexual relationships in the past year and the nature of assistance they had rendered each partner. The assistance was not limited to material transfers but included help with studies, advice or moral support. The Kisumu survey, as mentioned earlier, sampled 2,770 men aged twenty-one to forty-five in 2001, and asked respondents about their non-marital sexual relationships in

TABLE 7.2 Percentage of women who gave or received money, gifts or favours for sexual relations in the last twelve months, by age, marital status and country and date of the Demographic and Health Survey

	Age group (years)	Not currently married (%)	Currently married (%)
Mali, 1995–96†	15–19	25.6	9.1
	20–24	21.5	6.2
	15–49	21.8	4.9
Côte d'Ivoire, 1998–99†	15–19	7.2	2.9
	20–24	7.8	0.9
	15–49	6.4	1.2
Chad, 1996–97†	15–19	28.7	0.8
	20–24	10.3	1.0
	15–49	13.2	0.7
Burkina Faso, 1998–99†	15–19	19.8	4.0
	20–24	1.2	1.3
	15–49	10.1	1.2
Kenya, 1998*	15–19	20.9	4.2
	20–24	18.1	4.1
	15–54	17.3	3.0
Guinea, 1999*	15–19	16.3	2.9
	20–24	17.6	2.4
	15–49	14.8	2.4
Nigeria, 1999*	15–19	32.0	1.1
	20–24	25.8	2.1
	15–49	24.4	1.8
Zambia, 1996*	15–19	38.4	8.2
	20–24	28.4	4.9
	15–49	25.6	3.8
Zimbabwe, 1994 (last 4 weeks)*	15–19	12.8	1.8
	20–24	9.4	1.8
	15–49	10.3	1.2
Uganda, 1995 (last sexual encounter)	15–19	31.0	–

Source: Demographic and Health Survey website: <//www.measuredhs.com/> Zimbabwe and Uganda (PRB 2001)

Notes: * Those who ever had sexual intercourse † Those who had sexual intercourse in the last twelve months – Not reported

TABLE 7.3 Percentage of men who gave or received money, gifts or favours for sexual relations in the last twelve months, by age, marital status and country and date of the Demographic and Health Survey

	Age group (years)	Not currently married (%)	Currently married (%)
Mali, 1995–96†	15–19	19.2	41.5
	20–24	31.7	14.6
	15–59	30.6	4.8
Cote d'Ivoire, 1998–99+	15–19	3.9	–
	20–24	3.9	1.9
	15–59	7.9	4.1
Chad, 1996–97†	15–19	49.6	21.2
	20–24	41.4	14.3
	15–59	42.8	7.8
Burkina Faso, 1998–99†	15–19	28.1	–
	20–24	29.7	10.4
	15–59	27.6	4.3
Cameroon, 1998†	15–19	20.9	–
	20–24	35.2	17.7
	15–59	30.5	18.3
Guinea, 1999*	15–19	10.4	–
	20–24	5.4	5.8
	15–59	7.4	3.4
Nigeria, 1999*	15–19	28.4	–
	20–24	20.1	4.6
	15–54	24.0	7.2
Zambia, 1996*	15–19	39.3	–
	20–24	36.1	25.3
	15–64	38.7	13.6
Zimbabwe, 1999*	15–19	2.1	–
	20–24	11.1	6.1
	15–54	9.6	5.4
Zimbabwe, 1994 (last 4 weeks)*	15–19	8.0	–
	20–24	10.5	2.5
	15–54	11.2	4.3

Source: Demographic and Health Survey website: <www.measuredhs.com/>
Notes: * Those who ever had sexual intercourse † Those who had sexual intercourse in last 12 months – Few cases and figures suppressed

the year preceding the study as well as the type and value of material assistance given to each in the last month. As the Ondo Town and Kisumu studies did not tie the transfers to sexual activity, the assistance given could encompass either gift or commodity exchange.

Although is it difficult to compare the findings of these three studies as they cover different study populations and reference periods and the survey questions were framed differently, some crude comparisons can nevertheless be made. The main findings regarding the prevalence of exchange are reported in Table 7.4. The Soweto study, which is limited to commodity exchange relationships that are specifically motivated by financial gain, shows that 21.1 per cent of women were ever involved in such a partnership. The Soweto study also finds that 19.9 per cent of women had at some time a non-primary partnership in which they received cash, which is the category of items most exchanged. Looking across age groups of females, the prevalence of transactional sex among adolescents aged sixteen to twenty is lower than among women aged twenty-one and above.

Both the Ondo Town and Kisumu studies examine exchange across gift and commodity relationships among men. As seen in Table 7.4, the Ondo Town study found that in 94 per cent of men's non-marital sexual partnerships, men gave some form of help or assistance to their partners, and in 70 per cent of such partnerships men specifically gave material transfers. In Kisumu, similarly, men gave material transfers in 72.6 per cent of non-marital partnerships. As in Soweto, the category of items most exchanged in Ondo Town and Kisumu is cash. In Ondo Town, men gave money and other assistance[7] in 66.0 per cent of partnerships, and in Kisumu 51.2 per cent of the value of all transfers was monetary. The value of individual transfers in the last month is similar in both settings (approximately US$6–7). This is equivalent to approximately one-third of the per capita monthly income in Nigeria and approximately 9 per cent of men's monthly income in Kisumu. Finally, the Kisumu study finds that the prevalence and value of material transfers are lower in partnerships with adolescent girls aged less than twenty than in partnerships with women aged twenty and above.

In sum, the three studies reveal varying percentages of respondents reporting the experience of exchange relationships. One reason for these wide differences is the fact that settings vary in terms of the extent to which exchange behaviour occurs in the population, as well as across age groups and gender. Differences in survey design or instrument construction could also account for the variation. Moreover, the percentages reporting the experience of exchange may be lower among women than among men because women are less likely to engage in exchange behaviour or report it in surveys (see Gersovitz et al. 1998 for a study of males' and females' reporting of sexual behaviour). Unlike the Soweto study, the Ondo Town and Kisumu studies focused on both primary and non-primary partnerships, and this may account for the higher reporting in these two studies.[8]

TABLE 7.4 Prevalence rates for various measures of exchange

	Soweto, South Africa	Ondo Town, Nigeria	Kisumu, Kenya
Study population	Women aged 16–44 at antenatal clinics	Men aged 15–50	Men aged 21–45
Unit of analysis	Women with and without non-primary sexual partners in lifetime	Men's non-marital sexual partnerships in last 12 months	Men's non-marital sexual partnerships in last month
Prevalence of material transfers	21.1% of women ever had non-primary partnership motivated by financial gain	In 94% of non-marital partnerships, men gave help or assistance; in 70%, men gave material transfer	In 72.6% of non-marital partnerships, men gave material transfer
Prevalence with cash	19.9% of women ever had non-primary partnership where they received cash	In 66% of non-marital partnerships, men gave money and other assistance	51.2% of the value of all transfers was monetary
Value of transfers	–	Average Naira 70 (US$7) per non-marital partnership in last month	Average Ksh 445.7 (US$6.40) per non-marital partnership in last month
Prevalence among women by age group	20.9% women aged 16–20 and 24.4% women aged 21+ ever had a non-primary partnership motivated by financial gain	–	69.3% of non-marital partnerships with women aged <20 and 75.7% of non-marital partnerships with women aged 20+ had material transfer
Value of transfers among women by age group	–	–	Average Ksh 351.8 (US$5) to female partners aged <20 and Ksh 534.9 (US$7.65) to female partners aged 20+

Sources: Soweto, South Africa: Dunkle et al. 2004; Ondo Town, Nigeria: Orubuloye et al. 1992; Kisumu, Kenya: Luke 2005

Exchange relationships and reproductive health outcomes

In this final section we briefly review the hypotheses from our theoretical framework that have been tested with data from existing studies of exchange. Findings of two studies lend support to the hypothesis that larger transfers from male to female partners are associated with higher probabilities of risky sexual behaviour. Multi-variate regression analysis of the Kisumu data reveals a negative and significant association between both the presence and the value of a transfer that the male partner gave to his female partner in the month preceding the study and the likelihood of condom use at last sexual intercourse with this partner (Luke, 2005).[9] The Soweto study finds a significant bi-variate association between a woman ever having a transactional sexual partnership and testing positive for HIV infection at the time of the survey (Dunkle et al. 2004). As we cannot determine that the HIV infection, and thus unsafe sexual activity, came from the same man who gave the women a transfer, this finding only tentatively supports the hypothesis.

The Kisumu study tested the assumption that monetary transfers solely reflect commodity exchange (and therefore monetary transfers would have a significant effect on condom use) while non-monetary transfers reflect gift exchange (and therefore would have no effect on condom use). A multi-variate regression analysis, however, reveals no significant difference in the relationship between transfers and condom use by the type of transfer (Luke forthcoming). In other words, both monetary and non-monetary transfers are significantly related to unsafe sexual activity, which indicates that monetary and non-monetary transfers are substitutable in this context.

Commodity exchange is hypothesized to be associated with sexual coercion if one partner is forced to have sex owing to poverty or if the couple does not agree on the interpretation of the transfer. The Soweto study provides evidence to support this hypothesis. In a bi-variate analysis, Dunkle et al. (2004) find greater odds of transactional sex for women who live in substandard housing, which suggests that commodity exchange may be motivated by poverty in this setting. In addition, the study finds significant bi-variate associations between several measures of intimate partner violence, including physical and sexual abuse, and ever engaging in transactional sex. Again, a word of caution: we are not able to discern whether abuse occurred within a transactional sexual partnership, or whether women who are involved in transactional sex are also more likely to be abused in any of their relationships.

Study findings show mixed results regarding the hypothesis that there will be a higher prevalence of commodity exchange relationships among adolescent girls than among adult women. The hypothesis appears to be supported by the Demographic and Health Survey figures reviewed in Table 7.2 and not supported by the Soweto and Kisumu studies. The Kisumu results support the assumption that adolescent girls receive less in value of transfers than adult women. Finally, while it may be hypothesized that the effect of transfers on sexual activities for adolescent girls is greater than for older women, the Kisumu study finds no difference in the effect by the age group of the female partner (Luke forthcoming). These results suggest that all women, and not just adolescent girls, are at risk of unsafe sexual behaviour in exchange relationships.

Conclusion

In order to design programmes to modify risky sexual behaviour in exchange relationships, a greater understanding of the linkages between transfers and sexual activity is needed. This chapter outlines a theoretical framework of exchange in non-marital sexual relationships which can be used to operationalize exchange relationships and construct appropriate survey questions to test the association between transfers and sexual risk behaviour.

We argue that earlier studies have been limited in their conceptualization of exchange and their scope of enquiry, which has led to an under-reporting of commodity exchange relationships and an overestimation of the effect of transfers on sexual activity. To address these limitations, information needs to be collected on a range of exchange relationships, including gift and commodity exchange. Extensive data are also needed on the value and type of transfers across an individual's multiple sexual partnerships. Data that include gift exchange relationships provide conservative estimates of the effect of transfers on sexual activity and are perhaps appropriate for policy and programme planning. The methods used in the Kisumu study may be useful in addressing the limitations of earlier studies of exchange.

A review of the findings from existing studies of exchange relationships suggests that prevalence rates vary greatly across settings, gender and age groups. Several factors could account for these differences, including variation in the design of surveys and questions on exchange relationships. Limited data are available to test the linkages between exchange relationships, sexual activity and poor reproductive health outcomes. Nevertheless, available study findings show that transfers have a negative effect on safe sexual behaviour and reproductive health, and that the negative effect of exchange does not appear to be greater for adolescent girls than for adult women. Finally, there is some evidence that exchange is associated with sexual coercion. Future research should take into account lessons learned from these studies when designing surveys on exchange.

Our theoretical framework of gift and commodity exchange provides a two-pronged approach for policies and programmes aimed at increasing safe sexual behaviour within exchange relationships. On the one hand, our framework and the findings of studies reviewed underscore the fact that bargaining occurs in commodity exchange relationships – whether in formal prostitution or more informal exchange relationships. Thus, women are not simply passive pawns in commodity exchange relationships but they do have limited power to negotiate safe sexual practices. Programmes should be designed to help women and girls recognize the connection between transfers and sexual activity, increase their bargaining power to insist on safe sexual practices, or to empower them to forgo these relationships altogether. Recommendations include improving negotiating skills, increasing knowledge of the costs of risky sexual activities and facilitating opportunities for alternative sources of income. On the other hand, we hypothesize that transfers have no association with sexual activity in gift exchange relationships, where unsafe practices, such as low condom use, occur because partners love and trust one another, and not as a result of the gifts given. Aiming to reduce gift-giving within these relationships would prove ineffective in combating unsafe sexual practices; instead, programmes should seek to promote condom use and faithfulness to one sexual partner regardless of exchange behaviour.

Notes

This article is based on data from the Marriage and Sexual Behavior Project, directed by Kaivan Munshi and Nancy Luke, Population Studies and Training Center, Brown University. We gratefully acknowledge support from the National Institutes of Health, National Institute on Aging, grant number AG12836 through the Population Aging Research Center at the University of Pennsylvania, as well as the Mellon Foundation, the Center for AIDS Research and the University Research Foundation at the University of Pennsylvania. We would like to thank Francis Ayuka and the Survey Research Team, Nairobi, for their superb work in collecting the data.

1 Exchange also takes place in marital relationships but this topic is beyond the scope of this article.

2 Much of this general description of gift and commodity exchange relies on Carrier (1991), who offers a view of exchange from a sociological perspective.

3 Hunter nevertheless recognizes women's agency to gain control over their lives in 'economically coercive relationships' (Hunter 2002: 112).

4 One explanation for the greater vulnerability of adolescent girls to HIV is their biological susceptibility to infection (Glynn et al. 2001).

5 Non-primary sexual partners are non-marital sexual partners who are not serious dating partners, including 'roll-ons' (secret partnerships hidden from the primary partner) and 'one-off' partners (those with whom a woman has sex only once).

6 Of the men reporting non-marital sexual partners in the last year, 95 per cent had five or fewer partners.

7 Cash was not regarded as a separate category.

8 It should also be noted that the figures for women in Soweto are calculated using women as the denominator, and the figures for men in Ondo Town and Kisumu are calculated using men's non-marital partnerships as the denominator, although this difference does not necessarily lead to smaller estimates for women than for men.

9 Condom use at last sexual intercourse was limited to intercourse that took place in the last month.

References

Barker, G. K. and S. Rich (1992) 'Influences on adolescent sexuality in Nigeria and Kenya: findings from recent focus-group discussions', *Studies in Family Planning*, 23(3): 199–210

Bohmer, L. and E. Kirumira (1997) 'Access to reproductive heath services: participatory research with adolescents for control of STDS', Los Angeles: Pacific Institute for Women's Health Working Paper Summary

Caldwell, J., P. Caldwell, E. M. Ankrah et al. (1993) 'African families and AIDS: context, reactions and potential interventions', *Health Transition Review*, 3(suppl.): 1–16

Calves, A.-E. and D. Meekers (1997) 'Gender differentials in premarital sex, condom use, and abortion: a case study of Yaounde, Cameroon', Research Division Working Paper no. 10, Washington, DC: Population Services International

Campbell, C. (2000) 'Selling sex in the time of AIDS: the psycho-social context of condom use by sex workers on a Southern African Mine', *Social Science and Medicine*, 50: 479–94

Carrier, J. (1991) 'Gifts, commodities, and social relations: a Maussian view of exchange', *Sociological Forum*, 6(1): 119–36

Dunkle, K. L., R. K. Jewkes, H. C. Brown et al. (2004) 'Transactional sex among women in Soweto, South Africa: prevalence, risk factors and association with HIV infection', *Social Science and Medicine*, 59: 1581–92

Fuglesang, M. (1997) 'Lessons for life – past and present modes of sexuality education in Tanzanian society', *Social Science and Medicine*, 44(8): 1245–54

Gage, A. J. (1998) 'Sexual activity and contraceptive use: the components of the decision making process', *Studies in Family Planning*, 29(2): 154–66.

Gersovitz, M., H. G. Jacoby, T. Goetze et al. (1998) 'The balance of self-reported heterosexual activity in KAP surveys and the AIDS epidemic in Africa', *Journal of the American Statistical Association*, 93(443): 875–83

Glynn, J. R., M. Carael, B. Auvert et al. (2001) 'Why do young women have a much higher prevalence of HIV than young men? A study in Kisumu, Kenya, and Ndola, Zambia', *AIDS*, 15(suppl. 4): S51–S60

Görgen, R., B. Maier and H.J. Diesfeld (1993) 'Problems related to schoolgirls' pregnancies in Burkina Faso', *Studies in Family Planning*, 24(5): 283–94

Görgen, R., M. L. Yansane, M. Marx et al. (1998) 'Sexual behavior and attitudes among unmarried urban youths in Guinea', *International Family Planning Perspectives*, 24(2): 65–71

Haram, L. (1995) 'Negotiating sexuality in times of economic want: the young and modern Meru women', in K. I. Klepp, P. M. Biswalo and A. Talle (eds), *Young People at Risk: Fighting AIDS in Northern Tanzania*, Oslo: Scandinavian University Press, pp. 31–48

Hunter, M. (2002) 'The materiality of everyday sex: thinking beyond "prostitution"', *African Studies*, 61(1): 99–120

Jackman, M. R. (2002) 'Violence in social life', *American Review of Sociology*, 28: 387–415

Jejeebhoy, S. J. and S. Bott (2003) 'Non-consensual sexual experiences of young people: a review of the evidence from developing countries', Regional Working Paper no. 16, New Delhi: Population Council

Kaufman, C. E. and S. E. Stavrou (2004) '"Bus fare please": the economics of sex and gifts among young people in urban South Africa', *Culture, Health, and Sexuality*, 6(5): 377–91

Komba-Malekela, B. and R. Liljestrom (1994) 'Looking for men', in Z. Tumbo-Masabo and R. Liljestrom (eds), *Chelewa, Chelewa: The Dilemma of Teenage Girls*, Sweden: The Scandinavian Institute of African Studies, pp. 133–49

Konde-Lule, J. K., N. Sewankambo and M. Morris (1997) 'Adolescent sexual networking and HIV transmission in rural Uganda', *Health Transition Review*, 7(suppl.): 89–100

Leclerc-Madlala, S. (2003) 'Modernity, meaning and money: urban youth and the commodification of relationships', Paper presented at the 1st South African AIDS Conference, ICI, 6 August, Durban

Longfield, K., A. Glick, M. Waithaka et al. (2002) 'Cross-generational relationships in Kenya: couples' motivations, risk perception for STIs/HIV and condom use', Research Division Working Paper no. 52, Washington, DC: Population Services International

Luke, N. (2003) 'Age and economic asymmetries in the sexual relationships of adolescent girls in Sub-Saharan Africa', *Studies in Family Planning*, 34(2): 67–86

— (2005) 'Confronting the "sugar daddy" stereotype: age and economic asymmetries and risky sexual behavior in urban Kenya', *International Family Planning Perspectives*, 31(1): 6–14

— (forthcoming) 'Economic exchange and condom use in informal sexual relationships in urban Kenya', *Economic Development and Cultural Change*.

Luke, N. and K. Munshi (forthcoming) 'New roles for marriage in urban Africa: kinship networks and the labor market in Kenya', *Review of Economics and Statistics*

Meekers, D. and A.-E. Calves (1997a) '"Main" girlfriends, girlfriends, marriage, and money: the social context of HIV risk behavior in sub-Saharan Africa', *Health Transition Review*, 7(suppl.): 361–75

— (1997b) 'Gender differentials in adolescent sexual activity and reproductive health risks in Cameroon', Washington, DC: PSI Research Division Working Paper no. 4

Nnko, S. and R. Pool (1997) 'Sexual discourse in the context of AIDS: dominant themes on adolescent sexuality among primary school pupils in Magu District, Tanzania', *Health Transition Review*, 7(suppl. 3): S85–90

Nyanzi, S., R. Pool and J. Kinsman (2000) 'The negotiation of sexual relationships among school pupils in south-western Uganda', *AIDS Care*, 13(1): 83–98

Nzyuko, S., P. Lurie, W. McFarland et al. (1997) 'Adolescent sexual behavior along the trans-African highway in Kenya', *AIDS*, 11(suppl. 1): S21–S26

Orubuloye, I. O., J. C. Caldwell and P. Caldwell (1992) 'Diffusion and focus in sexual networking: identifying partners and partners' partners', *Studies in Family Planning*, 23(6): 343–51

Outwater, A., L. Nkya, G. Lwihula et al. (2000) 'Patterns of partnership and condom use in two communities of female sex workers in Tanzania', *Journal of the Association of Nurses in AIDS Care*, 11(4): 46–54

PRB (Population Reference Bureau) (2001) 'Sexual violence against young women', in *The World's Youth 2000*, Washington, DC: PRB, p. 10

Preston-Whyte, E. (1994) 'Gender and the lost generation: the dynamics of HIV transmission among black South African teenagers in KwaZulu/Natal', *Health Transition Review*, 4(suppl.): 241–55

Rasch, V., M. Silberschmidt, Y. Mchumvu et al. (2000) 'Adolescent girls with illegally induced abortion in Dar es Salaam: the discrepancy between sexual behavior and lack of access to contraception', *Reproductive Health Matters*, 8(15): 52–62

Silberschmidt, M. and V. Rasch (2001) 'Adolescent girls, illegal abortions and "sugar daddies" in Dar es Salaam: vulnerable victim and active social agents', *Social Science and Medicine*, 52: 1815–26

Ulin, P. R. (1992) 'African women and AIDS: negotiating behavioral change', *Social Science and Medicine*, 34(1): 63–73

Varga, C.A. (2001) 'Coping with HIV/AIDS in Durban's commercial sex industry', *AIDS Care*, 13(3): 351–65

Vos, T. (1994) 'Attitudes to sex and sexual behavior in rural Matabeleland, Zimbabwe', *AIDS Care*, 6(2): 193–203

Webb, D. (1997) *HIV and AIDS in Africa*, London: Pluto Press

White, L. (1990) *The Comforts of Home: Prostitution in Colonial Nairobi*, Chicago, IL: University of Chicago Press

Wojcicki, J. M. (2002) 'Commercial sex work or *Ukuphanda*? Sex-for-money exchange in Soweto and Hammanskraal area, South Africa', *Culture, Medicine and Psychiatry*, 26: 339–70

Wojcicki, J. M. and J. Malala (2001) 'Condom use, power and HIV/AIDS risk: sex-workers bargain for survival in Hillbrow/Joubert Park/Berea, Johannesburg', *Social Science and Medicine*, 53: 99–121

THREE | Young men as victims and perpetrators

8 | Assessing young people's non-consensual sexual experiences: lessons from Peru

CARLOS F. CÁCERES

Over the past decade, the issue of non-consensual sex has gained increasing attention in discussions on sexual and reproductive health, and its occurrence is regarded as both a sexual health and a human rights problem (Heise et al. 1999; Heise et al. 1995; PAHO/WHO 2000). One of the reasons for the greater focus on non-consensual sex is, no doubt, the spread of the HIV epidemic; and several studies have demonstrated the relationship between a history of non-consensual sex and the presence of HIV/sexually transmitted infection (STI) markers (Doll and Carballo-Diéguez 1998).

With research focusing on non-consensual sex, data from a number of communities across the world have shown that its occurrence is not rare (Heise et al. 1999). Evidence shows that non-consensual sex may take place among heterogeneous groups of young people across categories of gender, age, sexual orientation and type of relationship, including marital. In fact, non-consensual sex encompasses a range of circumstances where sexual activity occurs without the 'consent' of persons involved, from interactions that may be described as 'manipulation' to cases where violent force is used (often called rape or, in more generic terms, sexual violence). Sexual coercion and sexual abuse are the result of power imbalances determined by the social roles of the participants (for a list of related concepts see PAHO/WHO 2002). While experiences and consequences may vary, there are some common threads, which allow for a discussion of non-consensual experiences in general.

Our approach to understanding the phenomenon of non-consensual sex is, however, limited by methodology, as most studies rely solely on self-reported experiences. More significantly, reporting a sexual experience as non-consensual in a particular context is conditioned by norms governing gender roles and sexual scripts, for example those stating that all 'normal' men but no 'decent' women willingly engage in heterosexual activity. Thus men are more likely to under-report situations in which they have been sexually coerced by women and, conversely, would tend to over-report their homosexual experiences (if known to the interviewer) as non-consensual, or sometimes associated with alcohol consumption or transactional sex. In contrast, women may over-report any heterosexual experiences as forced.

This chapter discusses findings from two studies in Peru of sexually active young men's and women's accounts of their experiences of non-consensual sex, including both same-sex and opposite-sex experiences. It explores the frequency and correlates of non-consensual sex among young people, and discusses the ways in which young men and women perceive and interpret non-consensual sexual experiences.

Background

The studies reviewed in this chapter were conducted in the coastal cities of Lima, the capital of Peru, and Chiclayo and Trujillo (Cáceres 1999; Cáceres et al. 1997; Salazar et al. 2002). These three cities collectively comprise some 9 million of Peru's 28 million population. The coastal region is culturally homogeneous, and findings of this article are perhaps more representative of this part of the country than the Andean highlands or the Amazon area. At present, urban life expectancy is seventy-two years, with an ageing population as a result of decreasing birth and mortality rates. Young people aged fifteen to twenty-four represent 20 per cent of the total population (INEI 2000). The most common sexual health problems among young people include unplanned pregnancies (20 per cent of sexually active women aged fifteen to twenty-four reported a pregnancy, of which 64 per cent were unintended) (ibid.), STI/HIV (half of those diagnosed with AIDS during the period 1983–2000 are likely to have acquired the infection at the age of twenty-five or less) (Cáceres et al. forthcoming), and the experience of non-consensual sex, which is discussed in this chapter.

Recent studies from Peru indicate the high prevalence of sexual violence among young persons (Anicama et al. 1999; Cáceres et al. 2002; Escobedo 1999; Espinoza 2000; INEI 1998; León and Stahr 1995; Loli and Rosas 1995; Maraza and Maraza 2000; PROMUDEH 1998; MIMDES 2003; Montedoro 1996; Rosas 1990; Vargas 1997; Yáñez de la Borda 1998). The most recent and comprehensive evidence on sexual violence, however, has been presented in a multi-site study coordinated by the World Health Organization (Güezmes et al. 2003a, 2003b). In Peru, this research was conducted in Lima (covering a sample of 1,414 survey women) and Cuzco (covering 1,837 women in urban and rural areas). The findings of the study indicate that the lifetime experience of sexual violence (defined as being forced to perform a sexual act against their will) was 23 per cent in Lima and 47 per cent in Cuzco; and for the twelve months preceding the survey it was 7 per cent in Lima and 23 per cent in Cuzco. Among those reporting the experience of sexual violence in Lima and Cuzco, 20 and 18 per cent, respectively, reported the experience of sexual violence by age fifteen. By and large, women reporting the experience of sexual violence by age fifteen reported that they were acquainted with the perpetrators, and in only 24 per cent of cases in Lima and 21 per cent of cases in Cuzco were such acts perpetrated by strangers.

Methodology

The Lima study explores young men's and women's experiences of non-consensual sex perpetrated by partners of the same and opposite sex, draws a general picture of sexuality and gender among young people, and assesses the influence of gender, age and social class on the prevalence of non-consensual sex using a mix of qualitative and quantitative methods. Data for the qualitative component were collected in 1994/95. A total of forty in-depth interviews and twenty focus group discussions were conducted, covering eight strata defined by a combination of gender, age group (adolescents and young adults) and class (working-class and middle-class).

Data for the survey were collected in 1995–97. The survey covered a sample of 611 adolescents (309 males and 302 females) aged sixteen to seventeen, randomly recruited from among those obtaining military registration, which is mandatory, and 607 young adults (308 males and 299 females) aged nineteen to thirty, recruited from among persons requesting the issue of police certificates, to be used as work or study permits.[1]

The survey enquired about a range of issues including the frequency and context of sexual experiences of both young men and women. More specifically, the questionnaire explored non-consensual sexual experiences among all those reporting a heterosexual and homosexual experience as follows: 'Did you feel pressured to have this first sexual relationship?' and 'Have you ever had sex with a girl/boy because s/he pressured you to do it?' Responses included 'no pressure or force'; 'pressure but no force'; and 'force'. Non-consensual sex was then defined as any kind of sexual activity taking place against the respondent's will, as a result of force or pressure from others, with or without the use of physical violence.

The survey measured both non-consensual sexual initiation (for both heterosexual and homosexual experiences) as well as lifetime experience of non-consensual sex (ever having had sex with a girl/boy as a result of coercion). It also obtained information on the type of partner at first sex, including boy/girlfriend, fiancé/fiancée, acquaintance (peer or adult), 'easy' (easily available) girl/sex worker, or relative (same age or older); age at first sex; number of sexual partners; whether the respondent had ever paid or been paid for sex; whether sex had been experienced under the influence of alcohol or drugs; whether the respondent or partner had ever experienced an unplanned pregnancy; whether the respondent had ever experienced symptoms of STI or been diagnosed with an STI; sexual knowledge (measured on a scale of sixteen 'true'/'false'/'don't know' items relating to STIs, HIV/AIDS, reproduction and sexuality, recorded as 'correct'/'incorrect', and summed to form an index with scores ranging from 0–16, Cronbach alpha 0.75); and socio-demographic characteristics such as age, sex and socio-economic status (weighted score measuring household consumer goods/commodities; range 0–15, Cronbach alpha 0.73). Serological samples were also tested for HIV, hepatitis B virus (HBV) and syphilis.

The three-site study focuses on accounts of sexual experiences of young people in a working-class setting that highlight a variety of behaviours ranging from consensual to non-consensual, including group rape. This ethnographic study explores young people's vulnerability to sexual health problems in low-income *barrios* (neighbourhoods) and the relationship between local sexual norms and experiences and the transmission and prevention of HIV/STI in marginalized neighbourhoods. The findings of the study were used to adapt HIV prevention messages to the local context, and to apprise public opinion leaders in the community about local sexual norms and the risks they pose (Salazar et al. 2002).

Findings

Frequency and correlates of non-consensual sex In the survey of young people in Lima, 54 per cent of the 1,218 respondents (37 per cent of all women [N = 221] and 72 per cent of all men [N = 442]) were sexually experienced. The following discussion covers sexually experienced young men and women.

Findings suggest that by and large those sexually experienced tended to be older than other respondents. For example, 47 per cent of adolescent boys (aged sixteen to seventeen) and 91 per cent of young men (aged nineteen to thirty) reported heterosexual experiences, while among women the proportion reporting such experiences was 13 and 57 per cent respectively (not shown in tabular form). Of those reporting heterosexual experiences, 23 per cent reported that they or their partner had experienced an unplanned pregnancy. Homosexual experiences were common among men in the general sample, with 16 per cent of adolescents and 13 per cent of young adults reporting having had at least one homosexual experience. Among women, these figures were 3 and 4 per cent, respectively. Of those men reporting either heterosexual or homosexual experiences, 18 per cent reported ever having had symptoms of or being diagnosed with an STI.

Table 8.1 presents the percentage of young men and women reporting non-consensual heterosexual or homosexual sexual experiences at initiation and during their lifetime. As may be seen, 11 per cent of young men (N = 48) but 40 per cent of young women (N = 83) reported that their initiation was coerced by a perpetrator of the opposite sex. The proportion for young men includes 4 per cent who reported peer pressure. Over the course of their lifetime, some 20 per cent of young men and 46 per cent of young women reported a non-consensual sexual experience committed by an opposite-sex perpetrator. Among those who had homosexual experiences, 45 per cent of young men and 35 per cent of young women reported that their first homosexual experience was non-consensual, while 48 per cent of young men and 41 per cent of young women reported that they had had a non-consensual homosexual experience at least once during their lifetime.

As can be seen from Table 8.2 (col. 1), most men reported heterosexual initiation with a girlfriend or fiancée or with a peer or adult acquaintance; in addition

TABLE 8.1 Non-consensual sexual initiation and lifetime experience among sexually experienced young men and women

Variable	Young men aged 16–17 and 19–30	Young women aged 16–17 and 19–30
Total (N)	442	221
Number reporting a heterosexual experience	420	209
Reporting non-consensual initiation (%)	11	40
Reporting ever experiencing non-consensual sex (%)	20	46
Number reporting a homosexual experience	65	17
Reporting non-consensual homosexual initiation (%)	45	(35)
Reporting ever experiencing non-consensual sex (%)	48	(41)

Note: Figures in brackets denote numbers less than 20.
Source: Cáceres et al. 2000

some 14 per cent reported initiation with a sex worker or 'easy' woman and 6 per cent with a same-age or adult relative. Among females, by far the majority (91 per cent) reported that first sex occurred with a boyfriend or fiancé.

Where sexual initiation was non-consensual, young males and females reported a somewhat different set of perpetrators. For females, 38 per cent of those whose first sex occurred with a boyfriend or fiancé, seven out of ten whose first partner was an acquaintance and three out of eight whose first partner was a relative reported that the encounter was non-consensual. Among males, in contrast, only 13 and 10 per cent, respectively, of those reporting first sex with a girlfriend/fiancée or acquaintance reported that the encounter was non-consensual, as did six of twenty-five whose first sex occurred with a relative. In addition, three of the fifty-seven young males whose first sex was with a sex worker reported that they felt pressured, either by their peers or the sex worker herself, to have sex, as a result of the social norm to prove their manliness.

Age patterns are also evident, as seen in Table 8.2. Among both males and females who reported heterosexual initiation, those whose initiation had occurred at younger ages were more likely than those whose initiation had occurred at older ages to report the experience as non-consensual. We subsequently compared young men reporting (n = 48) and not reporting (n = 372) non-consensual heterosexual initiation (not presented here in tabular form). Significant differences were noted. The lifetime number of heterosexual partners was 3.7 for those whose sexual initiation was non-consensual and 5.7 for those who had not had such an experience ($p = 0.02$), while scores on the sexual knowledge index were reported as 5.8 for those whose sexual initiation was non-consensual and 7.8

TABLE 8.2 Non-consensual heterosexual initiation by type of partner and age at initiation among sexually experienced young men and women

Variable	Young men aged 16–17 and 19–30		Young women aged 16–17 and 19–30	
	Total number reporting first sex by:	% of col. 1 reporting non-consensual initiation	Total number reporting first sex by:	% of col. 3 reporting non-consensual initiation
Total	420	11	209	40
Type of partner*				
Boy/girlfriend or fiancé/fiancée	166	13	189	38
Acquaintance (peer or adult)	164	10	10	(70)
'Easy'/sex worker	57	(5)	–	–
Relative (same age or older)	25	(24)	8	(38)
Age at heterosexual initiation (years)**				
<15	122	15	21	62
15–17	218	10	74	39
18–21	67	10	79	39
22 or older	10	(10)	32	28

Notes: * 8 young men and 2 young women did not respond ** 3 young men and 3 young women did not respond. Figures in brackets denote numbers less than 20.
Source: Cáceres et al. 2000

for those for whom it was consensual (p = 0.0009). Up to 25 per cent of those reporting non-consensual sexual initiation, but only 14 per cent of those who had not had such an experience, reported having experienced symptoms of STIs (p = 0.04). While 25 per cent of those whose sexual initiation was non-consensual also reported homosexual experiences, only 16 per cent of those not reporting non-consensual initiation reported similar experiences.

A multiple logistic regression model was applied to explore factors distinguishing men who had and had not experienced non-consensual sex at initiation. Variables included age at first sex, experience of STI symptoms, sexual knowledge, the logarithm of the number of heterosexual partners, previous experience of commercial sex, age of first sexual partner, use of drugs or alcohol with sex, experience of unplanned pregnancy, socio-economic status, homosexual experience, and having had a steady first sexual partner (versus others). Among these, the following were significant: age at first sex (adjusted odds ratio 0.83 per year, 95 per cent CI 0.70–0.98), experience of STI symptoms (adj. OR 3.21, 95 per cent CI 1.26–8.20), index of sexual knowledge (0.86 per point, 0.77–0.97) and the logarithm of the number of heterosexual partners (0.35, 0.19–0.67). In other words, young men who reported a non-consensual sexual experience at initiation were, compared to others, more likely to have initiated sex early, more likely to have experienced an STI, less likely to be informed on sexual matters and less likely to report multiple heterosexual partners.

Among women, the picture is largely similar. Compared to those who experienced consensual heterosexual initiation (n = 126), those whose first sex was coerced (n = 83) were more likely than others to report early sexual initiation (mean age 17.5 versus 18.4, p = .03), more likely to have experienced an STI (33 per cent versus 17 per cent, p = 0.009) and less likely to know about sexual matters (index of 7.4 versus 8.4, p=0.04). A logistic regression model largely similar to that described for males above, with the exclusion of homosexual experience, suggests that significant factors distinguishing those whose first sex was non-consensual from those whose first sex was consensual were early age at first sex (adjusted odds ratio 0.87 per year, 95 per cent CI 0.77–0.97) and experience of STI (adj. OR 3.12, 95 per cent CI 1.44–6.73).

Young people's perceptions of non-consensual sex Both the three-site study and the Lima study included qualitative components from which we can draw insights into how young people perceive non-consensual sex. Findings suggest that perceptions are significantly influenced by sociocultural norms and attitudes towards gender roles.

Findings from the qualitative phase of the study conducted in Lima show that the definition of 'rape' (*violación*) varied between two extremes: from a general description of an act of 'forced penetration' to a more expanded definition whereby it was described as 'any episode of forced sex, including within marriage'. Young people reported that rape could not only be perpetrated by a man on a woman, but also by a woman, including an older woman, on a man, by a husband on a wife, and by a man on another man. Perspectives on how women and men perpetrate non-consensual sex are illustrated in the following quotes: 'I have heard of cases where young guys have been abused ... Well (in my case), if she is hot and offers herself to me I accept ... but if a man does it to a girl, then we put him in jail ... she is young, she doesn't know what rape is' (focus group discussion, working-class adolescent boys). Similarly, 'There is also male rape ... if she is thirty-eight and he is fifteen and she forces him, then it is rape as well' (focus group discussion, middle-class young men).

Young males also discussed marital rape: 'Rape doesn't only happen between uncles and nieces, but also between couples. If he forces her then it is rape' (focus group discussion, middle-class young men).

Several respondents described non-consensual sex as occurring within same-sex relationships, often evoking violent responses, as seen, for example, in the following quote: 'Once I took a taxi to the soccer stadium and the driver was homosexual; he came on to me, wanted to take me somewhere else. I freaked out and got pissed off, told him I was going to buy cigarettes, and got [out of] the car, then I started to throw stones at him' (focus group discussion, middle-class adolescent boys). Moreover, young people recognized that non-consensual sex could occur in unequal power relationships, such as within the family, at work or at school, where the less powerful person is forced or pressured to have sex in exchange for a benefit or to avoid harm. For example, in the course of discussions young males reported: 'Usually I have seen cases of uncles raping their nieces. Such cases are common' (focus group discussion, working-class adolescent boys); and 'rape within the home is common. When brothers and the mother go out, and the father stays with the daughter, he abuses her' (focus group discussion, working-class adolescent boys).

Indeed, young people appeared to be aware of the prevalence of non-consensual sex in their communities and reported that discussion of such incidents took place both in the media, and, especially among working-class respondents, within homes and neighbourhoods. While young people's familiarity with non-consensual sex was evident in all focus group discussions, there appears to be a tendency among middle-class respondents to perceive the occurrence of non-consensual sex as related to poverty, as shown in the following quote: 'It happens in places far away from here, still in the city, but in poor districts' (focus group discussion, middle-class adolescent boys).

In the three-site study, young people described perpetrators in a number of ways (Sandoval et al. 2004). Some described them as psychopaths, others as ordinary persons who did what others would have liked to do in their place. A number of commonly perceived underlying factors were also identified, including the attitudes of the victim/perpetrator and his/her parents, the use of alcohol and drugs, and exposure to pornography.

By and large, young males tended to agree that women were responsible for provoking a forced sexual heterosexual encounter and blamed the victim for her lack of responsibility. While women generally condemned rape, many young men adopted a light-hearted approach to the issue, reaffirming prevailing gender norms; they tended to justify violence on several grounds, notably if women were being 'difficult' or if they 'unfairly' denied sex to them. 'A guy I know, since his girl didn't want to have anal sex, made her get drunk and took her to his room. Since she fell asleep, he fucked her hard from behind. The next day she was feeling a bit of pain, but didn't know the reason. She used a cream, but it didn't work. She didn't go out for two or three days because she was ill, she couldn't walk [laughter]' (focus group discussion, working-class young man). In addition to blaming girls for provoking a coercive sexual encounter, young males tended to blame the victim's family, including fathers and stepfathers, for lack of appropriate supervision of the young girl. For example, they agreed: 'It was her parents' lack of care' (focus group discussion, middle-class adolescent boys).

An unexpected finding of the three-site ethnographic study was accounts of 'group rape' of a girl by several boys. Narratives were collected mainly from 'corner men', i.e. young men who spend time on street corners and who frequently consume alcohol and drugs (with a cocaine base or marijuana). In these narratives, young males described women (generally called *movidas* or 'easy girls') who would occasionally join 'corner' men, and drink and use drugs, and with whom young males would perpetrate group rape. Young males tended to condone group rape on the grounds that since the girls 'are not virgins, nobody would believe they were forced'.

Narratives discussed situations in which men revealed a sense of entitlement to force sex, including group sex, on a girl with whom they had been drinking. Alcohol and drug use by these women appears to be part of a ritual that is perceived to lead to both consensual and non-consensual forms of sexual activity. The following quotes from in-depth interviews with young men are illustrative: 'She got drunk and wanted to have sex with my friend, but he did not want to since he was with another girl'; 'Since they [the girls] are the ones who come to the neighbourhood, they are the ones who look for us'; and 'They come with that intention. If you come it's to win [with the intention of having fun, of having sex]. It can happen and, no big deal ... you can easily drink rum with a girl and she may be just thirteen, fifteen but it doesn't matter.'

Deceiving a girl into engaging in sex by drugging her was also perceived as acceptable and prevalent, as illustrated in the following description reflecting familiarity with mixing sleeping pills in a girl's drink:

'Tell me, are there several ways to have sex, or just one?'

'There are several ways.'

'Tell me about them.'

'Well, put a pill in her soda and you pick her up' (in-depth interview, young men).

Young people were well aware of the consequences of non-consensual sex, and reported that such incidents were likely to remain unreported and unpunished. They recognized, for example, that women who had experienced non-consensual sex faced stigma and discrimination, even from the family, as can be seen in the following quotes: 'She keeps it [rape by her stepfather] a secret because of shame and fear ... she fears that her mother will blame her for inciting her father' (focus group discussion, working-class adolescent boys); and: 'Her stepfather raped her, he suggested to her that she should not tell her mother because she would end up being worse off. And so it was. She told her mother and [her mother] said: "No, you are a loose girl, and want to catch my husband for yourself" and threw her out' (focus group discussion, working-class adolescent boys).

Young males' narratives, however, suggested that the consequences for men largely depended on whether the perpetrator was a man or a woman. Sexual advances/pressure by women on men were not commonly regarded as rape; in fact, in most cases such advances/pressure were perceived as being harmless and potentially pleasant. While male-on-male rape was recognized in focus group discussions, several points of view were expressed. Some, for example, tended to assume that the victim had provoked the incident. Others perceived the victim as being 'sexually possessed' by another man, at risk of losing his masculinity and becoming a homosexual. In both instances, homosexual rape was perceived to affect the victim's future sexual orientation. For example, 'if he liked it, then he can become homosexual'; 'both boys and girls are raped frequently ... when the boy is touched by a man, he becomes a queer' (focus group discussion, working-class adolescent boys); and: 'When a man is raped he becomes a queer. That happened to a friend who played soccer. He was raped and later he became a queer. Now he plays volleyball [a sport associated with women and gay men in Peru]' (focus group discussion, working-class young men).

Discussion and conclusions

Findings from the studies reviewed show that non-consensual sex is prevalent in Peru. Young people's perceptions of non-consensual sex may range, however, from condemnation to apathy or even justification. A number of contradictions characterize young people's interpretations of non-consensual sex experienced by youth. In a setting where traditional gender roles and attitudes are prevalent, gender and sexual scripts clearly influence both the ways in which young people identify and report a sexual experience as non-consensual and their attitude towards such experiences.

In the context of traditional gender roles, cultural scripts of non-consensual heterosexual experiences appear to be based on the classic conception of male heterosexual desire as uncontrollable. Consequently, the perception is that men are not to be blamed if they perpetrate non-consensual sex on women, as they are responding to the urges of their bodies. Conversely, female victims were perceived to have provoked the aggressive incident. Even the families of victims were blamed for not adequately protecting the victim.

Discussions of males as victims were less consistent. There was a perception that the perpetration of non-consensual sex on men by women was essentially contrary to the stereotypical image of the male as the aggressor, and thus such incidents occurred mainly with very young or mentally retarded boys, or young men with sexual dysfunction. Interpretations of non-consensual homosexual experiences also raised many questions, as young people had difficulty in associating the image of aggressiveness required of a perpetrator with the notion of a homosexual as 'passive'.

Clearly, much effort is needed to build an environment where sexual rights are promoted and protected for all, and traditional notions of masculinity are challenged (Cáceres et al. 2002; Kaufman 1999; Montoya 1998). Programmes are also needed that not only prevent the occurrence of non-consensual sex, but also mitigate its effects, with an emphasis on cases where the emotional impact and/or adverse life outcomes are most severe.

In addition, these complex, somewhat contradictory accounts lead us to recognize the need for studies that focus on and explore specific hypotheses of the contexts and patterns of non-consensual sex, and the manner in which young women and men define these experiences in the light of changing gender and sexuality norms. This would help us understand the role played by these and other sociocultural norms (as in the social construction of masculinity) in conditioning the interpretation and reporting of specific experiences as non-consensual or not. Research must devise ways of accommodating the likely under- and over-reporting of specific experiences and ascertain the extent to which responses represent timid attempts to start speaking out, or reflect socially desirable answers to questions that may challenge entrenched gender roles.

Note

1 Since these permits are generally required to study or work, we consider this sample to be representative of the population of Lima as a whole.

References

Anicama, J., S. Viscardo, J. Carrasco et al. (1999) *Estudio epidemiológico sobre la violencia y comportamientos asociados en Lima Metropolitana y Callao*, Lima: MINSA and UNFV

Cáceres, C. (1999) *La (re)configuración del universo sexual. Culturas sexuales y salud sexual entre los jóvenes de Lima a vuelta de milenio*, Lima: UPCH and REDESS Jóvenes

Cáceres, C., B. Marin and E. Hudes (2000) 'Sexual coercion among youth and young adults in Lima, Peru', *Journal of Adolescent Health*, 27: 361–7

Cáceres, C., B. Marin, E. Hudes et al. (1997) 'Young people and the structure of sexual risks in Lima', *AIDS*, 11(suppl 1): S67–S77

Cáceres, C., W. Mendoza, R. Leyva et al. (forthcoming) 'Re-estimating the PLHA population size in Peru for the implementation of a national HAART program: the Peru HAART study', Abstracts Book, XV International AIDS Conference, Bangkok

Cáceres, C., X. Salazar, A. Rosasco et al. (2002) *Ser hombre en el Perú de hoy: Una mirada a la salud sexual desde la infidelidad, la violencia y la homofobia*, Lima: REDESS Jóvenes

Doll, L. and A. Carballo-Diéguez (1998) 'Physical and sexual coercion and HIV risk: editorial', *AIDS Behavior*, 2: 31–2

Escobedo, T. R. (1999) *Agresión sexual: características del hecho, circunstancias y hallazgos físicos en la víctima en la Provincia de Piura*, Piura: Universidad Nacional de Piura

Espinoza, M. (2000) *Violencia en la familia en Lima y el Callao*, Lima: Ediciones del Congreso del Perú

Guezmes, A., N. Palomino and M. Ramos (2003a) *Violencia contra las mujeres en el Perú. ¿Es posible cambiar?*, <www.ciudadaniasexual.org/boletin/b3/articulos.htm>

— (2003b) *Violencia sexual y física contra las mujeres en el Perú*, Estudio Multicéntrico de la Organización Mundial de la Salud

Heise, L., M. Ellsberg and M. Gottemoeller (1999) 'Ending violence against women', Population Reports, Series L, no. 11, Baltimore, MD: Johns Hopkins University School of Public Health, Population Information Program, December

Heise, L., K. Moore and N. Toubia (1995) *Sexual Coercion and Reproductive Health: A Focus on Research*, New York: Population Council

INEI (Instituto Nacional de Estadística e Informática) (1998) *Encuesta de victimización de Lima Metropolitana*, Lima: INEI

— (2000) *Encuesta demográfica y de salud familiar 1999*, Lima: INEI

Kaufman, M. (1999) 'Las siete Ps de la violencia de los hombres', *International Association for Studies of Men*, 6(2), June

León, R. and M. Stahr (1995) *Yo actuaba como varón solamente*, Lima: DEMUS

Loli, S. and M. Rosas (1995) *Violencia contra las mujeres en el Perú*, Lima: Flora Tristan

Maraza, C. and H. Maraza (2000) *La violación sexual a menores y su influencia en la formación integral del educando secundario de la ciudad de Juliaca*, Puno: unpublished

MIMDES (Ministerio de la Mujer y Desarrollo Social) (2003) *Estado de las investigaciones en violencia familiar y sexual en el Perú*, Lima: MIMDES

Montedoro, F. (1996) *Violencia familiar en Chiclayo*, Chiclayo: Grupo Mujer–Chiclayo

Montoya, O. (1998) *Nadando contra corriente: buscando pistas para prevenir la violencia masculina en las relaciones de pareja*, Managua: Puntos de Encuentro

PAHO/WHO (Pan American Health Organization and World Health Organization) (2000) *Abuso sexual en mujeres adolescentes*, San José de Costa Rica: OPS/OMS – Programa Mujer, Salud y Desarrollo, <www.paho.org/Spanish/HDP/HDW/gph9.pdf>

— (2002) *Violencia sexual basada en género y salud: sistematización del taller introductorio*, San José de Costa Rica: OPS/OMS – Programa Mujer, Salud y Desarrollo, <www.paho.org/Spanish/HDP/HDW/gph13.pdf>

PROMUDEH (Ministerio de la Mujer y Desarrollo Humano) (1998) *Violencia familiar. Estadística y análisis de la línea de emergencia y de las comisarías de Lima Metropolitana*, Lima: PROMUDEH

Rosas, M. I. (1990) *Violación sexual: un crimen silenciado*, Lima: DEMUS

Salazar, X., A. Maiorana, M. Garate et al. (2002) 'Young people and vulnerability to HIV/STDs in Chiclayo, Peru', Abstracts Book, XIV International Conference on AIDS, Barcelona

Sandoval, C., C. Cáceres, X. Salazar et al. (2004) 'Sexual scripts and sexual violence: sexual coercion and consensual sexual transgression between women and men in Peru', Abstracts Book, International AIDS Conference, Bangkok

Vargas, M. (1997) *Agresiones sexuales contra mujeres: ¿responsabilidades compartidas?*, Lima: DEMUS

Yáñez de la Borda, G. (1998) *La violencia contra la mujer*, Lima: Ediciones Movimiento Manuela Ramos

9 | Non-consensual sexual experiences of young people in Kenya: boys as perpetrators and victims

CAROLYNE NJUE, IAN ASKEW AND JANE CHEGE

Results from the 2003 Kenya Demographic and Health Survey (KDHS 2003) indicate that physical and sexual abuse of women is a major problem in Kenya. Nationwide, 44 per cent of married, separated or divorced women aged fifteen to forty-nine years reported ever experiencing physical violence[1] by their partner, and 29 per cent reported such incidents in the twelve months preceding the survey. Moreover, 16 per cent of women reported ever being sexually violated by their husbands or partners,[2] with 12 per cent reporting such experiences during the previous year. Reports of physical and sexual violence were highest among women living in the neighbouring Western and Nyanza provinces in western Kenya.

As with most of sub-Saharan Africa, Kenya has a large population of young people, with more than 60 per cent of the 31 million population below the age of twenty-five, and 44 per cent under the age of fifteen (KDHS 1999). Nearly eight out of ten young people initiate sexual activity before the age of twenty, with the median age at first intercourse being 16.7 years for girls and 16.8 years for boys (ibid.). Studies show that, despite awareness, many young people continue to practise high-risk behaviours and, as a result, cases of early pregnancy, abortion, infection and HIV are observed (Ferguson 1988; Johns Hopkins Center for Communication Programs 1998; KDHS 1999; Nzioka 2001). Compounding their biological vulnerability is the fact that younger women are likely to be coerced into sex (vaginal or anal) or raped, often by someone older who has had exposure to the HIV virus (Buvé et al. 2001).

Given this context, non-consensual sex among young people in Kenya is relatively common. A study in Central Province, for example, found that 31 per cent of boys and 27 per cent of girls reported experiencing pressure to engage in sex, although it is usually the boys who exert this pressure on girls, either through peer pressure from other boys or by persuading or coercing girls (Erulkar 2004). A countrywide study shows that pressure starts at an early age, with 29 per cent of girls and 20 per cent of boys aged thirteen and below reporting one or more episodes of sexual harassment (Population Communication Africa and Pathfinder International 1999).

The World Health Organization has defined non-consensual sex as 'any sexual act, attempt to obtain a sexual act, unwanted sexual comments or advances, or acts to traffic, or otherwise directed against a person's sexuality using coercion, by any person regardless of their relationship to the victim' (Krug et al. 2002: 149). Other definitions include the act of forcing (or attempting to force) another individual through violence, threats, verbal insistence, deception, cultural expectations or economic circumstances to engage in sexual behaviour against her/his will (Ajuwon et al. 2001; Heise et al. 1995).

Several studies in Kenya highlight the fact that non-consensual sex has several forms, such as sexual insults and teasing, unwanted touching in public minibuses or discotheque halls, verbal and physical harassment when going to the shops or passing through dark places, forcing girls, and sometimes drugging them or gagging them to prevent them from screaming (Mensch 1996; Remes et al. 2002). Other forms of abuse include older boys/men beating their partners when they refuse to have sex, girls being forced into prostitution by their partners or parents/guardians, girl prostitutes being gang-raped by their clients and wife inheritance (where a dead man's relative forcibly inherits his wife) (Chege and Njue 1999). In schools, girls report being harassed or forced by male students and teachers to have sex (Ajayi et al. 1997; Njue and Vandenhoudt 2001).

Laumann et al. (1994) propose that the consequences of non-consensual sex are probably magnified at first sex because it comes at a turning point in a young person's life, making it a 'formative experience' for the adolescent. The object of this chapter is to examine non-consensual sex among youth, particularly the experiences of young men as victims and perpetrators, among the Luhya in Kenya. The article also discusses first sexual experiences among boys and girls.

Background

Socialization and non-consensual sex Gender relations among the Luhya are characterized by an unequal balance of power, with women having comparatively less access to influential positions and resources, which is reflected in definitions of masculinity and femininity. Motherhood and humility/submission are important aspects of femininity, whereas bravery/valour and sexual prowess are intrinsic elements of masculinity. So while boys are socialized into a role that recognizes and encourages their sexual freedom, girls are cautioned to avoid boys by their parents, teachers and other adults. Unmarried circumcised boys have a special hut within their parents' compound, while unmarried adolescent girls remain in their parents' house. Newly circumcised Luhya boys are told that, as men, they have the right to sexual intercourse with any unmarried woman: 'the door that is open [the unmarried woman] is yours, but that which is closed [the married woman] is not yours'. Girls, however, do not have a rite of passage into womanhood, but are socialized throughout adolescence into adopting a submissive role in public and in intimate relations with men.

Experiences of non-consensual sex can be categorized as tolerated (when based on sociocultural and gender stratification systems and expectations/norms) or as transgressive (where condemned by society) (Heise 1998). In Luhya culture, sweet-talking and persuasion are normally tolerated socially as they are often used to justify culturally acceptable expectations of male and female behaviour, and the belief that male sexuality is inherently predatory and female sexuality is essentially receptive and submissive. Coercion, such as violence, rape and incest, however, is considered transgressive behaviour and is abhorred by the community.

Methodology and the operationalization of non-consensual sex

The findings presented here are drawn from a survey conducted in two districts (Vihiga and Busia) in Western Province, Kenya, an area that is almost universally populated by the Luhya ethnic group. The survey was the baseline for an evaluation of a multi-sectoral intervention to address adolescents' reproductive health needs (Chege et al. 2001). Three locations (with an administrative area of approximately 15,000 people) in each district were selected through a multistage sampling procedure, and five enumeration areas (each with approximately 100–120 households) were randomly selected in every location. The sample sizes for the baseline survey were calculated to be able to detect changes in sexual experience over time due to the intervention rather than to estimate proportions within the population. As the estimated rates of sexual experience at the baseline were much lower among girls than boys, and among the younger than the older age groups, the sample sizes required to detect a significant change over time in each age group were significantly larger for girls than for boys, and for the younger age groups than for the older age groups.

A listing of all households and their members in each enumeration area was prepared and those households with adolescents aged ten to fourteen years and fifteen to nineteen were considered eligible. From households with more than one eligible adolescent, interviewers randomly selected one adolescent from each age and sex group. Face-to-face interviews were carried out individually and in privacy. The sample size, for those adolescents who clearly stated their age, was 3,522, categorized as follows:

Boys 10–14:	554	Girls 10–14:	1,408
Boys 15–19:	397	Girls 15–19:	1,163

Weighted percentages were presented to ensure that the responses represented the responses of the study population, as controlled by location, age and sex. The quantitative data were supplemented by qualitative information gathered through focus group discussions undertaken prior to the survey among groups of school-going and out-of-school adolescent boys, adolescent girls and parents in the study area. Despite study moderators' instructions to refrain from sharing personal experiences, participants in several focus group discussions shared their personal/intimate experiences, and given the insightful nature of these, we have opted to include such statements here.

The nature of the experience of first sexual intercourse was determined through the following closed-ended, single-response question: 'The first time people have sex, it can be for different reasons. For you, the first time you had sexual intercourse, did you want to have sex, were you forced to have sex, were you tricked or were you sweet-talked, were you threatened, or were you convinced with money or gifts?'

The interviewer read out the following response categories in the local language and asked for a single response, which was then recorded on the questionnaire:

- I wanted to have sex
- I was sweet-talked into having sex
- I was convinced to have sex with money/gifts
- I was tricked into having sex
- I was threatened into having sex
- I was forced (physically) to have sex
- No response

This question was asked also of the last time they had sex and for any other times they had had sex.

Respondents were also asked whether they had perpetrated any of these behaviours. Both girls and boys were asked: 'For all the times you have had sex, have you ever forced a boy/man [girl/woman] to have sex, have you ever tricked or sweet-talked a boy/man [girl/woman] against his/her will, have you ever threatened a boy/man [girl/woman], or have you ever convinced a boy/man [girl/woman] with money or gifts?'

Response categories included:

- I have sweet-talked a boy/man [girl/woman] into having sex
- I have convinced a boy/man [girl/woman] to have sex with money/gifts
- I have tricked a boy/man [girl/woman] into having sex
- I have threatened a boy/man [girl/woman] into having sex
- I have (physically) forced a boy/man [girl/woman] to have sex
- No response

Three categories of non-consensual sex are defined in this chapter:

1. 'Sweet-talked': defined as to be told 'sweet things', to be 'lured'.
2. Persuaded: includes those reporting they had been convinced with money/gifts or tricked.
3. Forced: includes those reporting they had been threatened or forced.

In this chapter, for reasons given shortly, 'sweet-talking' will not be categorized as non-consensual sex as it is difficult to define sweet-talking as definitely consensual or non-consensual from the data available. Non-consensual sex will include those reporting being persuaded or forced.

Findings

The survey found that 32 per cent all boys (N = 283) and 17 per cent of all girls (N = 436) aged ten to nineteen years reported ever having had sexual intercourse.

Consensuality of sex and experience of first sex As shown in Table 9.1, the majority of boys and girls (82 and 78 per cent respectively) reported having first sex with a boyfriend/girlfriend or a friend/acquaintance. While girls were more likely to have first sex with a casual acquaintance, however, boys more frequently reported first sex with a girlfriend or fiancée. Boys were also more likely than girls (15 versus 3 per cent respectively) to have first sex with a relative (aunt, cousin, elder sister, sister-in-law) or a housegirl, which supports the qualitative findings, presented later, that some boys experiment by having first sex with someone close to the family.

TABLE 9.1 Experience of first sex by type of partner among sexually active boys and girls aged ten to nineteen (%)

	Boys (n = 272)	Girls (n = 414)	Total (N = 686)
Girlfriend/boyfriend/fiancé	61	28	41
Friend/acquaintance	21	50	38
Another girl/boy	3	18	12
Relative	7	3	5
Housegirl/other	8	0	3

Note: Of the 283 boys and 436 girls who reported sexual experience, 11 and 22 respectively did not respond to this question.

Further analysis shows that, as in most settings, the majority of boys (66 per cent) had sex with someone younger, whereas for three-quarters of the girls sexual encounters were reported with an older person; only between one-quarter and one-third of girls and boys had first sex with someone their own age (not shown in tabular form).

For a substantial proportion of girls, the first sexual experience was coerced, in that they were either persuaded or forced to have sex (38 per cent); for the last episode, about one-quarter reported that they were either persuaded or forced (see Table 9.2). Only a small proportion of boys reported coerced sex at both first and last occasions (10 and 8 per cent respectively). When asked about all sexual experiences, 45 per cent of girls and 17 per cent of boys indicated that, on at least one occasion, they had experienced non-consensual sex.

The likelihood of girls, and to a lesser extent boys, having non-consensual sex

TABLE 9.2 Consensuality of first, last and any other sexual experiences among sexually active boys and girls aged ten to nineteen (%)

	First sex		Last sex		All times*	
	Boys N = 273	Girls N = 410	Boys N = 267	Girls N = 403	Boys	Girls
Wanted to have sex	77	36	85	52	68 (n = 265)	32 (n = 400)
Sweet-talked into having sex	13	26	7	22		
Persuaded to have sex	6	22	4	14	17 (n = 182)**	45 (n = 233)**
Forced or threatened to have sex	4	16	4	12		

Notes: *These proportions represent the responses from girls and boys concerning first, last and any other sexual encounter. ** These percentages are for persuaded or forced (i.e. they exclude sweet-talking). The denominators reflect that 101 boys and 203 girls did not answer one or more of the three questions on consensuality of first, last and any sex. Of the 283 boys and 436 girls who reported a sexual experience, 10 and 26 respectively did not respond to the question on first sex, 16 and 33 respectively did not respond to the question on last sex.

the first time varied depending on who the partner was (see Table 9.3). Almost one third of girls who first had sex within a romantic relationship reported that they had been persuaded or forced.

Among boys, levels of non-consensual first sex were considerably higher with 'other persons' compared to experiences with romantic partners or acquaintances. Unfortunately, when constructing the questionnaires, no allowance was made for the possibility of sexual experiences with persons of the same sex. As seen in the qualitative findings presented later, however, it is likely that some of these cases of persuasion and forced sex with 'other persons', including relatives, reflect incidents with same-sex partners.

In the following section, we will discuss the different contexts in which sex occurs. We start with the somewhat ambiguous experience of sweet-talking.

'Sweet-talking' As indicated in Table 9.2, a substantial proportion of girls (26 and 22 per cent respectively) and boys (13 and 7 per cent respectively) reported being sweet-talked into having sex at both first and last sexual experience. As discussed earlier, sweet-talking is difficult to categorize as definitely consensual or non-consensual, given the strong sociocultural expectations/norm that boys should take the lead in initiating sexual behaviour and that girls should wait for boys to seduce them. Thus, a girl reporting that she was 'sweet-talked' may be indicating that the boy had seduced her through 'sweet-talking', but that she participated consensually as she was following cultural norms in letting (and expecting) him go through the process of using words to convince her to have sex. Conversely, it may also reflect a situation in which a girl was 'sweet-talked' into having sex, but she did not really want it and regretted it after it had happened. As it is not possible to differentiate between these situations from the data available, 'sweet-talking' will not be categorized as non-consensual sex here.

Persuasion through gifts, money or trickery As Table 9.2 shows, 22 per cent of girls and 6 per cent of boys were persuaded through gifts or money or tricked to have first sex, indicating that the experience may have been non-consensual. A qualitative study in neighbouring Nyanza Province also shows that transactions involving sex are common among schoolgirls, but are rarely undertaken on a 'willing-buyer, willing-seller' basis (i.e. commercial sex). In most cases, 'sugar daddies'[3] or boys give girls financial or other material incentives (such as a plate of chips or a soda) to persuade them to have sex (Chege and Njue 1999). As indicated in Table 9.2, compared to girls reporting persuasion at first sex, somewhat fewer girls reported persuasion at last sex (14 per cent), suggesting that sexually active girls may be more able to counter the persuasion tactics used.

Forced sex In both the survey and qualitative studies, young people reported that they had been forced (including threatened) into engaging in sexual relations by

TABLE 9.3 Consensuality of first sex by type of partner among sexually active girls and boys aged ten to nineteen (%)

	Wanted	Sweet-talked	Persuaded	Forced	Total non-consensual
Girls (N = 402)					
Boyfriend / fiancé (n = 106)	34	35	19	12	31
Friend / acquaintance (n = 200)	43	17	27	14	41
Another person (n = 96)*	24	41	12	23	35
Boys (N = 268)					
Girlfriend / fiancée (n = 164)	80	12	6	2	8
Friend / acquaintance (n = 59)	79	14	4	4	8
Another person (n = 45)**	69	13	11	9	20

Notes: * Includes 15 cases reporting 'relatives'. ** Includes another girl, a relative, a housegirl and another person. Of the 283 boys and 436 girls who reported a sexual experience, 15 and 34 respectively did not respond to this question.

family or non-family members. As can be seen in Table 9.2, 16 per cent of girls and 4 per cent of boys reported being forced into first sex, while 12 per cent and 4 per cent respectively reported that their last sexual experience was forced.

FORCED SEX WITHIN FAMILIES In focus group discussions with both adolescents and parents/adults, participants identified incestuous relationships as an issue in Kenya. Indeed, as mentioned earlier, 7 per cent of boys and 3 per cent of girls reported having first sex with a 'relative' (Table 9.1), suggesting that this is clearly not insignificant behaviour.

Participants also talked of sexual relationships between girls and their brothers, cousins, fathers, uncles and grandfathers. Boys cited the desire to learn and practise how to have sex 'in safe grounds' as one of the reasons why boys have sex with their relatives. Indeed, the Luhya use cultural expressions to condone such behaviours. For example, 'A bull starts by eating the maize crop within its homestead'.

As one boy narrated his experience: 'My friends told me if you want to learn to cycle ... you train yourself in the home, meaning that if you want a lady for friendship you begin with your relative. Since I was young, I did exactly what my friends had told me to do' (focus group discussion, fifteen-to-nineteen-year-old out-of-school boys; Busia).

Discussions with key informants reveal that men who have had intercourse with their daughters justified their behaviour by blaming their daughters, their wives or the prevailing HIV situation. Girls were perceived as tempting their fathers because 'they look so much like their mothers' while mothers were perceived as having failed in their familial and sexual responsibilities to their husbands, leaving their husbands with no alternative but to be attracted to their daughters. Others reported that with the prevailing HIV/AIDS situation, men felt they should restrict their sexual activity to the women in their homes who 'they trust are safe from HIV infection'. Individuals and family members attempt to keep such relationships secret.

FORCED SEX OUTSIDE THE FAMILY Thirteen per cent of boys and 37 per cent of girls reported that they were persuaded or forced into sex by a peer or acquaintance (not shown in tabular form). Cultural definitions of masculinity justify the use of threats and force to have sex. For example, fears of being declared 'not man enough' or impotent or afraid of girls were cited as reasons why boys resorted to pressurizing girls to have sex: 'My elder brother was forced by his age-mates who used to tease him and ask him: "Are you truly a man? If you are, why don't you have a girlfriend?" This became too much, such that he could not leave the house, so he just decided to look for a girlfriend' (focus group discussion, ten-to-fourteen-year-old school-going boys; Busia). Moreover, boys also reported that when a girl is unwilling and refuses to succumb to sexual advances, they use physical threats or violence to have sex so as to prove their manhood. 'When a girl continuously refuses, this is often taken to mean that the girl is demeaning his manhood. The boy then has to use force' (focus group discussion, fifteen-to-nineteen-year-old out-of-school boys; Vihiga).

Young men openly admitted that they pressurize girls to have sex with them, and many could not understand why a girl would visit them and not be interested in having sex:

> And me, you know, the day she has come [she visits me], my body temperature changes and I feel like having sex with her ... and when I am drunk, I tell her that she just can't come visiting me and just go without us having sex. Sometimes she gets annoyed with me but later she gives in to my demand. (focus group discussion, husbands of adolescent girls; Busia)

> Yes ... I have even forced a girl to have sex around three to four times ... I insisted on having sex with her. In fact I had one who told me that she could not have sex with me until she completes her Form Four [secondary school]. I told her I was suffering, so I told her to give in so that I could satisfy my sexual desires not minding how she could feel (focus group discussion, nineteen-year-old spouse of an adolescent girl; Busia)

Some boys also believed that using force is an integral part of the seduction process: 'Girls want sex as much as boys, but they have to say "no" to maintain their reputation' (focus group discussion, fifteen-to-nineteen-year-old out-of-school boys; Vihiga).

Rape is frequently unreported and legal procedures to prosecute the perpetrator are rarely followed; if the rape is discovered, the families of both parties are likely to try to settle the matter between them. One girl narrated her experience when she accepted an invitation to visit an acquaintance in his hut:

> He came and grabbed me by force and I started screaming. When his parents and neighbours heard my screams, they came and requested him to open the door. He refused and went ahead to rape me. These people broke the door and entered the house but it was too late. He had already done it and hurt me badly ... I don't know how much he paid because the money was given to my father. Part of that money was used to pay for my hospital treatment and later to pay for my enrolment in a tailoring course ... My father and mother insisted that they use the money paid to them to procure an abortion. I refused ... they constantly abused and emotionally harassed me for refusing to have an abortion. (in-depth interview, eighteen-year-old unmarried mother)

Correlates of non-consensual sex among boys

Boys were asked whether they had ever persuaded or forced someone to have sex or whether they had been persuaded or forced to have sex (using the response categories listed earlier). As Table 9.4 shows, two-thirds of sexually active boys had never been involved in non-consensual sex, either as perpetrators or as victims. Of all the sexually active boys who responded to questions on experience and perpetration of non-consensual sex, 21 per cent reported that they had persuaded or forced a girl at least once to have sex with them, whereas 17 per cent reported ever having been victims of non-consensual sex in any of their sexual encounters, whether their first, last or any other time. Further analysis shows that boys reporting that they had suffered non-consensual sex at some time were 3.8 times more likely than those not reporting such experiences also to report that they had ever persuaded or forced a girl to have sex ($p < 0.01$).

TABLE 9.4 Sexually active boys who have ever perpetrated or suffered non-consensual sex (%)

		Ever been persuaded or forced to have sex		
	N = 182	No	Yes	Total
Ever persuaded or forced a girl to have sex	Yes	14	7	21
	No	69	10	79
	Total	83	17	100

Note: Of the 283 boys who reported a sexual experience, 101 boys did not respond to one or more of the four questions used to construct this table. All cases of boys reporting either sweet-talking or being sweet-talked have been dropped from the analysis.

As perpetrators Using multiple logistic regression analysis, the relative contribution of eight characteristics to the possibility of boys reporting ever coercing (that is, persuading or forcing) girls to have sex was determined and reported as odds ratios (see Table 9.5). These characteristics were derived from items in the survey questionnaire, and included characteristics that occurred prior to the coercive incident or characteristics that could be argued as proxies for long-term behaviour. They were divided into three categories to facilitate interpretation: family arrangements, schooling and experience at first sex. As this analysis has been undertaken using the existing data-set for the baseline survey rather than using data deliberately collected to address this issue, the items and categories included as potential determinants of such behaviour were selected on the basis of the researchers' judgement and experience in the field.

Five of the eight characteristics were significantly associated (higher than the 5 per cent confidence interval) with predicting an increased possibility of reporting ever having persuaded or forced a girl to have sex. Boys were significantly more likely to coerce a girl to engage in sex if they felt that it was acceptable for a man to hit his partner compared to boys who did not support wife-beating, and boys

TABLE 9.5 Logistic regression odds ratios predicting characteristics of boys reporting perpetrating or suffering non-consensual sex

Characteristics		Model I Perpetrators of non-consensual sex Odds ratios	Model I 95% CI	Model II Victims of non-consensual sex Odds ratios	Model II 95% CI
Family arrangements					
Living arrangements:	with both parents (Ref)	–		–	–
	Mother only	1.48	0.86–2.35	1.73	0.33–9.11
Parents have verbal arguments	Have arguments	1.69*	1.10–3.79	1.03*	0.38–2.78
	Never (Ref)	–	–	–	–
Acceptable for a man to hit partner	Agree	1.39*	1.10–1.54	1.65*	0.48–3.66
	Disagree (Ref)	–	–	–	
Schooling, currently attending school	Yes (Ref)	–	–	–	–
	No	1.59*	1.01–1.95	1.85*	0.59–5.82
Experience at first sex					
Age at first sex (years)	<13	1.29*	1.05–1.69	1.18*	0.21–2.45
	13–15	0.91	0.51–1.40	0.98	0.22–4.71
	>15 (Ref)	–	–	–	–
Wanted first sex	Yes (Ref)	–			
	No	2.42*	2.12–2.80	–	–
Protection at first sex	Yes	0.78	0.41–1.11	3.14	0.64–15.51
	No (Ref)	–		–	–
First sex with girlfriend	Yes (Ref)	–	–	–	–
	No	1.24**	0.98–1.50	0.84*†	0.32–2.19
Number		189		225	
R^2		0.45		0.35	

Notes: † Respondents may have been persuaded or forced to have sex with a girlfriend against their wishes * Significant at 0.05 level of significance ** Significant at 0.01 level of significance not attending school were much more likely to have perpetrated coercive sex than those attending school. Boys who initiated sex earlier, for whom first sex was unwanted and who did not have first sex with a girlfriend were significantly more likely to have ever persuaded or forced a girl to have sex.

Other associations were not significant but were revealing. Boys who live with only their mother were about 1.5 times more likely to have ever persuaded or forced a girl to have sex than boys living with both parents;[4] boys from families where parents frequently had arguments were more likely to have perpetrated non-consensual sex than boys whose parents did not argue in front of the children; and boys who did not use protection at first sex were more likely to have coerced someone to engage in sex at some time. These findings suggest that delaying sex and first having sex within the context of a wanted relationship appear to reduce the possibility of boys using persuasion or force for sex.

As victims As mentioned earlier, in constructing the questionnaires no allowance was made for reporting same-sex behaviours in the response categories because the researchers assumed heterosexual behaviour to be the norm. It should be noted, however, that when asked who their first sexual partner was, seven boys explicitly mentioned a male-to-male experience in the category of 'other person'; in five cases, the boys reported wanting to have sex with this male partner and in two cases the boys reported that they were forced. During a focus group discussion with young out-of-school girls an incident was narrated wherein 'a boy who was going to a funeral was forced by girls'. A married male adolescent similarly recalled during an in-depth interview: 'one day a girl tried to force me to have sex with her. Immediately we started having sexual intercourse, I got bored and this forced me to withdraw.' Thus whether boys reporting being coerced were persuaded or coerced by a female or male is not clear.

During focus group discussions, boys frequently mentioned being forced into same-sex liaisons in exchange for support or protection, including shelter and cash. For example, a young male reported that 'boys are cheated to come for a lift [given a ride], or to show [give directions to] a certain area, and they end up being abused. The boys are forced to have sex with these men and given money' (focus group discussion, ten-to-fourteen-year-old school-going boys; see also Njue and Vandenhoudt 2001).

As Table 9.5 shows, five of the seven[5] variables included in the multiple regression analysis were found to be significantly associated (at 95 per cent confidence intervals) with an increased possibility of reporting ever having been persuaded or forced to have sex.[6] As in the perpetrator model, early age at sexual initiation and non-attendance at school were significant risk factors for ever experiencing coerced sex. In addition, boys who witness frequent parental arguments and who justify partner violence are more vulnerable. This may suggest that domestic disharmony and violence are a normative situation for boys who suffer coerced sex. Another finding was that boys who report first sex with a girlfriend are more likely than other boys to have experienced coerced sex, suggesting that they may have been persuaded into having sex with their girlfriend against their will.

Limitations of the study

A number of methodological issues relating to non-consensual sex emerged from the study. First, as discussed earlier, the cultural norm (and one that is universal in most of sub-Saharan Africa) that the male is expected to take the lead in initiating intimate relationships, which may or may not involve sex, renders the category of being 'sweet-talked' into having sex difficult to interpret. This category was included in the study because respondents had used it frequently during formative research and it was perceived to be distinct from and intermediate to 'wanted to have sex' and 'convinced to have sex'. For future research, it is crucial that the nuances of the language involving phrases such as this are better understood so that the actual meaning for the respondent is clearly captured.

Second, the category of 'convinced with money or gifts' is also open to different interpretations, depending on the meaning and role that gifts play in developing intimate relationships and creating the conditions for sex to become part of the relationship. An instructive study of adolescents in Durban, South Africa, highlights the fact that although economic exchange often underpins sexual coercion and exploitation, especially when it is characterized by age and/or power differentials (see, for example, Luke and Kurz 2002), gift-giving among age-mates is integral to shaping the nature and direction of relationships (Kaufman and Stavrou 2002). The symbolism and expectations involved in giving and receiving gifts within the adolescent cultural context need to be better understood if programmes promoting abstinence and safe sex are to address this practice within the context of intimate relations.

Both these observations highlight the critical importance of thoroughly understanding concepts and pre-testing the language to be used as well as the need to understand the cultural context of social behaviour when undertaking research on non-consensual sex among adolescents.

The third methodological issue that emerged from this study reflects the naivety of the researchers, i.e. their failure adequately to detect and describe same-sex encounters in experiences of sex with relatives and 'other persons'. Clearly this information is sensitive and thus difficult to collect. The realization that such behaviours probably form a significant proportion of the experiences of non-consensual sex perpetrated or suffered by adolescent boys should motivate researchers to pay more attention to designing instruments that can collect valid information about stigmatized sex from adolescents in sub-Saharan Africa. Studies that have addressed this issue suggest that the audio computer-assisted self-interviewing (ACASI) methodology may be promising (Hewett et al. 2004).

Discussion and moving ahead

The findings of the study demonstrate that a large proportion of adolescent girls and boys report having experienced non-consensual sex at some time, especially at sexual initiation. First sex was less likely to be reported as coerced if it occurred in the context of a romantic relationship, that is with a boyfriend or girlfriend, than if it occurred with an acquaintance, relative or 'other person'.

Our findings have also suggested that boys who witnessed violence and discord among parents, who held traditional gender role attitudes and who were out of school were significantly more likely to coerce a girl to engage in sex than were other boys. The nature of the first sexual experience was also important in influencing subsequent coercive behaviour: those whose initiation was early and unwanted, or occurred with someone other than a girlfriend, appeared to be significantly more likely to have ever persuaded or forced a girl to have sex than others.

A significant finding of the study is the link between the experience of coerced first sex and subsequent perpetration of forced sex. Given the belief that boys should take the lead with girls in initiating sex, boys who report unwanted first sex may feel pressured to adhere to these traditional norms and start coercing girls. Even when these experiences are recognized as abuse, the victims may be viewed as having been 'weak' or 'not man enough' because they were unable either to stop the incident or defend themselves (Lisak 1994; Lisak et al. 1996; Munro 2002; Myers 1989). Abused boys may become angry and defensive – socially acceptable emotions for men. Male survivors may cope by drinking heavily, using drugs, practising unsafe sexual behaviours and avoiding intimate relationships; an increase in the frequency and intensity of drinking are both associated with sexually aggressive behaviour. These factors can trigger coercive behaviours in male victims as a way of camouflaging their pain and as revenge (Koss and Gaines 1993; Myers 1989). Sexually abused males may attempt to 'prove' their masculinity by having multiple partners, sexually victimizing others and/or engaging in dangerous or violent behaviours (Bruckner and Johnson 1987; Lew 1988).

The process of socialization for Luhya boys appears to sanction the practice of non-consensual sex through definitions of masculinity ingrained in the language, jokes and even through the media. Boys begin to learn at an early age that men are expected to be strong, emotionally tough, daring, virile, self-reliant, aggressive, competitive and a little 'reckless' in their sexual behaviour, otherwise they may be seen as soft, too timid and not 'macho' enough. These cultural definitions of masculinity account for the use of threats and force to have sex and may explain the results of the 2003 Kenya Demographic and Health Survey, which shows that domestic, physical and sexual violence suffered by women is particularly high in Western Province. Qualitative research among adolescent men in Latin America, Asia, North America and sub-Saharan Africa suggests that viewing women as sexual objects, using coercion to obtain sex and viewing sex from a performance-oriented perspective begin in adolescence and often continue into adulthood (Brown et al. 2001).

Clearly, the growing efforts of concerned national and international organizations to raise awareness of the magnitude and consequences of non-consensual sex in Kenya need to advocate for interventions to be initiated among adolescents before they become sexually active (i.e. between the ages of ten to fourteen) if they are to influence the timing and the nature of their formative first sexual activity. The results of this study indicate that boys brought up in families where both parents are present can provide an environment conducive to promoting such values.

The data also suggest that in many cases when boys were persuaded or forced into having sex, this pressure may have been from other boys or men. The Luhya (and all other cultures in Kenya) abhor same-sex relations, however, and the community does not know how to handle these situations; consequently, little is done to prevent such incidents or to punish the perpetrators. Evidence of boys as victims of non-consensual sex tends to be mixed and tentative. While 17 per cent of boys reported having been victims of non-consensual sex, it is unclear whether this coercion was perpetrated by a female or male, but data from focus group discussions indicate that same-sex coercion may be more common than is generally acknowledged in this society. While tentative, findings suggest that delayed sexual debut in a supportive family environment could protect young males from suffering non-consensual sex.

More research is needed better to understand not only the magnitude of sexual exploitation by and of adolescent boys, but also the context in which such behaviour occurs. Such an understanding is critical to guide the formulation of appropriate policies and programmes that explicitly recognize this reality and address both the prevention of such incidents and care for victims.

A second issue that needs further research is a better understanding of the range of persons who perpetrate forced sex, particularly in the context of the finding that non-consensual first sex is largely perpetrated by known persons, including relatives. Whether this is sexual experimentation among age-mates, or is coercion by an adult relative or acquaintance of a young girl or boy, this study suggests that both types of behaviour are more common than is generally recognized and more needs to be known about their frequency and context.

For both these issues, the cultural norm of not discussing sexuality within the family, social group or community (and often not within personal relationships) has prevented the open acknowledgement that these transgressive behaviours are not uncommon and can lead to serious psychological, social and health problems. Likewise, the development of mainstream public sector interventions to address these issues has been inhibited because of the sociocultural taboos in Kenya against a public discussion about sexuality. Moreover, the fact that one-quarter of adolescent boys openly persuade and force girls to have sex is perhaps even harder to address, as this behaviour is tolerated and even sanctioned as part of the coming-of-age process among Luhya adolescents, both male and female. Furthermore, in view of the fact that fewer than one-third of girls report having first sex within the context of a romantic relationship, it is clear that the idealized conception of sex as a physical expression of love is clearly not the norm for these girls.

In the short term, skills to exercise assertiveness to resist physical and psychological pressure to have unwanted sex are urgently needed, for both girls and boys. For a longer-term approach to reducing non-consensual sex among adolescents and adults, efforts are clearly needed to provide young people, their families and the wider community with opportunities to talk openly about issues related to adolescent sexuality. Such forums and venues, perhaps using the existing institutions of the Church, schools and community groups, could also help boys and girls develop egalitarian attitudes towards gender roles and communication skills in male–female relations.

Notes

1 Acts of physical harm include pushing, slapping, punching, kicking, attempting to strangle, burning or threats to use weapons against women.

2 Physically forcing a woman to have sexual intercourse or to perform other sexual acts when they did not want to.

3 Much older men who have sexual relations with younger girls in exchange for money, gifts or favours.

4 Similarly, a study undertaken in the slums of Nairobi found that the presence of the father (with or without the mother) was associated with adolescent girls having more positive reproductive health behaviours (Ngom et al. 2003).

5 The variable 'wanted first sex' included in the perpetrator model was omitted from this analysis because of its interrelationship with the dependent variable.

6 This variable was constructed using a combination of three questions concerning coerced sex: at first sex, at last sex and at any other time.

References

Ajayi, A., C. Wesley, A. Erulkar et al. (1997) *Schooling and the Experience of Adolescents in Kenya*, Republic of Kenya: Population Council and Ministry of Education

Ajuwon, A., I. Akin-Jimoh, B. Olley et al. (2001) 'Perceptions of sexual coercion: learning from young people in Ibadan, Nigeria', *Reproductive Health Matters*, 9(17): 128–36

Brown, A. D., S. J. Jejeebhoy, I. Shah et al. (2001) *Sexual Relations among Young People in Developing Countries: Evidence from WHO Case Studies*, Geneva: World Health Organization

Bruckner, D. F. and P. E. Johnson. (1987) 'Treatment for adult male victims of childhood sexual abuse', *Social Casework*, 68: 81–7

Buvé, A., M. Caraël, J. Chege et al. (2001) 'Comparison of key parameters of sexual behaviour in four African urban populations with different levels of HIV infection', *AIDS*, 15(suppl. 4): S41–S50

Chege, J. and C. Njue (1999) *Insights into Youth Sexual Networking*, Presentation at the 11th ICASA Meeting, Lusaka, additional qualitative data for the Multicentre Study on Factors determining the Differential Spread of HIV in 4 African Towns: Kisumu-Kenya, Site Report

Chege, J., I. Askew, C. Warren et al. (2001) *Improving the Reproductive Health of Adolescents in Kenya. A Report on the Baseline Study in Two Districts in Western Kenya*, Nairobi: Population Council

Erulkar, A. (2004) 'The experience of sexual coercion among young people in Kenya', *International Family Planning Perspectives*, 30(4): 182–9

Ferguson, A. (1988) *Schoolgirl Pregnancy in Kenya*, Nairobi: Ministry of Health, Division of Family Health

Heise, L. (1998) 'Violence, sexuality and women's lives', Presentation at the SIECUS Board Meeting, New York, February

Heise, L., K. Moore and N. Toubia (1995) *Sexual Coercion and Reproductive Health. A Focus on Research*, New York: Population Council

Hewett, P., B. Mensch and A. Erulkar (2004) 'Consistency in the reporting of sexual behaviour by adolescent girls in Kenya: a comparison of interviewing methods', *Sexually Transmitted Infections,* 80(suppl. II): ii43–ii48

Johns Hopkins Center for Communication Programs (1998) 'Advocacy and mass media: a winning combination for Kenyan youth', *Communication Impact*, no. 2, Center Publications, Baltimore, MD: Johns Hopkins University, June

Kaufman, C. and S. Stavrou (2002) '"Bus fare, please": the economics of sex and gifts among adolescents in urban South Africa', Policy Research Division Working Paper no. 166, New York: Population Council

KDHS (Kenya Demographic and Health Survey) (1999) National Council for Population and Development (NCPD), Central Bureau of Statistics (CBS), Kenya, and Macro International Inc. (MI), Calverton, MD

— (2003) Central Bureau of Statistics, Ministry of Health, Kenya Medical Research Institute/Centres for Diseases Control, Kenya, Measure DHS+, Calverton, MD

Koss, M. and J. Gaines (1993) 'The prediction of sexual aggression by alcohol use, athletic participation, and fraternity affiliation', *Journal of Interpersonal Violence*, 8(1): 94–108

Krug, E. G., L. L. Dahlberg, J. A. Mercy et al. (2002) *World Report on Violence and Health*, Geneva: World Health Organization

Laumann, E. O., J. H. Gagnon, R. T. Michael et al. (eds) (1994) *The Social Organization of Sexuality: Sexual Practices in the United States*, Chicago, IL and London: University of Chicago Press

Lew, M. (1988) *Victims No Longer: Men Recovering from Incest and Other Child Sexual Abuse*, New York: Nevraumont

Lisak, D. (1994) 'The psychological impact of sexual abuse: content analysis of interviews with male survivors', *Journal of Traumatic Stress*, 7: 525–48

Lisak, D., J. Hopper and P. Song (1996) 'Factors in the cycle of violence: gender rigidity and emotional construction', *Journal of Traumatic Stress*, 9: 721–43

Luke, N. and M. Kurz (2002) *Cross-generational and Transactional Sexual Relations in Sub-Saharan Africa: Prevalence of Behavior and Implications for Negotiating Safer Sexual Practices*, Washington, DC: International Center for Research on Women and Population Services International

Mensch, B. (1996) 'Locating adolescence: an overview of adolescents' reproductive behaviour and its social consequences', Presented at the World Bank, Washington, DC

Munro, K. (2002) 'Male sexual abuse victims of female perpetrators: society's betrayal of boys', <http://www.kalimunro.com/articles>

Myers, M. F. (1989) 'Men sexually assaulted as adults and sexually abused as boys', 13th Annual Canadian Sex Research Forum Conference, Vancouver, *Archives of Sexual Behavior*, 18: 203–15

Ngom, P., M. Magadi and T. Owuor (2003) 'Parental presence and adolescent reproductive health among the Nairobi urban poor', *Journal of Adolescent Health*, 33(5): 369–77

Njue, C. and H. Vandenhoudt (2001) *What Do Youth Themselves Think about Their Reproductive Health Problems? A Rapid Assessment in Nyanza Province, Kenya*, Project report, Kisumu/Antwerp: Centres for Diseases Control/Institute of Tropical Medicine

Nzioka, C. (2001) 'Perspectives of adolescent boys on the risks of unwanted pregnancy and sexually transmitted infections: Kenya', *Reproductive Health Matters*, 9: 108–17

Population Communication Africa and Pathfinder International (1999) *Child Abuse in Kenya: A National Survey*, Cited in *Fact Sheets on ARH*, Centre for the Study of Adolescence and the Kenya Association for the Promotion of Adolescent Health

Remes, P., C. Njue and H. Vandenhoudt (2002) *Study on Adolescents' Sexual Behaviour in Kisumu*, Project report, Kisumu/Antwerp: Ministry of Health/Institute of Tropical Medicine

10 | Youth gang rape in Phnom Penh

DAVID JOHN WILKINSON, LUKE SAMUEL BEARUP AND TONG SOPRACH

There is growing international concern regarding the incidence of non-consensual sex among youth. In Cambodia, for example, rape is largely an experience of youth. LICHARDO, a non-governmental organization, reported that in 2003 89 per cent of rape victims who sought their assistance were aged under nineteen. Approximately 40 per cent were girls aged between eleven and fifteen, while 61 per cent of all males accused of rape were below the age of nineteen years (LICHARDO 2001). Also disturbing is emerging evidence of a growing form of non-consensual sex, namely gang rape, perpetrated by young men and adolescent males. In this phenomenon, colloquially known as *bauk*, literally meaning 'plus' in Khmer, groups of youths are reported to have coercive sex with the same woman.

This chapter explores the context of *bauk* and the perspectives and experiences of young male perpetrators. It presents findings from three recent studies conducted in Cambodia, which examined issues of sexual risk among young people and, in this context, shed light on the phenomenon of gang rape. The findings are limited to the capital city of Phnom Penh; the extent of *bauk* in Phnom Penh, and whether it occurs elsewhere in the country, is presently unclear.

Bauk *in the context of Cambodia's sociocultural milieu*

The phenomenon of sexual violence and coercion among youth should be viewed in Cambodia's cultural context, as well as in the light of its recent history of civil conflict, which resulted in the neglect of education, religion, culture, ethics and the law for over twenty years.

Although it has been twenty-five years since the overthrow of the Democratic Khmer (Khmer Rouge) regime, the executive, legislative and judicial systems are still frail and vulnerable to financial and political pressure, and law enforcement is consequently weak (Mansfield and MacLeod 2002). Ordinary citizens have little recourse to the judiciary, and the rights guaranteed by the constitution are neutralized by the fear created by powerful figures who operate in a culture of impunity. There are growing indications that the sons of wealthy, and even middle-class, families also believe that they operate within this culture.

Many parents of today's adolescents grew up during the Democratic Khmer regime, a period when the institution of the family was systematically destroyed. For the majority, during this period, survival was their main concern, and they did not have the opportunity to experience a 'normal' adolescence. It is possible that this collective experience of trauma has had an adverse impact upon the ability of a generation of parents to act as positive role models to the new generation of young people.

Cambodia is currently undergoing rapid social and economic change. A more stable society, greater access to local and international media and a rise in disposable income have helped to fuel a rapidly increasing birth rate and an emerging youth culture. There are indications that young Cambodians (especially in Phnom Penh) have vastly different expectations to their parents regarding free time, recreational activities and social bonding. Young Cambodians are being introduced to notions of individuality and materialism, and are experiencing a greater level of urban wealth and sexual freedom than ever before (Fordham 2003). Increased disposable income has also allowed young men greater access to commercial sex, with the attendant risks of acquiring sexually transmitted infections (STIs).

Women in Cambodia who are raped often face discriminatory attitudes from a society that considers them to be 'fallen women'. Social stigma, family dishonour and corrupt and indifferent legal authorities often prevent women who have been raped from trying to seek legal redress or gain access to healthcare for the physical injuries and the psychological trauma they have suffered. Women who do seek medical care for injuries as a result of rape are often reluctant to reveal the cause to health practitioners or to the police. Convictions, or indeed prosecutions for any kind of sexual abuse, are rare. Sex workers are even less likely to report incidents of sexual abuse because of their low status.

Findings

The three studies reviewed in this article examined various issues related to young people's sexual and reproductive heath. One study was intended to explore condom use in committed relationships, the second was on youth attitudes and the third focused on the sexual and reproductive health needs of adolescents.

These studies are among the few that provide evidence of *bauk* among adolescent men in Cambodia. What is notable is that while none of them specifically focused on *bauk*, each study shed light on this phenomenon. During interviews and discussions, the issue of *bauk* emerged in all the studies and many young men and adolescent boys readily spoke of their own involvement in this practice.

The findings of each of the studies are explored in the following section.

A study of condom use in committed relationships Although there have been sporadic reports of incidents of *bauk* in Cambodia over the past five years, the nature and extent of the practice came to light only in 2002, somewhat accidentally, during a study that explored condom use in 'sweetheart' (committed) relationships in Phnom Penh (PSI 2002; Wilkinson and Fletcher 2002). The study used the peer ethnographic method, which derives from the anthropological approach to studying social interactions, where a relationship of trust is established between the researcher and the community (Hawkins and Price 2000; Price and Hawkins 2002). This methodology is based on training members of a particular social group or network to become peer ethnographic researchers (PERs).

Ten waitresses/beer promoters and ten male university students were trained as PERs. Each PER interviewed three to four peers. All the interviews were conducted in the third person, i.e. respondents were asked not to talk about themselves but rather to talk about what other people in their social networks say and do. This approach allowed respondents to speak more freely about sensitive issues. In addition, debriefing sessions and synthesis workshops were also held. The data gathered from the interviews, together with results of the debriefing sessions and synthesis workshops provided the raw data for the study.

In the course of debriefing sessions, the PERs provided in-depth information about their own perspectives and experiences of *bauk*. The male PERs described how students, either singly or in pairs, arrange to have sex with a woman, often a mobile sex worker. The students take the woman to a guesthouse, where a group of their friends are waiting. This group generally consists of between four and ten students, although up to thirty have been reported. The young men then force the woman to have sex with all of them. The students reported that *bauk* usually involves verbal violence and the threat or use of physical violence to coerce the woman into having sex with all the men.

The student PERs cited the following reasons for participating in *bauk*: group bonding: 'It's a shared secret'; convenience: 'Although there are many *srey kalip* [modern women], not all of them are pretty and we don't want to waste time having to attract one woman each'; economy: 'Freelance sex workers are too expensive for students to afford one each, so we share the woman and the cost. Also, you can have sex more than once without having to pay more'; safety in numbers: 'We don't have to worry about our motorbikes being stolen by someone else while we are having sex, or about the women drugging us and stealing our bikes.'

There were varied responses to the frequency of participating in *bauk*. One student PER estimated that a group of his friends engage in *bauk* once or twice a month, either with sex workers or 'karaoke women' (women who act as hostesses in karaoke bars). Another student reported going out with three or four friends and gang-raping sex workers about once a week. A third stated that he and his friends participate in *bauk* about once a month, generally with park-based sex workers. One student in this group reported taking part in *bauk* when his girlfriend refuses to have sex with him.

The findings of the peer ethnographic research suggest that a number of university students regularly participate in *bauk* with sex workers or with *srey kalip*. These women are perceived by the students as being sexually available, which appeared to be sufficient justification for the students for gang rape.

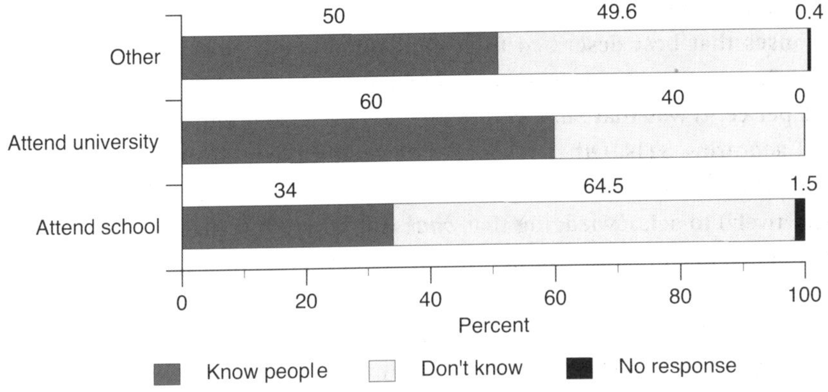

Figure 10.1 Males who know others involved in *bauk* (Source: Bearup 2003; Note: N = 580)

While the limited number of cases covered in this study cannot allow us to conclude that the practice of *bauk* is widespread, it should be noted that the waitress/beer promoter PERs independently reported that *bauk* occurs almost every day with at least one park-based sex worker (PSI 2002).

A study of perceptions and attitudes among youth Further evidence for the prevalence of gang rape emerged from a study of young people's attitudes toward gangs, violence, rape, drugs and theft in Phnom Penh (Bearup 2003). The research involved a survey of the attitudes of 580 young people aged between thirteen and twenty-eight, and semi-structured interviews with fourteen youth gang members.

In conducting the survey, researchers recognized the sensitivity of eliciting information on criminal behaviours; hence rather than their own behaviours, respondents were asked about their knowledge of others involved in *bauk* (see Figure 10.1). While the level of knowledge of *bauk* was lower among women than among men, still a significant proportion of women – 19.1 per cent of out-of-school girls, 14.5 per cent of female school students and 4.6 per cent of female university students – stated that they knew others involved in *bauk* (not shown in tabular form). Interviews with males revealed that 34 per cent of high school students knew others involved in *bauk*, while for out-of-school males the corresponding figure was almost 50 per cent (see Figure 10.1). The highest proportion (60 per cent) stating that they knew others involved in *bauk*, however, was male university students (ibid.). It is acknowledged that some caution should be exercised while interpreting young men's reported knowledge of others' involvement in sexual activities, as it is well known that young men tend to exaggerate their own and their peers' sexual experiences.

The survey questionnaire also included a definition of *bauk* with a prostitute, and respondents (N = 580) were asked to choose one out of seven possible responses that best described their perception about *bauk* (ibid.) (see Figure 10.2). The most common response among both males (33.4 per cent) and females (40.7 per cent) was that *bauk* was dangerous because it enhanced the possibility of acquiring STIs. Other responses covered a range of perspectives, which varied from viewing *bauk* as a fun male bonding activity (11.1 and 6.7 per cent respectively) to acknowledging that *bauk* was wrong but that it was better that it happened to a prostitute rather than to other women in society (12.7 and 16.7 per cent respectively). Although respondents recognized *bauk* as a dangerous activity in terms of the risk of acquiring infection, however, few recognized it as an infringement of a woman's rights – only 13.7 per cent of males and 13.4 per cent of females categorized *bauk* as an act of rape, or as being wrong because the woman does not give consent.

The qualitative phase of the study involved in-depth semi-structured interviews with fourteen middle-to-upper-class youth gang members to enquire about their experiences of *bauk* and the techniques employed while participating in gang rape. The method of critical discourse analysis (CDA) was used to examine English translations of interview transcripts. CDA has been described as being 'similar to the micro concerns of literary criticism combined with a broader sociological political perspective' (Lupton 1994: 28). The aim of using this method of analysis was to develop insights into the generative factors that underlie gang activity.

In Khmer, the word *bauk* is a mathematical reference to plus ('+') and the act of gang rape is equated with 'additional' value for the perpetrators. This perception of extra economic value was evident in gang members' accounts of *bauk*. Also evident is that in describing the number of people involved in an act of *bauk*, the gang members acknowledged only the perpetrators, while the victim, and her feelings, were almost invariably not considered.

As in the earlier study, young gang members reported little recognition of the human rights of the victims, be they sex workers or other women who are perceived to be sexually available. The following quotations highlight the way in which gang members describe and justify their actions:

> I have money but I don't want to pay for the prostitute; I want to spend my money on eating and drinking, or drugs. My team and I do it like this because we need sex and want to have fun together. The girl who we rape is only a prostitute. (male university student, aged twenty-two)

> This word [*bauk*] we use for sex with the prostitute, but for me and my friends we also use with the student. First I just flirt normally with a student two or three times and she likes fashion so she follows. Two or three times we go out together and eat corn. First I just have sex with the girl like *songsar* [sweetheart] two or three times. After that I call to my friends to *bauk* her and then I break up with her. (high school student, aged twenty)

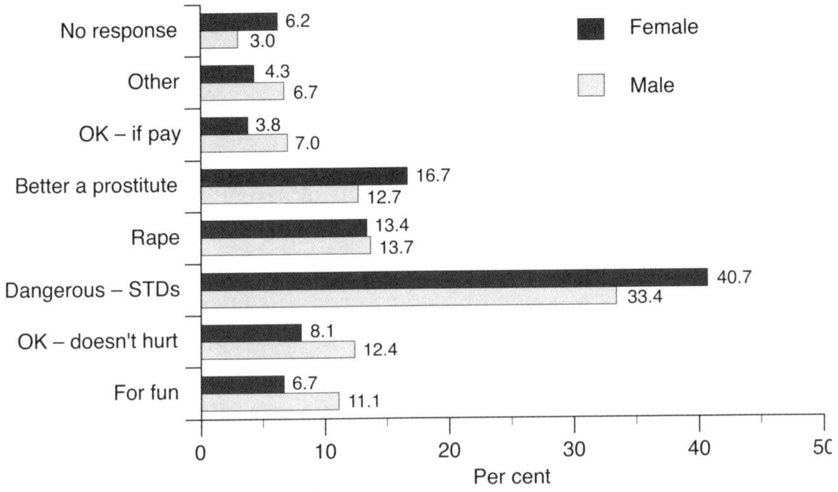

Figure 10.2 Young people's opinions about *bauk* (Source: Bearup 2003; Note: N = 580)

Similarly, 'I have never experienced *bauk* with a good girl, just only with prostitutes and beer girls' (university student, aged twenty-three).

Taking part in *bauk* is linked to perceptions of masculinity, and peers put pressure on young men to participate in *bauk*. The following quotes are illustrative: 'I like *bauk* because I follow my friends to be a man' (university student, aged seventeen); '*Bauk* is my skill. I am very horny and need sex a lot ... I have money but I don't want to pay. I want fun with my friends' (businessman, aged twenty-two); and 'I like to join in *bauk* to be happy, [and] have fun with my friends. I know that *bauk* is not good ... I have a sister too ... but my friends force me. [For] Example, there are ten friends and nine go. I cannot stay by myself' (unemployed male, aged twenty-two).

The study suggests that males perceive *bauk* as enhancing value, and as reinforcing traditional notions of masculinity and power. At the same time, there is little recognition among males of the rights of victims. The evidence underscores the recommendation that awareness of human rights should be incorporated in education on HIV and sexual and reproductive health.

A study of the sexual and reproductive health needs of adolescents Further data on gang rape emerged from a qualitative study on the sexual and reproductive health needs of adolescents in Phnom Penh (Wilkinson 2003). While not specifically focused on sexual violence, the study findings revealed that in eight focus group discussions (N = 64) with adolescent boys and girls, respondents in all groups unanimously agreed that 'information on management of sexual violence' was very important to them.

In order better to understand what the respondents meant by this, the research team conducted two follow-up focus group discussions with groups of male and female out-of-school adolescents in Phnom Penh, who had earlier participated in the study. The participants were asked to explain what they understood by the term 'sexual violence' and to give examples. They were also asked what they understood by 'management of sexual violence', and again asked to provide examples. Finally, participants were asked whether they had heard of *bauk*.

The focus group discussions with adolescent girls (aged sixteen to twenty) revealed that the phenomenon of *bauk* is well known, and provided an indication that this practice is not restricted to sex workers: 'We know that *bauk* often happens to beer-promotion girls; it is occasionally the case with other types of girls too. It might happen to the female factory worker as well. Men would possibly catch her and take her to *bauk*. Women are powerless to act in this situation' (female focus group discussion participant).

In the focus group discussions with adolescent boys, the majority of participants admitted to taking part in *bauk*. For example, 'My friend took a girl for sex, telling her that there was only him. However, five more people were ready waiting in the room. When the girl refused, they seriously beat her' (male focus group discussion participant); 'My elder brother [and I] ... took a girl for sex. But when we were ready for sex, there were ten other people waiting to have sex with her. After the fourth man, she refused to go further with the fifth one. Then we beat her and forced her to agree. This means doing *bauk*' (male focus group discussion participant).

The responses of some of the boys highlighted a widely held belief about masculinity – that once sexually aroused, men are unable to control themselves. For example, 'Although we know that raping will end up with us being in prison, we still do it because we are blindly stricken by passion' (male focus group discussion participant); and 'I don't think it [*bauk*] is good, but at that time my passion was too strong. I was blindly driven, and the sorrow only comes too late' (male focus group discussion participant).

The concept of masculinity is associated with the practice of *bauk*, as rape appears to act as an affirmation of masculinity. As reported by a male focus group discussion participant, 'He wouldn't be a man if he was unable to rape her.'

As in the previous studies, although a number of male focus group discussion participants admitted that *bauk* was wrong, they justified it on the basis of sharing experiences with friends. They also appeared to feel little responsibility to try to curtail either their own participation or that of their friends. According to male focus group discussion participants, '*Bauk* is not good for us and it also causes problems. However, we still do it as we follow our friends who ask us to join. We want our friends to enjoy with us. Close friends always share things together'; and 'We think we will not be able to stop [*bauk*] as long as we still have many friends who encourage us to do so to prove our faithfulness to them. However, we never do this with our lovely girlfriends.'

While the study provided indications that *bauk* is a bonding experience for many young men, not all the respondents reported engaging in *bauk*, despite high levels of peer pressure. As a male focus group discussion participant testified: 'I used to go along with them and see them do *bauk* with my own eyes, but I did not join with them.'

It should be noted that these accounts represent the perspectives of the participants of one focus group discussion each with boys and girls, and should be interpreted with caution. As with all group-interviewing techniques, allowance should be made for the possibility that outcomes may be influenced by peer pressure. Despite requests not to disclose personal experiences, boys provided accounts of their experiences of *bauk* freely, in a matter-of-fact manner, and without any sense of boasting or embarrassment. Furthermore, these accounts are consistent with the findings from the two other studies reviewed in this article, and taken together these findings provide a body of evidence that indicates that the practice of *bauk* may be prevalent among a number of young males in Phnom Penh.

Discussion

Given the paucity of research presently available on *bauk*, it would be premature to draw any firm conclusions regarding the reasons for the occurrence of *bauk* and the extent of this practice among young males in Cambodia. Yet the findings of the three studies reviewed in this article consistently suggest that *bauk* is an issue of significance in Cambodia.

Two further research initiatives on gang rape have supported these findings. One study, which examined gang rape from the perspective of the survivors through a review of interviews conducted in 2002 with twenty-two park-based sex workers in Phnom Penh (Grant 2004), reveals that some of the women reported being raped and abused by between twenty and thirty males. A rapid countrywide survey has also been conducted (Soprach 2004), in which eight moto-taxi-drivers in each of Cambodia's twenty-four urban centres were asked whether they had heard of local instances of gang rape. The survey provides the first indications that gang rape is an issue in almost all of Cambodia's major urban centres.

The three studies reviewed in this chapter suggest two underlying factors associated with *bauk*. One derives from traditional Khmer perspectives of gendered hierarchy and the unequal role of women in society, while the second is related to male bonding and the associated notion of masculinity. These factors are explored in the following sections.

'Men are gold, women are cloth': gender differentials and double standards

Cambodian society imposes significant double standards of behaviour for males and females, especially during the period of adolescence. Young girls are expected to uphold the honour of their family by retaining not only their actual virginity but also their imputed sexual reputation (Ledgerwood 1990). Conversely, it is expected that young men will seek out multiple partners, both prior to and after marriage, and especially when their wife is pregnant, because it is believed that their irrepressible sexual needs must be met. The stark gender differentials that pervade Cambodian society are illustrated by the Khmer proverb 'men are gold, women are cloth', which suggests that, when soiled by their actions, men can easily be cleaned, but women are tainted for ever (Phan and Patterson 1994).

This proverb also highlights the stereotypical 'good woman/bad woman' dichotomy surrounding the sexual behaviour of women. The studies reviewed provide evidence that sex workers are perceived to be fundamentally different from other women and therefore not entitled to human rights. The studies further suggest, however, that any woman who is perceived as sexually active may fall into the category of 'bad woman' and becomes fair game for gang rape.

The young men interviewed demonstrated a disregard for the human rights of their victims, and in particular a disregard for the dignity of women. The studies suggest an assumption of impunity among the young males – the idea that you can do what you like to a sex worker and get away with it. This situation is further exacerbated by the lack of confidence among victims in the capacity of the police and judicial system to provide justice (Bearup 2003).

Male bonding and the affirmation of masculinity The studies provide evidence that male bonding is a major factor underlying the practice of *bauk* by young men and appears to be closely associated with peer pressure to prove their masculinity.

In Cambodia, as in many cultures, the transition from boyhood to manhood is often marked by an initiation into a sexual experience. For many young men in Cambodia, this initiation occurs with a sex worker, and he is often accompanied by his friends, who facilitate, and sometimes pay for, the encounter. Evidence from the studies indicates that early sexual experiences sometimes involve *bauk*. Through this behaviour, a precedent is set that associates the concept of masculinity with sexual experiences, often in the form of forced sex.

For some young men, a shortage of willing sexual partners and the necessary financial resources to purchase sex may lead to a crisis in male identity. Young men overcome the social and economic obstacles to realizing their sense of masculinity through the practice of gang rape. The experience also appears to enhance male bonding, which provides a sense of belonging as well as fulfilling the need for sexual release.

It is necessary to understand these sexual practices in the context of the social construction of gender and sexuality, which has significant implications for behaviour change interventions targeted towards violent sexual behaviour and the linkages between gender, sexuality, poverty, hierarchy and power. The findings of these three studies highlight stark gender differentials in social expectations of sexual activity, social acceptance of certain sexual behaviours and practices, and the social consequences of rape and violence.

Possible future directions

Within this context, the challenge for politicians, policy-makers, programmers and human rights workers, and indeed for Cambodian society, is to identify entry points and strategies that help propagate the social changes needed to ensure that this pattern of behaviour does not become normative among young males.

There is a strong case for further research on *bauk* and the associated demonstrations of power and violence. Research perhaps needs to be set within the broader context of a study of 'masculinity' and its effect on sexual behaviour. At the same time, there are a number of programmatic interventions that could be initiated to address the issue of gang rape. It is clear, however, that interventions would need to be reinforced by a significantly stronger legal and regulatory environment, and political commitment at the highest level.

Given the consistent findings of the disregard for the human rights of women, a key intervention will be to strengthen young people's understanding of human rights issues, and particularly the rights of women, including sex workers. Human rights education in Cambodia is currently targeted towards politicians, policy-makers and older members of society. To address the lack of understanding of human rights among young people, an approach could be developed to include human rights education in adolescent sexual reproductive health initiatives.

There is also a need to improve access to counselling and health services for survivors of rape and sexual abuse, especially for women involved in the sex trade.

Public education strategies should be initiated that seek to change prevailing attitudes towards rape and public perceptions of rape survivors. The stigma associated with rape survivors should be transferred to the perpetrators of sexual assault.

Using role models to stimulate positive behaviour change among young people has proved successful in many contexts. While role models in other countries have been drawn from political leaders, sports stars and media personalities, Cambodia's recent emergence from years of conflict, together with growing disillusionment with political leadership, has greatly reduced the number of positive role models for adolescent males to emulate. One initiative under consideration is the creation of fictional role models through television programmes. A key objective is to help empower young men to make more positive decisions in the face of negative peer influences.

Despite the massive social and economic changes that have taken place in Cambodia during the last decade, there are few leisure activities geared to young people, and limited opportunities for young people to meet socially. Addressing these social and recreational gaps may allow young males to achieve a healthy personal sense of fulfilment and to experience a sense of identity and bonding through involvement in such activities.

The studies reviewed in this chapter have recently received attention in the national and international press, and have stimulated public debate on the emerging issues of gang rape and other aspects of youth-related sexual violence. This chapter provides advocacy for research and interventions that will help to address the issue of coercive and violent sexual behaviour in all settings.

References

Bearup, L. S. (2003) *Paupers and Princelings: Youth Attitudes toward Gangs, Violence, Rape, Drugs and Theft*, Phnom Penh: Gender and Development for Cambodia

Fordham, G. (2003) *Adolescent Reproductive Health in Cambodia: Status Policies, Programs and Issues*, Phnom Penh: POLICY Project

Grant, L. (2004) *From Cotton to Precious Gems: The Use and Abuse of Commercial Sex Workers in the Context of Police, Law and Society in Cambodia*, Phnom Penh: Oxfam Hong Kong and CARE International, EU/UNFPA

Hawkins, K. and N. Price (2000) *A Peer Ethnographic Tool for Social Appraisal and Monitoring of Sexual and Reproductive Health Programmes*, Swansea: Centre for Development Studies, University of Wales

Ledgerwood, J. (1990) 'Changing Khmer conceptions of gender: women, stories, and the social order', PhD thesis, Cornell University

LICHARDO (2001) *Rape and Indecent Assault: Crimes in the Community*, Phnom Penh: LICHARDO

Lupton, D. (1994) *Analysing News*, London: Taylor & Francis

Mansfield, C. and K. A. MacLeod (2002) *Advocacy in Cambodia: Increasing Democratic Space*, Phnom Penh: Pact

Phan, H. and L. Patterson (1994) *Men are Gold, Women are Cloth: A Report on the Potential for HIV/AIDS Spread in Cambodia and Implications for HIV/AIDS Education*, Phnom Penh: CARE International

Price, N. and K. Hawkins (2002) 'Researching sexual and reproductive health behaviour: a peer ethnographic approach', *Social Science and Medicine*, 55: 1327–38

PSI (Population Services International) (2002) *Love, Sex and Condoms in the Time of HIV – Sweetheart Relationships in Cambodia*, Phnom Penh, PSI

Soprach, T. (2004) *Gang Rape: The Perspectives of Moto-Taxi-Drivers across Cambodia*, Phnom Penh: CARE International, EU/UNFPA

Wilkinson, D. J. (2003) *A Model for Adolescent-friendly Sexual and Reproductive Health Services in Cambodia*, Phnom Penh: WHO

Wilkinson, D. J. and G. Fletcher (2002) *Sex Talk: Peer Ethnographic Research with Male University Students and Waitresses in Phnom Penh*, report prepared for PSI, Cambodia

FOUR | Outcomes of non-consensual sex

11 | Childhood and adolescent sexual abuse and incest: experiences of women survivors in India

ANUJA GUPTA AND ASHWINI AILAWADI

There is increasing evidence that a significant number of women experience non-consensual sex in childhood and adolescence, yet their experiences remain poorly documented and their needs rarely addressed. Of the various forms of non-consensual sex, sexual abuse perpetrated by persons in positions of trust, including a member of the immediate or extended family (incest), or someone who is known to the child or adolescent or the family (such as a domestic helper, neighbour, family friend or teacher), remains shrouded in silence and there is a tendency at the family, community and national levels to deny its existence. The objectives of this article are to share insights on the experience of incest and sexual abuse in childhood or adolescence by persons in positions of trust among middle-class Indian women, address the multiple facets of the abuse experience and explore women's own reports of the effects of such experiences.

In this chapter we focus on abuse that occurred before the respondent was aged eighteen. Sexual abuse and incest include all forms of sexualized contact and non-contact behaviours imposed on a child or adolescent by someone older or bigger, in a position of power or authority over the child or adolescent, and with whom she shares a relationship of trust. Non-contact behaviours include suggestive sexual looks, talk and comments, exposure to pornographic material, masturbation and exhibitionism in front of the child or adolescent. Contact behaviours include hugging, kissing, brushing and rubbing against the child or adolescent suggestively, insertion of fingers and objects in the vagina, and oral and penetrative sex.

Data

Data for this chapter are drawn from a variety of sources, including a survey of women who were exposed to awareness programmes on sexual abuse of the RAHI Foundation[1] or were randomly selected through the RAHI network, a series of in-depth interviews and ogoing individual and group interactions with survivors of childhood or adolescent incest in particular who sought support at RAHI. The respondents included middle/upper-middle-class English-speaking women aged fifteen to sixty-seven.

In the survey, self-administered questionnaires were distributed to a total of 1,000 women residing in urban settings, largely Mumbai and New Delhi (RAHI Foundation 1998). Some 626 women returned the questionnaire; of these twenty-six were incomplete. Hence the response rate was only 60 per cent. Of the 600 survey respondents, 457 reported the experience of sexual abuse by age eighteen; of these, 181 were sexually abused by a family member, another 144 by individuals with whom the respondent was acquainted and the remaining 132 by strangers. In this chapter, we present survey findings on the experience of sexual abuse, including incest, perpetrated by persons in positions of trust.

We acknowledge that because of the methodological and ethical difficulties of conducting research on sexual abuse perpetrated by persons in positions of trust, the experiences reported here are by no means representative of Indian women or even urban women. Study participants were self-selected on the basis not only of their contact with RAHI but also their willingness to participate in the study. As mentioned above, the significant non-response rate raises additional questions of selectivity.

Survey data are supplemented by qualitative data from one group of survivors, namely those who experienced incest. These data are drawn from in-depth interviews (RAHI Foundation 1999; unpublished findings) and from our individual and group work, with thirty-three survivors aged eighteen to sixty-seven at the time of interview. The evidence is gathered retrospectively from women who recalled experiences of incest that occurred in childhood or adolescence (prior to age eighteen). Most of the interviews were recorded and transcribed; some women gave written narratives of their experiences. The interviews were conducted at RAHI, in the homes of the women or at clinics of mental health professionals. Data also comprise counselling session notes of women who provided consent for the use of such information under conditions of anonymity.

Notwithstanding the limitations described above, findings offer rare insights into the experience of childhood and adolescent sexual abuse, including incest, underscore the myriad ways in which it has damaging consequences and highlight that it is a problem of major social significance that requires considerable further research and programmatic attention.

The abuse

Socio-demographic characteristics of the sample A socio-demographic profile of the 325 women who experienced abuse at the hands of family members or other persons in positions of trust is presented in Table 11.1. Respondents were largely young, urban and well educated. Two out of three grew up in nuclear families.

Relationship of the perpetrator to the woman As seen in Table 11.2, in the majority of cases (82 per cent), perpetrators were people close to and trusted by the child or adolescent, who enjoyed a position of power, authority and respect in the household. Perpetrators were mainly male family members (36 per cent), predominantly uncles and cousins, although some 4 per cent reported a father or brother as the perpetrator and some 3 per cent reported other more distant

TABLE 11.1 Socio-demographic profile of women who reported non-consensual sexual experiences in childhood or adolescence perpetrated by family members or other persons in positions of trust (N = 325)

Characteristics		Per cent
Current age	15–17	5
	18–25	73
	26–70	22
Current education status	Students	75
	Non-students	25
City where incident/s took place*	Mumbai	35
	New Delhi	22
	Other	45
Family type in adolescence	Nuclear	68
	Joint	17
	Extended	15

Note: * Percentages may exceed 100 due to multiple responses

family members, including a brother-in-law and sister's prospective father-in-law, stepfather and stepbrother (Table 11.2). In addition, some 46 per cent of perpetrators were other persons in positions of trust, largely neighbours, family friends and domestic help. In-depth interviews highlight the extent to which women reported a close relationship with their abusers which existed outside of the abuse. Frequently, these were people with whom the study participant had grown up and interacted on a daily or frequent basis. In many cases, the perpetrator/s had lived in the same home as them, and if not, they had visited and stayed over at each other's homes frequently, as is often the case in Indian families.

Indeed, as qualitative data show, for many women the abuser was a special person in their lives, someone for whom they reported admiration, awe, respect, love, a 'close bond' and, for some, a 'crush'. One woman described her adolescent adulation for her abuser who was her favourite cousin's husband: 'He was the man I loved the most in the world ... He stood for perfection and correctness par excellence ... the ultimate in goodness, kindness and devotion to those he loved' (twenty-eight-year-old woman, postgraduate, employed, married, abused between ages of twelve and twenty-one approximately).

Another woman reported abuse by her brother, highlighting the bonds that formed the basis of their relationship: 'Apart from this, we were like normal brother and sister, we were good friends, we'd fight, he'd help me out in my studies, we'd play together and were good company for each other. We always

TABLE 11.2 Percentage distribution of reported perpetrators (N = 561)

Reported perpetrators	Per cent
Family member	36
Uncle	15
Cousin	15
Father	2
Brother	2
Others, e.g., brother-in-law	3
Other persons in positions of trust	46
Neighbour	12
Family friend	11
Domestic help	11
Teacher	5
Friend	4
Doctor	2
Other persons in positions of trust	2
Strangers and others	18

stuck by each other' (eighteen-year-old woman, college student, abused between the ages of five and fourteen).

The circumstances of abuse Table 11.3 reports selected characteristics of the abusive incident. As can be seen from the table, abuse occurred at a young age, and by age ten for over one-quarter of respondents. The youngest reported age of abuse was two, although for the majority it occurred at older ages.

Qualitative data shed light on women's first or early experiences of abuse, in every case the woman's first experience of any form of sexual activity. For example, one woman, who was abused by her father from a very young age, described an incident of abuse when she was thirteen years old, and had just returned from school: 'I had just started wearing a bra ... I remember that he actually put his hand inside my blouse ... and touched me and said, "Oh, you've become very big" ... I remember he had this really strange expression on his face ... So I just moved away and remember feeling very uncomfortable' (Thirty-year-old woman, postgraduate, single, employed, abused between the ages of six and thirteen approximately).

Another woman recalled the first time her uncle attempted to rape her when she was ten years old during one of her regular weekend visits to his house. She was sleeping with his daughters in their room: 'There was no space on the bed, so he lay on top of me ... I found it difficult to breathe. I was wearing a short nightie. I don't remember having any leggings on because he put his fingers in

TABLE 11.3 Characteristics of the abusive experience (N = 325)

Characteristics	Per cent
*Age at which abuse occurred (years)**	
<4	3
4–6	16
7–8	17
9–10	24
11–12	29
13–14	31
15–16	33
17–18	26
Number of abusers	
1	48
2	30
3+	22
Frequency of abuse	
Once	11
More than once	87

Note: *Percentages exceed 100 because abuse spanned many age groups; in addition, 8% were unsure or did not respond.

very easily. Then he half undid his pyjamas and tried to insert his penis. It was painful, very, very painful' (forty-two-year-old woman, postgraduate, married, employed, abused between the ages of ten to fifteen approximately).

As seen in Table 11.3, as many as half of all survey respondents reported more than one abuser. Abuse occurred frequently, and some 87 per cent of respondents reported that it occurred on more than one occasion. Most women could not recall the exact number of times a single abuser had abused them, but reported in such qualitative ways as 'often enough' or 'every time he got a chance'. For many women the abuse was prolonged in that it took place over a number of years. Several reported that it continued well into their early twenties.

Qualitative data suggest that there was a preceding phase when the child or adolescent was 'groomed' or prepared for the abuse in a variety of ways. The abuse often progressed from milder to more severe acts. One study participant described how her brother would fondle and pet her from the time she was very young; later this progressed to 'using very specific language to describe sexual acts', to finally 'taking off my clothes and doing everything he wanted to do' by the time she was twelve years old. Another woman recounted how 'the abuse began harmlessly ... with small passes, the little squeezes, the protective arm around the shoulders, an affectionate hug, the gentle pat on the bottom' and went on to rape.

Threats and physical force were frequently mentioned as preceding the abuse. Women described being bullied and threatened as children and adolescents by their abusers. In some cases, outright physical violence was used. One woman recounted being abused when she was sleeping with her stepbrother in the same room: 'the brute' would hit her to overpower her and then molest her. Another woman described being physically overpowered by her brother-in-law when she was inadvertently forced to spend the night in the same room with him: ' ... he offered me a drink ... then he tried. He first requested me to allow him to hug me. Then he begged for it and when after repeated refusals I was on the verge of tears of disbelief that it was happening again, he forcibly hugged me. It was a very tight hug. I could hardly breathe. I had crossed my arms over my chest ... I became numb' (twenty-eight-year-old woman, postgraduate, employed, married, abused between the ages of twelve to twenty-one approximately).

Another woman described the cajoling and emotional blackmail by her brother that preceded the abuse. At times, he would take off her clothes and at other times persuade her to let him have sex with her. When she protested and attempted to stop the abuse, she was made to feel responsible for the abuse: 'My protests didn't really didn't deter my brother. Like when I'd say "no" he wouldn't listen. He'd say things like "please, just this once" and coerce me into it. I would give in ... When I told him that if he made one more move, then I'd tell our parents, he'd turn around and say go ahead, tell them, you're equally guilty, you want it too, so go ahead' (eighteen-year-old woman, college student, abused between the ages of five and fourteen).

Women also frequently mentioned being given gifts and presents as children or adolescents, favoured over siblings and made to feel special in a variety of ways preceding the abuse. One woman spoke about how her brother-in-law brought her boxes of chocolates every time he visited and would 'feel' her while giving them to her. Another woman recounted how her uncle made her feel 'like a woman, special and wanted' and treated her differently from his own daughters. Another woman remembered being singled out for attention and affection by her father while growing up. She was the only one he would take out for long walks and who could sit on his lap and be cuddled. She was also allowed the 'privilege' of sleeping in his room, which enabled him to perpetuate the sexual abuse.

Abuse was inextricably woven into the daily routine of the child or adolescent and happened as part of her everyday life. Most of the abuse took place in the home of the child or adolescent or that of the abuser. It occurred unpredictably and in 'normal' circumstances such as when the child/adolescent encountered the abuser accidentally in a corridor, when watching television with other siblings, when visiting her relatives' place for a weekend, when learning how to drive a car or when going out for a drive with her abuser. Many women reported that the elders were 'downstairs', 'in the other room' or 'cooking', and siblings and cousins were 'playing outside', and that they could hear the voices and laughter of other family members while they were being abused.

In-depth interviews highlight that while appearing 'normal', many of these families were characterized by strained relationships between parents, alcoholism, neglect, emotional abuse and domestic violence.

Immediate reactions and disclosure Survey and in-depth interview participants reported a sense of confusion, bewilderment and unreality as they juxtaposed the apparent normalcy of life with the trauma of the abuse they had just suffered. As Table 11.4 suggests, the main feelings that the incident evoked at the time of the abuse were largely those of confusion, anger, disgust, guilt and self-blame, helplessness, fear and shame; somewhat fewer reported a sense of sadness and an experience of pleasure.

Survey findings are corroborated by in-depth interviews. For example, one woman remembered the scene the day after her uncle had penetrative sex with her at night in the room she shared with his two daughters: 'The next day I remember feeling very strange. There was a sense of unreality as if nothing had happened. I was confused. Everything seemed so normal that I wondered if I had imagined it' (forty-two-year-old woman, postgraduate, married, employed, abused between the ages of ten and fifteen approximately).

Another woman described the scene when, after managing to disengage from a sexually abusive situation with two young male neighbours that could have led to forced penetration, she ran back into her garden and felt a complete sense of unreality when she saw her mother sitting with her friends and calmly knitting. She found it difficult to correlate the two scenes: 'What is clearly etched in my mind is my mother's calm, peaceful face as she bent and knitted ... Suddenly the scene seemed so odd. I just stood there and stared at the calm, undisturbed scene. Somehow it didn't fit in with or relate to what I had gone through' (forty-one-year-old woman, postgraduate, employed, single, abused between the ages of four and eleven approximately).

Although the majority of women reported that at the time they did not fully understand the abusive incident or coherently articulate their feelings, all identified the experience of an overriding feeling of discomfort, a sense that a 'wrong' act had been committed. For example: 'Something told me that whatever it was, it was not normal' (forty-two-year-old woman, postgraduate, married, employed, abused between the ages of ten and fifteen approximately); 'I had been held and kissed before, but I just knew that this time it was wrong' (thirty-year-old woman, graduate, married, employed, abused between the ages of six and fifteen approximately); and 'something that should not have happened had happened' (twenty-seven-year-old woman, postgraduate, single, employed, abused between the ages of seventeen and nineteen).

A few women reported experiencing sexual stimulation and pleasure during

TABLE 11.4 Reactions to and disclosure of the abusive incident

Type of reaction and disclosure status	Per cent
Feelings at the time of abuse	
Confusion	54
Anger	51
Disgust	49
Helplessness	43
Fear	42
Shame	34
Humiliation	30
Guilt	26
Self-blame	21
Sadness	16
Pleasure	15
Other responses (dirty, mistrust, pain, curiosity)	1
No response	3
Disclosure	
Never disclosed	36
Partially disclosed	10
Fully disclosed	54
*Person/s disclosed to:**	
Friend	30
Mother	26
Sister	12
Parent/s	9
Cousin	4
Aunt	4
Husband	4
Other family member	5
Other non-family member	7
Not specified, not answered	1
Main reason for non-disclosure (among those who did not disclose to anyone)	
I want to forget it happened	23
Feared what people would think	14
Felt it was my fault	11
Don't trust anyone	11
It is not that important	9
I feel guilty as it gave me pleasure	7
I would not have been believed	7
I was a willing participant so it was not an issue	3
I was threatened, bribed	3
Others**	12

Notes: *Multiple responses **Includes: stopped the abuse/the abuse stopped, did not know whom to tell, confused the abuse (see Table 11.4). This response of pleasure was itself a source of shame, self-blame, conflict and self-hatred for women who reported this reaction. One woman recounted how the fact that she derived pleasure from the abuse was 'a major part of my guilt trip'. She wondered how she could 'do something like that just for the sake of some physical pleasure' and 'what kind of person does that make me'. Another woman described her conflicting feelings at the time of the abuse by her brother: 'I cannot find the words to explain the state I would be in. Shock, arousal, intense hate ... wishing it would stop, wishing it would continue, wishing it would finish ... hopes, dreams shattering, helplessness ... so many things' (twenty-seven-year-old woman, postgraduate, single, employed, abused between the ages of seventeen and nineteen).

Many women recalled the strategies they employed to resist the abuse, usually ineffectively. For example, they would pretend to be asleep, hoping the abuser would not approach them, or pretend not to hear the abuser calling them. One woman recalled placing a pillow between her brother and herself when they slept on the same bed. Another woman recalled how she would change the places where she slept. One woman described her futile attempts to escape from her elder sister's husband: 'When I saw him head towards me, I would duck into a room that had people in it. I tried as much as possible not to be alone in his company ... But I was only a child and alone in this battle' (sixty-seven-year-old woman, married, housewife, abused between the ages of six and eleven).

As indicated in Table 11.4, over one-third of all abused women did not disclose the abusive experience to anyone. Women reported a number of reasons for this: primarily a desire to forget the abusive incident and, more importantly, fear of other people's reactions, including a fear of being disbelieved or held responsible for provoking the incident, or a sense of guilt and self-blame. In the in-depth interview, one woman recalled: 'I could never pluck up the courage to tell anyone about what was happening. Fear and doubt would assail me ... I sensed that even if I were believed I would pay a heavy price for it. I would be severely reprimanded or held responsible for being within reach of the abuser. Silence would be demanded of me' (sixty-seven-year-old woman, married, housewife, abused between the ages of six and eleven).

Qualitative data show that everal women reported fears that disclosure would upset the equilibrium in the family. Some feared the effect disclosure would have on their parents. For example, one woman resisted disclosure for fear that it would 'break her mother to pieces'. Another woman recounted her reaction when her counsellor discussed the idea of disclosure to her: 'I was appalled. I was sure that they could not handle it ... that it would grievously injure them' (twenty-seven-year-old woman, postgraduate, single, employed, abused between the ages of seventeen to nineteen).

For many women, these fears did indeed prove well founded. They experienced negative and unsupportive reactions from those in whom they confided, exacerbating their trauma and leading to feelings of revictimization. For example, one woman who mentioned to her mother that a neighbour had taken her to a park and done 'something with her' was told by her mother that she was a dirty girl who had a vivid imagination and that she must not tell such lies. This left her confused and betrayed. She never disclosed subsequent abuse to her mother or anyone else. Another woman described her father's response to her disclosure about abuse perpetrated by her brother as of one of denial and anger: 'My father ... accused me of lying to conceal my madness. He went ahead to claim that his son was not capable of doing any such thing' (twenty-seven-year-old woman, postgraduate, single, employed, abused between the ages of seventeen to nineteen).

Yet another woman who disclosed to her parents that she had been abused by the family's loyal domestic help recounted their response and her reaction to this: 'My parents didn't believe me ... my mother said I was imagining it. My father said, " ... I don't believe this. You're ... jolly lucky if a man lays his hands on you" ... I felt completely violated ... It was like a double whammy. First the abuse, and then not being believed by my parents ... After that I ... didn't talk about it for the next ten to twelve years' (thirty-eight-year-old woman, postgraduate, married, employed, abused between the ages of eleven and sixteen approximately).

Clearly, then, a repeated theme among victims of sexual abuse, including incest in childhood or adolescence, is a feeling of confusion, anger, fear, betrayal and a sense that they would be held responsible for having provoked the incident. No more than half of all survivors reported disclosing the abusive incident, and the leading factor underlying non-disclosure was, again, fear that they were, or would be, held responsible for provoking the incident.

Reported outcomes of sexual abuse in childhood and adolescence

Studies of non-consensual sexual experiences of young people have identified a number of adverse health and social outcomes of abuse (see, for example, Koenig et al., this volume; Patel and Andrew, this volume). Outcomes include gynaecological disorders, sexually transmitted infection and unintended pregnancy followed often by unsafe abortion. They also include severe mental health consequences including anxiety, depression and suicidal tendencies, and such social and relational outcomes as an inability to trust or have stable relationships with others.

Women in our study reported the experience of all these outcomes. The abusive experience affected their emotional, psychological, sexual and reproductive well-being. It shaped the way in which they perceived themselves, others and the world around them, and how they conducted themselves within relationships. It also shaped subsequent sexual relationships and coping mechanisms.

Compromised ability to develop subsequent trusting relationships The majority of women reported a sense of betrayal by not only their abusers but also their parents or other close family members for denying them protection. Issues of trust were repeatedly highlighted ('not trusting any man'; 'not trusting too easily'; 'mistrusting the entire male race'; 'easily suspicious'; 'having great problems with trust'; 'no one can be trusted'; 'the world is not a safe place'; 'keeping a distance from men because they invariably want sex'; and 'not having many friends'). One woman spoke of her difficulty in forming trusting relationships: 'The one thing that abuse does to people is to destroy their ability to relate to other people with love and trust ... When I look back at that phase I think I was damaged most critically in my ability to trust ... I had experienced too many adult betrayals, without experiencing enough adult love' (twenty-seven-year-old woman, postgraduate, single, employed, abused between the ages of seventeen and nineteen).

Other women spoke of indiscriminate trust ('allowing people to walk over me and to be fooled by overt gestures'; 'expecting all older men to abuse me'; 'being too trusting'; or 'trusting everyone').

Social and intimate relationships invariably suffered. Many women reported conflicting emotions – seeking love and care on the one hand and thwarting or rejecting other people's attempts to develop relationships with them on the other. A sense of isolation was frequently acknowledged. Several women highlighted this conflict: 'I was scared of and avoided intimacy. I believed that love came with a price, that people I loved and trusted would betray me ... This belief was rooted in my abuse as a child. So strong were these roots ... that I laughed at, spurned even, the few men who came close to loving me ... all the time wanting them to stay, I was effective in seeing that they left me' (thirty-nine-year-old woman, graduate, single, employed, abused between the ages of six and nineteen approximately).

Another woman reported: 'One of the most damaging effects my childhood abuse has had on my emotional and mental well-being is my inability to develop stable relationships ... Whenever I get close, I start withdrawing' (forty-two-year-old woman, postgraduate, married, employed, abused between the ages of ten and fifteen approximately).

Risky sexual behaviours The abuse also had an adverse effect on women's sexual and reproductive health and on healthy sexual development. For many, consensual sexual relationships were initiated at an early age and many reported multiple sexual partners: '[As I had] overnight become a woman, by the time [I] was fourteen or fifteen years old, [I] was leading a very promiscuous existence and had no qualms about entering into sexual relationships with men if I found them attractive' (forty-two-year-old woman, postgraduate, married, employed, abused between the ages of ten and fifteen approximately). Another reported: '[I] had been sleeping around with so many men since an early age, it didn't really matter if there was one more' (twenty-four-year-old woman, graduate, single, employed, abused between the ages of six and twenty-one approximately).

Many continued to associate sex with secrecy and furtiveness. One woman, who had been abused by her father's younger brother, said she grew up having 'furtive one-night stands' in 'seedy hotels with semen-stained bed-sheets'. She explained: 'My uncle taught me by his terrible acts that sex was furtive, it took place ... in a quick shifty manner' (thirty-nine-year-old woman, graduate, single, employed, abused between the ages of six and nineteen approximately).

Women recognized the sexual risks to which they were exposed, and several reported the experience of repeated vaginal infections, unintended pregnancies and abortions, as well as persistent fears of unwanted pregnancy and infection, including HIV.

Several women reported that they identified their own sense of self-worth with the number of sexual partners they had. Indeed, women reported that they felt compelled to have sex because not to be sexually active was equated with rejection. At the same time, sex enabled them to overcome feelings of powerlessness. As one woman said: 'Sex is my ultimate winning weapon' (thirty-three-year-old woman, postgraduate, married, employed, abused between the ages of four and fourteen approximately). According to another: 'With every lover I acquired I would feel a sense of triumph, victory almost. Nothing in my life has given me greater or more overwhelming power ... I needed men, their approval, their furtive looks and sordid sex to make me whole. Till then I felt incomplete, unwanted' (thirty-nine-year-old woman, graduate, single, employed, abused between the ages of six and nineteen approximately).

Other women reported that they could neither refuse sexual advances nor protect themselves from unintended outcomes. Many of these women reported that they were exploited or violated in subsequent relationships.

Experiences in engaging in consensual sexual relationships Women reported that they tended to avoid touch and sex in consensual sexual relationships. For example, one woman spoke about how she hated it when her boyfriend touched her and yet did not know how to explain this to him 'when other people seemed to do such things so naturally and normally'. Another explained: 'I don't think I was able to enjoy sex ... I was always very scared that I would be violated ... I think there was always something stopping me from deriving sexual pleasure from a sexual act ... there was a certain amount of discomfort with one's own body, one's own admission to pleasure' (thirty-eight-year-old woman, postgraduate, married, employed, abused between the ages of eleven and sixteen approximately).

Another woman spoke of the intrusive images of her abuse and abusers coming in the way of her enjoyment of sex. She said that every time she had sex with her partner, she could 'see the faces of all my five abusers in between my husband

and me'. According to one survivor: 'The abuse taught me ... that I had no control or right over my body. I was trained as a child to understand my sexuality in ways that made no place for my own wishes and desires. I learnt therefore to accommodate the demands of men' (thirty-nine-year-old woman, graduate, single, employed, abused between the ages of six and nineteen approximately).

Negative body images Abusive experiences also affected the way women perceived their own bodies. Several perceived that it was their bodies, notably their breasts, which provoked the abuse; many associated their breasts with feelings of shame and, in one case, 'the external manifestation of all my sordid crimes'. Many women described their bodies in disparaging terms, or reported hating their bodies. Women reported wearing 'layers and layers of clothes', or 'dark loose clothes that resembled a bag and completely hid my body' to 'negate my femininity', or walking with a stoop and hunched shoulders in order to 'hide and protect myself'.

Mental health outcomes Several women reported severe mental health outcomes ranging from compulsive behaviours, substance abuse and eating disorders to self-inflicted injuries and suicide attempts. Obsessive behaviours were reported that 'seemed to have taken a grip over my life and I had no control over them'. For at least one woman, this fear developed into an obsessive-compulsive disorder: 'I still want to clean myself. I wash my hands at least fifty times a day. There is a need in me to rid myself of any smell or contamination, and remain every moment of the day clean and pure' (sixty-seven-year-old woman, married, housewife, abused between the ages of six and eleven); and 'I found myself terribly anxious with worries about getting contaminated. My rituals of cleaning became excessively strong. I had to wash everything and myself' (forty-one-year-old woman, postgraduate, employed, single, abused between the ages of four and a half and eleven).

Eating disorders were also reported. Women described how eating was a way of coping with feelings. In an extreme case, one woman reported requiring hospitalization for malnutrition. Eating disorders were reported as follows: 'I found solace in food. I used food to stuff down my feelings, perhaps to defocus from what I was going through' (thirty-nine-year-old woman, graduate, single, employed, abused between the ages of six and nineteen approximately).

Another woman recalled how in order to deal with her flashbacks of abuse she almost stopped eating: 'I so completely suppressed my hunger that I didn't feel hungry at all ... This thing went on for some years and it was only when I was in my early twenties or something that I was able to see it as a problem' (thirty-year-old woman, postgraduate, single, employed, abused between the ages of six and thirteen approximately).

Several women reported substance abuse as a means by which they sought to cope with low self-esteem and the pain of sexual abuse, including incest in childhood or adolescence, and, for some, of ongoing abusive relationships. Women acknowledged that alcohol abuse appeared to exacerbate sexual risk-taking: one woman recalled that she 'made passes at men and had to get laid' every time she was drunk. Another woman said that often while drinking she ended up having sex with men whom she otherwise disliked and would have nothing to do with in 'normal circumstances'. Yet another woman said that often under the influence of alcohol she had sex with more than three or four men at the same time and, when sober, felt 'revolted' by her behaviour.

A number of women reported mutilating themselves or contemplating suicide. Some women made several suicide attempts. One woman spoke of cutting herself and beating herself with a belt and watching the welts rise. Another woman, who was abused by multiple family members, described how she frequently slashed her wrists in order to divert her attention from the pain of the abuse to the more physical pain: 'Somehow, cutting myself helps. It helps me focus on a more different and bearable pain, the physical pain I experience ... It is better than the pain inside me, which I don't know what to do about' (twenty-two-year-old woman, college student, single, abused between the ages of six and fourteen). Another reported: 'Certainly I contemplated suicide and planned it in elaborate detail. I found out ways to hurt myself, to turn the anger that was in me towards me, for there was no one else ... in college I was deeply suicidal and self-destructive ... There were times I would lock myself in my hostel room and beat myself' (twenty-seven-year-old woman, postgraduate, single, employed, abused between the ages of seventeen and nineteen).

Conclusion

Findings presented in this chapter, while by no means representative of urban Indian women, shed light on a significant but poorly researched and poorly addressed topic. Indeed, they shatter the belief that the family provides a safe environment and protects female children and adolescents from sexual advances. Collectively, these findings illustrate that sexual abuse of children and adolescents perpetrated by family members and other trusted persons does indeed take place in Indian society and allow us to understand women's own perceptions of their abuse experiences and how such experiences have influenced their lives. They reveal the unique features that characterize such abuse and highlight the ways in which it is a significant psychological, emotional, reproductive and sexual health hazard both in the short and the longer term.

Clearly, the consequences of sexual abuse, including incest, in childhood or adolescence are severe and continue well into adulthood. Multiple consequences have been articulated by victims. These include a sense of betrayal and compromised ability to trust others and a loss of self-esteem. They also include sexual risk-taking or, alternatively, difficulties in engaging in sex in subsequent consensual relationships. And finally, they are associated with severe mental health repercussions including anxiety, depression, eating disorders, substance abuse, compulsive behaviours, self-inflicted injury and suicidal tendencies. Many survivors felt that they had yet to overcome some of these adverse consequences.

Findings call for interventions at the level of adult women victims, children and adolescents themselves, as well as their families, teachers, healthcare providers and society more generally. Actions need to be two-pronged. Prevention efforts that sensitize children and adolescents to good and bad touch, including bad touch by those they like and trust, are essential. Adults must also be sensitized to abusive behaviours within families, and exposed to appropriate parenting skills and the need to communicate with children and adolescents on sexual matters. Particular efforts must be directed towards those mothers who have themselves been victims of sexual abuse or incest in childhood or adolescence. At the same time there is a need for a comprehensive law in the country to address such abuse, and interventions at the family, school and health service level that enable the detection of abuse in childhood or adolescence, supports those who have experienced abuse and provide confidential and non-threatening legal and health-related services to them.

For any effective work therefore in the fields of mental, sexual and reproductive health, it is vital that clinicians, researchers and social workers begin to address the problem of incest and other forms of sexual abuse among young people. Special efforts, in terms of appropriate health information, counselling and support services, must be made available to adults who have experienced sexual abuse, including incest, during childhood or adolescence. In designing programmes to address such abuse, it is important to draw insights from their experiences. A combined effort of this nature will undoubtedly influence the discourse on childhood and adolescent sexual abuse and incest, shape empirical research on the subject, drive social policy and develop services for victims and survivors in our country.

Note

1 The RAHI (Recovering and Healing from Incest) Foundation is a Delhi-based support and resource centre for women survivors of childhood/adolescent incest and sexual abuse.

References

RAHI Foundation (1998) *Voices from the Silent Zone: Women's Experiences of Incest and Childhood Sexual Abuse: The RAHI Findings*, New Delhi: RAHI.

— (1999) *The House I Grew Up In: Five Indian Women's Experiences of Childhood Incest and its Impact on their Lives: The RAHI Testimonies*, New Delhi: RAHI.

12 | Coerced first intercourse and reproductive health among adolescent women in Rakai, Uganda

MICHAEL A. KOENIG, IRYNA ZABLOTSKA, TOM LUTALO, FRED NALUGODA, JENNIFER WAGMAN AND RON GRAY

Over the past decade, the issue of domestic violence has received increasing international recognition and attention. The World Health Organization defines domestic violence as 'the range of sexually, psychologically and physically coercive acts used against adult and adolescent women by current or former male intimate partners' (WHO 1997). There is also growing awareness of the importance of sexual violence and coercion as a component of overall domestic violence.

Most research on sexual violence is based on data from reproductive-age women in intimate partnerships. Studies have indicated high rates of non-consensual intercourse in developing countries, where as many as one-fifth to one-half of all female respondents report having been coerced into sexual intercourse by an intimate partner (Coker and Richter 1998; Ellsberg et al. 2000; Haj-Yahia and Edleson 1994; Ilkkaracan and Women for Women's Human Rights 1998; Martin et al. 1999b; van der Straten et al. 1998; Watts et al. 1998). Comparatively few studies from developing countries, however, have explored the prevalence of sexual abuse and coercion specifically among adolescent women.

One indication that sexual violence is common among female adolescents is the substantial proportion of women who report that their first sexual intercourse (also referred to as 'first sex' in this chapter) was coerced; this finding has been documented by a number of studies, although definitions of coercion have varied. Although the reported prevalence of coerced first sex is relatively low (less than 10 per cent) in several developed and developing country studies (Abma et al. 1998; Ajuwon et al. 2001b; Dickson et al. 1998; Mulugeta et al. 1998), in a number of other studies, largely from sub-Saharan Africa, it typically ranged from 20 to 30 per cent of all women (Buga et al. 1996; Glover et al. 2003; Matasha et al. 1998; Somse et al. 1993) and in some cases exceeded 40 per cent (Cáceres et al. 2000; Rwenge 2000). These quantitative results have been reinforced by qualitative findings from sub-Saharan Africa that underscore the important role that coercion frequently plays in compelling young women to engage in sexual intercourse (Ajuwon et al. 2001a; Hulton et al. 2000; Wood et al. 1998).

Concern over the issue of coerced sex among adolescent women has been elevated by a growing body of research – much of it from developed countries

– that has reported significant associations between coerced sex and a range of negative health and reproductive health outcomes for women of reproductive age (García-Moreno and Watts 2000; Heise et al. 1995; Krug et al. 2002). One of the strongest associations to emerge from the literature is the link between sexual abuse and the risk of unintended pregnancy, a relationship found in a number of studies from the United States (Boyer and Fine 1992; Brown and Eisenberg 1995; Butler and Burton 1990; Cokkinides et al. 1999; Curry et al. 1998; Dietz et al. 1999; Gazmararian et al. 1995; Roosa et al. 1997; Stewart and Cecutti 1993). Studies from South Africa, Tanzania and India have also found a significant association between physical violence and coerced sex and the occurrence of unintended pregnancy (Hof and Richters 1999; Jewkes et al. 2001; Martin et al. 1999b). Other relevant work has documented a reduced likelihood of contraceptive use among women who have prior or current exposure to physical or sexual abuse by an intimate partner, or who are afraid of such violence (Bawah et al. 1999; Folch-Lyon et al. 1981; Martin et al. 1999b).

Other studies from developed countries have reported a significant link between physical or sexual abuse among reproductive-age women and a range of gynaecological problems, including vaginal bleeding, pain during intercourse, chronic pelvic pain, urinary tract infection and medically treated pelvic inflammatory disease (Eby et al. 1995; Schei 1990, 1991; Schei and Bakketeig 1989). Another set of studies has highlighted the possible association between women's experience of physical or sexual violence and their risk of contracting a sexually transmitted infection (STI) (Amaro et al. 1990; Martin et al. 1999a), including HIV (García-Moreno and Watts 2000; Maman et al. 2000); in several studies from sub-Saharan Africa, HIV-positive women were significantly more likely to report prior physical abuse or coerced sex than were HIV-negative women (Maman et al. 2002; Quigley and Morgan 2000; van der Straten et al. 1995). Consistent with these results are findings from studies from the United States that indicate elevated levels of sexual risk behaviour among women who have experienced coerced sex (Choi et al. 1998; He et al. 1998; Somse et al. 1993), along with decreased levels of condom negotiation or use (He et al. 1998; Kalichman et al. 1998; Wingood and DiClemente 1997; Wingood et al. 2000).

Evidence concerning the reproductive health sequelae of physical and sexual violence thus remains limited and has been drawn largely from studies in the United States or other developed countries. Moreover, most studies have focused on women of all reproductive ages rather than on adolescents specifically. Many of the existing studies have also used data from special, high-risk populations rather than from more broadly representative samples. Finally, existing studies display substantial variability in methodological rigour with respect to study design and controls for potentially confounding risk factors.

Data collected in rural Uganda in 2001/02 provide a unique opportunity to explore in greater depth the issue of coerced sex and its reproductive health sequelae among young women in a community-based sample. In this chapter, we present findings on the linkages between coerced first sex and selected reproductive health behaviours and outcomes in a sample of 575 sexually experienced adolescent women.

Methods

Setting and data The setting for this study is rural Uganda. Premarital sex is common in Uganda and is a widely accepted behaviour for young people of both genders (Ntozi and Lubega 1991; Olowo-Freers and Barton 1992). One-quarter of Ugandan women have had sex by age fifteen, and two-thirds have done so by age eighteen (UBOS and ORC Macro 2001); a significant proportion initiate sex prior to marriage (Blanc and Way 1998). Although many young women's sexual relationships appear to be volitional, some qualitative evidence from Uganda suggests that force and coercion may also frequently be a factor (Hulton et al. 2000).

Data for the present study came from the ongoing Rakai Project, which was started in 1987 as a collaborative intervention research initiative to understand and reduce HIV transmission in rural Uganda. Rakai, a rural district in south-western Uganda that borders Tanzania and Lake Victoria, has been at the centre of the country's HIV/AIDS epidemic, with an estimated HIV prevalence of 16 per cent in the mid-1990s (Wawer et al. 1999). In 1994, fifty-six communities located on secondary roads in Rakai were randomly selected and aggregated into ten clusters; each cluster was randomly assigned to an intervention arm, which received mass STI treatment, or to a control arm (ibid.).[1] Interviews were conducted in respondents' homes at regular ten-month intervals and used a detailed questionnaire that collected data on demographic characteristics, health status and sexual behaviour and partnerships. Respondents were also asked to provide blood and urine samples to be tested for HIV and selected STIs. All participants in both arms were educated about HIV, other STIs and family planning; given condoms free of charge; and provided with HIV test results, HIV/STI counselling, and treatment for general health problems and STIs on request (Lutalo et al. 2000). No financial incentives were provided to respondents for their participation in the study. The study was approved by one institutional review board in Uganda and two in the United States.

Between March 2001 and February 2002, all fifteen-to-forty-nine-year-old women who had been enrolled in the Rakai surveillance system prior to the 2001/02 round were asked a series of questions concerning their experience of physical and sexual violence during their lifetime and in the last twelve months (Koenig et al. 2003a). Respondents were specifically asked whether force had been used the first time they had sex. Those who replied affirmatively were asked about the specific actions (both verbal and physical) that accompanied coercion at first sex. Respondents were also asked how willing they had been to engage in sex the first time. In this study, all women who reported that force had been used to compel them into first intercourse were classified as having had coerced first sex.[2] The 2001/02 survey round also collected information on current use of contraceptives, pregnancy history, experience with unintended pregnancy, lifetime number of sexual partners, condom use at last sex, consistency of condom use in the last six months, and current symptoms of STIs and genital tract morbidity.

Procedures carefully established over the last decade in the Rakai Project for the collection of sensitive information included safeguards to protect the confidentiality of information provided by respondents and to minimize potential risks associated with participation in the study. Consent to participate was obtained from all respondents at enrolment and at each follow-up contact. Interviews were conducted in complete privacy by highly trained, same-sex interviewers, and no information from the survey was disclosed to respondents' family members. Completed questionnaires were kept in secure facilities, and interview schedules were coded with participants' study identification; no personal identifiers were included. In 2001/02, only limited domestic violence services existed in this rural setting, but the Rakai Project has subsequently expanded both violence prevention efforts and counselling and support services for abused women.

Our primary study population consisted of all sexually experienced women who were aged between fifteen and nineteen at the time of the 2001/02 survey, had been enrolled in the surveillance system prior to this round,[3] and provided information on their first sexual intercourse. These selection criteria yielded a sample of 575 young women.

Statistical analysis We used Pearson chi-square tests to assess significant differences in the prevalence of reproductive health outcomes among women who reported coerced first sex and among those who did not. We used multi-variate logistic regressions, stratified by marital status, to evaluate associations between coerced first intercourse and dichotomous variables designed to measure reproductive health behaviours and outcomes: current use of modern contraceptive methods,[4] condom use at last intercourse, consistent condom use with all partners during the last six months, reporting one or more current genital tract symptoms and, among ever-pregnant women, reporting the current or most recent pregnancy as unintended (i.e. mistimed or unwanted). The following demographic characteristics were included as categorical variables in all adjusted regression models: educational level (fewer than five years of schooling, five to seven years and eight or more years), age at first intercourse (younger than fourteen, fourteen to fifteen and sixteen or older), religious affiliation (Catholic, Muslim or other) and current marital status (marriage was defined as either legal or consensual union). The statistical package of STATA 8.1 was used for all analyses (STATA Corporation, STATA Statistical Software, 2001, release 8.1.).

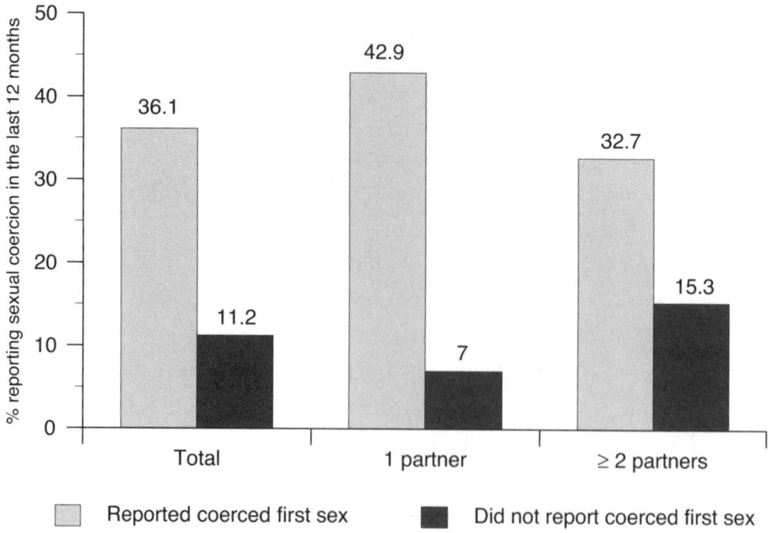

Note: Difference between those who reported coerced first sex and those who did not was significant at p≤.01 for each comparison.

Figure 12.1 Among sexually experienced women aged fifteen to nineteen, percentage who reported having experienced sexual coercion in the twelve months preceding the survey, by experience of coerced first sex, according to cumulative number of partners

Results

Overall, 19 per cent of young women had had fewer than five years, 49 per cent had had five to seven years and 33 per cent had had eight or more years of schooling. Nineteen per cent reported that they were still attending school; thus, levels of education ultimately attained are likely to be somewhat higher than the levels reported in the survey. Roughly three in five participants were Catholic, one in five were Muslim, and the remainder reported other religious affiliations. In this population of sexually experienced young women, 13 per cent said that they had first had sex before the age of fourteen, 46 per cent at age fourteen or fifteen, and 41 per cent at age sixteen or older. At the time they were interviewed, 52 per cent of women were married, 44 per cent were never-married and 4 per cent were previously, but not currently, married.

Prevalence of coerced first sex Fourteen per cent of all respondents reported that their first sexual intercourse had been coerced (not shown). The likelihood of a respondent's first intercourse having been coerced was strongly associated with the age at which it occurred: although 26 per cent of young women who had first had sex when they were younger than fourteen described that experience as coerced, this proportion fell to 15 per cent among respondents whose age at first intercourse was fourteen or fifteen, and to 10 per cent among those who had first had sex at age sixteen or older. Differences among the three sub-groups were statistically significant.

Figure 12.1 shows the association between young women's reports of coerced first intercourse and experience of sexual coercion in the last twelve months. Respondents who reported that their first intercourse had been coerced were significantly more likely than those who did not to report that they had experienced recent coercion (36 per cent versus 11 per cent). Because this difference may be attributable in part to cases in which respondents' first and most recent partners were the same person, we further stratified young women by their reported cumulative number of partners. Among respondents who reported having had only one partner – and whose most recent partner was therefore presumably also the first partner – those whose first sex had been coerced were significantly more likely to report recent coercion than those whose first sex had not been forced (43 versus 7 per cent). Even among women who reported two or more cumulative partners – whose first and most recent partners were probably different[5] – the proportion experiencing recent coercion was significantly higher among those who reported coerced first sex than among those who did not (33 versus 15 per cent); this suggests that women whose first intercourse was coerced may be vulnerable to continued sexual coercion, even within subsequent partnerships.

Coerced first sex and reproductive behaviour Table 12.1 examines the relationships between coerced first intercourse and current contraceptive use, pregnancy and unintended pregnancy, overall and by marital status. Among all respondents, those who reported coerced first intercourse were significantly less likely than those who did not to be currently using contraceptives (18 versus 34 per cent). Although a similar pattern appeared among both currently married and unmarried young women, the difference was statistically significant only among the latter sub-group (30 versus 50 per cent).

A significantly higher percentage of young women who had been coerced into first intercourse than those who had not been coerced reported having ever been pregnant (81 versus 65 per cent). This difference was also significant among unmarried women (57 versus 31 per cent) but not among married women, almost all of whom had experienced at least one pregnancy.

To measure unintended pregnancy, ever-pregnant women were asked to recall whether their current or most recent pregnancy had been wanted then, wanted later or unwanted. Among ever-pregnant young women, a significantly higher percentage of those who reported coerced first sex than of those who did not indicated that their current or most recent pregnancy had been unintended (52 versus 37 per cent). This differential was of borderline significance among currently married young women (45 versus 29 per cent, $p = .069$), and was not statistically significant among unmarried young women.

TABLE 12.1 Percentage distributions of sexually experienced Ugandan women aged fifteen to nineteen, by selected measures of reproductive behaviour, according to marital status and experience of coerced first sex

Measures	All Coerced first sex Yes	 No	Married Coerced first sex Yes	 No	Unmarried Coerced first sex Yes	 No
Current contraceptive use	(N=83)	(N=492)	(N=46)	(N=249)	(N=37)	(N =243)
Yes	18.1	33.5	8.7	17.7	29.7	49.8
No	81.9	66.5	91.3	82.3	70.3	50.2
χ^2 *p-value*	*.005*		*.130*		*.023*	
Ever pregnant	(N=82)	(N=492)	(N=45)	(N= 249)	(N=37)	(N=243)
Yes	80.5	64.6	100.0	97.2	56.8	31.3
No	19.5	35.4	0.0	2.8	43.2	68.7
χ^2 *p-value*	*.005*		*.255*		*.002*	
Intendedness of current or most recent pregnancy+	(N=66)	(N=316)	(N=45)	(N=242)	(N=21)	(N=74)
Intended	40.9	58.5	46.7	64.9	28.6	37.8
Unintended	51.5	36.7	44.5	29.3	66.7	60.8
No preference	7.6	4.8	8.9	5.8	4.8	1.4
χ^2 *p-value*	*.031*		*.069*		*.500*	
Total	100.0	100.0	100.0	100.0	100.0	100.0

Note: + Restricted to ever-pregnant women.

Further analysis revealed that among all ever-pregnant respondents, both unwanted and mistimed pregnancies were more common among young women who had been coerced than among those who had not (15 versus 6 per cent and 36 versus 31 per cent, respectively; data not shown).

Coerced first sex and sexual risk behaviour Table 12.2 shows distributions of married and unmarried women by three indicators of sexual risk behaviour – reported cumulative number of sexual partners, condom use at last sex and the consistency of condom use during the last six months – according to experience of coerced first intercourse. Overall, a modest but significant difference in cumulative number of partners was evident between respondents who had been coerced and those who had not: young women whose first intercourse had been coerced were significantly more likely than those who had not been coerced to report having had two or more sexual partners (66 versus 51 per cent). This difference was of borderline statistical significance among both married and unmarried respondents.

A significant relationship was evident between coerced first intercourse and

TABLE 12.2 Percentage distributions of sexually experienced Ugandan women aged fifteen to nineteen, by selected measures of sexual risk behaviour, and according to marital status and experience of coerced first sex

Measures	All		Married		Unmarried	
	Coerced first sex		Coerced first sex		Coerced first sex	
	Yes	No	Yes	No	Yes	No
Cumulative number of partners	(N = 83)	(N = 492)	(N = 46)	(N = 249)	(N = 37)	(N=243)
1	33.7	49.2	32.6	46.2	35.1	52.3
≥2	66.3	50.8	67.4	53.8	64.9	47.7
χ^2 p-value	*.001*		*.088*			*.052*
Condom use at last sex						
No	86.7	67.1	95.6	94.8	75.7	38.4
Yes	13.3	32.9	4.4	5.2	24.3	61.6
χ^2 p-value	*.004*		*.804*		*.001*	
Consistent condom use over last 6 months*						
Always	7.2	25.3	0.0	1.6	16.2	49.6
Sometimes	18.1	15.5	8.7	11.2	29.7	19.8
Never	74.7	59.3	91.3	87.2	54.1	30.6
χ^2 p-value	*.001*		*.592*		*.001*	
Total	100.0	100.0	100.0	100.0	100.0	100.0

Note: * Total N for this measure was 574.

condom use at last sex: respondents who reported coerced first intercourse were less likely than those who did not to say that they had used a condom at last intercourse (13 versus 33 per cent). Young women who reported coerced first sex were also less likely than other respondents to report that they had always used condoms with all sexual partners in the preceding six months (7 versus 25 per cent), and were more likely to report that they had never used condoms (75 versus 59 per cent) during that time. Both associations were statistically significant.

Stratification by marital status revealed that the relationships between coerced first sex and both measures of condom use remained significant only among unmarried women. Twenty-four per cent of unmarried women who reported coerced first sex had used a condom at last sex, compared with 62 per cent of those who reported no coercion at that time. When asked about condom use during the last six months, 16 per cent of women who had been coerced had always used them, 30 per cent had used them sometimes and 54 per cent had never used them. Among women who had not been coerced, those proportions were 50, 20 and 31 per cent. Condom use among married young women was extremely low in both coercion categories.

TABLE 12.3 Percentages of sexually experienced Ugandan women aged fifteen to nineteen who reported at least one genital tract symptom and who reported specific symptoms, by marital status and experience of coerced first sex

Symptom	All Coerced first sex Yes	All Coerced first sex No	Married Coerced first sex Yes	Married Coerced first sex No	Unmarried Coerced first sex Yes	Unmarried Coerced first sex No
	(N = 83)	(N = 492)	(N = 46)	(N = 249)	(N = 37)	(N=243)
At least one symptom	42.2***	20.5	43.5*	28.1	40.5***	12.8
Lower abdominal pain	19.3**	9.4	17.4	14.1	21.6***	4.5
Discharge	10.8	7.3	8.7	10.0	13.5*	4.5
Vaginal itching or unpleasant odour	18.1*	9.8	17.4	11.7	18.9*	7.8
Frequent or painful urination	9.6	5.7	10.9	8.8	8.1	2.5
Pain during intercourse	3.6	2.9	6.5	4.0	0.0	1.7
Genital ulcer	2.0*	0.6	4.4	0.8	2.7	0.4
Genital warts	2.4	1.2	2.2	1.6	2.7	0.8

Notes: * Difference from those who did not report coerced first sex significant at $p \leq .05$ **Difference from those who did not report coerced first sex significant at $p \leq .01$ *** Difference from those who did not report coerced first sex significant at $p \leq .001$

Coerced first sex and genital tract symptoms Overall, the proportion of adolescent women who reported at least one genital tract symptom was twice as high among those who had experienced coerced first sex than among those who had not (42 versus 21 per cent), a statistically significant difference (Table 12.3). Moreover, the prevalence of specific symptoms was consistently higher among young women whose first intercourse had been coerced than among other respondents (2–19 versus 1–10 per cent); differences between the two groups were statistically significant for lower abdominal pain, vaginal itching or unpleasant odour, and genital ulcers. The proportion of married respondents who reported at least one genital symptom was significantly higher among young women whose first intercourse had been coerced than among others (44 versus 28 per cent). This relationship was even stronger among unmarried respondents (41 versus 13 per cent).

Multi-variate analyses The relationships of risk behaviours and reproductive health outcomes with coerced first sex that were found at the bi-variate level remained significant in the multi-variate models, which controlled for education, religious affiliation, age at first sex and marital status (Table 12.4). Compared with young women who did not report coerced first intercourse, those who did had significantly reduced odds of current contraceptive use (odds ratio 0.5). This

TABLE 12.4 Odds ratios (and 95 per cent confidence intervals) from multiple logistic regressions assessing the association of reproductive health behaviours and outcomes with coerced first sex among sexually experienced Ugandan women aged fifteen to nineteen

Behaviour and outcome	Current contraceptive use (N = 575)	Condom use at last sex (N = 574)	Consistent condom use during last 6 months (N = 574)	≥1 Genital tract symptom (N = 575)	Current or most recent pregnancy unintended† (N = 384)
Coerced first sex					
No	1.00	1.00	1.00	1.00	1.00
Yes	0.47(0.25–0.88)*	0.26(0.12–0.55)***	0.19(0.08–0.50)***	2.60(1.57–4.32)***	2.06(1.17–3.63)*
Education level (yrs)					
<5	1.00	1.00	1.00	1.00	1.00
5–7	1.34(0.72–2.52)	1.33(0.58–3.04)	2.54(0.79–8.15)	0.97(0.58–1.62)	1.26 (0.75–2.12)
≥8	2.90(1.49–5.63)**	3.98(1.72–9.26)***	7.38(2.31–23.61)***	0.57(0.30–1.08)	1.94(1.00–3.78)*
Religious affiliation					
Other	1.00	1.00	1.00	1.00	1.00
Catholic	2.11(1.28–3.45)**	1.57(0.90–2.74)	1.82(1.00–3.34)	0.84(0.52–1.36)	1.65(0.97–2.82)
Muslim	1.33(0.71–2.50)	1.17(0.57–2.40)	0.78(0.35–1.70)	0.82(0.43–1.54)	1.29(0.65–2.58)
Age at first sex					
<14	1.00	1.00	1.00	1.00	1.00
14–15	1.22(0.65–2.32)	0.98(0.46–2.09)	1.17(0.49–2.83)	0.73(0.42–1.27)	1.04(0.58–1.88)
≥16	1.32(0.63–2.78)	1.33(0.56–3.17)	1.74(0.65–4.66)	0.52(0.25–1.09)	0.70(0.32–1.55)
Marital status					
Unmarried	1.00	1.00	1.00	1.00	1.00
Married	0.29(0.19–0.44)***	0.05(0.03–0.10)***	0.02(0.01–0.06)***	1.80(1.15–2.81)**	0.40(0.24–0.65)***

Notes: *p≤.05 **p≤.01 ***p≤.001 †Restricted to ever-pregnant women

negative relationship was even stronger for condom use at last intercourse (0.3) and for consistent condom use in the last six months (0.2). The risk of reporting one or more genital tract symptoms was significantly higher among women who had experienced coerced first intercourse than among those who had not (2.6). Among ever-pregnant women, coercion was associated with significantly elevated odds of reporting the current or most recent pregnancy as unintended (2.1). In addition, having had eight or more years of schooling was strongly associated with contraceptive use, condom use at last sex and consistent condom use in the last six months (2.9–7.4). Catholic women had significantly higher odds of reporting current contraceptive use relative to those in the 'other' religious affiliation category (2.1). Compared with unmarried respondents, currently married women had significantly decreased odds of current contraceptive use, condom use at last sex, consistent condom use and unintended pregnancy (0.02–0.40), and had significantly increased odds of reporting at least one genital tract symptom (1.8).

Discussion

At least three plausible mechanisms have been put forward to explain the potential association between physical or sexual violence and adverse reproductive health outcomes. One mechanism concerns the direct biological effects of coerced intercourse, such as unintended pregnancy, abortion and STIs and their sequelae (Heise et al. 1995). A second mechanism suggests that physical or sexual violence may disempower women in negotiating safer sex and may negatively affect protective behaviours related to fertility regulation and STIs, including contraceptive use, STI treatment-seeking, use of condoms and ability to affect their partners' risk-taking behaviour (ibid.; Maman et al. 2000). A third mechanism relates to sexual coercion and abuse during childhood, which may increase women's propensity to subsequently engage in high-risk sexual behaviour during adolescence (Handwerker 1993; Maman et al. 2000).

Whether an indicator of subsequent elevated risk or a direct contributing factor, coerced first sex was strongly and systematically associated with a number of adverse reproductive health outcomes in our study: decreased contraceptive use, condom non-use at last sex, inconsistent condom use during the last six months, unintended pregnancy and genital tract symptoms, which may indicate the presence of an STI. Other research from Rakai has highlighted the significant association between coerced first intercourse and young women's risk of HIV infection (Koenig et al. 2004). That these associations may arise not solely from coercion at first sex but from repeated acts of coerced intercourse is suggested by our finding that young women whose first intercourse had been coerced were at increased risk of recent coercion, regardless of whether their first and current partners were the same person.

This is one of the first developing-country studies to present evidence on the association between coerced first intercourse and adverse reproductive health outcomes among adolescent women; still, several limitations merit discussion. First, under-reporting associated with respondents' reluctance to acknowledge a highly sensitive experience may have led to an underestimate of the prevalence of sexual coercion. The prolonged exposure of respondents to the Rakai Project and its interviewers over the past decade, however, the rapport that has been established between respondents and interviewers as a result of this exposure, and the safeguards for privacy and confidentiality of information are likely to have increased respondents' willingness to discuss the issue of sexual coercion. The order of questions on coerced first sex may also have contributed to under-reporting: respondents were initially asked whether their first sex had been coerced, which left them to define what constitutes coercion. Only those who answered affirmatively were asked about the range of coercive acts that accompanied first intercourse. If the order of questions had been reversed, more women might have identified coercive actions that had accompanied first sex and subsequently defined that experience as 'coerced'.

Second, our study is limited by the measurement of several reproductive health outcomes included in the analyses. For example, retrospective assessments of pregnancy intendedness often underestimate the prevalence of unintended pregnancy, largely because mothers tend to rationalize unintended births as having been intended (Joyce et al. 2002; Santelli et al. 2003). Moreover, the correspondence between self-reported genital tract symptoms and clinically identified or laboratory-confirmed gynaecological morbidity has been shown to be quite low (Jejeebhoy et al. 2003). Nevertheless, self-reported symptoms are useful in assessing women's perceptions of gynaecological problems and in many cases may indicate the presence of an STI. A related concern is that women with adverse reproductive health outcomes (for example unintended pregnancy and genital tract symptoms) may be more likely to view their first sexual experience in a negative light and to classify it as coerced. Although we cannot rule out this possibility, the absence of such response bias is supported by the findings from another study in Rakai, which revealed that the relationship between coerced first intercourse and HIV infection was statistically significant whether or not women were aware of their HIV status (Koenig et al. 2004).

Finally, we are unable to assume temporality or causality in the relationships between sexual coercion and the outcomes considered. Many of these observed associations may be attributable to unmeasured antecedent factors (for example, unstable family environment or economic adversity) that both place young women at increased risk of sexual coercion during adolescence and increase their vulnerability to subsequent adverse reproductive health behaviours or outcomes. Moreover, the cross-sectional nature of the data complicates our ability to establish temporality or causality in many of the observed relationships, although this issue is addressed somewhat by our consideration of coercion at first intercourse as the exposure variable. Before assumptions of causality can be attributed to these associations, further quantitative and qualitative research is required to elucidate the specific pathways through which sexual coercion increases young women's vulnerability to adverse outcomes.

Our findings highlight the magnitude of the problem of sexual coercion among adolescent women in this rural Ugandan population. Coerced intercourse represents only one of the more extreme forms of sexual abuse, however. Had the survey also included questions about attempted sexual coercion and forms of sexual abuse other than penetrative intercourse, the prevalence of sexual violence in our study would most likely have been substantially higher. In addition, it is noteworthy that the levels of coerced intercourse reported here are significantly lower than those reported by many studies from sub-Saharan Africa. Other research suggests that the prevalence of sexual coercion – at least at first intercourse – appears to have significantly declined across successive age cohorts in Rakai (Koenig et al. 2003b). It is of interest to consider the role this trend may have played in the apparent decrease in HIV prevalence that has recently taken place in Uganda (Kilian et al. 1999).

The issue of sexual coercion and violence remains largely overlooked within current family planning and reproductive health service programmes. Although sexual abuse is an important social and public health issue in its own right, the results of our study strongly suggest that such behaviour has major adverse consequences for important aspects of young women's sexual and reproductive health. Our study highlights the potential importance of addressing the issue of sexual coercion and violence as an integral component of current reproductive health service programmes.

Notes

The authors gratefully acknowledge the assistance of Mark Emerson, Feng Zhao, Eva Bazant and Mary Shields in the preparation of this paper. Permission to reprint Koenig, M. A. et al. (2004) 'Coerced first intercourse and reproductive health among adolescent women in Rakai, Uganda', *International Family Planning Perspectives*, 30(4): 156–63, is gratefully acknowledged.

1 In 1999, twelve communities from the original Rakai surveillance area were dropped, and twelve new communities were added.

2 This measure exhibited a high level of internal consistency with the measure of how willing respondents had been to have sex the first time: 84 per cent of young women who reported that their first sexual experience had been coerced also stated that they had been unwilling to engage in sex at that time.

3 New entrants into the surveillance system – many of whom had recently turned fifteen – were interviewed separately and not included in the follow-up survey; as a result, newly sexually active women may be under-represented.

4 Modern methods include oral contraceptives, condoms, spermicides, injectables, intra-uterine devices (IUDs), male and female sterilization and the implant.

5 For women reporting two or more cumulative partners, some current primary partners may also have been the initial sexual partners.

References

Abma, J., A. Driscoll and K. Moore (1998) 'Young women's degree of control over first intercourse: an exploratory analysis', *Family Planning Perspectives*, 30(1): 12–18

Ajuwon, A. J., L. Akin-Jimoh, B. J. Olley et al. (2001a) 'Perceptions of sexual coercion: learning from young people in Ibadan, Nigeria', *Reproductive Health Matters*, 9(17): 128–36

Ajuwon, A. J., B. J. Olley, A. J. Iwalola et al. (2001b) 'Experience of sexual coercion among adolescents in Ibadan, Nigeria', *African Journal of Reproductive Health*, 5(3): 120–31

Amaro, H., L. H. Fried, H. Cabral et al. (1990) 'Violence during pregnancy and substance abuse', *American Journal of Public Health*, 80(5): 575–9

Bawah, A. A., P. Akweongo, R. Simmons et al. (1999) 'The impact of family planning on gender relations in northern Ghana', *Studies in Family Planning*, 30(1): 54–66

Blanc, A. B. and A. Way (1998) 'Sexual behavior, contraceptive knowledge, and use', *Studies in Family Planning*, 29(2): 106–16

Boyer, D. and D. Fine (1992) 'Sexual abuse as a factor in adolescent pregnancy and child maltreatment', *Family Planning Perspectives*, 24(1): 4–19

Brown, S. S. and L. Eisenberg (1995) *The Best Intentions: Unintended Pregnancy and the Well-being of Children and Families*, Washington, DC: National Academy Press

Buga, G. A., D. H. Amoko and D. J. Ncayiyana (1996) 'Sexual behaviour, contraceptive practice and reproductive health among school adolescents in rural Transkei', *South African Medical Journal*, 86(5): 523–7

Butler, R. J. and L. M. Burton (1990) 'Rethinking teenage childbearing: is sexual abuse a missing link?', *Family Relations*, 39(2): 73–80

Cáceres, C.F., B. V. Marin and E. S. Hudes (2000) 'Sexual coercion among youth and young adults in Lima, Peru', *Journal of Adolescent Health*, 27(5): 361–7

Choi, K. H., D. Binson, M. Adelson et al. (1998) 'Sexual harassment, sexual coercion, and HIV risk among U.S. adults 18–49 years', *AIDS and Behavior*, 2(1): 33–40

Coker, A. L. and D. L. Richter (1998) 'Violence against women in Sierra Leone: frequency and correlates of intimate partner violence and forced sexual intercourse', *African Journal of Reproductive Health*, 2(1): 61–72

Cokkinides, V. E., A. L. Coker, M. Sanderson et al. (1999) 'Physical violence during pregnancy: maternal complications and birth outcomes', *Obstetrics and Gynecology*, 93(5): 661–6

Curry, M. A., N. Perrin and E. Wall (1998) 'Effects of abuse on maternal complications and birth weight in adult and adolescent women', *Obstetrics and Gynecology*, 92(4): 530–34

Dickson, N., C. Paul, P. Herbison et al. (1998) 'First sexual intercourse: age, coercion, and later regrets reported by a birth cohort', *British Medical Journal*, 316(7124): 29–33

Dietz, P. M., A. M. Spitz, R. F. Anda et al. (1999) 'Unintended pregnancy among adult women exposed to abuse or household dysfunction during their childhood', *Journal of the American Medical Association*, 282(14): 1359–64

Eby, K. K., J. C. Campbell, C. M. Sullivan et al. (1995) 'Health effects on experiences of sexual violence for women with abusive partners', *Health Care for Women International*, 16(6): 563–75

Ellsberg, M., R. Pena, A. Herrera et al. (2000) 'Candies in hell: women's experiences of violence in Nicaragua', *Social Science and Medicine*, 51(11): 1595–610

Folch-Lyon, E., L. de la Macorra and S. B. Schearer (1981) 'Focus group and survey research on family planning in Mexico', *Studies in Family Planning*, 12(2): 409–32

García-Moreno, C. and C. Watts (2000) 'Violence against women: its importance for HIV/AIDS', *AIDS*, 14(3): S253–65

Gazmararian, J. A., M. M. Adams, L. E. Saltzman et al. (1995) 'The relationship between pregnancy intendedness and physical violence in mothers and newborns', *Obstetrics and Gynecology*, 85(6): 1031–8

Glover, E. K., A. Bannerman, B. W. Pence et al. (2003) 'Sexual health experiences of adolescents in three Ghanaian towns', *International Family Planning Perspectives*, 29(1): 32–40

Haj-Yahia, M. M. and E. L. Edleson (1994) 'Predicting the use of conflict resolution tactics among engaged Arab-Palestinian men in Israel', *Journal of Family Violence*, 9(1): 47–62

Handwerker, W. P. (1993) 'Gender power differences between parents and high-risk sexual behavior by their children: AIDS/STD risk factors extend to a prior generation', *Journal of Women's Health*, 2(3): 301–16

He, H., H. V. McCoy, S. J. Stevens et al. (1998) 'Violence and HIV sexual risk behaviors among female sex partners of male drug users', *Women and Health*, 27(1/2): 161–75

Heise, L., K. Moore and N. Toubia (1995) *Sexual Coercion and Reproductive Health: A Focus on Research*, New York: Population Council

Hof, C. and A. Richters (1999) 'Exploring the intersections between teenage pregnancy and gender violence: lessons from Zimbabwe', *African Journal of Reproductive Health*, 3(1): 51–65

Hulton, L. A., R. Cullen and S. W. Khalokho (2000) 'Perceptions of the risks of sexual activity and their consequences among Ugandan adolescents', *Studies in Family Planning*, 31(1): 35–46

Ilkkaracan, P. and Women for Women's Human Rights (1998) 'Exploring the context of women's sexuality in eastern Turkey', *Reproductive Health Matters*, 6(12): 66–75

Jejeebhoy, S. J., M. A. Koenig and C. Elias (eds) (2003) *Reproductive Tract Infections and Other Gynaecological Disorders*, Cambridge: Cambridge University Press

Jewkes, R., C. Vundule, F. Maforah et al. (2001) 'Relationship dynamics and teenage pregnancy in South Africa', *Social Science and Medicine*, 52(5): 733–44

Joyce, T., R. Kaestner and S. Korenman (2002) 'On the validity of retrospective assessments of pregnancy intention', *Demography*, 39(1): 199–213

Kalichman, S. C., E. A. Williams, C. Cherry et al. (1998) 'Sexual coercion, domestic violence, and negotiating condom use among low-income African American women', *Journal of Women's Health*, 7(3): 371–8

Kilian, A., H. D. S. Gregson, B. Ndvanabangi et al. (1999) 'Reduction in risk behavior provides the most consistent explanation of declining HIV-1 prevalence in Uganda', *AIDS*, 13(3): 391–8

Koenig, M. A., T. Lutalo, F. Zhao et al. (2003a) 'Domestic violence in Rakai, Uganda: evidence from a community-based survey', *Bulletin of the World Health Organization*, 81(1): 53–60

— (2003b) 'Risk and protective factors for coercive first sex in Rakai, Uganda', Paper presented at the Annual Meeting of the Population Association of America, Minneapolis, 1–3 May

Koenig, M. A., I. Zablotska, T. Lutalo et al. (2004) 'First coercive sex and subsequent HIV risk among young women in Rakai, Uganda', Unpublished paper

Krug, E. G., L. L. Dahlberg, J. A. Mercy et al. (2002) *World Report on Violence and Health*, Geneva: WHO

Lutalo, T., M. Kidugavu, M. Wawer et al. (2000) 'Trends and determinants of contraceptive use in Rakai District, Uganda, 1995–98', *Studies in Family Planning*, 31(3): 217–27

Maman, S., J. Campbell, M. D. Sweat et al. (2000) 'The intersections of HIV and violence: directions for future research and interventions', *Social Science and Medicine*, 50(4): 459–78

Maman, S., J. K. Mbwambo, N. M. Hogan et al. (2002) 'HIV-positive women report more lifetime partner violence: findings from a voluntary counseling and testing clinic in Dar es Salaam, Tanzania', *American Journal of Public Health*, 92(8): 1331–7

Martin, S. L., L. S. Kupper, L. L. Thomas et al. (1999a) 'Domestic violence and sexually transmitted diseases: the experience of prenatal care patients', *Public Health Reports*, 114(3): 262–8

Martin, S. L., B. Kilgallen, A. Ong Tsui et al. (1999b) 'Sexual behaviors and reproductive health outcomes: associations with wife abuse in India', *Journal of the American Medical Association*, 282(20): 1967–72

Matasha, E., T. Ntembelea, P. Mayaud et al. (1998) 'Sexual and reproductive health among primary and secondary school pupils in Mwanza, Tanzania: need for intervention', *AIDS Care*, 10(5): 571–82

Mulugeta, E., M. Kassaye and Y. Berhane (1998) 'Prevalence and outcomes of sexual violence among high school students', *Ethiopian Medical Journal*, 36(3): 167–74

Ntozi, J. and M. Lubega (1991) 'Patterns of sexual behaviour and the spread of AIDS in Uganda', in T. Dyson (ed.), *Sexual Behaviour and Networking: Anthropological and Socio-Cultural Studies on the Transmission of HIV*, Liege: Derouaux-Ordina Publications

Olowo-Freers, B. P. and T. G. Barton (1992) *In Pursuit of Fulfilment: Studies of Cultural Diversity and Sexual Behaviour in Uganda*, Kisubi, Uganda: Marianum Press

Quigley, M. A and D. Morgan (2000) 'Case-control study of risk factors for incident HIV infection in rural Uganda', *Journal of Acquired Immune Deficiency Syndrome*, 23(5): 418–25

Roosa, M. W., T. Jenn-Yun, C. Reinholtz et al. (1997) 'The relationship of childhood sexual abuse to teenage pregnancy', *Journal of Marriage and Family*, 59(1): 119–30

Rwenge, M. (2000) 'Sexual risk behaviors among young people in Bamenda, Cameroon', *International Family Planning Perspectives*, 26(3): 118–23, 130

Santelli, J., R. Rochat, K. Hatfield-Timajchy et al. (2003) 'The measurement and meaning of unintended pregnancy', *Perspectives on Sexual and Reproductive Health*, 35(2): 94–101

Schei, B. (1990) 'Psycho-social factors in pelvic pain: a controlled study of women living in physically abusive relationships', *Acta Obstetricia et Gynecologia Scandinavica*, 69(1): 67–71

— (1991) 'Physically abusive spouse – a risk factor of pelvic inflammatory disease', *Scandinavian Journal of Primary Health Care*, 9(1): 41–5

Schei, B. and L. S. Bakketeig (1989) 'Gynaecological impact of sexual and physical abuse by spouse: a study of a random sample of Norwegian women', *British Journal of Obstetrics and Gynaecology*, 96(12): 1379–83

Somse, P., M. K. Chapko and R. V. Hawkins (1993) 'Multiple sexual partners: results of a national HIV/AIDS survey in the Central African Republic', *AIDS*, 7(4): 579–83

Stewart, D. E. and A. Cecutti (1993) 'Physical abuse during pregnancy', *Canadian Medical Association Journal*, 149(9): 1257–63

UBOS (Uganda Bureau of Statistics) and ORC Macro (2001) *Uganda Demographic and Health Survey 2000–2001*, Calverton, MD: UBOS and ORC Macro van der Straten, A., R. King, O. Grinstead et al. (1995) 'Couple communication, sexual coercion and HIV risk reduction in Kigali, Rwanda', *AIDS*, 9(8): 935–44

— (1998) 'Sexual coercion, physical violence, and HIV infection among women in steady relationships in Kigali, Rwanda', *AIDS and Behavior*, 2(1): 61–73

Watts, C., M. Ndlovu, E. Koegh et al. (1998) 'Withholding of sex and forced sex: dimensions of violence against Zimbabwean women', *Reproductive Health Matters*, 6(12): 57–65

Wawer, M. J., N. K. Sewankambo, D. Serwadda et al. (1999) 'Control of sexually transmitted diseases for AIDS prevention in Uganda: a randomised community trial', *Lancet*, 353(9152): 525–35

WHO (World Health Organization) (1997) *Violence against Women: A Priority Health Issue*, Geneva: WHO

Wingood, G. M. and R. J. DiClemente (1997) 'The effects of an abusive primary partner on the condom use and sexual negotiation practices of African-American women', *American Journal of Public Health*, 87(6): 1016–18

Wingood, G. M., R. J. DiClemente and R. Anita (2000) 'Adverse consequences of intimate partner abuse among women in non-urban domestic violence shelters', *American Journal of Preventive Medicine*, 19(4): 270–75

Wood, K., F. Maforah and R. Jewkes (1998) '"He forced me to love him": putting violence on adolescent sexual health agendas', *Social Science and Medicine*, 47(2): 233–42

13 | Coercive sex and psycho-social outcomes in adolescents: exploring the role of parental relationships

VIKRAM PATEL AND GRACY ANDREW

Sexual abuse and violence embrace a continuum of behaviours ranging from threats and insults to unwanted touch and rape. Thus sexual violence may be defined as 'any sexual act, attempt to obtain a sexual act, unwanted sexual comments or advances, or acts of traffic, or otherwise, directed against a person's sexuality using coercion, by any person regardless of their relationship to the victim' (Krug et al. 2002: 149). Sexual abuse and violence in childhood and adolescence have been found to be strongly associated with adverse mental health outcomes in studies in developed countries (e.g. Diaz et al. 2002). Adverse mental health outcomes include depression, attempted suicide, medically unexplained symptoms, eating disorders and substance abuse. Surveys consistently show significantly higher rates of experiences of childhood sexual abuse in adults with mental health problems (e.g. Coid et al. 2003; Coxell et al. 1999; Edwards et al. 2003).

Recent research from developed countries has demonstrated that psycho-social health is profoundly influenced by contextual factors, in particular parental relationships. For example, a survey of 8,667 adults that reported a strong association between childhood abuse and poor mental health also reported an association between family environment and these factors, in that an emotionally abusive family environment accentuated the decrements in mental health scores (Edwards et al. 2003). Furthermore, adolescents exposed to severe adversity (such as sexual abuse) may have different outcomes based on the presence of other risk and protective factors in four social contexts, namely school, family, peer group and the neighbourhood (Jessor et al. 2003). There is, however, little comparable evidence on the impact of sexual abuse from developing countries.

This chapter explores the hypothesis that the quality of an adolescent's parental relationship influences the association between exposure to coercive sex and the risk of adverse psycho-social health outcomes.

The chapter draws on the findings of an adolescent health study conducted in Goa, India, that assessed the health and educational needs of adolescents in high school and explored linkages between sexual health, mental health and risk behaviours. The research was carried out in two stages, using a research design that combined qualitative and quantitative methods.

Only the findings of the quantitative study (a cross-sectional survey) are discussed in this chapter. Details of the qualitative findings are published elsewhere (Andrew et al. 2003).

Setting

Goa is one of the smallest states in India, with a population of 1.3 million. In 1998/99, Goa recorded a relatively low total fertility rate of 1.77 (compared to an all-India average of 2.85), a relatively high rate of women participating in decisions about their own healthcare (62 versus 52 per cent for India) and low levels of female illiteracy (25 versus 49 per cent). The rates of reproductive health complaints were high, however, with 40 per cent of women reporting a current reproductive health problem (IIPS and ORC Macro 2001).

The study was conducted among students in Standard XI of eight higher secondary schools in South Goa. Two schools out of a total of three in Margao, the largest town in Goa, made up the urban schools in the study, and six schools out of a total of eleven in the semi-urban and rural areas of Salcete district the rural schools. These schools were purposively selected with a view to sample similar numbers of urban and rural students and boys and girls.

Significant differences were observed between the urban and rural schools. In the urban schools, there were more students in each class and the classroom size was larger than in the rural schools. Students in the rural and semi-urban schools were more likely to speak Konkani and come from a lower socio-economic background, while in the urban schools students were more likely to speak English and come from a middle-class background.

A draft questionnaire was developed based on the information generated in the first stage. In the first stage, free lists, focus group discussions with students and teachers and key informant interviews were conducted. The draft questionnaire was then discussed with groups of adolescents and teachers to examine face validity and wording. Different versions were prepared for boys and girls to take into account gender differences regarding sexual relationships and sex-specific issues such as menstrual health. The questions were mainly closed-ended. Konkani translations of the draft questionnaire were prepared using translation–back-translation and consensus methods (Flaherty et al. 1988). The draft questionnaire was piloted with thirty students and revised for content and style in a pilot study. The revised questionnaire was then presented to the principals of all the participating schools (excluding the school that participated in the pilot study), with a request to discuss with and obtain consent from the respective Parent–Teacher Associations. The questionnaire was modified once again to incorporate suggestions and comments from parents and principals.

The sample covered all the students in Standard XI present in the selected schools on the day of the survey. The survey was conducted during school hours. Students were seated, as if in an examination hall, to ensure confidentiality of responses. Members of the study team explained the purpose of the survey, and students were given the opportunity to leave the room if they did not want to participate and to ask the study team questions. All the questionnaires were completed anonymously. Experienced professionals (psychologists and social workers) were present throughout the ninety-minute period allotted for completion of the questionnaire. If students were unclear about any question, they were requested to seek clarifications with one of the professionals present. At the end of the questionnaire, each respondent was provided with the name and contact telephone numbers of professional counsellors associated with Sangath, a non-governmental organization that works with young people and provides youth-friendly health services.

Three variables are of key relevance in our analysis: coercive sex, psycho-social outcomes and parental relationships.

Coercive sex Coercive sex was assessed on the basis of responses to the question determining whether the respondent had been forced to have sex in the past twelve months. This question was the last of five questions enquiring into forms of sexual abuse (someone talking to you about sex in a manner that made you uncomfortable; someone purposely brushing their private parts against you; someone forcing you to touch their body parts against your wishes; someone touching you in a sexual manner without your permission).

Psycho-social outcomes Five psycho-social outcomes were evaluated: the score on the twelve-item General Health Questionnaire (GHQ) (whose Konkani version has been validated in Goa; see Patel et al. 1998) as a measure of depression and anxiety; thoughts that life is not worth living in the past month; use of alcohol in the past month; cigarette smoking in the past month; and experience of frequent discharge from the genitals in the past month. The latter variable was included because there is growing evidence suggesting that complaints of sexual discharge are reflective of psycho-social stressors (Patel and Oomman 1999). Among adolescent boys, a well-described psychosomatic syndrome – the *dhat* syndrome – has been found to be associated with seminal discharge (Malhotra and Wig 1975). Each of the twelve items of the GHQ was coded to equal 1 if the response suggested depression and anxiety and 0 if it did not. The total score therefore ranged from 0 to 12. Based on the validity data for the GHQ, scores of 5 or more suggested clinically significant levels of symptoms of depression and anxiety, and a cut-off of 4/5 was used to define 'probable' case status for depression/anxiety (Patel et al. 1998).

Parental relationships Six items enquired about the nature of adolescents' relationships with their parents. Five of these – whether parents understood them; whether they felt neglected by their parents; whether they felt their parents spent enough time with them; whether they could talk freely with their father;

whether they could talk freely with their mother – were coded as dichotomous variables, assigned 0 if the relationship was reported to be positive and 1 if not. The sixth variable, whether they argued a lot with their parents, was an ordinal variable with scores of 0–2 (i.e. not at all/a little/a lot). A composite index of parental relationship was then computed by adding the scores of all six items. Thus, the index ranged from 0 to 7. The definition of a dichotomous outcome of good and poor parental relationships was based on the cut-off of the seventy-fifth centile of the composite score; on this rationale, those who attained a score of 4 or more were classified as having poor parental relationships and those who scored 0–3 were classified as having good parental relationships.

Findings

Of the 812 students present on the day of the survey, 811 agreed to participate. The average age was sixteen (range fourteen to nineteen; two students were aged twenty and twenty-one years respectively). Just over half (53 per cent) were boys. About half were Christian (49 per cent), and the rest (46 per cent) mainly Hindu. Students from the two urban schools made up 63 per cent of the sample. The majority of respondents belonged to literate families as more than half reported that their fathers and mothers had completed high school.

Experiences of sexual coercion were common; about one in three reported at least one of five different types of sexual abuse, and 6 per cent reported being forced to have sex in the past twelve months (Patel and Andrew 2001). The only demographic association with coercive sex was age; thus, 49 per cent of adolescents who had experienced coercive sex were over seventeen as compared to 29 per cent of younger adolescents (OR 2.3, 1.3–4.1, $p = 0.004$). Despite this, focus group discussions with adolescents and teachers (not reported here) revealed little awareness of the scale of the problem of sexual abuse in schools (ibid.).

Association between coercive sex and psycho-social variables, and parental relationships The hypothesis that parental relationships would influence the association between coercive sex and adverse psycho-social outcomes was tested and the findings of the step-wise analysis are presented separately for boys and girls in Tables 13.1 and 13.2 respectively. While for boys analyses were conducted on all five outcome indicators, for girls analyses were carried out for three outcomes as only a small number had consumed alcohol ($N = 4$) or smoked cigarettes ($N = 4$).

First, bi-variate analyses were carried out between coercive sex and each outcome (col. 3). Next, adjustments were made for age and school setting (urban/rural) in multi-variate logistic regression models (col. 4). Finally, the composite measure of parental relationship (dichotomously categorized as good/poor as discussed earlier) was added to the model as an explanatory dichotomous variable (col. 5). Column 6 shows the association of poor parental relationships

TABLE 13.1 Bi-variate and adjusted association of psycho-social health with coercive sex among boys (N = 430)

Psycho-social outcome	% reporting psycho-social outcome listed in col. 1	Bi-variate association with coercive sex	Adjusted for age and school setting	Adjusted for age, school setting and parental index	OR for parental index in the final model
Depression/anxiety	29.1	2.43	2.40	1.91	2.12
	(125)	1.1–5.2	1.1–5.2	0.8–4.4	0.9–5
(GHQ)		0.02	0.03	0.1	0.08
Life not worth living	23.0	1.55	1.62	1.40	2.52
	(99)	0.7–3.5	0.7–3.8	0.6–3.4	1.1–5.7
		0.2	0.2	0.4	0.02
Alcohol consumption	9.5	2.72	2.58	2.41	2.55
	(41)	1–7.1	0.9–7.1	0.9–6.7	1.1–5.7
		0.04	0.06	0.08	0.02
Cigarette smoking	9.1	1.67	1.46	1.2	2.59
	(39)	0.5–5,1	0.4–4.7	0.4–3.9	1.1–5.9
		0.3	0.5	0.7	0.02
Sexual discharge	9.8	3.32	5.43	4.44	2.18
	(42)	1.3–8.3	1.9–15.2	1.5–12.7	0.9–5.1
		0.01	0.001	0.006	0.07

Note: Figures in brackets are actual numbers of respondents in each category. Values for the associations with coercive sex and parental index are odds ratios, 95 per cent confidence intervals and two-tailed p test results.

with the outcome in the final model. Odds ratios and 95 per cent confidence intervals are reported. Tests of significance are two-tailed.

Table 13.1 shows that among boys, on bi-variate analysis, statistically significant associations emerged between the experience of coercive sex and three adverse psycho-social outcomes, namely anxiety and depression, alcohol use and sexual discharge. There was no marked change in the odds ratios after adjustment for age and school setting (urban versus rural) (col. 4). In the final model (cols 5 and 6), however, where parental relationship was included as a risk factor, only one association (with sexual discharge) remained significant. In contrast, in the same model poor parental relationships remained significantly associated with most of the psycho-social outcomes even after adjustments were made for age and school setting.

Among girls, on bi-variate analysis, statistically significant associations emerged between the experience of coercive sex and two of three psycho-social outcomes (see Table 13.2). As in the findings for boys, significant associations were noted with depression and anxiety and the experience of sexual discharge, and there was no marked change in the odds ratios after adjustment for age and school setting. In the final model, none of the associations between coercive sex and psycho-social outcomes was significant; in the same model, poor parental relationships were significantly associated with all three psycho-social outcomes.

Discussion

This chapter reports secondary analysis of data collected in a study of adolescent health among students attending higher secondary schools in Goa, India. The analysis focused on the influence of parental relationships on the association between coercive sex and adverse psycho-social outcomes. The results of the study suggest that a considerable number of adolescents have experienced some form of sexual abuse, and those who have experienced coercive sex are significantly more likely to have poorer mental health, and more likely to abuse alcohol and to experience physical health problems such as sexual discharge compared to others (Patel and Andrew 2001).

Approximately one in twenty students reported experiencing coercive sex in the previous year. Boys and girls were equally affected. Those who had experienced coercive sex had a higher risk of a range of adverse psycho-social outcomes, including higher rates of non-specific physical complaints such as sexual discharge, poorer mental health including depression and anxiety, greater suicidal tendencies and, among boys, greater alcohol abuse. These findings remained significant even after adjusting for age and school setting. On adjusting for parental relationships, however, all the associations were attenuated, becoming non-significant for most of the outcomes in both sexes. The effect of this attenuation was more marked for girls. This finding suggests that the association

TABLE 13.2 Bi-variate and adjusted association of psycho-social health with coercive sex among girls (N = 381)

Psycho-social outcome	(%) reporting psycho-social outcome (listed in col. 1)	Bi-variate association with coercive sex	Adjusted for age and school setting	Adjusted for age, school setting and parental index	OR for parental index in the final model
Depression/anxiety	40.4	2.73	2.75	1.96	5.7
	(154)	1.1–6.7	1.1–6.7	0.8–4.9	2.1–15.3
(GHQ)		0.02	0.03	0.1	<0.001
Life not worth living	28.9	2.15	2.21	1.27	6.1
	(110)	0.9–5.1	0.9–5.3	0.5–3.2	2.2–16.7
		0.08	0.07	0.6	<0.001
Sexual discharge	15.2	2.81	2.80	2.05	6.01
	(58)	1.1–6.7	1.1–7.2	0.8–5.5	2.3–15.9
		0.02	0.03	0.1	<0.001

Note: Proportions are rounded off to the nearest full integer. Figures in brackets are actual numbers of respondents. Values for the associations with coercive sex and parental index are odds ratios, 95 per cent confidence intervals and two-tailed p test results.

between coercive sex and adverse psycho-social outcomes is influenced by the effect of parental relationships.

There are three possible mechanisms for this relationship between the three variables. One pathway leads from poor parental relationships to a heightened vulnerability to experience of coercive sex in adolescents; in this model, poor parental relationships are the cause of poor psycho-social outcomes, with coercive sex being a mediating or proximal risk factor. The second mechanism is when poor parental relationships are associated with both coercive sex and the psycho-social outcome, i.e. poor parental relationships are a confounder in the association between coercive sex and psycho-social outcomes. A third mechanism is where coercive sex is a cause of adverse psycho-social outcomes, but the quality of parental relationships modifies this effect such that, if the relationship is good, then the adverse impact of coercive sex is mitigated. Irrespective of which pathway is the most plausible explanation, it is evident from the study that the quality of parental relationships is an important variable in studying the risk of experiencing coercive sex and the impact of coercive sex on adolescent psycho-social health.

A limitation of this study is its cross-sectional design, which makes causal interpretations difficult; thus, it is possible to interpret some associations in the reverse direction, for example adolescents who abuse alcohol finding themselves in situations where coercive sex is more likely to occur, or adolescents who are depressed finding solace in relationships that are abusive. Other limitations include the use of screening questionnaires for the assessment of mental health and the use of a school sample that renders the data of limited generalizability, especially in terms of comparing environmental contexts.

New evidence from a community cohort study may throw fresh light on the influence of parental relationships on the prevalence and impact of sexual violence/coercion among adolescents. A study of approximately two thousand twelve-to-sixteen-year-old adolescents in Goa is in progress. In addition to quantitative data on the environmental and parental context, the study includes a qualitative component investigating parental relationships among adolescents who have experienced abuse or violence. This study uses structured, diagnostic interviews for depressive and anxiety disorders.

In conclusion, the analysis presented in this chapter suggests preliminary evidence that the adverse impact of coercive sex on psycho-social outcomes, such as depression and substance abuse, is considerably influenced by the quality of parental relationships. These findings highlight the interaction between psycho-social factors and sexual violence/coercion and the quality of the relationship that adolescents have with their parents. It is notable that most adolescents in all parts of the world live with their parents, and the family environment is a powerful influence on psycho-social development. It is perhaps not surprising that the family environment should influence both the vulnerability of adolescents to experiencing coercive sex and the adverse impact of coercive sex. Clearly, research on coercive sex must take into account this developmental aspect of adolescents in its study design, for example by using valid measures of parental relationships in quantitative studies, and to explore the gender differences in parental relationships and their impact on risk behaviours.

From a programme perspective, the findings of the study reported in this chapter suggest that there is a need for a broad approach to adolescent health which considers the diverse influences and pathways to risk behaviours. Interventions aimed at improving reproductive health must also ensure personal safety and prevention of abuse, enhance mental health and self-esteem, discourage substance abuse and improve communication skills, particularly with parents. From a public health perspective, educating parents about healthy communication with adolescents may well be the single most important prevention strategy for facilitating a safe, pleasurable and healthy transition to adulthood.

Note

We acknowledge the NIMHANS Small Grants Program for supporting the study, the WHO Special Program of Research, Development and Research Training in Human Reproduction for supporting the adolescent cohort study in progress, the MacArthur Foundation for supporting our advocacy and training work in adolescent health and the Wellcome Trust for supporting the community cohort study of psycho-social predictors of women's reproductive health. (For more on Sangath and to download the study report visit: <www.sangath.com>.)

References

Andrew, G., V. Patel and J. Ramakrishna (2003) 'Sex, studies or strife? What to integrate in adolescent health services', *Reproductive Health Matters*, 11: 120–29

Coid, J., A. Petruckevitch, W. S. Chung et al. (2003) 'Abusive experiences and psychiatric morbidity in women primary care attenders', *British Journal of Psychiatry*, 183: 332–9

Coxell, A., M. King, G. Mezey et al. (1999) 'Lifetime prevalence, characteristics, and associated problems of non-consensual sex in men: cross sectional survey', *British Medical Journal*, 318: 846–50

Diaz, A., E. Simantov and V. I. Rickert (2002) 'Effect of abuse on health: results of a national survey', *Archives of Pediatrics and Adolescent Medicine*, 156: 811–17

Edwards, V. J., G. W. Holden, V. J. Felitti et al. (2003) 'Relationship between multiple forms of childhood maltreatment and adult mental health in community respondents: results from the adverse childhood experiences study', *American Journal of Psychiatry*, 160: 1453–60

Flaherty, J. A., F. M. Gaviria, D. Pathak et al. (1988) 'Developing instruments for cross-cultural psychiatric research', *Journal of Nervous and Mental Disease*, 176: 257–63

IIPS (International Institute for Population Sciences) and ORC Macro (2001) *National Family Health Survey-2, 1998–99: India*, Mumbai: IIPS

Jessor, R., M. Turbin and F. Costa (2003) 'Adolescent problem behaviour in China and the US: a cross-national study of psycho-social protective factors', *Journal of Research on Adolescence*, 13: 329–60

Krug, E. G., L. L. Dahlberg, J. A. Mercy et al. (2002) *World Report on Violence and Health*, Geneva: World Health Organization

Malhotra, H. K. and N. N. Wig (1975) 'Dhat syndrome: a culture-bound sex neurosis of the Orient', *Archives of Sexual Medicine*, 4: 519–28

Patel, V. and G. Andrew (2001) 'Gender, sexual abuse and risk behaviours: a cross-sectional survey in schools in Goa', *National Medical Journal of India*, 14: 263–7

Patel, V. and N. M. Oomman (1999) 'Mental health matters too: gynecological morbidity and depression in South Asia', *Reproductive Health Matters*, 7: 30–38

Patel, V., J. Pereira and A. Mann (1998) 'Somatic and psychological models of common mental disorders in primary care in India', *Psychological Medicine*, 28: 135–43

FIVE | Legal, education and health system responses

14 | The vulnerability of adolescence: legal responses to non-consensual sexual experiences of young persons in India

INDIRA JAISING

While it is recognized that a considerable number of young people experience non-consensual sex in India, the legal responses to these issues remain limited. This chapter explores the issue of young people's experiences of non-consensual sex within the Indian legal framework and discusses possible legal responses. Reforms in the existing law are also suggested.

Under Indian law, the issue of consent to sexual activity is immaterial for persons below the particular age of majority, defined differently under particular laws. The law criminalizes all sexual activity of all persons below the relevant age, which affects minors engaged in both consensual and non-consensual sexual activity. While the Indian Penal Code (IPC) punishes non-consensual sexual activity with women, including rape (Section 375, IPC), child prostitution (Section 372, IPC) and indecent assault upon women (Section 354, IPC), all sexual intercourse with girls below the age of sixteen is also criminalized (Section 375 [6], IPC).

For the purposes of this chapter, the term 'non-consensual sexual experiences of young persons' refers to sexual violence perpetrated against persons below the age of majority. 'Sexual violence' is an umbrella term that refers to any unwanted act of a sexual nature, ranging from exhibitionism to penetration, that causes a person to feel uncomfortable, humiliated, frightened or intimidated. Offences of sexual violence are also committed when the victim is unaware of or confused about his/her reactions to such offences and may not recognize these acts as sexual coercion.

International jurisprudence, including the Statute of the International Criminal Court (Article 7[9], Statute of the International Criminal Court [Rome Statute]) and judgments of the International Criminal Tribunal for Rwanda (*Prosecutor* v. *Akayesu [Judgment]*, ICTR-96-4-T, T Ch I [2 September 1998]), has adopted comprehensive interpretations of acts of sexual violence which cover penetrative and non-penetrative forms of abuse. The Declaration on the Elimination of Violence against Women (DEVAW) defines violence to include all threats or acts of gender-based violence that result in physical, sexual or psychological harm (Article 1, DEVAW; <www.iwhc.org>). 'Sexual violence' is, therefore, a comprehensive term incorporating all intentions, words, gestures and acts of a sexual but unwanted nature.

Adolescents and young persons are vulnerable to sexual violence because of their age. The forms of sexual violence they face include (but are not limited to) rape, child sexual abuse, criminal intimidation and insults, threat or the use of criminal force, sexual harassment, forced prostitution and trafficking. Women and girls form the majority of victims of sexual violence, and the specific acts perpetrated particularly on girls include marital rape, indecent assault, outrage to modesty and female genital mutilation.

International conventions have recognized that governments have an obligation to adopt aggressive measures to protect all young persons (especially women and girls) from all forms of violence, including sexual violence, and to punish such violence (see DEVAW, adopted by the UN General Assembly at the 85th Plenary Meeting, 20 December 1993, UN Doc. A/Res/48/104). The obligation of states to protect children from sexual exploitation by providing special measures has been recognized under the International Covenant on Civil and Political Rights (ICCPR) (Article 24), the International Covenant on Economic, Social and Cultural Rights (ICESCR) (Articles 10[3], 12), and the Convention on the Rights of the Child (CRC) (Articles 19, 34, 39). The Programme of Action of the International Conference on Population and Development (ICPD) (Principles 4, 8, 9, 11) and the Convention on the Elimination of All Forms of Discrimination against Women (CEDAW) (Articles 1, 5) recognize the principle of gender equality and the need to eliminate violence against women. In India, in addition to these international conventions, the obligations of the state to protect children are also enshrined in the Constitution of India (Articles 14, 21, 23, 39[f], Constitution of India, 1950).

Definitions of 'child', 'adolescent' and 'young person'

The provisions in international law have not provided a comprehensive definition of 'child', 'adolescent' or 'young person'. The leading covenants on human rights, including the ICCPR and the ICESCR, also do not provide a definition, although they have provisions dealing explicitly with 'children', 'young persons' and 'juveniles'. The CRC defines a child as anyone under the age of eighteen, unless majority has been attained earlier under the concerned law of specific countries (Article 1, CRC). In a joint statement in 1998, the World Health Organization (WHO), the United Nations Children's Fund (UNICEF) and United Nations Population Fund (UNFPA) agreed on the following categorization: adolescent (ten to nineteen years), youth (fifteen to twenty-four years) and young person (ten to twenty-four years) (CRLP 1999: 2).

In contrast, under Indian law there is no definition of 'adolescent' or 'young person', and the law primarily deals with one category – that of legal minority, which usually includes all individuals aged eighteen years or younger. Under the Indian Majority Act, 1875, a minor is deemed to have attained majority on reaching eighteen years of age (Section 3). Similarly, minority extends to eighteen years in the definition of 'child' under the Juvenile Justice Act, 2000 (Section 2[k], Juvenile Justice [Care and Protection of Children] Act, 2000) or the definition of a minor or a female child under the Child Marriage Restraint Act, 1929 (Section 2[d] and Section 2[a] respectively). The Child Marriage Restraint Act, 1929, however, follows a dual definition of 'child' based on sex. A child, if male, is a person under twenty-one years of age, and if female, under eighteen years of age (Section 2[a]). It also recognizes a special category of 'minor' as a person under eighteen (Section 2[d]). The Indian Penal Code does not have a specific definition of an adolescent or a young person. Section 10 of the Indian Penal Code defines a 'man' and a 'woman' as a male human being or female human being of any age (Section 10, IPC). The age of the victim is relevant under the Indian Penal Code for particular offences committed on minors, including kidnapping (Sections 361, 363-A, 366, 366-A, 366-B, 369, IPC) and rape of a girl under sixteen (Section 375[6], IPC). There are, however, significant exceptions to definitions of the age of majority. For example, while the age of consent for a woman under the rape law is sixteen (see Section 375, IPC), the relevant age of a female victim in an offence of marital rape is fifteen (exception to Section 375, IPC).

Types of sexual violence

One of the most extreme forms of sexual violence is rape, which is often defined as penile–vaginal penetration. A restrictive definition of sexual violence would seriously underestimate the number of children and adolescents who have experienced such abuse.

The offence of rape or forced sexual intercourse has no statutory definition in India (see, for example, Justice Mallimath Committee on Reforms of Criminal Justice System, 2003: 192). Under Section 375 of the Indian Penal Code, any male who penetrates a female's vagina with his penis, in the absence of valid consent, is guilty of rape. As Section 375 is limited to penile–vaginal penetration, rape as described in this section is a gender-specific offence, which means that only a male can be a perpetrator and only a female can be a victim. Existing forms of sexual assault, however, are not restricted to male-to-female offences. Section 377 of the Indian Penal Code punishes 'carnal intercourse against the order of nature'. In the context of sexual violence, this section has also been used to penalize practices of sexual assault that are not strictly penile–vaginal (see *Brother John Antony* v. *State*, 1992 Cr LJ 1352 [Mad]) and do not fall under the rubric of Section 375. The creative use of Section 377 can be applied to child abuse, and especially the abuse of girls and women, where the abuse may not fall within the traditional understanding of rape under Section 375. Male children and adolescents who have been sexually assaulted can also file complaints under this provision.

The use of Section 377 has, however, been widely criticized because it seeks to outlaw even consensual sexual relations that do not fall within the traditional understanding of sex. In 1971 the Law Commission of India favoured retaining this provision, thereby enabling the prosecution of private and consensual sexual conduct perceived as immoral (Law Commission of India Report 1971: 281). In 2000, however, the Law Commission recommended the deletion of Section 377 (Law Commission of India Report 2000: 34).

There is an urgent need to amend Section 377 to exclude consensual sexual relations from its ambit, while it should continue to prohibit the sexual abuse of children and adolescents under the age of eighteen. The provision must also prosecute non-consensual sex that is not defined as rape under Section 375, particularly sexually violent acts against minors. The problem remains, however, that at present Section 377 is restricted to penetrative abuse (Explanation to Section 377, IPC), and the actual sentences imposed by courts in these cases are usually not heavy (for example, in Fazal Rab Choudhary, 1983 Cr LJ 632[SC], the sentence was reduced to six months of imprisonment; and in Charanjit Singh, 1986 Cr LJ 173 [H & P], the offence of committing sodomy twice with a minor was punished with one year's imprisonment and a fine of Rs 500). In addition, there are difficulties in determining the issue of consent in sexual relations. In *Rameshwar* v. *State of Rajasthan* (AIR 1952 SC 54), the court held that in the case of 'unnatural offences' the issue of consent was immaterial if the person was under the age of consent. If the person was over the age of consent, however, the court would consider the testimony of the victim as suspect as coming from an accomplice to the offence.

As discussed above, the main limitation of the existing laws on rape under Section 375 and 'unnatural offences' under Section 377 is that they are confined to penetrative abuse (see Explanation to Section 375, 377, IPC). In a recent judgment, the Supreme Court has shown its reluctance to redefine rape as an act that goes beyond penile–vaginal penetration. In *Sakshi* v. *Union of India* ([2004] 5 SCC 518), the court held that only sexual intercourse involving penetration of the vagina by the penis fell within the purview of Section 375 of the Indian Penal Code, adding the explanation that penetration is sufficient to constitute the sexual intercourse necessary for the offence of rape.

In 2000, the Law Commission of India suggested replacing the offence of rape under Section 375 with the offence of graded sexual assault, which would include not only penile penetration but also penetration by any other part of the body (such as fingers or toes) or by any object (Law Commission of India Report 2000: 19). Additionally, the Justice Mallimath Committee on Reforms of Criminal Justice has suggested that all other forms of forcible penetration, including penile/oral, penile/anal, object or finger/vaginal and object or finger/anal, should be made a separate offence with punishment similar to that under Section 376 of the Indian Penal Code (Justice Mallimath Committee on Reforms of Criminal Justice System 2003: 192–3). It must be noted that both these proposals require the act of penetration, even though not limited to penile–vaginal penetration, as an essential element of the offence. Thus, even these definitions would continue to exclude many offences, including unwanted touch, sexual harassment and other non-penetrative forms of sexual abuse.

The Law Commission of India has, however, recommended the inclusion of a new section (Section 376E) in the Indian Penal Code that will deal exclusively with the offence of 'unlawful sexual contact' (Law Commission of India Report 2000: 34) and cover a wide variety of offences, including sexual harassment and other forms of non-consensual sex at the workplace and elsewhere. The new section would deal with the following. Sub-section (1) would cover non-consensual touching of any part of the body by persons who are not the spouse of the person. Non-consensual touching can occur directly, or indirectly with an object. Sub-section (2) would deal specifically with sexually suggestive and offensive touch perpetrated on young persons, and would invite a more severe punishment. It should be noted that 'young person' in this proposed section is defined as a person under the age of sixteen.

In addition to other existing provisions, Section 354 of the Indian Penal Code punishes assault or the use of criminal force upon a woman with the intent to outrage her modesty. This section can be used to punish the perpetration of non-consensual sex on young women, beyond the separate offence of rape. Although the word 'modesty' is not defined in the Indian Penal Code, the Supreme Court, in *Rupan Deol Bajaj* v. *Kanwar Pal Singh Gill* ([1995] 6 SCC 194), emphasized that the ultimate test for ascertaining whether modesty has been outraged is if the action of the offender is such as could be perceived as capable of shocking the decency of a woman. Section 509 of the Indian Penal Code makes the intention to insult the modesty of a woman the essential element of the offence. Both Sections 354 and 509 exclude male children and adolescents/young men from the ambit of these offences. On the other hand, Section 506 punishes criminal intimidation, and male victims and women who suffer offences that do not fall within the ambit of Section 509 may file a complaint under this section.

Sexual violence in fiduciary and non-fiduciary relationships

Fiduciary relationships Minors may experience sexual violence in fiduciary relationships, which are relationships involving trust. Sexual violence perpetrated in fiduciary relationships includes abuse in custodial situations and within the family, such as between a husband and wife or in incestuous relationships, for example by a parent, more powerful sibling or other relative. It also encompasses offences committed by an authority figure or those who are close enough to be 'as if' family or are involved with the child in a functional role, involving trust (RAHI 1998: 6). Unfortunately, while minors have been and continue to be sexually abused by their fathers, brothers, grandfathers, uncles and other trusted people, the Indian Penal Code does not define the offence of incest or punish the offence as such.

Minors may also experience sexual violence in custodial situations. Section 376C of the Indian Penal Code penalizes superintendents or managers of jails, remand homes and other places of custody who have taken advantage of their official position and authority to have coerced or induced sexual intercourse with their female inmates. This provision also covers offences committed in women's and children's institutions, whether an orphanage or home for the care of women and children (Explanation 2, Section 376, IPC). Section 376D of the Indian Penal Code punishes intercourse by any member of the management or staff of a hospital with any woman in that hospital. The offence is committed if the intercourse was conducted within the precincts of the hospital or any institution for the admission and medical treatment of people during convalescence and rehabilitation (Explanation 3 to Section 376, IPC). These provisions would also cover the context of specialized institutions, where caretakers sexually abuse mentally ill children or other children in their care. It should be noted that these provisions are limited to the act of sexual intercourse and do not cover the full range of sexually coercive behaviour. Further, these offences are categorized as 'sexual intercourse not amounting to rape' and hence carry a less severe punishment than rape.

Another example of a fiduciary relationship is that between a husband and wife. As mentioned earlier, the Indian Penal Code does not recognize marital rape as an offence if the woman is older than fifteen (Exception to Section 375, IPC). Section 376A, however, recognizes an offence of rape when a man has sexual intercourse with his wife at a time when she was living separate from him under a legal decree of separation or custom. It makes clear, therefore, that all other instances of marital rape are not punishable under the existing law. Representatives of NGOs have recommended the deletion of Section 376A, along with the marital rape exception to Section 375, to avoid the discriminatory classification between an offending husband and other offenders. The Law Commission of India has not, however, recommended the deletion of the exception to Section 375, citing its reluctance to interfere when the bond of marriage has not been severed (Law Commission of India Report 2000: 28). The commission has, however, suggested an enhancement of the punishment under Section 376A from the current two years to seven years' imprisonment (ibid.: 28–9).

The Child Marriage Restraint Act of 1929 was enacted to prevent the occurrence of child marriages (Section 5). Although the act attempts to outlaw marriages of young women and men under the ages of eighteen and twenty-one respectively, such marriages do frequently occur. In 2000, there were ninety-two reported cases of child marriage, which reflected a 58.6 per cent increase over the previous year (NCRB 2002: 213). The mild sentences imposed under the act on parents or guardians of the minor who have abetted or permitted such marriages (Section 6) have not deterred prospective offenders from forcing minors into marriage. The act also excludes women offenders from imprisonment. As the exception to Section 375 does not punish marital rape over the age of fifteen, it is clear that girls over this age have no legal protection. Further, although international safeguards under CEDAW require the registration of all marriages (Article 16[2]), the Indian government has declared its inability to comply with this requirement, making it more difficult to eliminate exploitative practices such as child marriage.

In the light of instances of sexual violence in fiduciary relationships coming before the courts, the Law Commission has suggested a modification to Section 376 to prescribe severe punishment when sexual assault is committed by a father, grandfather, brother or 'any other person being in the position of trust or authority towards the other person' (Law Commission of India Report 2000: 23). A foreseeable problem with this provision is that it does not define 'position of trust or authority'. The United States Code Section 2243 (b)(2), which deals with sexual abuse of a minor or ward, elaborates on the definition of authority, as 'under the custodial, supervisory, or disciplinary authority'. The adoption of a similar definition in Indian law would cover situations of incest within the family as well as abuse by teachers and other disciplinary authorities.

Non-fiduciary relationships Minors may also face sexual coercion and violence in non-fiduciary relationships. The most common among such types of sexual exploitation are economic coercion due to poverty, particularly in developing countries, organized crime, including sex tourism and trafficking, and socially exploitative practices.

Minors and young people may be coerced into prostitution and trafficking in exchange for gifts and money. In addition to poverty, the factors contributing to the trafficking of girls include their low status, lack of education, inadequate or non-existent legislation relating to trafficking and the lack of law enforcement (<www.iwhc.org/uploads/wsc-10traffickingfactsht.pdf>).

The CRC forbids the sexual exploitation and trafficking of children (Articles 11, 21, 34, 35, CRC). It also ensures the child's right to physical and psychological recovery after abuse (Articles 32, 34, 36, 398, CRC). Article 6 of CEDAW allows state parties to take appropriate measures to suppress all forms of trafficking of women and the exploitation or prostitution of women. Article 23 of the Constitution of India prohibits trafficking of human beings.

Although the Indian Penal Code punishes forcing a child into prostitution (Section 372, IPC), there was a 15 per cent increase in the number of cases of girls being sold for prostitution in 2000 over 1999 (NCRB 2002). Despite the presence of special legislation, the Immoral Traffic (Prevention) Act, 1956, there has been a steady increase in the trafficking of girls under the law since 1997, with an increase of 1.6 per cent in 1999 (ibid.: 211). Cases registered under this Act showed an increase of 27.8 per cent during 2002 (ibid.). There has also been a rise in specialized categories of organized prostitution, such as sex tourism, in states such as Goa that cater solely to the demand of tourists. The victims of child prostitution in Goa are mostly migrants from other states (O'Connell Davidson and Sanchez Taylor 1996: 3).

Other socially coercive practices and customs, such as the *devdasi* cult (the practice of 'giving' girls to the temple), are also responsible for the sexual exploitation and abuse of young persons. The courts have held that illegal trafficking of women and children includes making them *devdasis*, and violates Article 23 of the Constitution of India (*Gaurav Jain* v. *Union of India*, AIR 1997 SC 3021).

Minors as perpetrators of sexual violence

Special circumstances arise when the perpetrator of sexual violence is a minor himself. The Indian Penal Code does not include in its purview any offences committed by a child under seven (Section 82, IPC). If the perpetrator is between seven and twelve, the Indian Penal Code ignores such offences, provided the child was incapable of comprehending its consequences (Section 83, IPC). The question arises, however, as to the liability of minors between twelve and eighteen for offences of sexual violence, including rape. Under the existing laws on rape, a minor can be convicted of rape even if he has consensual sex with a girl below under sixteen. This is a particular area of concern, especially when teenage consensual sex is increasing.

Procedures in court for minor victims

Testimony of the child witness The Indian Evidence Act, 1872, allows all persons to testify in a court of law (Section 118). This includes children, and therefore the provision is of critical importance for prosecutions in which the victim is a minor. In *Rameshwar* v. *State of Rajasthan* (AIR 1957 SC 54), the court held that children can give evidence provided they are found able to understand questions put to them and to give rational answers (AIR 1957 SC 54).

A prosecutrix complaining of having been a victim of rape is not an accomplice to the crime (*State of Rajasthan* v. *N.K*, 2000 SCC Cri 898, 907, para. 11; *Bodhisattwa Gautam* v. *Subhra Chakraborty*, 1996 1 SCC 490, 403, para. 21). There is no rule of law that prevents her testimony being acted upon without corroboration by material facts. In *Narayanamma* v. *State of Karnataka* ([1994] 5 SCC 728, 733, para. 5), the court held that the word of a fourteen-year-old prosecutrix could not be disbelieved on mere generalities. Earlier, the law contained in Section 155(4) of the Indian Evidence Act, 1872, linked the credibility of the prosecutrix with her 'general immoral character'. This provision was used to belittle the credibility of some young persons as witnesses. The Supreme Court, in *State of Maharashtra* v. *Madhukar* ([1991] 1 SCC 57), has laid down that the 'unchastity' (implying a woman of immoral character) of a woman does not make her 'open to any or every person to violate her person as and when he wishes' and that she is equally entitled to the protection of the law. The Law Commission of India has also recommended the deletion of Section 155(4) of the Indian Evidence Act, 1872, citing the absence of a connection between an offence of sexual assault and general immoral character (Section 155[4] of the Indian Evidence Act; Law Commission of India Report 2000: 73). Following these developments, Section 155(4) was removed from the statute books by an amendment in 2003.

A child victim of sexual violence enjoys the right to privacy, and therefore the procedures of in-camera trials ought to be encouraged to secure her testimony. Section 327 of the Criminal Procedure Code (CrPC) provides for in-camera trials for certain types of rape within custodial situations. This provision helps shield victims from publicity during and post-trial, as anonymity is important in the Indian context because victims of rape are often shunned by society. In *State of Punjab* v. *Gurmit Singh* ([1996] 2 SCC 384), the court held that trials for rape ought to be held in-camera as a rule, and open trials can only be the exception. It has, however, been pointed out that as the lawyers for both parties remain present during in-camera proceedings, the child victim continues to provide her testimony in a hostile environment.

Special protocols on video conferencing could ensure that a child victim is not in the vicinity of the accused and his counsel. In *State of Maharashtra* v. *Praful Desai* ([2003] 4 SCC 601), the Supreme Court held that recording of evidence by video conferencing was permissible in cases in which the attendance of the witness cannot be procured without delay, expense and inconvenience. The practice of video conferencing to record evidence is prevalent in the USA and has been upheld by the US Supreme Court in *Maryland* v. *Santra Aun Craig* (497 US 836 [1990]).

In its most recent judgment on the issue of sexual violence to date (2004), the Supreme Court has categorically recognized the importance of effective procedures that are sensitive to victims in trials of sexual assault. The court observed: 'Rules of procedure are the handmaiden of justice and are meant to advance and not to obstruct the cause of justice. It is therefore permissible for the court to expand or enlarge the meanings of such provisions in order to elicit the truth and do justice to the parties' (*Sakshi* v. *Union of India* [2004] 5 SCC 518).

In the Sakshi judgment, the court laid down that in trials of sexual assault the following could also be implemented in addition to existing procedures for the protection of the victim.

A screen or a similar arrangement may be made available whereby the victim or witnesses (who may be as vulnerable as the victim) do not see the body or the face of the accused.

The questions posed in the cross-examination on behalf of the accused, in so far as they relate directly to the incident, should be given in writing to the presiding officer of the court, who may put them to the victim or witnesses in a language that is clear and not embarrassing.

The victim of child abuse or rape, while giving testimony in court, should be allowed sufficient breaks as and when required (*Sakshi* v. *Union of India* [2004] 5 SCC 518).

The question that arises is whether the provision of such special protocols to protect the victim violates the right of the accused to a fair trial under the constitution and the law governing criminal procedure. In *State of Maharashtra* v. *Praful Desai* ([2003] 4 SCC 601), the court held that the recording of evidence by video conferencing was a 'procedure established by law' under Article 21 of the constitution, and did not violate the rights of the accused. The court went on to say that although the rights of the accused must be safeguarded, they should not be overemphasized to the extent of forgetting that the victim has rights too. The jurisprudence of the European Court of Human Rights also indicates that 'various ways are conceivable in which the right to adversarial proceedings are ensured, as long as the other party is aware and gets a real opportunity to comment' (Eur. Court HR, case of *Brandsetter* v. *Austria*, Judgment of 28 August 1991, Series A, no. 211, pp. 27–8, para. 67).

Other provisions The legal system protects minor by appointing a guardian *ad litem* in civil law (Section 146, Code of Civil Procedure, 1908) and providing for an expeditious trial in criminal law (Section 309, Code of Criminal Procedure, 1973). In addition, the Law Commission has recommended a special statutory provision for the interrogation of child victims of sexual violence by female police officers alone, and, in their absence, by qualified female social workers (Section 160[3], Criminal Procedure Code, Law Commission of India Report 2000: 41–3). It should be noted that in decisions pertaining to sentencing for acts of sexual violence against minors, the age of the minor remains relevant (*State of Karnataka* v. *Krishnappa* [2000] 4 SCC 75). The younger the victim, the more severe the punishment.

Procedures for minors as perpetrators

There are instances when a minor can be the perpetrator of sexual violence against another minor. In such a case, the Juvenile Justice Act, 2000, requires that certain measures are taken for the protection of the juvenile offender. For example, it provides that the privacy of the individual offender is maintained by ensuring confidentiality of the proceedings and reports (Sections 21, 51).

General remedies

In addition to the specific penalties under criminal law, there are certain remedies available to victims of sexual violence under general criminal and civil law. Section 357 of the Criminal Procedure Code allows for limited compensation to be paid to victims of crime. The remedy is generally available if the victim is entitled to relief in a civil court (Tandon and Tandon 1993: 271). In instances of custodial rape, the obligation of the state to protect its citizens has been invoked, and the state has also been directed to pay compensation to victims of rape (*P. Rathinam* v. *State of Gujarat*, 1994 SCC [Cri] 1163; *Arvinder Singh Bagga* v. *State of U.P.* [1994] 6 SCC 565). In addition, the High Courts possess inherent powers under Section 482 of the Criminal Procedure Code to pass any orders necessary to prevent the abuse of such processes in any court and to secure the ends of justice.

Ethical concerns

There is an urgent need for an ethical response to the offence of sexual violence, especially among young people. On the one hand, for example, while the existing law does not criminalize incest as such, the sexual exploitation of minors in familial settings continues. At the same time, on the other hand, the rise in the practice of consensual sex among young people demands ethical and social responses. While the existing law criminalizes all sexual intercourse with young women under the age of sixteen, there are innumerable instances of consensual sexual intercourse between adolescents. The existing dichotomy between the law and practice needs to be addressed.

Conclusion

The law in India does not adequately recognize the issue of non-consensual sexual experiences of young persons or the special vulnerability that adolescents face by virtue of their age in situations of sexual coercion. What is therefore required is a simultaneous process of legislative and judicial reform to incorporate this recognition in the laws and judicial processes of the country.

A first step in this direction would be the adoption of a comprehensive definition and understanding of both 'sexual violence' and 'coercion', based on the particular experiences of adolescent communities and on developments in international and national law. This understanding of sexual violence must be based on the different fiduciary and non-fiduciary relationships that adolescents experience which involve coercion. Any process of reform must emphasize sensitive and effective procedures that recognize the reality of adolescents' vulnerability, and ensure that this vulnerability is not aggravated in courts of law.

References

CRLP (Center for Reproductive Law and Policy) (1999) *Implementing Adolescent Reproductive Rights through the Convention on the Rights of the Child*, New York: CRLP

Justice Mallimath Committee on Reforms of Criminal Justice System (2003) vol. 1 (March), New Delhi: Ministry of Home Affairs, Government of India

Law Commission of India Report (1971) (no. 42) *Indian Penal Code*, New Delhi: Law Commission of India, Ministry of Law and Justice, Government of India

— (2000) (no. 172) *Review of Rape Laws*, New Delhi: Law Commission of India, Ministry of Law and Justice, Government of India

NCRB (National Crime Records Bureau) (2002) *Crime in India, 2000*, New Delhi: Ministry of Home Affairs, Government of India

O'Connell Davidson, J. and J. Sanchez Taylor (1996) 'Child prostitution and sex tourism – Goa', Paper prepared for the World Congress against the Commercial Sexual Exploitation of Children, ECPAT International, Bangkok

RAHI Foundation (1998) *Voices from the Silent Zone: Women's Experiences of Incest and Childhood Sexual Abuse: The RAHI Findings*, New Delhi: RAHI

Tandon, M. P. and R. Tandon (1993) *The Code of Criminal Procedure*, 8th edn, Allahabad: Allahabad Law Agency

15 | Synchronizing traditional legal responses to non-consensual sexual experiences with contemporary human rights jurisprudence

CHARLES NGWENA

Coercive sexual experiences occur among both males and females in all age groups. Historically, coercive sexual experiences have been regulated through the application of criminal law, mainly through the law pertaining to the crime of rape. Traditionally, rape has been narrowly defined in virtually all jurisdictions, and has nearly always required the insertion of the penis by a male into the vagina of a female who has not granted consent (Burchell and Milton 1997). Moreover, when applying laws pertaining to the crime of rape, courts have nearly always required, as a constituent element of proving rape, proof of the use or threat of physical violence. Criminal courts, however, have generally not attached the label of rape where sexual intercourse has been achieved through the use of emotional or economic pressure (ibid.; Whitney 1996).

Traditionally, coercive sexual experiences have also been regulated by laws other than those pertaining to the crime of rape. The law addressing indecent assault, for example, has been used to regulate coercive sexual experiences falling short of rape. The law has also prescribed the age for consenting to sexual intercourse and the age for consenting to marriage. The law pertaining to the crime of incest has been another tool to regulate proscribed sexual acts.

The question, however, is whether traditional legal approaches and responses to coercive sexual experiences are adequate and comprehensive enough to take into account the peculiarities as well as the variety of non-consensual sexual experiences among young people, including economically coerced sexual experiences. In this chapter, it is argued that the traditional legal approaches are inadequate, not least because they are oblivious to the modern concept of human rights. Traditional legal approaches have yet to embrace the notion of sexual rights as fundamental rights.

Drawing, *inter alia*, from the experiences of South Africa, this chapter discusses the potential of the application of human rights norms, including norms derived from the Convention on the Rights of the Child, 1989 (CRC) (UN 1989) and the Convention of the Elimination of All Forms of Discrimination against Women, 1979 (CEDAW) (UN 1979), to formulate more comprehensive legal/judicial responses to non-consensual sexual experiences.

The meaning of 'non-consensual' in sexual experiences

As this chapter is situated in a human rights paradigm, it is important to shed light on the meaning and forms of non-consensual sexual experiences at a conceptual level within the context of reproductive and sexual health rights.

The Programme of Action (POA) that emanated from the International Conference on Population and Development (ICPD) held in Cairo in 1994, and the International Conference on Women held in Beijing in 1995, contributed significantly to the conceptualization and popularization of the idea of sexual rights (UN 1994, 1995). In doing so, they also laid out a framework for the conceptualization of non-consensual sex as the antithesis of the free exercise of sexual rights. The meaning of 'non-consensual' in sexual experiences of young people can thus be understood if one begins by appreciating the notion of sexual rights as human rights.

The language of sexual rights entered the debates at Cairo and Beijing through the language of reproductive health rights. The innovation in the debates was the emphasis on women as subjects with human dignity and fundamental rights rather than as objects of population control policies. The following definition of reproductive health, which was adopted at Beijing, unambiguously cast reproductive health as a fundamental right that was inextricably linked with sexual health:

> Reproductive health is a state of complete physical, mental and social well-being and not merely the absence of disease or infirmity, in all matters relating to the reproductive system and to its functions and processes. Reproductive health therefore implies that people are able to have a satisfying and safe sex life and that they have the capability to reproduce and the freedom to decide if, when and how often to do so. Implicit in this last condition are the rights of men and women to be informed and to have access to safe, effective, affordable and acceptable methods of family planning of their choice, as well as other methods of their choice for regulation of fertility which are not against the law, and the right of access to appropriate health-care services that will enable women to go safely through pregnancy and childbirth and provides couples with the best chance of having a healthy infant. (UN 1995: para. 94)

From this definition it is possible to arrive, by extrapolation, at a definition of sexual rights. Sexual rights, as in the definition above, implies a state of complete physical, mental and social well-being and not merely the absence of disease or infirmity in matters relating to sexual health. It also implies the ability to express sexuality free from discrimination, coercion or violence.

It needs to be borne in mind, however, that attaching the language of rights to sexuality is problematic for a number of reasons (Ngwena 2002). For one, the concept of sexual rights itself is fairly novel, and has only recently intersected with human rights jurisprudence (Parker 1997; Petchesky 1996). Moreover, sexual rights might be misunderstood as implying the absence of all restraints and the lack of protection of vulnerable groups, and tantamount to licensing the right of anyone to have sex with whomever they desire, including children (defined as those under eighteen). It is, thus, important to emphasize that sexual rights are not an alternative jurisprudence; rather, they emanate from and affirm existing human rights norms.

Cook et al. (2003) have defined sexual health rights to comprise the following: the ability to enjoy mutually fulfilling sexual relationships; freedom from sexual abuse, coercion or harassment; safety from sexually transmitted infection (STI); and success in achieving or in preventing pregnancy. This approach to sexual rights is comprehensive and is situated within contemporary human rights norms that not only seek to secure the realization of civil and political rights, but also the realization of the socio-economic rights of the individual.

Sexual rights should be conceived as composite rights and not merely in terms of the absence of rape and indecent assault, protection from which is the sole preserve of the criminal courts. They comprise all those rights that are integral to the expression of sexuality. Thus, a host of rights, including the right to equality, sexual orientation, human dignity, life, reproductive decision-making, bodily integrity, freedom of association, freedom of expression, access to information, access to education, healthcare and other socio-economic goods, are all constituent elements of sexual rights (Ngwena 2002). An absence of one or more of these rights may render a sexual experience non-consensual.

Non-consensual sexual experiences of young people in South Africa

Studies of the sexual health of young people in South Africa, and similar settings, incontrovertibly demonstrate the existence of non-consensual sexual activity among young people (Mart 2000). Many young people in South Africa, however, lack adequate knowledge about basic reproductive and sexual health. Teenage pregnancies are common. Many young people are alienated from the public health system and are reluctant to seek professional support. Violence, fear, coercion, abuse and peer pressure are part of the currency of sexual experiences of young people.

Violence against girls and women in South Africa is a particular obstacle in the realization of sexual rights and has also been a fuelling factor in the spread of HIV. South Africa has a particularly high incidence of rape and other forms of sexual violence (Van Rensburg et al. 2001). A survey conducted in 2001 found that among women in the age group seventeen to forty-eight, the annual incidence of rape was 2,000 per 100,000 of the population (South African Institute of Race Relations 2001). In studies conducted across the country among teenage mothers to discover reasons for sexual debut, coercion or pressure by a partner accounted for the greatest percentage (Ehlers et al. 2000; Rutenberg et al. 2001; Van Rensburg et al. 2001). There is substantial evidence to suggest that a significant number of boys and young men have normalized violence as a routine tool for procuring sex from girls and women (South African Institute of Race Relations 2001; Van Rensburg et al. 2001). Victimization through sexual violence is particularly marked among black teenage women. A study of black townships in Cape Town reveals that a third of the respondents had been raped on their sexual debut. Even more alarming is the finding that a large proportion of these teenagers (72 per cent) reported experiences of rape and other forms of coercion in subsequent sexual encounters as well (Vundule et al. 2001).

It is not only physical violence which is used to gain unwanted sex, but other forms of coercion are used as well. The following is a summary of the context in which young people in South Africa experience coercive sex (Mart 2000; South African Institute of Race Relations 2001; Van Rensburg et al. 2001).

- Gender inequality and the subordination of women to men in society create fertile conditions for coercive sexual experiences. The patriarchal system requires women to be subservient to men in sexual matters and the economic subordination of women disempowers young girls and women in negotiating safe sex. Only a minority of women believe that they can refuse to have sex with their husband or partner.
- Poverty and economic adversity are fuelling factors underlying coerced sexual experiences, which adversely affect females and young people.
- Young girls, many of whom are minors, are trafficked into prostitution and sexual slavery. Some may have entered the country illegally and are thus disadvantaged as they are illegal immigrants working illegally and have little or no access to healthcare and other social services.
- Parents may sometimes coerce their daughters into transactional sex as a means of generating and sustaining family income.
- Young girls, including schoolgirls, are vulnerable to sexual exploitation by teachers and older men, particularly in rural areas where poverty is more pronounced. In these situations, economic or other benefits may be exchanged for sex.
- Young homeless children are particularly vulnerable to exploitation in commercial sex and sexual abuse and are coerced into sex in exchange for basic necessities, including shelter and food.

Legal responses in the South African context

Responses to coercive sexual experiences need to be multi-faceted and aim to reform archaic legal doctrines. The law relating to rape in particular, as discussed earlier, has remained unchanged and does not include many forms of coercive sexual experiences. What is needed is a broadening of the scope of the law pertaining to the crime of rape to include coercive circumstances other than the use or threat of blatant force.

A number of states have begun to follow this route, and South Africa is a case in point. The South African Law Commission proposed the reform of the rape law (South African Law Commission 1999), which culminated in the Criminal Law (Sexual Offences) Amendment Bill of 2003.

In its preamble, the bill takes cognizance of the fact that the country's common law and statutory law have failed to respond effectively and in a non-discriminatory manner to sexual exploitation, which is more pronounced among vulnerable populations, particularly women and children. The bill seeks to strengthen the commitment of the state to eliminate all forms of violence and sexual exploitation. It also takes cognizance of the international human rights obligations of the state in that it seeks, *inter alia*, to align the existing law on sexual offences with the provisions under CEDAW and CRC.

The substantive provisions of the bill bear testimony to the objectives articulated in the preamble. Owing to limitations of space, however, it is possible to comment only briefly on some of the provisions.

Clause 2, which defines the crime of rape, is a clear illustration of the broadening of the scope of the law. Rape is defined, *inter alia*, as follows:

1) A person who intentionally and unlawfully commits an act which causes penetration to any extent whatsoever by the genital organs of that person into or beyond the anus or genital organs of another person, or any act which causes penetration to any extent whatsoever by the genital organs of another person into or beyond the anus or genital organs of the person committing the act, is guilty of the offence of rape.

2) An act which causes penetration is *prima facie* unlawful if it is committed –
    a) in any coercive circumstances;
    b) under false pretences or by fraudulent means; or
    c) in respect of a person who is incapable in law of appreciating the nature of the act which causes penetration.

4) Coercive circumstances, referred to in subsection (2)(a), include any circumstances where there is
    a) a use of force against the complainant or another person or against the property of the complainant or that of any other person;
    b) a threat of harm against the complainant or another person or against the property of the complainant or that of any other person; or
    c) an abuse of power or authority to the extent that the person in respect of whom an act which causes penetration is committed is inhibited from indicating his or her resistance to such an act, or his or her unwillingness to participate in such an act; or
    d) false pretences or fraudulent means, referred to in subsection (2)(b), are circumstances where a person –

i) in respect of whom an act which causes penetration is being comitted, is led to believe that he or she is committing such an act with a particular person who is in fact a different person;
ii) in respect of whom an act which causes penetration is being committed, is led to believe that such an act is something other than that act; or
iii) intentionally fails to disclose to the person in respect of whom an act which causes penetration is being committed, that he or she is infected by a life-threatening sexually transmissible infection in circumstances in which there is a significant risk of transmission of such infection to that person.

In addition to providing a new definition of rape, the bill identifies new offences such as sexual violation, oral–genital sexual violation and child prostitution. According to the bill, a person commits the offence of sexual violation if he or she unlawfully and intentionally commits an act that causes penetration to any extent whatsoever by any object, including any part of the body of an animal, or any part of the body of that person, other than the genital organs of that person, into or beyond the anus or genital organs of another person. Oral–genital sexual violation is committed when a person unlawfully and intentionally commits an act that causes penetration to any extent whatsoever by the genital organs of that person, or the genital organs of an animal, into or beyond the mouth of another person.

The definition of rape in Clause 2 applies *mutatis mutandis* to sexual violation and oral–genital violation. A person who, in relation to a child, for financial or other reward, favour or compensation to such a child, engages in acts that are tantamount to participating in, promoting, encouraging or facilitating the commission of indecent acts or acts that cause penetration with such a child is guilty of the offence of being involved in child prostitution.

There is little doubt that the bill is set to introduce new values into the legal system to meet new challenges. The bill makes it clear that coercion in sexual penetration can emanate from circumstances other than the use of physical force, such as the abuse of authority. It also takes cognizance of the fact that sexual penetration of the victim can be achieved other than by the insertion of a penis into a vagina. Both females and males can be victims of rape, in contrast to the historical position, whereby only women can be victims of rape. The bill also seeks to abolish discrimination between boys and girls in terms of age of consent. It abolishes the presumption of common law that girls under the age of twelve are incapable of consenting to sexual intercourse, and instead provides that a person under the age of twelve (whether a boy or a girl) is incapable of appreciating the nature of an act of sexual intercourse. As discussed earlier, the protection of children from sexual exploitation, including child prostitution, is given a special place in the bill.

The application of international human rights norms within the state

It would be an empty victory if responses to coercive sexual experiences of young people did not also seek to address the underlying socio-economic circumstances of such experiences. To this end, it is necessary to apply the social obligations of states under international human rights instruments, such as the International Convention on Economic, Social and Cultural Rights, CEDAW and CRC, domestically. Official interpretations of the obligations of the state under these treaties provide important guidelines as to how states can enhance the sexual rights of young people and eliminate factors that lead to coercion.

Several potential coercive situations have been addressed by the Committee on the Rights of the Child in its General Comments. A case in point is General Comment no. 4 of the CRC on *Adolescent Health and Development*, which, *inter alia*, requires states to recognize the vulnerability of adolescents, and the factors underlying these vulnerabilities. For example, the General Comment has observed that as the health and development of adolescents are strongly determined by their environment, creating a safe and supportive environment would entail addressing the attitudes and actions of the immediate environment (family, peers, school and services) and the wider community. Early marriage and pregnancy are significant factors related to sexual and reproductive health, including HIV/AIDS. The Comment suggests that where necessary, states should reform legislation and practice to increase the minimum age at marriage for both boys and girls.

With regard to the issue of coercion, the Comment says that states must take effective measures to ensure that adolescents are protected from all forms of violence, neglect and exploitation, paying attention to specific forms of abuse that affect young people. In addition, states should adopt special measures to ensure the physical, sexual and mental integrity of adolescents with disabilities who are particularly vulnerable to abuse and neglect.

Homeless adolescents are also vulnerable to violence and sexual exploitation. The Comment recommends that states should develop policies and enact and enforce legislation that protect adolescents from violence. States should also develop strategies for the provision of appropriate education and access to healthcare, and build opportunities for the development of livelihood skills.

The CRC has also noted that adolescents who are sexually exploited through prostitution, pornography and other means are exposed to significant health risks, including infection and HIV/AIDS, unwanted pregnancies, unsafe abortions, violence and psychological distress, and have a right to physical and psychological recovery and social reintegration in an environment that fosters health, self-respect and dignity.

The Comment also requires that states enact and enforce laws to prohibit all forms of sexual exploitation and related trafficking; collaborate with other states to eliminate inter-country trafficking; and provide appropriate health and counselling for young victims of violence.

In short, the Comment notes that adolescents who have been sexually exploited should be treated as victims and not offenders. States must take appropriate legislative, administrative and other measures for the realization and monitoring of the rights of adolescents with regard to their health.

The Committee on the Rights of the Child, in General Comment no. 3 of 13–31 January 2003, *HIV/AIDS and the Rights of the Child*, has also recognized in the context of HIV/AIDS that children have legal rights and that they have a right to be free from sexual coercion and exploitation.

Conclusion

In this chapter, the responses of the legal system in South Africa to non-consensual sexual experiences have been situated in the context of the human rights paradigm. It is argued that the starting point for legal responses to non-consensual sexual experiences of young people must be the recognition of their basic human right to sexual health and sexuality. The efficacy of the responses of the state to non-consensual sexual experiences among young people will crucially depend on the extent to which a state has embraced contemporary human rights norms, including those that are espoused in CEDAW and CRC. To afford maximum protection to vulnerable groups, national constitutions and domestic laws must incorporate universal human rights values in form as well as in substance. This will require overhauling archaic legal doctrines so that sexual offences reflect a society that is committed to eliminating unfair discrimination, protecting the vulnerable and achieving substantive equality. In this way states will be able to effectively discharge their obligation to respect, protect, promote and fulfil the right of all peoples to enjoy fundamental rights, including the right to equality, human dignity, privacy, freedom and security, which includes the right to be free from all forms of violence, and to protect the rights of children, whose interests are of paramount consideration.

References

Burchell, J. and J. Milton (1997) *Principles of Criminal Law*, Kenwyn: Juta and Co. Ltd

Cook, R. J., B. M. Dickens and M. F. Fathalla (2003) *Reproductive Health and Human Rights*, Oxford: Oxford University Press

Ehlers, V. J., T. Maja, E. Sellers et al. (2000) 'Adolescent mothers' reproductive health services in the Gauteng province of the Republic of South Africa', *Curationis*, 23(3): 43

Mart, B. (2000) 'Risky business: issues affecting adolescent health in South Africa', *Development Update*, 3(2): 144–59

Ngwena, C. (2002) 'Sexuality rights as human rights in southern Africa with particular reference to South Africa', *South Africa Public Law*, 15(2): 1–21

Parker, R. (1997) 'Sexual rights: concept and action', *Health and Human Rights*, 2(3): 31–7

Petchesky, R. (1996) 'Sexuality rights: inventing a concept, mapping international practice', Unpublished paper presented at the Conference on Conceiving Sexuality, Rio de Janeiro, 14–18 April

Rutenberg, N., C. Kehus-Alons, L. Brown et al. (2001) *Transitions to Adulthood in the Context of AIDS in South Africa: Report of Wave 1*, New York: Population Council

South African Institute of Race Relations (2001) *South Africa Survey, 2000/2000*, Johannesburg: South African Institute of Race Relations

South African Law Commission (1999) *Sexual Offences: Substantive Law*, Pretoria: South African Law Commission

UN (United Nations) (1979) *Convention on the Elimination of All Forms of Discrimination against Women*, General Assembly Resolution 34/180, New York: UN

— (1989) *Convention on the Rights of the Child*, General Assembly Resolution 44/25, New York: UN

— (1994) *Programme of Action Adopted at the International Conference on Population and Development*, Cairo, 5–13 September

— (1995) *Platform for Action and Beijing Declaration: Fourth World Conference on Women*, Beijing, 4–15 September

Van Rensburg, H. C. J., I. Friedman, C. Ngwena et al. (2001) *Strengthening Local Government and Civic Responses to the HIV/AIDS Epidemic in South Africa*, Bloemfontein: Centre for Health Systems Research and Development

Vundule, C., F. Maforah, R. Jewkes et al. (2001) 'Risk factors for teenage pregnancy among sexually active black adolescents in Cape Town', *South African Medical Journal*, 91(1): 73–80

Whitney, C. A. (1996) 'Non-stranger, non-consensual sexual assaults: changing legislation to ensure that acts are criminally punished', *Rutgers Law Journal*, 27(2): 417–45

16 | Developing opportunities within the education sector to prevent non-consensual sexual experiences: an emerging issue for human rights, public health and education development goals

JUDITH MIRSKY

This chapter focuses on the need to address non-consensual sexual experiences within and through the education sector. It reviews evidence of promising interventions in the sector and raises issues that need to be addressed in the future.

The term non-consensual sexual experience is used in this article to refer to a variety of behaviours, including sexual violence that can be prosecuted under existing laws on child abuse, rape and indecent assault, and behaviours that more easily fall under the rubric of sexual harassment and sexual bullying. Sexual harassment is a term commonly used in the tertiary education sector while sexual bullying is more usually encountered in the secondary education sector (Duncan 1999).

The features common to all definitions of sexual harassment are that the behaviour is known to be unwanted or unreasonable, and that it hampers an individual's advancement or well-being (Aeberhard-Hodges 1995). The definition most commonly cited is contained in the European Commission's Recommendation on the protection of the dignity of women and men at work and its accompanying code of practice, which states that 'sexual attention becomes sexual harassment if it is persisted in once it has been made clear that it is regarded by the recipient to be offensive', while adding the caveat that 'one incident of harassment may constitute sexual harassment if sufficiently serious' (European Commission 1992). In South Africa, the Promotion of Equality and Prevention of Unfair Discrimination Act, 2000, defines harassment as being 'unwanted conduct which is persistent or serious and demeans, humiliates or creates a hostile or intimidating environment or is calculated to induce submission ... and which is related to sex, gender or sexual orientation' (Republic of South Africa 2000). Thus, behaviour that is sexual in nature and is clearly welcomed or reciprocated, such as flirting between peers, is not sexual harassment. Supervisory bodies of both the International Labour Organization (ILO) and the United Nations have classed sexual harassment as a form of sex-based discrimination (ILO 1998).

Sexual harassment in educational settings may occur in two ways. One, 'quid pro quo' (something for something) harassment occurs, for example, when a student is offered grades or a grant in return for sex. Second, the creation of an 'intimidating', 'hostile' or 'offensive' environment occurs, for example, when students face repeated sexual comments in class.

Non-consensual sexual experiences are a serious concern for young people, and sexual coercion is often the root cause of other sexual and reproductive health problems, such as unintended pregnancy and sexually transmitted infections (STIs), including infection with HIV.

There are two primary reasons to focus on non-consensual sexual experiences in the education sector. First, a growing body of research from settings across the world documents the existence of behaviours ranging from verbal abuse to rape within educational institutions which violate the human rights of students, damage their health and undermine their educational advancement. Girls and young women are disproportionately affected, and there is a substantial gender gap in the frequency, severity and outcomes of such behaviours. Young people themselves have prioritized sexual coercion and harassment as an important concern in school and university life in a number of studies (Demise et al. 2002; Kaim et al. 1999; Mgalla et al. 1998), frequently rating it higher than their concern with either HIV/AIDS or unintended pregnancy. Given this background, educational institutions have an ethical and legal obligation urgently to address this issue.

Second, epidemiological research suggests that non-consensual sexual experiences are a serious concern for young people, particularly young women, in the wider sociocultural context as well. Studies document significant levels of sexual violence between young people (Krug et al. 2002) and endorsement of sexually coercive attitudes among youth (Burton et al. 1998; Duvvury et al. 2002). Children and young people are also at risk of sexual abuse from adults (Finkelhorn 1994). Research from different settings on the extent of sexual violence affecting youth and its impact provides a compelling rationale for the provision of primary prevention through the education sector, irrespective of the extent to which it is perceived as a problem in particular institutions.

The extent and impact of non-consensual sexual experiences within the education sector

Research on non-consensual sexual experiences within the education sector has largely focused on the USA and other developed countries (AAUW 1993, 2001; Duncan 1999, Larkin 1994, Stein 1995). Sexual harassment and violence have more recently been researched in developing countries in the context of development goals concerned with human rights, sexual and reproductive health and education. In sub-Saharan Africa, the battle against HIV/AIDS has opened a window on sexual violence experienced in the education sector. Studies in Botswana, Ethiopia, Ghana, Kenya, Malawi, South Africa, Uganda and Zimbabwe document violence faced by young women at school and university from peers and staff, ranging from harassment to rape (Ajayi et al. 1997; Demise et al.

2002; George 2001; Jewkes et al. 2002; Leach et al. 2000, 2002; Mirembe and Davies 2001; Nhundu and Shumba 2001; Rivers 2000). Data are also emerging from other regions, including South Asia (Bajpai 1999; Finney Hayward 2000; Gender Study Group 1996). While studies are not comparable across countries or regions owing to differences in sample population groups, definitions used of violence and harassment and methodologies employed, the weight of evidence taken together shows that non-consensual sexual experiences within schools and higher education institutions are an issue of considerable global concern.

The effects of sexual violence on health and well-being are well documented (García-Moreno and Watts 2000; Krug et al. 2002). Sexual violence and harassment in schools and colleges can lead to physical and mental health problems as well as adverse social outcomes such as avoiding/not attending school/college, dropping out of school/college, not attending classes, and underachievement. Students may refrain from participating in class; have difficulty concentrating; lose trust in school officials; avoid certain areas such as toilets, libraries and canteens; and become isolated (AAUW 2001; FAWE 2000; Finney Hayward 2000; Leach et al. 2000, 2002; Stein 1995). There is also an impact on the entire institution, undermining its educational effectiveness. Staff morale may be eroded and the institution, by failing to be accountable to the community, can lose its credibility, resulting in young women being kept out of education. Thus, an opportunity to close the gender gap in education is lost. Indeed, if issues of sexual violence and harassment are not addressed in these institutions, a message is given to students and the wider community that such gendered norms are upheld by society.

A multi-level approach to addressing non-consensual sexual experiences within the education sector

In analysing the determinants of gender-based violence in society and identifying appropriate opportunities for intervention, many researchers have used an ecological model that identifies influences operating at various levels, i.e. the individual, family, community and society (Heise et al. 1999). When addressing sexual violence and harassment within and through the education sector, interventions can likewise be made at different levels.

Currently, interventions in the education sector that address sexual violence and harassment, especially in resource-poor settings, tend to be restricted to the level of students. Multi-level interventions that focus at the same time on teachers, parents and the wider community more generally are likely to be more effective in reducing violence. Broadly, interventions in the education sector can be classified in two groups: those that are student-based and those that bring about systemic change. Gender norms can be addressed at both these levels. Student-level interventions can be provided by teachers, peers and external groups, such as non-governmental organizations (NGOs), and focus on the curriculum and extra-curricular activities. Interventions for systemic change include teacher training, building awareness of national legislation and guidelines, establishing effective institutional policies and support strategies, establishing external links with the wider community, including groups with experience of gender-based violence and human rights, and child protection networks, modifying the school environment to promote gender equality and female leadership, and ensuring safety in the physical environment.

Programmes that report some success in addressing non-consensual sexual experiences in educational institutions can be seen to have an impact in one or more of three dimensions. At an individual level they enhance agency. They also promote systemic change in the education sector to support teachers and modify the characteristics/features of education systems that perpetuate discriminatory sexual norms. Finally, they promote communication and solidarity between students, between students and staff, and between educational institutions and communities. Change can be achieved in these three areas only by working holistically at multiple levels within the education sector.

Cross-sector collaboration is needed for interventions to be effective. Addressing non-consensual sexual experiences within and through educational institutions is integral to human rights, public health and education policies, which aim to uphold women's rights, to enable adolescents to deal in a positive and responsible way with their sexuality and to close the gender gap in education. It is also integral to three of the Millennium Development Goals, i.e. those concerning education, gender and HIV/AIDS. Addressing sexual violence is also a priority for other key stakeholders, including child protection networks, community organizations, local communities and young people themselves, whose direct participation in designing interventions will ensure that they are contextually relevant and meaningful.

The following section discusses interventions that appear promising, or that have the potential of being acceptable and effective. Little evaluation research has, however, been conducted on initiatives to prevent sexual violence and harassment within and through the education sector in developing countries, and further research is required.

Student-oriented interventions Issues related to non-consensual sexual experiences can be introduced into the curriculum in existing courses on life skills, sexuality, HIV/AIDS or family life education, and can be linked to wider issues of gender-based violence, male-on-male violence, bullying and harassment. This would provide an additional avenue to engage young men in discussing how norms of male dominance, toughness and aggression contribute to male-on-male and male-on-female violence, as well as distort intimate relationships between young people. The dynamics and motivations that underlie male-on-male violence, gender battery and sexual violence reflect a range of gender norms that need to be explicitly addressed within such a curriculum. For example, men's rationale for sexual violence may be different from their justification for battery, and would need to be separately addressed. As a result, while integrating violence into existing curricula, the issue of non-consensual sexual experiences must be clearly and independently addressed.

Student-oriented interventions can be delivered by NGOs. Some NGOs have developed innovative strategies for working with students to provide support and offer educational initiatives that cannot be provided by schools because of a lack of knowledge and skills (Mirsky 2003). These include dissemination of information through drama and other media such as magazines and radio programmes, mentoring schemes, discussions based on case studies of men who have campaigned against violence perpetrated on women and girls, and informing youths of their rights. Where NGOs work with students, teacher involvement is essential to enable staff to engage with the new material as well as address issues that may arise after the NGO has left.

An example of a promising initiative is the Girls' Power Initiative (GPI), an NGO in Nigeria, and the Coordinating Centre for Reaching Out to New Generations of Amanitare (the African Partnership for Sexual and Reproductive Health and Rights of Women and Girls). GPI promotes comprehensive sexuality education that includes personal empowerment; human rights; anatomy and physiology; sexual health; gender, society and culture; and livelihood skills. The initiative focuses primarily on increasing young women's agency, and helping them recognize that, despite societal constraints, they can be effective initiators and leaders of change. Weekly meetings using a range of methods and techniques begin with girls recounting and discussing their experiences and role-playing possible strategies to respond to these situations. These meetings also provide a socially supportive network. The programme's reach is extended through courses in the holidays, a newsletter and a radio programme. An enabling environment is also promoted by teacher training, and by organizing public meetings and programmes for boys, parents, teachers, healthcare providers and policy-makers that aim to increase communication between them and girls on issues of concern to girls.

The programme has yet to be formally evaluated; however, widespread mobilization within communities and participants' reflections on changes in their knowledge, attitudes and skills over time offer powerful testimony that 'adolescent girls can make important changes in their self-perception, in their intimate relationships, in the ways in which they handle discrimination, and in the course their lives take' (GPI 2000: 11).

Conscientizing Male Adolescents (CMA) is another promising initiative in Nigeria, which is complementary to and draws technical support from the GPI project. Within sexuality education, while conventional topics, such as preventing unintended pregnancy, STIs and HIV, condoms and contraception, are discussed, a major focus is on violence. CMA, like other programmes that address sexual violence, believes that helping young men to understand the concept of 'consent' is particularly important (SECRU 2002). Questions that are addressed include: What does 'consent' mean in particular contexts? How does a boy know if he has consent? What should he do if he is not sure? Why is consent important? Can consent be withdrawn? Through historical and contemporary studies young men are encouraged to explore their own experiences of injustice so that they are sensitized to the injustices faced by girls. CMA has developed a complementary counselling service for boys and a newsletter, and boys are also guided to improve their reasoning and communication skills.

While rigorous evaluation has not been conducted, preliminary information has been obtained on knowledge and attitudes at baseline, mid-term and end of year. In addition, in-depth interviews with boys, girls, school staff and the community were carried out by an external evaluator. Findings tentatively suggest that participation in these interventions reduced harassment of girls by boys, increased support among boys for gender equality and led to the greater involvement of boys in domestic work. At school, boys gained prestige as a result of their newly acquired skills, and for their ability to articulate their views, listen and debate. They reported the development of friendships with both boys and girls and greater comfort in forming non-sexual relationships with girls (Girard 2003).

Another promising intervention is the Auntie Stella project in Zimbabwe, developed by the NGO TARSC (Training and Research Support Centre). The project used participatory reflection and action research with adolescent girls and boys aged thirteen to seventeen to ensure the development of a curriculum package that reflected their concerns. As students had identified 'agony aunts' in magazines as an enjoyable source of information, the project uses discussion cards, compiled with the help of professionals, adopting the format of letters to an 'agony aunt', accompanied by replies and supplementary information for students and teachers. Preparatory research had revealed that adolescents are most at ease when talking to peers of the same sex, but feel inhibited in discussions with larger groups, with the opposite sex or in the presence of a teacher, so the cards, which support up to ten forty-minute class periods, are discussed in small groups, usually single-sex, with teachers intervening minimally. The package has subsequently been made available on the Web. Both boys and girls had identified a number of pressures they experienced to engage in sex; pleasure was not identified as a major factor in most sexual activity. Of the thirty-three issues addressed in the pack, those that focused on issues of sexual violence and coercion included: 'I pay for [her] lunches and bus fares – surely my girlfriend should have sex with me?'; 'We made our girlfriend pregnant to punish her – now I'm worried'; 'I'm scared of rape – what can I do?'; 'Should I have sex to pay for my school fees?'; 'What can I do when my teacher wants to have sex with me?' and 'Is it possible to kiss and hug but not have sex?' (Kaim et al. 1999).

Participatory evaluation of the project was supplemented by an external evaluation in eight schools using surveys of students and teachers. Findings suggest that students appreciated the format and solution-oriented content. They felt more aware and better able to resist pressure, to make friends with and advise peers, and to talk to parents. The majority, especially the girls, appreciated working in single-sex groups. Most students felt that the group discussions in which they practised decision-making helped them solve their own problems. Teachers found the discussion cards easy to understand and use, and less stressful and embarrassing than traditional methods of imparting reproductive and sexual health information. They noticed changes in the behaviour of both girl and boy students, including less abuse and more caring attitudes. Some teachers, however, found the student-led nature of the discussion a challenge to their authority within the classroom, and felt the need for further training in participatory styles of teaching (Harnmeijer 1999).

Dealing with sensitive issues in classrooms requires new styles of teaching. Innovative activity-based methods of learning encourage critical thinking and flexibility in students, and encourage them to ask questions and challenge the status quo. Simply opening up spaces for student discussion is not enough. When innovative approaches, such as peer education, are employed, it is important to include materials that can generate a critical analysis of prevailing gender norms and factors that impede behaviour change among young students. An evaluation of an HIV prevention programme based on peer education in South Africa, for example, found that without this focus the programme reaffirmed rather than transformed existing norms. Female peer educators felt bullied if they challenged their male colleagues. Boys dominated groups with joking discussions on the desirability of frequent sex soon after meeting girls and focusing on male pleasure. A young female peer educator resigned because the 'guys were treating the girls so badly'. Although researchers tried to create opportunities for young women to talk, 'this occurred infrequently' (Campbell and MacPhail 2002).

Alternative models to explore masculinity are also required as challenges to group norms are likely to be resisted unless the costs of nonconformity are lowered and the costs of conforming to discriminatory norms raised. Research documents the considerable pressure felt, particularly by young men, to conform to norms of male dominance and to police each other's attitudes and behaviour, even when personal views are in conflict with those of the group. Studies show that in one-to-one interviews, many young men express views that they are reluctant to express in larger groups, such as a peer group or focus group setting (Wight 1994).

Systemically oriented interventions IN-SERVICE TEACHER TRAINING The personal attitudes and experiences of staff relating to non-consensual sexual experiences are key to implementing successful interventions in the education sector. Initiatives in the health sector have found that it is important to address the experiences and attitudes of health staff to enable them to deal with gender-based violence experienced by their clients (Haaland and Vlassoff 2001; Kim and Motsei 2002); similarly teachers, too, need assistance to be able to address these issues effectively. It is particularly important to reach head teachers/principals and district education officials, as they influence and encourage commitment. Motivated teachers with the necessary information, skills and confidence can then provide leadership within the profession to successfully implement new curricula.

Teachers, like students, also experience violence in their personal and professional lives. An evaluation of teacher training with a 'gender and conflict' component developed for the school curriculum in South Africa found that training which stimulated self-reflection as well as reflection on the school environment led to attitudes less accepting of gender-based violence and greater competence and comfort in addressing the issue at school (Dreyer et al. 2001). Before training only 30 per cent of teachers felt that schools could play a meaningful role in addressing gender-based violence; 70 per cent reported such an attitude after training. Likewise, 26 per cent of teachers before training and 74 per cent after training felt they would know what to do to address incidents of gender-based violence within a school. Before training, one quarter of teachers felt that women provoked their partners to beat them, for example by disobeying them; this figure fell to just 5 per cent after training.

In the study, two models for teacher training were explored: (a) the training-of-trainers model, in which two teachers from selected schools participated, and (b) the 'whole school' training model, in which all staff, from the principal to the secretaries and cleaning/support staff, participated. Both models led to significant changes in teachers' perceptions of the role of schools in addressing gender-based violence as well as in their own attitude. The whole school model, however, was found to be more effective in operationalizing the training, leading to a higher level of commitment by the school management in addressing the issues raised. In contrast, teachers trained in the training-of-trainers model expressed difficultly in requesting other teachers to allocate time to receive training from them, a problem perhaps exacerbated by the subject matter.

Teachers' attitudes influence the success of programmes. Addressing sexual harassment and violence necessitates teachers being able to explore their own attitudes and beliefs. A programme in the UK on the prevention of domestic violence in schools by Zero Tolerance, an NGO, in partnership with the Scottish Executive, the devolved government for Scotland, found that before training some staff held attitudes endorsing violence against women. For example, 22 per cent of staff agreed that, at least sometimes, 'girls can provoke violence and abuse because of how they dress or behave' (SECRU 2002). In Nigeria, qualitative research in a teacher training college documented an ethos that marginalized female staff: male teachers routinely and publicly refer to female colleagues in sexually demeaning terms such as 'a pot of honey', 'my urine jug', 'an edible fruit' and 'bottom heavy' (personal communication, Salihu Bakari).

Harassment and violence, though not endorsed, are frequently not addressed because staff, like students, are not aware of the means for recourse. Harassment often occurs in public places in schools and colleges, including classrooms, hallways/corridors, libraries and cafeterias. When such behaviour is ignored, it is considered normative and tacitly accepted. Providing support to staff in schools and universities is a first step towards changing such norms and attitudes and addressing the needs of students.

NATIONAL LEGISLATION AND GUIDELINES Staff need to be guided by national legislation and directives, and made aware of existing sanctions against educational staff who sexually exploit students. Existing legal standards and professional codes of conduct may need to be updated. In the UK, for example, the Sexual Offences (Amendment) Act 2000 introduced a new criminal offence, 'abuse of a position of trust', making it illegal for any person aged eighteen or over to have sexual intercourse – or any other form of sexual activity – with a person aged seventeen or under in their care. Though the age of consent for sexual intercourse in the UK is sixteen, consensual sexual acts are outlawed in an educational setting, in addition to those that could be prosecuted under the existing act (Hamilton 2002). In the USA, a 1999 Supreme Court decision held that a school board aware of but indifferent to sexual harassment could be held liable for damages (Supreme Court of the United States 1999). This ensures that the prevention of harassment is not contingent upon individual interpretations by school administrators of what behaviours are or are not acceptable. In South Africa, similarly, guidelines on HIV/AIDS from the Department of Education underscore the fact that sexual relations between teachers and students are against the law as educators are in a position of trust. They further state that if a staff member is aware that a colleague is having sexual relations with a student, failure to report this could in some circumstances lead to being charged with being an accessory to rape (Jewkes 2000).

Some reports of sexual violence and harassment in the education sector (George 2001; Omale 2000) describe no action being taken or teachers being moved to other jobs after having sexual relations with students, which is a case of simply transferring the problem elsewhere. To be effective, national legislation and guidelines must be perceived as being effectively implemented.

INSTITUTIONAL POLICIES AND SUPPORT STRATEGIES Staff and students also need to be backed by institutional policies and support strategies. At the university level, policies that exist focus on sexual harassment. In India, universities have collaborated through a National Consultation on Sexual Harassment on University Campuses, and in southern Africa the Network of Tertiary Educational Institutions Challenging Sexual Harassment and Violence was established in 1997. In the USA, sexual harassment policies in schools commonly define harassment as 'unwanted and unwelcome behaviour of a sexual nature that interferes with the right to receive an equal educational opportunity' (Stein 1995). For younger students, designing an approach in the context of bullying is considered a more age-appropriate way of generating shared codes of conduct: 'If educators and advocates pose and present the problem as "bullying" to young children rather than labeling it immediately as "sexual harassment", we can engage children and universalize the problem as one that boys as well as girls will understand and accept as problematic' (ibid.: 150–51).

Crucial to the effectiveness of policies is identifying sources of support to whom individuals can be referred. If these do not exist then new mechanisms may need to be created. An example from Tanzania is the female guardian programme, a school-based initiative involving parents and the community. The programme aims to reduce sexual harassment and coercion as well as reduce schoolgirl pregnancies. It also seeks to prevent girls from being blamed or expelled from school if they become pregnant. One guardian or *mlezi* is chosen per primary school by colleagues and trained to provide advice on sexual and reproductive health concerns. The focus is on girls, but boys can approach them too. In the first eight months of the programme's operation, 61 per cent of girls in 185 schools consulted a *mlezi*, 59 per cent regarding harassment by a boy and 9 per cent regarding harassment by a teacher. A comparison of schools with and without *mlezis* revealed that 52 per cent of girls in schools with a guardian said they would approach a *mlezi* if they were harassed by a teacher whereas none of the girls in schools without a *mlezi* would approach any member of staff, including female teachers (Mgalla et al. 1998).

LINKS WITH THE WIDER COMMUNITY Establishing links with the wider community, such as with NGOs and experts, can strengthen and broaden the scope of interventions. Working with communities raises the opportunity to address factors in the environment outside school that contribute to harassment in school, such as the disproportionate lack of access to economic resources of female students. For example, a study of abuse of schoolgirls in Zimbabwe found that boys had significant opportunities to earn money at weekends through casual labour, which was not considered an option that was acceptable or feasible for girls because of their domestic workload. As many as 26 per cent of girls interviewed said they regularly went hungry. Researchers documented how the school cafeteria became a site where young girls could unwittingly be drawn into friendships with boys who bought them food and later pressurized them for sex (Leach et al. 2000). In Uganda, Stepping Stones, a community-based training programme on gender, HIV, communication and relationship skills that specifically addresses gender violence, enabled young women to galvanize community action to challenge harassment by older men and consequently resulted in their being able to walk to and from school without fear (Renton et al. 2000).

MODIFICATION OF THE WIDER SCHOOL ENVIRONMENT Efforts to build egalitarian values in the sphere of sexual relationships must be complemented by parallel efforts to challenge discriminatory gender norms and acceptance of violence in the school ethos more generally. Currently, in many school settings, young women are denied leadership roles – for example, they are discouraged from becoming prefects (Mirembe and Davies 2001), and are expected to perform domestic chores such as cleaning in schools (Omale 2000); moreover, there is a lack of female teachers and punitive policies are implemented against young women who become pregnant (Hallam 1994). All of these hamper efforts to develop critical thinking and agency on the part of students, and fail to challenge norms of male dominance and female submissiveness among both staff and students. The continuing use of corporal punishment even when it is illegal (Ehrenreich et al. 1999) undermines efforts to promote non-violent relationships among students.

Initiatives on sexual violence with students can themselves have an impact on the wider school environment. The UK Zero Tolerance 'Respect' campaign found that positive evaluations from students included the fact that post-intervention, teachers were much less likely to shout and students felt they had become closer to their teachers (SECRU 2002).

Attending to the physical and temporal organization of the school can also result in a positive change in the school environment. School toilets and unlit areas on university campuses have been found to be sites for sexual harassment, which can inhibit their use (Ajayi et al. 1997; Gender Study Group 1996). The structuring of the school timetable can also expose students to risk: in some situations it is common practice for final-year primary school students, who are under pressure to prepare for final examinations, to be detained after school for extra lessons, resulting in journeys home much later in the evening (Omale 2000).

Safety and ethical considerations

A range of ethical principles have been elucidated that guide research in areas such as domestic violence against women (WHO 1999) and trafficking of women and girls (Zimmerman and Watts 2003). Many of these principles are also relevant to research and interventions with young people in the education sector, of which protecting the safety of those involved and ensuring confidentiality are of paramount importance. In an educational setting, care is needed not to expose students who disclose incidents of violence and harassment to the risk of reprisals after the researchers or visiting NGOs have left. In order to support the health and well-being of staff and students, where problems are reported, referral mechanisms must also be put in place. Researchers investigating domestic violence also stress the importance of building rapport with respondents and designing appropriate methodological approaches that will reduce under-reporting of violence.

In educational settings, additional context-specific ethical concerns include the need to respect the emotional and cognitive development of students, which is especially challenging in mixed-age classrooms. In some developing countries, late starting and repetition of academic years mean the age range can be considerable (Ajayi et al. 1997). A further consideration is to ensure that interventions are rights-based and do not attempt to reduce violence by further curtailing young women's freedom of movement or action, for example by locking female students into their hostels at night (Omale 2000). Such measures do little to challenge norms endorsing male violence and encourage blaming the victim.

Problems may also arise if interventions focus on imparting knowledge and awareness of sexual violence without a parallel focus on enhancing agency by creating a space for positive discussions of young men's and women's relationships and supporting young people to critically analyse and take steps to transform inequitable gender norms that condone violence. Furthermore, there remains the ethical imperative to address systemic factors that allow teacher–student sexual exploitation to continue unchallenged, that undermine behaviour change among students, and which fail to alleviate the personal costs to students who defy discriminatory norms.

Conclusion

Non-consensual sexual experiences, ranging from verbal harassment to rape, occur within educational institutions, perpetrated not just by students but also by staff, in contravention of existing legal and professional codes. Few interventions have been designed to address these issues in educational settings. Neither are students equipped to transform a world outside the school or college gates where physical, sexual and psychological gender-based violence are far from uncommon (Krug et al. 2002).

Sexual violence and harassment are a violation of human rights, a public health problem and, when they occur in educational institutions, a drain on efforts to close the gender gap in education. Schools and higher education institutions can play an active role in prevention. The salient features of a successful intervention include increasing personal agency and awareness of rights among students, particularly girls and young women. Also needed is the creation of an enabling environment through systemic change at all levels of the education system, from the local to the national, including the provision of support for teachers to deliver new curricula and effective sanctions against staff and students who sexually harass or are violent towards others. Interventions also need to focus on enhancing solidarity among students, between students and staff, and between educational institutions and the community by promoting dialogue, communication and gender-equitable attitudes and behaviours.

Educational institutions are already in the front line of providing sexuality, HIV/AIDS and life skills education programmes to young people in many settings. Activities aimed at preventing sexual violence and harassment can be included as part of this package. Addressing non-consensual sexual experiences will assist young people in transforming, rather than being subject to, social norms that sanction gender inequality or gender-based violence and will enhance existing education programmes. If sexual violence and harassment are ignored, existing education programmes could reinforce discriminatory norms and will miss opportunities to enable young people to embark on intimate relationships in a spirit of equality, mutual respect and caring. Educational institutions are uniquely placed to deliver such programmes at a time in young people's lives when they are forming their sexual identities.

Addressing non-consensual sexual experiences within and through the education sector is necessary to achieve internationally agreed development goals of upholding young people's human rights, protecting their health and well-being and closing the gender gap in education. It is a strategically important component of wider efforts to prevent gender-based violence and HIV infection and to promote sexual and reproductive health and rights, and should form part of national plans to address these issues.

References

AAUW (American Association of University Women) (1993) *Hostile Hallways: The AAUW Survey on Sexual Harassment*, Newton: AAUW Educational Foundation

— (2001) *Hostile Hallways: Bullying, Teasing and Sexual Harassment in School*, Newton: AAUW Educational Foundation

Aeberhard-Hodges, J. (1995) 'Sexual harassment in employment: recent judicial and arbitral trends', *International Labour Review*, 135(5): 499–533

Ajayi, A., W. Clark, A. Erulkar et al. (1997) *Schooling and the Experience of Adolescents in Kenya*, Nairobi: Ministry of Education/Population Council

Bajpai, A. (1999) 'Sexual harassment in university and college campuses in Mumbai', *Indian Journal of Social Work*, 60(4): 606–23

Burton, S., J. Kitzinger et al. (1998) *Young People's Attitudes toward Violence, Sex and Relationships*, Edinburgh: Zero Tolerance Charitable Trust

Campbell, C. and C. MacPhail (2002) 'Peer education, gender and the development of critical consciousness: participatory HIV prevention by South African youth', *Social Science and Medicine*, 55(2): 331–45

Demise, A., R. Shinebaum and K. Melesse (2002) 'The problems of female students at Jimma University, Ethiopia, with some suggested solutions', *Ethiopian Journal of Health Development*, 16(3): 257–66

Dreyer, A., J. Kim and N. Schaay (2001) *What Do We Want to Tell Our Children about Violence against Women?* Evaluation report for the project developing a model 'Gender and Conflict' component for the primary school curriculum, School of Public Health, University of the Western Cape

Duncan, N. (1999) *Sexual Bullying: Gender Conflict and Pupil Culture in Secondary Schools*, London: Routledge

Duvvury, N., M. Nayak and K. Allendorf (2002) 'Links between masculinity and violence: aggregate analysis', in *Men, Masculinity and Domestic Violence in India: Summary Report of Four Studies*, Washington, DC: International Center for Research on Women

Ehrenreich, R., A. Marx, M. Simons et al. (1999) *Spare the Child: Corporal Punishment in Kenyan Schools*, New York: Human Rights Watch

European Commission (1992) Commission Recommendation of 27 November 1991 on the Protection of the Dignity of Women and Men at Work (92/131/EEC), Brussels: European Commission Official Journal L 049, 24/02/1992, pp. 1–8

FAWE (Forum for African Women Educationalists) (2000) 'Sexual harassment – a major hindrance to learning', *FAWE News*, 8(3): 21–7

Finkelhorn, D. (1994) 'The international epidemiology of child sexual abuse', *Child Abuse and Neglect*, 18(5): 409–17

Finney Hayward, R. (2000) *Breaking the Earthenware Jar: Lessons from South Asia to End Violence against Women and Girls*, Nepal: UNICEF Regional Office for South Asia

García-Moreno, C. and C. Watts (2000) 'Violence against women: its importance for HIV/AIDS', *AIDS*, 14(suppl. 3): S253–S265

Gender Study Group (1996) *Sexual Harassment in Delhi University: A Report*, Delhi: Delhi University Study Group

George, E. (2001) *Scared at School: Sexual Violence against Girls in South African Schools*, New York: Human Rights Watch

Girard, F. (2003) *'My Father Didn't Think This Way': Nigerian Boys Contemplate Gender Equality*, New York: Population Council

GPI (Girls' Power Initiative) (2000) Nigeria End of Grant Year Report, vol 2: Programme Execution Team Members' Evaluation, Benin City: 'Girls' Power Initiative', cited in A. Irvin, *Taking Steps of Courage: Teaching Adolescents about Sexuality and Gender in Nigeria and Cameroon*, New York: International Women's Health Coalition (IWHC)

Haaland, A. and C. Vlassoff (2001) 'Introducing health workers for change: from transformation theory to health systems in developing countries', *Health Policy and Planning*, 16(Suppl. 1): 1–6

Hallam, R. (1994) *Crimes without Punishment: Sexual Harassment and Violence against Female Students in Schools and Universities in Africa*, London: African Rights

Hamilton, C. (2002) *Working with Young People: Legal Responsibility and Liability*, Colchester: University of Essex, Children's Legal Centre

Harnmeijer, J. (1999) *Adolescent Reproductive Health Education Project 'Auntie Stella' Phase 1 Evaluation*, Harare: Training and Research Support Centre (TARSC)

Heise, L., M. Ellsberg and M. Gottemoeller (1999) *Ending Violence against Women: The Hidden Health Burden*, Population Reports, Series L, no. 11, Baltimore, MD: Johns Hopkins University School of Public Health

ILO (International Labour Organization) (1998) Governing Body 271st Session, Geneva, March 1998, Agenda item 4, GB.271/4/1, paras 146–8

Jewkes, R. (2000) *The HIV/AIDS Emergency: Department of Education Guidelines for Educators*, Pretoria: Department of Education

Jewkes, R., J. Levin, N. Mbananga et al. (2002) 'Rape of girls in South Africa', *Lancet*, 359 (9303): 319–20

Kaim, B. et al. (1999) *Auntie Stella: Teenagers Talk about Sex, Life and Relationships*,

Adolescent Reproductive Health Pack, Harare: Training and Research Support Centre (TARSC)

Kim, J. and M. Motsei (2002) '"Women enjoy punishment": attitudes and experiences of gender violence among PHC nurses in rural South Africa', *Social Science and Medicine*, 54(8): 1243–54

Krug, E. G., L. L. Dahlberg, J. A. Mercy et al. (2002) *World Report on Violence and Health*, Geneva: WHO

Larkin, J. (1994) 'Walking through walls: the sexual harassment of high school girls', *Gender and Education*, 6(3): 263–80

Leach, F. and P. Machakanja with J. Mandoga (2000) *Preliminary Investigation of the Abuse of Girls in Zimbabwean Junior Schools*, Education Research Paper no. 39, London: DFID

Leach, F., V. Fiscian, E. Kadzamira et al. (2002) *An Investigative Study of the Abuse of Girls in African Schools* (draft), London: DFID

Mgalla, Z., D. Schapink and J. Ties Boerma (1998) 'Protecting school girls against sexual exploitation: a guardian programme in Mwanza, Tanzania', *Reproductive Health Matters*, 7(12): 19–30

Mirembe, R. and L. Davies (2001) 'Is schooling a risk? Gender, power relations, and school culture in Uganda', *Gender and Education*, 13(4): 401–16

Mirsky, J. (2003) *Beyond Victims and Villains: Addressing Sexual Violence in the Education Sector*, London: Panos Institute

Nhundu, T. and A. Shumba (2001) 'The nature and frequency of reported cases of teacher perpetrated child sexual abuse in rural primary schools in Zimbabwe', *Child Abuse and Neglect*, 25: 1517–34

Omale, J. (2000) 'Tested to their limit: sexual harassment in schools and educational institutions in Kenya', in J. Mirsky and M. Radlett (eds), *No Paradise Yet: The World's Women Face the New Century*, London: Zed Books

Renton, L., J. Bataringaya and C. Millar (2000) *Safe Crossing: The Stepping Stones Approach to Involving Men in the Prevention of Violence and HIV Transmission*, London: Action Aid

Republic of South Africa (2000) Promotion of Equality and Prevention of Unfair Discrimination Act, 2000, Pretoria: Parliament of the Republic of South Africa

Rivers, R. (2000) *Shattered Hopes: Study of Sexual Abuse of Girls – a Survey on Sexual Abuse of Students in Botswana Schools*, Mochudi: Metlhaetsile Women's Information Centre

SECRU (Scottish Executive Central Research Unit) (2002) *Evaluation of the Zero Tolerance 'Respect' Pilot Project*, Edinburgh: Stationery Office

Stein, N. (1995) 'Sexual harassment in school: the public performance of gendered violence', *Harvard Educational Review*, 65(2): 145–61

Supreme Court of the United States (1999) *Davis* v. *Monroe County Board of Education*, *United States Reports*, 526 US 629 (1999), Washington, DC: Supreme Court of the United States

WHO (World Health Organization) (1999) *Putting Women First: Ethical and Safety Recommendations for Research on Domestic Violence against Women*, Geneva: WHO, WHO/EIP/GPE/99.2

Wight, D. (1994) 'Boys' thoughts and talk about sex in a working class locality of Glasgow', *Sociological Review*, 42: 703–37

Zimmerman, C. and C. Watts (2003) *WHO Ethical and Safety Recommendations for Interviewing Trafficked Women*, Geneva: World Health Organization

17 | The health service response to sexual violence: lessons from IPPF/WHR member associations in Latin America

SARAH BOTT, ALESSANDRA C. GUEDES AND ANA GUEZMES

Research suggests that substantial proportions of young people have experienced forced sexual debut, child sexual abuse or other forms of sexual violence in virtually every setting of the world (Heise et al. 1995; Krug et al. 2002). Both males and females report sexual coercion, but the majority of victims are female (for example, see CDC 2003), and the vast majority of perpetrators are male (Heise et al. 1995). Sexual violence has been linked to a host of health consequences and risk behaviours for victims of abuse, including unwanted pregnancy, sexually transmitted infections (STIs)/HIV/AIDS, chronic pain and gastrointestinal disorders, post-traumatic stress, suicidal thoughts and depression, high-risk sexual behaviour, substance abuse, and a higher risk of subsequent victimization (National Research Council 1996). Research suggests that survivors of sexual abuse in childhood and early adolescence face a higher risk of early (consensual) sexual debut, substance abuse, multiple sexual partners and failure to use contraception to prevent unwanted pregnancy (Felitti et al. 1998; Heise et al. 1999; Walker et al. 1999).

In light of this evidence, it is likely that most providers of sexual and reproductive health services will need to provide care to survivors of violence at some point in their practice. Unfortunately, many healthcare institutions are inadequately prepared to address issues related to their care. They may not protect clients' privacy or respect the confidentiality of personal information. Many do not have written policies for managing cases of violence, including child abuse, rape or sexual harassment. Healthcare providers are often unprepared to recognize the signs and consequences of violence. They often see violence against women as a social problem that has little to do with medical care, believe that physical violence against women is normal, or feel that sexual violence is often the fault of the victim (Ferdinand n.d.; Heise et al. 1999; Kim and Motsei 2002). Many healthcare providers do not know the legal requirements for reporting incidents of coercion, procedures for gathering forensic evidence or where to refer survivors of abuse who need legal assistance or counselling.

In recent years, many health programmes have made an effort to improve their response to sexual and physical violence (e.g. Billings et al. 2002; Velzeboer et al. 2003). Few of these efforts in developing countries have been rigorously evaluated, however. Even fewer studies have investigated whether these efforts meet the specific needs of young people.

This chapter summarizes lessons from an initiative launched by the regional office of the International Planned Parenthood Federation, Western Hemisphere Region (IPPF/WHR) and three member associations – PLAFAM (Venezuela), PROFAMILIA (the Dominican Republic) and INPPARES (Peru). The aim of the initiative was to improve the health service response to violence against women. The initiative did not focus exclusively on young people, as only three of the twelve participating clinics were youth clinics. Nor did it focus exclusively on sexual violence, but rather it addressed gender-based violence more broadly, including physical and psychological violence within the family, sexual violence by any perpetrator, and a history of childhood sexual abuse among adolescent and adult women. Nevertheless, the resulting case study presented many lessons learned about improving the health service response to violence, including some specific findings related to sexual violence against young people.

History of the IPPF/WHR initiative

Following the Cairo and Beijing conferences in 1994 and 1995, IPPF/WHR worked to encourage its member associations to incorporate the principles and recommendations of the Cairo Programme of Action into their work (Newman and Helzner 1999; Ortiz-Ortega and Helzner 2000; UN 1994). During training and evaluations that focused on gender, clients and providers repeatedly mentioned physical and sexual violence as an issue that merited attention. To this end, the IPPF/WHR regional office and the three member associations launched a four-year regional initiative in 1999, with four main objectives: to improve the capacity of sexual and reproductive health services to care for women who experience violence; to raise awareness of violence against women as a public health problem and a violation of human rights; to improve laws related to gender-based violence and their application; and to increase knowledge about effective health service interventions in the area of violence.

This chapter focuses on the first objective – building the capacity of health services to care for survivors of violence. The three member associations introduced a broad package of reforms, including sensitizing and training all staff; improving clinic infrastructure to ensure privacy during consultations; strengthening policies and increasing staff awareness on issues related to confidentiality; adjusting patient flow, information systems and clinic policies to allow routine screening with written questions about violence; introducing policies and procedures to guide the process of detecting, referring and providing services to women who have experienced violence; establishing stronger alliances with referral services in the community; and providing specialized in-house services for survivors such as counselling, legal assistance and support groups. The member associations also changed their hiring procedures by asking about candidates' views on gender-based violence during job interviews, seeking out candidates with expertise in the area and communicating the organization's commitment to these issues from the beginning. This was a significant component of the initiative given that the associations hired a relatively large number of new staff during the course of the initiative owing to unrelated staff turnover or expansion. In addition, the three associations developed or strengthened sexual harassment policies.

To standardize their approach, the member associations developed common operational definitions and screening questions using the United Nations definition of violence against women as a starting point.[1] Four broadly worded screening questions were designed to initiate a dialogue with clients rather than to measure prevalence (see Table 17.1). The participants in the initiative also developed follow-up questions about the victim's relationship to the perpetrator, the time frame in which the event(s) occurred and women's level of danger.

TABLE 17.1 Screening questions for clients visiting the PLAFAM, PROFAMILIA and INPPARES clinics

Emotional abuse:	Have you ever felt harmed emotionally or psychologically by your partner or another person important to you? (For example, through constant insults, humiliation at home or in public, destruction of objects you felt close to, ridicule, rejection, manipulation, threats, isolation from friends or family members, etc.)
Physical violence:	Has your partner or another person important to you ever caused you physical harm? (For example, hitting, burning or kicking you)
Sexual violence:	Have you ever been forced to have sexual contact or intercourse?
Sexual abuse in childhood:	When you were a child, were you ever touched in a way that made you feel uncomfortable?

Note: Questions translated from Spanish.

Evaluation methods

To ensure an independent evaluation, external consultants carried out baseline, mid-term and follow-up studies at each site using standardized instruments. In addition, IPPF/WHR provided technical assistance to enable member associations to upgrade their information systems to gather routine service statistics on screening levels, detection rates, referrals and specialized services.

In early 2000, consultants collected baseline information on provider knowledge, attitudes and practices (KAP) related to violence through seventy-nine face-to-face interviews with all front-line service providers involved in the initiative.

'Provider' was broadly defined to embrace all staff members who had direct contact with female clients, and included physicians, midwives, nurses, counsellors, social workers, psychologists and, in some cases, receptionists. The questionnaire primarily collected quantitative data; at one site, however, the consultants complemented these data with qualitative field notes on provider perspectives. The baseline evaluators also conducted structured observations of participating clinics using a standardized observation/staff interview guide to gather information on the human, printed and physical resources available in each clinic.

In late 2001, an exit survey was carried out among 691 female clients, and mid-term qualitative data were collected through discussions with six groups of providers, five groups of external key informants and eight groups of women who had experienced violence. In addition, evaluators carried out fourteen in-depth interviews with survivors and fourteen in-depth interviews with key informants from the member associations and other organizations in each country. To ensure comparability, the same external consultant collected and analysed the qualitative data from all three associations.

A final evaluation was conducted in late 2002. A team of two consultants travelled to each country and fielded the KAP survey used at baseline through ninety-eight face-to-face interviews with all staff that met the baseline eligibility requirements. Throughout the evaluation, every effort was made to follow the ethical guidelines for conducting research on gender-based violence published by the World Health Organization (WHO 1999).

During the course of the initiative, all three associations experienced staff turnover and two experienced staff expansion. Therefore, the baseline respondents were not necessarily the same as the follow-up survey respondents. For example, just under one-third (29 per cent) of those interviewed at follow-up had not been working at the associations at baseline. IPPF/WHR had anticipated a certain degree of staff turnover, so the evaluation had been intentionally designed to capture the KAP profile of the staff as a group at the beginning and end of the initiative.

Evaluators also reapplied the clinic observation guide in all the clinics and carried out a random record review of medical charts at two different points in time to evaluate the adequacy of the written record of screening, documentation and referrals.

The initiative placed a high priority on evaluation, but it was not primarily designed as a research project. As a result, the monitoring and evaluation strategy had certain limitations. For instance, the three consultants who collected and analysed the baseline data met only after the data were collected. Owing to logistical problems, eight providers at one site filled out the questionnaire in a self-administered way rather than through face-to-face interviews; at another site, a couple of eligible providers were unavailable at baseline, and one small clinic did not join the initiative until after baseline data collection was over. In addition, as the sample size was small (fewer than one hundred service providers), it was impossible to conduct sophisticated statistical analyses.

Moreover, differences in screening policies and information systems made it difficult for the three associations to collect strictly comparable information on the percentage of clients detected as survivors of violence.[2] While measuring the number of women identified as survivors was straightforward, the associations found it difficult to measure the number of clients who attended the clinic who were eligible for screening or the number of clients who were asked all four screening questions. Therefore, detection rates did not measure prevalence among the clinic population; rather they were a composite indicator of screening levels (never perfect) combined with reported prevalence of emotional, physical and sexual harm.

Finally, although IPPF/WHR and the member associations invested heavily in developing, field-testing and documenting several tools and pilot strategies, the initiative did not gather information on the costs of replicating this approach. The lack of well-documented models from other Latin American settings made the initiative more time-consuming – and therefore more costly – as did the associations' commitment to carry out these reforms in a coordinated and participatory way.

Findings

Clinic facilities and resources At baseline, many clinics lacked essential resources. In some settings, consultation rooms lacked privacy, conversations with clients could be overheard or staff filled out clinical history forms in the reception area. Most clinics lacked printed information about referral services, screening questions, educational materials and protocols for caring for women who had experienced violence. In addition, many clinics did not have referral arrangements with other services, and the majority of providers (85 per cent) had not received any kind of training on issues related to physical or sexual violence. Some clinics did not provide emergency contraception (EC) or have protocols for prescribing EC.

By follow-up, the three associations had strengthened policies and procedures, and training and support for providers, and established referral networks. Printed materials and EC were made available in all twelve clinics, and nearly all (96 per cent) providers reported that they felt prepared to counsel women about EC. Both providers and clients cited enhanced privacy and confidentiality as a major achievement of the initiative which improved the quality of care throughout the services. Some problems persisted, however, including frequent interruptions during consultations and the lack of opportunities to speak to clients, particularly young clients, without partners or family members present.

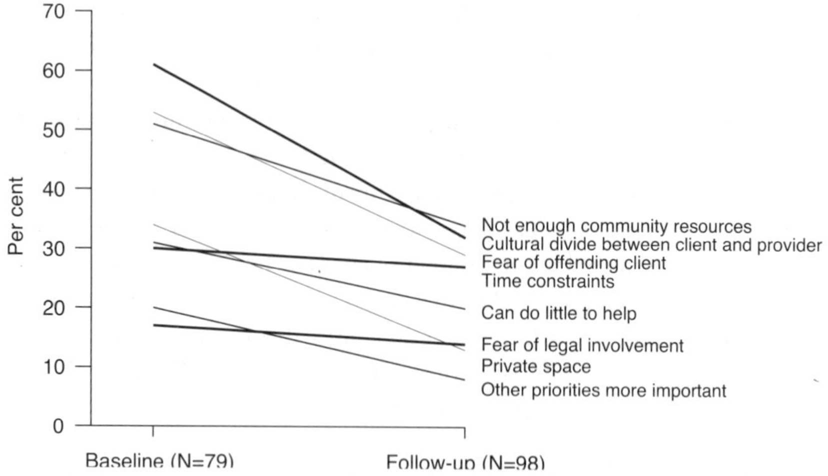

Figure 17.1 Providers' perceived barriers to asking women about violence: findings from baseline and follow-up surveys at the PLAFAM, PROFAMILIA and INPPARES clinics

Provider practices The baseline study found that even before the initiative began many providers had begun to discuss sexual and physical violence with clients, and many clients disclosed the experience of sexual violence without being asked. Just over half of providers (58 per cent) (versus 86 per cent at follow-up) had asked a direct question about violence in the past year (usually in response to a sign or symptom), and a large majority (85 per cent at baseline versus 97 per cent at follow-up) reported that clients had disclosed physical or sexual violence (not shown in tabular form). Interviews, service statistics and random record reviews indicate that provider practices improved throughout the participating clinics and perceived barriers to screening decreased between baseline and follow-up data collection. As Figure 17.1 suggests, however, several barriers remained.

Detection rates rose sharply after standardized questions were introduced within the first year of the initiative (Guedes et al. 2002). Over the following three years of the initiative, screening and detection levels varied from clinic to clinic, even within the same association, but remained fairly constant or in some cases rose. In contrast, some programmes have had difficulty sustaining screening levels over time owing to lack of institutional support (e.g. see García-Moreno 2002).

Over the course of the initiative, over 168,000 adolescent and adult women sought services at the participating clinics. Of these, just over 10 per cent reported some kind of physical or sexual abuse, 3 per cent reported forced sexual contact/intercourse and 3 per cent reported uncomfortable (sexual) touch in childhood (not shown in tabular form). Similar percentages were reported by the three clinics that exclusively serve youth (see Table 17.2).

At baseline, some providers in large clinics expressed concern that document-

TABLE 17.2 Female clients who reported emotional, physical or sexual violence as a percentage of clients who were eligible for screening at the PLAFAM, PROFAMILIA and INPPARES youth clinics, 2001/02

Type of violence included under the screening policy	Female clients at the PLAFAM youth clinic reporting violence	Female clients at the PROFAMILIA youth clinic reporting violence	Female clients at the INPPARES youth clinic reporting violence	Total
	New clients only	New clients and returning clients who had never been screened	New clients and returning clients regardless of whether they had been screened	
Any type of violence	18	23	7	11
Emotional harm	12	20	5	8
Physical violence	6	13	2	4
Forced sexual contact/intercourse	4	8	1	2
Uncomfortable (sexual) touch in childhood	3	8	3	4
No. of clients served*	2,871	1,377	8,802	13,050

**Note*: The associations had some difficulty collecting comparable service statistics. See note 2 in text.

ing violence in medical records would make sensitive information available to other staff members. Others noted that when the client was a minor, parents sometimes demanded that information about violence not be included in their child's records. Providers also expressed concern that a parent or guardian who had perpetrated the abuse might demand access to medical records through legal intervention. These concerns were resolved in most sites by strengthening the policies that protected the confidentiality of medical records, by giving providers more accurate information about legal issues and by challenging the idea that a history of abuse is more sensitive or stigmatizing than other confidential medical information such as a girl's family planning or STI/HIV history.

Provider–client interaction Surveys, group discussions and in-depth interviews with providers and clients explored the extent to which they felt comfortable discussing sexual violence. At baseline, providers were reluctant to discuss both physical and sexual violence, but over the course of the initiative their discomfort appeared to decline (see Figure 17.2), and the proportion of providers who said that most victims of sexual violence would deny the abuse if asked dropped by half (from 67 to 32 per cent) (not shown in tabular form). When interviewers probed the reasons for providers' discomfort, some suggested that discussing sexual violence was even more likely to evoke emotional distress among their clients than physical violence.

Nearly all women interviewed (96 per cent) in the mid-term exit surveys said that they felt comfortable/good ('*se sintieron bien*') when asked the screening questions, and nearly all (97 per cent) felt that healthcare providers should ('*debe*') address the issue of violence against women (not shown in tabular form). Not surprisingly, clients felt more comfortable discussing physical rather than sexual violence. In-depth interviews and group discussions at mid-term with survivors of violence suggested that shame and fear kept many women from talking about sexual violence. Women repeatedly mentioned childhood sexual abuse as the most difficult to disclose. While many survivors of physical violence joined support groups, survivors of sexual violence were often hesitant to share their experiences in a group setting. Barriers to disclosure were particularly complex for adolescent girls for legal and social reasons. For example, an adolescent girl who lived apart from her mother described her conflict over how to deal with sexual abuse by her father. Though she was distressed, she feared that her father would be arrested if she revealed the abuse to anyone, including her mother.

Women consistently mentioned four issues when asked about the positive experience of discussing violence with healthcare providers in the participating clinics: non-judgemental attitude – 'the good thing is that they don't judge you and this enables you to talk'; confidentiality, especially for young clients – 'We feel comfortable because we know that others will not find out'; being believed – 'This was the first time I felt that I was taken seriously and that they believed my

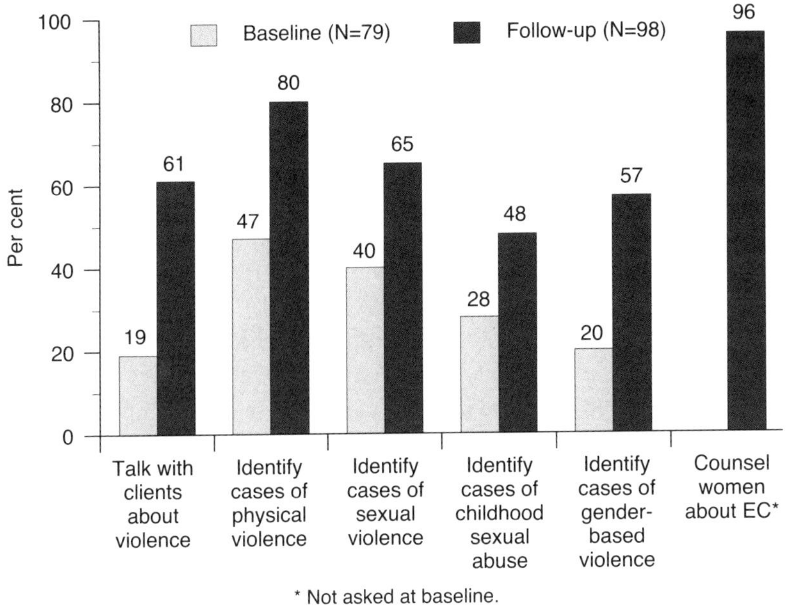

Figure 17.2 Extent to which providers in the three member associations of IPPF/WHR felt 'sufficiently' prepared to discuss violence and identify cases at baseline and follow-up

story'; and finally, emotional support – 'When I told my story to the provider, she gave me security, she gave me courage, she gave me strength.'

Many providers and clients believe that providers have a fundamental responsibility to help women recognize physical and sexual force as 'abuse' rather than as a normal or 'acceptable' part of their lives. Specifically, they noted that providers could raise awareness that violence could put a woman (and her children) at risk of health problems, injury and in some cases even death. Providers reported that many women do not see themselves as victims of violence and often the first time a woman recognizes a problem in her relationship and the idea that she is not to blame for the violence is while discussing violence with a healthcare provider. As one provider said, 'If we don't ask, it might take them many more years to start on the road to recovery.'

During interviews and discussions, survivors of intimate partner violence talked about the difficulty of leaving abusive relationships, but agreed that once a healthcare provider helped them become aware that violence is a serious problem, 'nothing is ever the same'. The ability of providers to reframe sexual and physical abuse as a health issue was cited by some women as a major catalyst for deciding to confront their situation and seek ways to change it. One woman explained: 'I was dying without realizing it. When the physician told me that my health problems were related to what was happening in my house, I started to understand what was going on with me. It was as if a screen was lifted from my eyes and I started to think that I didn't deserve this' (survivor of intimate partner violence, the Dominican Republic).

Negative aspects of provider–client interaction In-depth interviews, group discussions and exit surveys found that women were generally positive about their experiences at the member association clinics. When asked about the negative experiences of disclosing violence to health professionals in general, however, not necessarily at the participating associations – women mentioned providers who seemed rushed, uninterested, judgemental or sceptical of their story. Women complained about providers who discounted the significance of the emotional, sexual or physical harm they had experienced. They also described providers who ignored their broader situation, focused only on physical lesions and simply told them to submit a police report. Women in all three countries (especially survivors of sexual violence) complained about the poor treatment received from forensic physicians. Finally, survivors of sexual violence mentioned shame and frustration when asked to repeat their story many times: 'They ask and ask the same thing. I felt ashamed after everything that had happened to me' (adolescent survivor of sexual violence).

Perceptions of adolescent and young adult clients While the evaluation did not investigate the specific needs of young survivors of sexual violence, several findings emerged from the qualitative data. Young survivors frequently expressed feelings of fear, insecurity and guilt. In contrast to older women, young women often mentioned conflicts with parents and broader problems such as access to education and employment. They expressed the need to reduce the impact of violence on their health, to have sexual relations without fear, and to accept and live with what happened to them. Risk-taking behaviour was frequently mentioned; for instance, a young woman in the Dominican Republic who had been sexually abused by her cousin said: 'I am with many lovers as a way to demonstrate that what happened to me did not affect me much.' Conversely, some young women described avoiding sexual relationships altogether. Young women who had been sexually abused, particularly victims of sexual violence, stressed the need for emotional support and counselling services.

Providers' knowledge about legal issues At baseline, only 14 per cent of healthcare providers could explain what the law requires of healthcare providers who encounter a case of 'family violence' (see Figure 17.3). Few were aware of their obligation to report sexual abuse against a minor. Some providers – including physicians who had cared for survivors of rape – were unaware that only physicians licensed in forensic medicine could gather legal evidence of rape, and eight out of thirty-six physicians (22 per cent) cited fear of getting involved in legal proceedings as a barrier to asking about sexual or physical violence. One

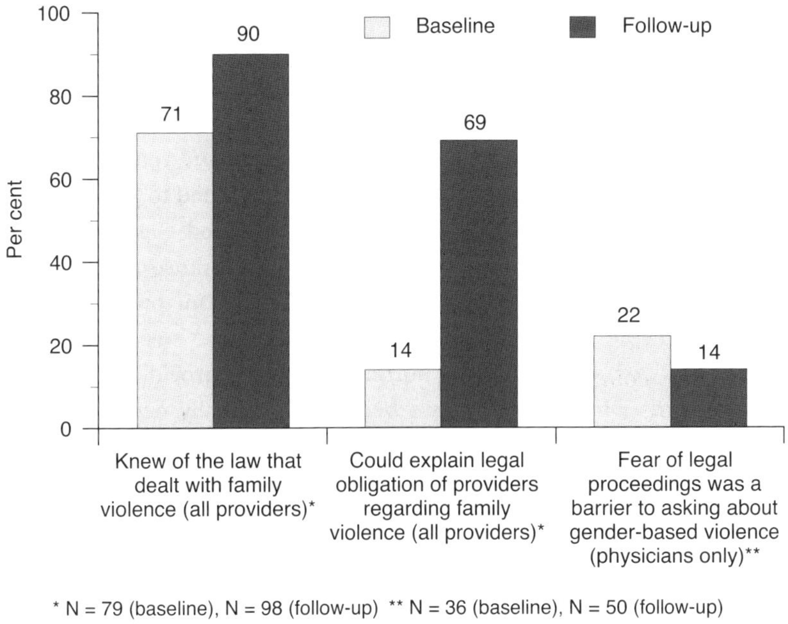

Figure 17.3 Change in providers' knowledge of the law and perceived fear of legal proceedings: baseline and follow-up findings from the PLAFAM, PROFAMILIA and INPPARES clinics

provider said, 'There are many incoherent aspects of the law governing our work.' According to another provider, 'in the end, each [provider] interprets the law as they wish'. None of the providers mentioned any negative consequences of ignoring the law.

Providers' knowledge of relevant laws increased over the course of the initiative (see Figure 17.3). By follow-up, the proportion of providers who were able to explain their legal obligations rose from 14 to 69 per cent, and the proportion of physicians who cited fear of legal proceedings as a barrier to enquiring about violence fell slightly, from one in five to one in seven (22 to 14 per cent). As part of the initiative, each association hired a lawyer, and providers valued the opportunity to have access to information about the law. In PROFAMILIA the lawyer was also responsible for reporting cases of sexual violence against minors and for legal follow-up; according to providers, this approach made it easier to report cases of sexual violence and lessened their fear of getting involved with the legal system. Nevertheless, at follow-up some healthcare providers continued to express confusion about their legal obligations. Only four of the twelve clinics had printed material about the laws relevant to clients, and most physicians did not have printed materials in their consultation rooms, even though these materials had been distributed during training.

Providers' attitudes towards survivors of sexual and physical violence Baseline interviews revealed that a substantial proportion of healthcare providers reported attitudes that held girls and women responsible for violence, such as the belief that some women enjoy being treated with violence, that sexual abuse is the result of inappropriate behaviour by adolescent girls, and that mothers are to blame for their daughters' sexual abuse because they failed to provide adequate supervision (see Figure 17.4). Some providers expressed classic stereotypical attitudes, suggesting that young women bring sexual abuse upon themselves 'by the way that they dress and the places that they go'. One provider said: 'I am partially in agreement because the young girls of today see everything as normal; they have anal contact as if it was nothing.'[3] Another provider agreed, saying, 'adolescent girls who provoke abuse behave in generally negative ways; they drink; they escape from the house; they join gangs; they are girls with dubious [*controvertida*] sexuality'. According to a male gynaecologist, the anatomy of the vagina makes it 'impossible for a man to rape a woman if she wants to avoid it'. One doctor explained that before the initiative began, when female clients spoke to him about intimate partner violence, he had often defended the man. At follow-up, a small group of providers continued to express negative attitudes, but in general the proportion of providers reporting blame-the-victim attitudes dropped substantially, and many described in detail how much their attitudes and beliefs had changed.

Before training, many providers believed that sexual and physical violence

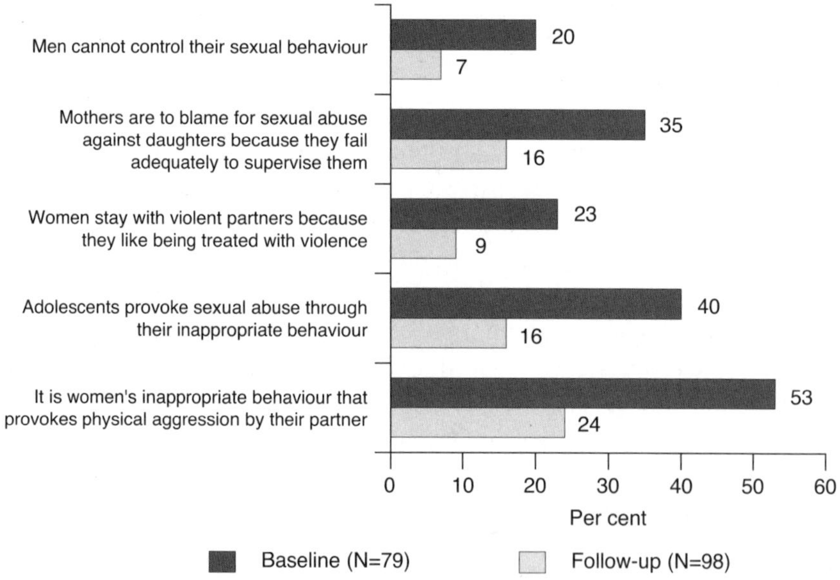

Figure 17.4 Attitudes related to physical and sexual violence, baseline and follow-up: findings from the PLAFAM, PROFAMILIA and INPPARES clinics

was a problem that was best dealt with by psychologists, who they assumed had the skills to address these issues with clients. The baseline study, however, found that the ten psychologists working in the associations were not necessarily knowledgeable about issues concerning violence against women and only six felt that they were sufficiently prepared to talk about violence with their clients. Several expressed misconceptions or negative attitudes about victims, sometimes drawing on their training in psychology to blame women for abuse. For example, some viewed violence against women as the result of 'masochistic' tendencies of women's personalities rather than a violation of human rights. Some interpreted women's psychological symptoms as the result of their individual emotional profile rather than a normal reaction to external trauma. At follow-up, all the psychologists reported feeling 'sufficiently' prepared to discuss violence with clients and many reported that their views had changed substantially over the course of the initiative. For example, one said that she had previously held the 'belief that only strangers could be perpetrators of sexual violence'. Another described realizing for the first time that 'anyone can be raped'. Another said that over the course of the initiative she had learned to be more empathetic towards survivors and to shed the 'neutral' stance that had been part of her professional training.

Integrating concerns about violence into sexual and reproductive health services The evaluation also explored whether providers integrated concerns about physical and sexual violence into broader aspects of their services. During baseline interviews, physicians in several clinics believed that they should concentrate strictly on physical complaints. As one physician explained, 'people do not come for those reasons [violence]; one must treat only what they require [the physical aspects]'. When asked whether he ever observed signs of physical abuse, one male gynaecologist said that he would not know because he 'concentrated on looking at the vagina'. When the initiative began, some physicians assumed that their role was simply to ask about violence and refer women elsewhere. By mid-term, however, many providers described how they had begun to integrate concern for violence into sexual and reproductive healthcare more broadly. One physician explained, 'Before we focused on the health problem for which she came; now the care is more holistic.' According to another physician, 'In addition to being more humane, now I see the patient as a whole. Before I saw problems that did not fit into what I had learned, now I am more efficient ... I know that many pathologies for which I did not find an explanation are caused by violence' (female gynaecologist, the Dominican Republic).

Lessons learned from training IPPF/WHR initially expected to use a 'training-of-trainers' approach. While that strategy was feasible for developing specific provider skills, such as prescribing EC, it quickly became clear that it would not be adequate to prepare providers to address broader issues related to sexual and physical violence. As others have noted (e.g. Heise et al. 1999), a one-time training workshop seldom changes provider practices, much less attitudes; preparing providers to address issues of sexual and physical violence is a long-term task that requires multiple training sessions over a period of time.

Another finding was that while many staff members had previously participated in training on gender, this had not always translated into a belief that women have the right to live free of violence. Emphasizing a human rights framework proved to be critical for reducing providers' tolerance of violence. Finding the appropriate person to carry out training was also essential. IPPF/WHR found that critical qualities of a trainer included a strong grasp of epidemiological evidence and human rights theory, the confidence to speak in front of physicians, the ability to communicate potentially threatening ideas in an unthreatening manner, and extensive experience of the nexus of medicine, law and psychology in the Latin American context.

Another finding was that many providers reported that training had transformed their attitudes towards women and men in their professional life. For example, in the follow-up survey the majority of providers said that training had increased their knowledge (77 per cent), changed their way of thinking (82 per cent) and the way they carried out their job (81 per cent) (not shown in tabular form). Many spoke of a greater recognition of women's rights. A female counsellor (*orientadora*) said, 'Before I justified violence; I said that women should cater to their husbands.' Some spoke about transformations in their personal lives. As a gynaecologist from the Dominican Republic explained, 'I arrived at the training looking to learn about technical issues; afterwards, my life, my relationship with my wife and two children can never be the same.' Another gynaecologist from the Dominican Republic explained:

> I began to change. First, by changing at home. I began not to speak so harshly to my daughters, not to fight as much with my wife. Because I thought, how can it be that I argue and I am violent at home and then I am telling women, 'I know how you feel, if I were in your place, I would feel the same'? ... So for me the change has been wonderful. I feel like I have become enriched as a person, like I have grown. I have learned things that I didn't understand before.

Finally, an important lesson was that some providers would not change, irrespective of the training they received. At follow-up, a small core of staff continued to express negative attitudes about victims of gender-based violence, and two associations fired staff members who violated sexual harassment policies. In contrast, staff members who joined the associations after the initiative began often had more positive attitudes and better knowledge than many staff who had been with the organizations for a long period of time, owing perhaps to the incorporation of awareness of gender-based violence into the hiring process.

Discussion and programme recommendations

Specific recommendations for health programmes that aim to address non-consensual sex among young people can be drawn from the evaluation of the IPPF/WHR initiative. These include:

All sexual and reproductive health care organizations, not just those that have a routine screening policy, should be prepared to respond to the needs of survivors of sexual violence Recent articles have highlighted the potential risks that routine screening may pose to women when providers are not prepared to respond appropriately (García-Moreno 2002; Ramsay et al. 2002). The IPPF/WHR experience confirms the need for caution, but also suggests that most women's healthcare providers will care for survivors of rape and sexual violence at some point. Thus, preparing providers to respond to violence is an essential component of ensuring quality care for women, regardless of whether clients are routinely screened.

Health services cannot ensure quality of care for girls and women unless they address the specific health and safety implications of sexual and physical violence among their clients Many 'youth friendly' services have sought to raise awareness of gender issues among their staff and to prepare them to provide non-judgemental counselling for young people. While raising awareness of gender issues is important, it may not be sufficient to ensure an adequate response to survivors of violence. Programmes need to make an additional effort to ensure that providers have the knowledge, skills and attitudes to respond appropriately to young survivors who disclose sexual violence, ideally within the framework of both a human rights and a gender perspective.

Changing provider behaviour requires a comprehensive package of reforms throughout the healthcare organization As others have argued (Heise et al. 1999), sustained behaviour change among providers requires a comprehensive package of reforms throughout the organization. Providers need policies, procedures, written resources, referral networks, ongoing support and training. Health programmes may be tempted to implement routine screening without comprehensive reforms, but such short cuts are unlikely to produce sustainable change and have the potential to endanger women's safety and well-being.

Changing provider attitudes about violence against women is a challenging, long-term task Preparing health providers to discuss sexual violence with clients often requires changing deeply rooted attitudes about women and men, sexuality and women's right to live free of abuse. This is a long-term task that requires ongoing sensitization and training. A single training session is rarely sufficient to change provider behaviour, much less attitudes. Health programmes should identify trainers with a grasp of human rights and gender issues, lest they exacerbate existing misconceptions and cause more harm than good. Moreover, some staff members will not change, irrespective of the training they receive. Hiring and firing practices can play an important role in changing the professional culture over time. Managers who simply cannot fire staff members with negative attitudes should never ask them to screen women for violence.

The legal implications of sexual and physical violence are complex and pose a serious challenge to healthcare programmes In many settings, even lawyers are unfamiliar with the nuances of laws related to sexual violence and health services. Moreover, translating legal issues into a language that is comprehensible to medical providers is challenging. IPPF/WHR has had some success in training health workers to recognize their legal obligations and understand the procedures for handling cases of sexual violence, and in imparting the basic information that abused women need. The follow-up evaluation suggests, however, that much remains to be done in this area.

Conclusion

In recent years, researchers and programmers have written extensively about efforts to make health programmes more 'youth friendly' (for example, Focus on Young Adults 2001). Many programmes have strengthened their commitment to privacy and confidentiality, gender issues and counselling – all of which are components of quality of care for young survivors of sexual violence. Few youth-friendly programmes, however, have evaluated how this commitment translates into providers' specific attitudes, beliefs and skills regarding sexual violence.

Despite the recent international attention to gender-based violence, young women who experience sexual violence often face a poor institutional response, whether from health, social or law enforcement services. The evaluation of the IPPF/WHR initiative found that member associations were able to improve the quality of care for women by improving the institutional resources available and by educating providers to view violence against women as a public health problem and a violation of human rights. By documenting and publishing the lessons learned and tools developed from this initiative, IPPF/WHR hopes to assist other health programmes in developing-country settings improve the health service response to gender-based violence.[4]

Notes

1 'Any act of gender-based violence that results in, or is likely to result in, physical, sexual, or psychological harm or suffering for women, including threats of such acts, coercion, or arbitrary deprivations of liberty, whether occurring in public or private life' (UN 1993).

2 Owing to differences in information systems, patient flow and screening policies, the definition of 'clients served' and clients eligible for screening varied from site

to site. In PLAFAM, it was restricted to new clients, in PROFAMILIA it covered new and returning clients who had never been asked about gender-based violence, and in INPPARES this denominator included all new and returning clients regardless of whether or not they were eligible for screening. Thus, the percentages of women detected as survivors are not strictly comparable, although they were internally consistent over time.

3 In Peru, past sexual history is deemed admissible in court against victims of sexual violence. If evidence of anal sex is recorded in a girl's medical chart, this can be used against her as evidence of 'reprehensible behaviour' in court, as documented by the Center for Reproductive Rights (2002) and Cabal et al. (2001).

4 All the major tools developed during the course of the initiative have been revised and are available on the IPPF/WHR website (<www.ippfwhr.org>) and in Bott et al. (2004).

References

Billings, D. L., C. Moreno, C. Ramos et al. (2002) 'Constructing access to legal abortion services in Mexico City', *Reproductive Health Matters*, 10(19): 86–94

Bott, S., A. Guedes, C. Claramunt et al. (2004) *Improving the Health Sector Response to Gender-based Violence: A Resource Manual for Health Care Professionals in Developing Countries*, New York: IPPF/WHR

Cabal, L., M. Roa and J. Lemaitre (eds) (2001) *Cuerpo y derecho: legislación y jurisprudencia en América Latina*, Bogotá: Editorial Temis and Centro Legal para Derechos Reproductivos y Políticas Públicas

CDC (Centers for Disease Control) (2003) 'Sexual violence factsheet', Atlanta, GA: <www.cdc.gov/ncipc/factsheets/svfacts.htm>

Center for Reproductive Rights (2002) *Bringing Rights to Bear: An Analysis of the Work of UN Treaty Monitoring Bodies on Reproductive and Sexual Rights*, New York: Center for Reproductive Rights

Felitti, V. J., R. F. Anda, D. Nordenberg et al. (1998) 'Relationship of childhood abuse and household dysfunction to many of the leading causes of death in adults: the Adverse Childhood Experiences (ACE) study', *American Journal of Preventive Medicine*, 14(4): 245–58

Ferdinand, D. L. (n.d.) *Indicadores de calidad de atención en los servicios de salud para los casos de violencia sexual y doméstica*, Santo Domingo: Centro de Apoyo Aguelarre

Focus on Young Adults (2001) *Advancing Young Adult Reproductive Health: Actions for the Next Decade*, Washington, DC: Focus on Young Adults

García-Moreno, C. (2002) 'Dilemmas and opportunities in the health sector response to violence against women', *Lancet*, 359: 1509–14

Guedes, A., S. Bott and Y. Cuca (2002) 'Integrating systematic screening for gender-based violence into sexual and reproductive health services: results of a baseline study by the International Planned Parenthood Federation, Western Hemisphere Region', *International Journal of Gynecology and Obstetrics*, 78 (suppl. 1): S57–S64

Heise, L., K. Moore and N. Toubia (1995) *Sexual Coercion and Reproductive Health: A Focus on Research*, New York: Population Council

Heise, L., M. Ellsberg and M. Gottemoeller (1999) *Ending Violence against Women*, Population Reports Series L no. 11, Baltimore, MD: Johns Hopkins University School of Public Health, Population Information Program

Kim, J. and M. Motsei (2002) '"Women enjoy punishment": attitudes and experiences of gender-based violence among PHC nurses in rural South Africa', *Social Science and Medicine*, 54(8): 1243–54

Krug, E. G., L. L. Dahlberg, J. A. Mercy et al. (eds) (2002) *World Report on Violence and Health*, Geneva: WHO

National Research Council (1996) *Understanding Violence against Women*, Washington, DC: National Academy Press

Newman, K. and J. Helzner (1999) 'IPPF charter on sexual and reproductive rights', *Journal of Women's Health and Gender-based Medicine*, 8(4): 459–63

Ortiz-Ortega, A. and J. Helzner (2000) 'Opening windows to gender: a case study of a major international population agency', IPPF/WHR Working Paper no. 1

Ramsay, J., J. Richardson, Y. H. Carter et al. (2002) 'Should health professionals screen women for domestic violence? Systematic review', *British Medical Journal*, 325: 314–26

UN (United Nations) (1993) General Assembly, *Declaration on the Elimination of Violence against Women, Article 1*, Proceedings of the 85th Plenary Meeting, Geneva, 20 December

— (1994) Programme of Action adopted at the International Conference on Population and Development, Cairo, 5–13 September, UN Document no. A/CONF. 177/13 of October 1994

Velzeboer, M., M. Ellsberg, C. Clavel Arcas et al. (2003) *Violence against Women: The Health Sector Responds*, Washington DC: Pan American Health Organization

Walker, E., A. Gelfand, W. Katon et al. (1999) 'Adult health status of women HMO members with histories of childhood abuse and neglect', *American Journal of Medicine*, 107(4): 332–9

WHO (World Health Organization) (1999) 'Putting women first: ethical and safety recommendations for research on domestic violence against women', Geneva: WHO, document WHO/EIP/GPE/99.2

18 | Non-consensual adolescent sexual experiences: policy implications

ALAN J. FLISHER

Other chapters in this volume address important gaps in knowledge of the prevalence of non-consensual sexual experiences of adolescents in different contexts, and the risk or protective factors with which they are associated. While such knowledge is essential to provide a core of scientific knowledge on which to base a rational response to the challenge posed by non-consensual sex, however, it is not sufficient to change or influence behaviour at the individual or collective level, for which it is necessary to frame and implement specific policies. Policy initiatives can also achieve other objectives, including ensuring that priority is assigned to the issue of non-consensual sex among adolescents; establishing a set of goals to be achieved upon which future action can be based; improving procedures for developing and prioritizing services and activities for adolescents affected by non-consensual sex; identifying the principal stakeholders in the field with a view to designating clear roles and responsibilities; and achieving consensus for action among the different stakeholders (Pillay and Flisher forthcoming).

This chapter identifies guiding concepts for framing policies for non-consensual sex among young people, describes general intervention strategies at the individual and community level to address this issue and outlines steps to formulate policies for non-consensual sex.

Guiding concepts

A set of fundamental guiding concepts that should inform the development of policies to address non-consensual sex among adolescents (WHO 1999) is discussed in this section.

A complex web of causation of non-consensual sex For the purpose of policy development, it is useful to consider the interrelated effects of aetiological factors for non-consensual sex at three levels: at the level of the individual, including behaviours and characteristics; within the proximal context, including interpersonal factors and the physical and organizational environment; and within the distal context, including cultural and structural factors (Figure 18.1) (Eaton et al. 2003). This framework can be used to identify risk factors associated with exposure to sexual violence and the perpetration of non-consensual sex. In trying to understand the reasons why young people become perpetrators of

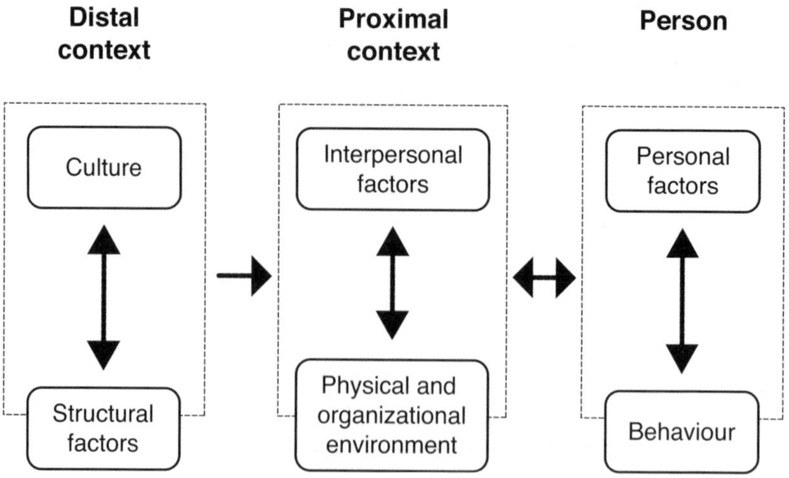

Figure 18.1 Aetiological framework for non-consensual adolescent sexual experiences (*Source*: Eaton, Flisher and Aaroe 2003)

non-consensual sex, for example, one may need to consider individual factors such as alcohol and drug use, fantasies about coercive sex, attitudes and beliefs that support sexual violence, impulsive and antisocial tendencies, and a history of sexual abuse and witnessing family violence. The proximal context would also need to be considered, including interpersonal factors such as identification with aggressive peers, a family environment characterized by physical violence and limited resources, patriarchal family or intimate relationships, emotionally unsupportive family relationships, and physical and organizational environmental factors such as limited leisure resources, living on the street and incarceration. Such behaviours could also be influenced by the distal context, including cultural factors such as patriarchal norms, perceptions of the biological need for males to have sex (for example, with a girlfriend) and their right to force sex, and structural factors such as poverty and limited access to legal resources (ibid.; Krug et al. 2002).

Clearly, these domains overlap to some extent and reciprocally influence each other. Poverty, for example, can influence the experience of non-consensual sex though several pathways (Eaton et al. 2003). It contributes to homelessness, which places young people at risk of non-consensual sex, either through the need to engage in transactional sex or through physical vulnerability (Adams and Marshall 1998; Kelly and Parker 2000). It may also be linked to perceptions that support an unequal distribution of sexual power between men/boys and women/girls. Whitefield (1999) reports that adolescent girls from Cape Town, South Africa, from advantaged socio-economic backgrounds, did not endorse sexist beliefs and discourses about relationships while girls from less advantaged backgrounds supported sexist beliefs to the same extent as their male peers. The study also shows that adolescent girls of low socio-economic status experienced eight times more physical abuse and four times more attempted rape and actual rape in dating relationships compared to their peers of higher socio-economic status.

These issues have important implications for policy formulation. For one, they indicate that policies should be comprehensive, in that they should be multi-faceted. Particular efforts should be made on three fronts. Efforts should aim at primary prevention, i.e. to prevent violence before it occurs. Other critical responses that are more widespread in certain countries but need to be strengthened are secondary prevention, i.e. the immediate response to address the needs of those who experience non-consensual sex along with tertiary activities, i.e. long-term care for consequence (Krug et al. 2002). While secondary and tertiary responses are critical, they should not be undertaken at the expense of primary prevention. Prevention activities call for the need to address the individual, proximal and distal context, including social norms that condone the perpetration of non-consensual sex among young males. Such comprehensive interventions have the potential to bring about changes in a large number of individuals across a range of settings.

Second, partnerships with a wide range of individuals and organizations are crucial in framing a comprehensive policy to address non-consensual sex among adolescents (ibid.). For example, the issue of poverty can be addressed in collaboration with, or by supporting the efforts of, government officials, development experts, economic planners and housing authorities, together with non-governmental organizations (NGOs) working in these fields. Such collaborations should be beneficial to all the sectors involved, otherwise they will not be sustainable and may even have a negative impact by absorbing energy and time that could have been more profitably used elsewhere. The advantages of such an approach would include avoiding duplication of efforts, increasing the resources available through a pooling of funds and personnel in joint actions, and allowing research and prevention activities to be conducted in a more collective and coordinated manner (ibid.).

Non-consensual sexual experiences among young people cannot be addressed in isolation Being a victim or perpetrator of non-consensual sex is closely associated with a number of other risk behaviours and adverse social and health outcomes. For example, one factor that increases the vulnerability of female adolescents to non-consensual sex is the use of alcohol and other addictive substances (Crowell and Burgess 1996). If an adolescent who is abusing alcohol presents for counselling or some other intervention following a non-consensual sexual encounter, both the sequelae of the sexual encounter and the problem of alcohol abuse would need attention. Additionally, exposure to a non-consensual sexual experience may have consequences such as physical injury, HIV and other sexually transmitted infection (STI), post-traumatic stress disorder and other psychopathology, and social exclusion (Krug et al. 2002). Clearly, what is required is a comprehensive policy and programmes that are delivered in an integrated way. For example, interventions to address non-consensual sex should be integrated into other policies and interventions, such as those that address adolescent health or violence, keeping in focus their impact on the prevalence and consequences of non-consensual sex.

Strengthening the underlying protective factors Also needed are efforts to promote the healthy development of all young people, irrespective of whether or not they are at risk or have experienced non-consensual sex (WHO 1999). These efforts should focus on the positive potential of young people and strengthen the underlying protective factors rather than the 'problems' that they manifest. Protective factors can be categorized into three groups: connectedness, autonomy and regulation (to establish that there are explicit limits on behaviour and to help parents and other authority figures recognize the stage of physical or psychological development).

Strategies to promote the healthy development of young people include building life skills; establishing a sense of self, identity and values; ensuring meaningful participation in safe and supportive peer groups, schools and communities; developing income-generating opportunities; providing education; promoting positive role models; and fostering supportive relationships with families.

Non-consensual sexual experiences among adolescents are diverse There are diverse forms of non-consensual sex among adolescents, including rape or sexual harassment by strangers, family members or intimate partners; unwanted sexual advances; sexual abuse by older people; unwanted sex agreed to as a result of blackmail, threats or persistent pleading; and transactional sex caused by poverty (Krug et al. 2002). In addition, the nature of non-consensual sexual experiences depends on factors such as the age of the 'victim', whether it was a single episode or part of an ongoing relationship, whether there was a single perpetrator or multiple perpetrators (for example, a gang), where the incident(s) took place (for example, at home, in school or on the street) and the sex of the 'victim'.

It is important that policies and other interventions recognize and address this diversity. For example, if policies and interventions focus only on adolescent girls, they will ignore the needs of adolescent boys who have experienced non-consensual sex. This would be a critical omission, as the prevalence of non-consensual sex among adolescent boys may be higher than generally recognized and the denial and shame that frequently accompany sexual violence against boys may require a different strategy than for girls (ibid.). Thus, a policy that does not address the fact that adolescent boys can also experience non-consensual sex may unwittingly exacerbate the problem. Similarly perpetrators of violence should not be excluded from policies and other interventions that address non-consensual sex among adolescents. Indeed, some perpetrators of non-consensual sex may also have been victims, as males who are victims of child abuse are at increased risk of perpetrating abuse in adolescence or later (De Ridder 1997; Krug et al. 2002).

General intervention strategies

A comprehensive policy to address the issue of non-consensual sex among young people must include the following five general intervention strategies (WHO 1999).

Promote a culturally sensitive, safe and supportive environment RELATION SHIP WITH THE FAMILY, ADULTS AND FRIENDS Intervention strategies are needed that aim to influence the proximal context (Figure 18.1). For example, interventions for parents might address the need to ensure that adolescents develop within a safe and supportive family environment. These interventions can promote positive family relationships and provide positive role models as well as provide emotional support and encouragement to enhance autonomy and inculcate values that are contrary to the perpetration of non-consensual sex. These interventions operate mainly at the level of enhancing interpersonal relationships (Figure 18.1), and can meet the basic physiological and emotional needs of the child from infancy, provide training for good parenting, and facilitate effective communication with children on various issues including sexuality.

SOCIAL NORMS AND CULTURAL PRACTICES As mentioned earlier, perceptions of the biological need for males to have sex and their 'right' to force sex may contribute to an environment in which non-consensual sex among adolescents is implicitly tolerated or even encouraged. Cultural practices, such as forced early marriage, represent an extreme manifestation of unequal gender norms.

A comprehensive approach to reducing the prevalence of non-consensual sex among adolescents and mitigating the adverse consequences of exposure to such experiences should include systematic and rigorous interventions that aim to change social norms to make them more consistent with human rights. Although this is a huge challenge, in the long term it is such social changes that will have the greatest potential to reduce non-consensual sex among adolescents. It is important to emphasize that cultural practices can be positive (such as the sexuality education that takes place in certain initiation rituals) and, in such cases, should be encouraged and promoted.

A promising approach to changing social norms is the use of opinion leaders.

Opinion leader interventions can identify and educate influential members in a community to catalyse changes in social norms, at first within the leader's social network and eventually in the larger community. A social network is a group of people who have a shared culture, set of values and behavioural norms. These behavioural norms change relatively slowly, as each sub-group adopts them through a process of diffusion. This process of change is facilitated, however, when individuals observe the behaviour or standards of popular opinion leaders in their own peer group (Fisher and Misovich 1983). Compared to their peers, opinion leaders are among the first to adopt new ideas, have greater recognition and higher social status, are more exposed to the mass media, and are more likely to communicate new norms through their interpersonal networks. Opinion leader interventions have the potential to influence social norms that would prevent non-consensual sex among adolescents. The promotion of positive social norms by opinion leaders is likely to be more effective than if it is carried out by professionals who may have limited affinity with the community (Mathews et al. 2000/01).

MASS MEDIA The media, notably television, play a significant role in the lives of young people. Interventions should aim to use television and other media, including the radio, films, flyers, newspapers, puppet shows, theatre and dance, magazines, videos and the internet to raise awareness about issues relating to non-consensual sex. An example of such an integrated approach is Soul City, a project of the Institute for Health and Development Communication in South Africa, which attempts to provide a supportive environment by influencing healthy behaviour choice by changing attitudes and social norms (CASE 1997; Krug et al. 2002). The lead media are prime-time television and radio dramas, backed by newspaper inserts and life skills and education packages. Some of the issues that have been addressed so far are rape and sexual harassment, domestic violence, gang violence and bullying.

ACCESS TO KEY OPPORTUNITIES This intervention strategy includes enhancing access to a wide range of services, including education, tutoring, affordable and quality healthcare, and facilities for sports and recreation. It thus addresses the distal factor of poverty as a cause of non-consensual sex among young people. Related to this is the need to improve the physical infrastructure and organizational environment. If, for example, it is found that non-consensual sex among young people is more common in specific locations (for example, unsupervised areas of a school building), attention should be given to the particular aspects of these locations that result in such incidents, and these should be rectified.

LEGISLATION Efforts at advocacy are often necessary when implementing this intervention strategy. Advocacy 'consists of organized efforts and actions that use the instruments of democracy to establish and implement laws and policies that will create a just and equitable society. These instruments include elections, mass mobilization, civil action ... lobbying, negotiations, bargaining and court actions' (Kwawu 1999: 4). While advocacy is necessary to lay the groundwork for the promulgation of legislation, however, it is often even more important, after promulgation, to ensure that the legislation is implemented.

While developing legislation to address non-consensual sex among young people, one is obliged to take into consideration treaties, conventions and other instruments to which one's country is committed. Examples of such instruments are the Convention on the Rights of the Child (CRC), the Programme of Action of the International Conference on Population and Development (ICPD), and the Programme of Action adopted at the United Nations Fourth World Conference on Women.

Provide information Over and above the information that would be provided through the mass media, in interventions that enhance opportunities for adolescents and in programmes for parents, more direct efforts for providing information are also required. An important means of achieving this strategy is by providing information, education and communication (IEC) materials. Adolescents need information on a variety of issues related to non-consensual sex, such as risk behaviours, including the use of alcohol and other substances; the risks of non-consensual sex, including exposure to HIV and other STIs; how to defend oneself if assaulted; legal steps to prevent further episodes of non-consensual sex or to bring perpetrators of previous episodes before the judicial system; where one can access physical resources such as leisure facilities and shelter; where to obtain post-coital contraception; and where to seek mental health and legal services if vulnerable to non-consensual sex.

Parents can also benefit from access to accurate information. For example, they can be made aware of the links between domestic violence and non-consensual sex. Moreover, if they are aware of the issues and extent of non-consensual sex among young people, they could help to reduce their children's vulnerability and be more sensitive to the possibility of exposure to such incidents.

Build skills Skill-building refers to the interactive process of teaching competencies to influence behaviour through a set of structured activities such as brainstorming, workshops, role play, games and debates. Key elements in the process of developing new skills are demonstration and practice, self-assessment, supportive and constructive feedback, and follow-up practice sessions.

There are many different types of skills, such as livelihood skills and life skills, that need to be built to reduce vulnerability to or perpetration of non-consensual sex. Life skills refer to adaptive and positive proficiencies that enable one to deal with the challenges in everyday life (De Jong et al. 1995). They include decision-making, problem-solving, creative and critical thinking, effective communication, interpersonal relations, self-awareness, the ability to communicate with empathy, coping with emotions, stress management, conflict resolution, the ability to act assertively in responding to problems, the capacity to pursue goal-directed behaviour, and the ability to evaluate the effectiveness of one's actions and pursue other options if necessary.

Clearly, building generic social skills is an important aspect of promoting healthy adolescent development as a high level of proficiency in these skills may reduce the likelihood of being a victim or perpetrator of non-consensual sex. In addition, there are skills that are specifically relevant to experiences of non-consensual sex. For those vulnerable to non-consensual sex, these would include self-defence, the ability to withstand pressure from others and to seek help from the health or legal systems, while for actual or potential perpetrators, they would include relationship-building skills.

Provide counselling Counselling is typically characterized by one person assisting another person (or a group of people) to gain an understanding of themselves and their situation, thus enabling individuals to make and implement appropriate decisions. A counsellor is generally a professional, and may be a teacher, health worker or religious leader. In situations characterized by a shortage of such resources, however, peers or other lay persons may act as effective counsellors (Flisher and Isaacs 1987). In the case of non-consensual sex, for example, rape crisis organizations have been established that are often staffed entirely by lay persons. It is important to recognize the need for counselling for both those who have experienced non-consensual sex and those who perpetrate such acts. This may take the form of court-ordered treatment.

Ensure access to health services Ensuring access to health services is an important component of a comprehensive response to the problem of non-consensual sex among young people. Adolescents who have experienced non-consensual sex may need treatment for the physical sequelae of such incidents, such as vaginal or anal injuries. They may also need prophylactic antibiotics or anti-retroviral agents, and/or post-coital contraception. In addition, they may benefit from an intervention to assist them to come to terms with the psychological or psychiatric consequences of the episode(s).

In many developing countries, however, there are a number of barriers to accessing health services (Eaton et al. 2003), particularly for young people, the poor and those living in rural areas. Few facilities specifically cater to young people; rather, they tend to cater to babies, adults or the elderly. In some contexts, young people report that staff at facilities scold or mock them when they seek reproductive health services (MacPhail and Campbell 2000; Richter 1996; Wood et al. 1997). Clinic facilities may lack privacy and confidentiality and hence young people may feel inhibited from seeking help from health services, resulting in

TABLE 18.1 Examples of interventions for each general strategy in the health system

Promote a culturally sensitive, safe and supportive environment

- Facilitate the development of adolescent forums to identify community-specific causative factors for non-consensual sexual experiences among young people.
- Use information and experience derived from the clinical situation to assist the media in ensuring that cultural norms that are inconsistent with non-consensual sex are promoted.

Provide information

- Provide education to the public on the causes and consequences of non-consensual sexual experiences among young people.
- Conduct research that addresses diverse aspects of non-consensual sex among young people, including incidence, causes and consequences, and the efficacy and effectiveness of interventions.
- Contribute to education campaigns to inform adolescents on substance use.
- Incorporate information related to non-consensual sex in the curricula of health professionals, which should include a focus on gender issues.

Build skills

- Collaborate with other sectors and NGOs to develop, implement and evaluate life skills programmes.

Provide counselling

- Support NGOs and other sectors to provide counselling to adolescents who have engaged in/suffered non-consensual sexual encounters and the perpetrators of such acts. This support can be in the form of ensuring supervision, providing a destination for referral, or encouraging research on the efficacy of counselling.

Improve health services

The strategies listed below relate to health services that are offered at health facilities. In addition, the strategies discussed above are clearly relevant for improving health services and are implicit in many of the specific strategies listed below.

- Develop appropriate health services that address the challenge of non-consensual sexual experiences of young people at the primary, secondary and tertiary levels.
- Develop an appropriate information system for evaluation, auditing and monitoring interventions that address the non-consensual sexual experiences of young people, including the development of indicators.
- Ensure that health programmes for adolescents at all levels address the non-consensual sexual experiences of young people.
- Take steps to ensure that services that are appropriate for the management of non-consensual sexual experiences of young people are available at all levels, including, for example, post-coital contraception, anti-retroviral agents, psychotropic medication for the treatment of post-traumatic stress disorder and other possible psychopathology that may be precipitated by young people's exposure to such experiences.
- Ensure the comprehensive integration of services that address non-consensual sex with other services.
- Where appropriate, involve communities (including disadvantaged and rural communities) at all levels in the planning and implementation of services that address the non-consensual sexual experiences of young people.

TABLE 18.1 Continued

- Increase the number of people engaged in developing services that address non-consensual sex at the national and provincial levels, and improve their managerial skills.
- Develop rules and protocols to prevent the perpetration of non-consensual sex in health facilities.
- Improve emergency response systems for victims of non-consensual sex.
- Ensure that health services avoid secondary victimization of young people who have experienced non-consensual sex.
- Improve prenatal and perinatal care for mothers who are victims of non-consensual sex.

missed opportunities for treatment and the provision of information. Clearly, any attempt to maximize the potential of health facilities as sites for the provision of services for victims of non-consensual sex should aim to address these barriers to service utilization. By so doing, health facilities would become more accessible and 'youth friendly'.

Settings for the implementation of interventions

There are a number of settings in which these general intervention strategies can be implemented, including community-based organizations, the health system, the media, the political/legislative system, residential centres, schools, the street, the workplace and youth groups. Each of the general intervention strategies discussed earlier can be implemented in any of these settings (WHO 1999). For example, the general intervention strategy of providing information can be implemented in homes, schools and the media.

For each general intervention strategy in each setting, one can consider interventions that address each aetiological level (Figure 18.1), i.e. the personal, proximal and the distal context. Indeed, some settings may be more appropriate for a specific aetiological level; for example, the political/legislative system is particularly suitable for addressing factors in the distal context, while the family is more suitable for addressing interpersonal factors in the proximal context.

Table 18.1 discusses possible interventions for each of the five general strategies listed above in one of the settings, namely the health system.

Developing policies for non-consensual sex among young people

It has been argued in this chapter that a comprehensive policy for non-consensual sexual experiences among young people should include all five general intervention strategies, and be implemented in different settings. The available resources, however, may be inadequate, even in the most resource-rich settings, to implement all these strategies. Eight steps are suggested to provide a rational framework for developing a policy for non-consensual sex among young people at all levels of society, including at the national, provincial and district levels. This section draws on the child and adolescent mental health module of the World Health Organization (WHO) Mental Health Policy Project (WHO 2005).

Step 1: Assess the population's needs It should be a priority to enhance the national capacity for collecting data on non-consensual sexual experiences of young people (Krug et al. 2002). These data can be used to inform policy, monitor the impact of interventions and support advocacy efforts. It would be efficient and economical if these data on non-consensual sex were subsumed into national data-gathering efforts, for example on the incidence or prevalence, causes and consequences of violence, and adolescent risk behaviours.

With regard to the incidence and prevalence of non-consensual sex, efforts to synthesize and interpret findings from small-scale epidemiological studies, regional, country or international data and other qualitative studies of adolescents, parent groups, educators, paediatricians, the clergy and court officials would also be valuable. In gathering information on the incidence and prevalence of non-consensual sex among young people, one should bear in mind the full range of such experiences.

Step 2: Gather evidence on promising interventions After gathering information on the needs of the population (Step 1), it is necessary to gather information on interventions that have been effective in addressing these needs. Ideally, the evidence should be based on methodologically sound research and evaluation studies. NGO programmes may provide a variety of models that could be tested.

Pilot projects are especially relevant at this stage of the policy planning cycle as they can provide information on successful interventions as well as reveal why certain programmes failed. Policy planners may know of pilot projects in their districts or provinces, or they may consult colleagues from other districts or even other countries. NGOs may also be a good source of information on relevant pilot projects. As NGOs generally focus their efforts on a well-defined area, they would be able to offer suggestions and guidelines for policy development within their area of expertise. Clearly, the more closely the conditions from which the evidence is obtained approximate the conditions in the setting for which services are planned, the more likely that the evidence will be relevant. Where there are wide differences, policy planners would need to make appropriate modifications to suit their sociocultural setting.

Step 3: Consultation and negotiation As mentioned earlier, to develop a comprehensive policy to address non-consensual sex among young people it is crucial to forge partnerships with a wide range of individuals and organizations. Such an approach is necessary at every stage of the policy-making cycle and effective policy-makers can use the initial information-gathering step as an opportunity to begin to build consensus. It is also important to ensure the involvement of key stakeholders throughout the policy-making cycle.

Step 4: Interaction with other countries Interaction with other countries can also be mutually beneficial. It is essential that international scientific advances and intervention experiences inform policies for non-consensual sex, which is possible when there is ongoing contact between policy-makers and their counterparts in other countries. International consultations can make an important contribution, especially when participants can share experiences of several countries that are similar in terms of the level of economic development and the organization of the health and government systems. Interaction between national and international organizations can be instrumental in providing support and promoting networking. Interaction with other countries can also include visits to sites where interventions or pilot interventions have been launched.

Step 5: Determine the vision, values, principles and objectives of the policy Policy-makers need to develop the core of a policy which is informed by the outputs of the first four steps. The policy would need to have a vision, values, principles and objectives, which are discussed below.

As mentioned earlier, a policy for non-consensual sex would need to address the twin goals of preventing and responding to the problem as well as promoting healthy development. The former would need to include the provision of services, such as counselling for adolescents who have suffered such experiences, while the latter would include legislation, media campaigns, promoting a supportive family environment and school-based life skills programmes.

The vision of the policy would represent the expected future goals vis-à-vis non-consensual sex. While it should specify what is desirable and for what it strives, it should at the same time be realistic. The vision should serve to motivate and unite all stakeholders by appealing to their highest idealistic and altruistic motivations. The vision may address aspects such as accessibility, affordability, equitability, inter-sectorality and the quality of services.

Values refer to intrinsic worth, quality or usefulness. They would need to be consistent with and flow from the vision. Examples of values that could guide policy formulation include addressing adverse outcomes of non-consensual sex, encouraging family involvement and community participation, and addressing the needs of young people.

Principles are the broad actions that are implied by values. For example, a significant principle may be the need to provide health services specifically for adolescents (as opposed to providing such services in settings designed for children or adults), which flows from the value of developmental appropriateness.

Objectives are more specific than principles, and refer to what the policy sets out to achieve. In other words, they are the *raison d'être* of the principles and hence also of the values and vision. Objectives may, for example, include the promotion of healthy transition to adulthood, including the promotion of safe consensual sex.

Step 6: Determine areas for action In this step, the policy objectives are transformed into areas for action. A policy for non-consensual sex should include action in several areas to avoid isolated developments that would have limited impact.

Actions in different areas would mutually reinforce each other in a synergistic manner. There are two conditions necessary for this to occur. First, there needs to be a clear understanding of how all the actions are manifestations of a single comprehensive policy for non-consensual sex. Second, there needs to be a high degree of inter-sectoral collaboration and avoidance of unnecessary competition. Clearly, synergy is more likely if the process of stakeholder consultation has been inclusive and exhaustive.

One way of organizing a set of areas of action would be to assess which of the five general intervention strategies and nine settings could be prioritized. Any choice would imply an opportunity cost, however, as the resources allocated to that choice cannot be directed elsewhere.

Step 7: Identify the major roles and responsibilities of different stakeholders and sectors Interventions that address young people must be multi-sectoral and involve the full range of stakeholders. Those involved in the consultation process outlined in Step 3 should take responsibility in implementing interventions. As mentioned earlier, the different sectors are best placed to address the areas of action in their spheres.

It is essential to identify potential stakeholders and the most appropriate setting through which to implement the strategy. All those who were potentially involved in the consultation process could be considered to a play a role or take responsibility as the areas of action are addressed.

Step 8: Undertake pilot projects Projects must be undertaken and evaluated before a new policy is rolled out or diffused on a large scale. Specifically, pilot projects can demonstrate the feasibility and perhaps efficacy of the policy; help to identify aspects that require further development; assist with cost estimations; test the extent to which and the harmony with which people from different sectors can cooperate; and assess attitudes to change. A review of pilot projects that failed to produce the desired outcomes may also be useful, as they may suggest which aspects of the project should be addressed to prevent a repetition of such failure.

Concluding comments

Although this chapter has focused on the process of policy development, it is important to recognize that this is merely the first step in formulating a response to the problem of non-consensual sex among young people. Policy needs to be translated into plans, which are sets of strategies that represent the line of action that has the highest probability of achieving the policy objectives in a specific population. If policies are not thus translated, they will remain of trivial consequence for the lives of young people who are affected by non-consensual sex.

References

Adams, H. and A. Marshall (1998) 'Off target messages – poverty, risk and sexual rights', *Agenda*, 39: 87–92

CASE (Community Agency for Social Enquiry) (1997) *Soul City Evaluation Report*, Series II, unpublished report

Crowell, N. A. and A. W. Burgess (eds) (1996) *Understanding Violence against Women*, Washington, DC: National Academy Press

De Jong, T., L. Ganie, S. Lazarus et al. (1995) 'Proposed general guidelines for a lifeskills curriculum framework', in A. Gordon (ed.), *Curriculum Framework for the General Phase of Education*, Johannesburg: Centre for Education Policy Development, pp. 91–108

De Ridder, T. (1997) 'Boys pay unbearable price to survive prison', in S. R. Boikanyo and P. Donnell (eds), *Children and Youth at Risk into the 21st Century*, Pietermaritzburg: Masakhane Youth Consultancy, pp. 30–36

Eaton, L., A. J. Flisher and L. Aarœ (2003) 'Unsafe sexual behaviour in South African youth', *Social Science and Medicine*, 56: 149–65

Fisher, J. D. and S. J. Misovich (1983) 'Social influences and AIDS preventive behavior', in J. Edwards, R. S. Tindall and R. S. Prosauce (eds), *Social Influence Processes and Prevention*, New York: Free Press, pp. 39–70

Flisher, A. J. and G. M. Isaacs (1987) 'The evaluation of a training programme in rape crisis intervention', *South African Journal of Psychology*, 17: 40–46

Kelly, K. and P. Parker (2000) *Communities of Practice: Contextual Mediators of Youth Response to HIV/AIDS*, Pretoria: Department of Health

Krug, E. G., L. L. Dahlberg, J. A. Mercy et al. (2002) *World Report on Violence and Health*, Geneva: WHO

Kwawu, J. (1999) 'Advocacy: The concept', *Africa Link*, 4–6 March

MacPhail, C. and C. Campbell (2000) '"I think condoms are good but *aai* I hate those things": condom use among adolescents and young people in a southern African township', *Social Science and Medicine*, 52: 1613–27

Mathews, C., S. Guttmacher, A. Hani et al. (2000/01) 'The identification of student opinion leaders for an HIV prevention programme in Cape Town high schools', *International Quarterly of Community Health Education*, 20: 369–79

Pillay, Y. and A. J. Flisher (forthcoming) 'Policy issues', in K.-I. Klepp, A. J. Flisher, S. Kaaya (eds), *Promoting Adolescent Sexual and Reproductive Health in Eastern and Southern Africa*, Uppsala: Nordic Africa Institute

Richter, L. (1996) *A Survey of Reproductive Health Issues among Urban Black Youth in*

South Africa (Final grant report), Pretoria: Centre for Epidemiological Research in South Africa

Whitefield, V. J. (1999) 'A descriptive study of abusive dating relationships among adolescents', Unpublished Masters dissertation, University of Cape Town

WHO (World Health Organization) (1999) *Programming for Adolescent Health and Development*, Geneva: WHO Technical Report Series 886

— (2005) *Child and Adolescent Mental Health Policies and Plans. Mental Health Policy and Service Guidance Package*, Geneva: World Health Organisation.

Wood, K., J. Maepa and R. Jewkes (1997) *Adolescent Sex and Contraceptive Experiences: Perspectives of Teenagers and Clinic Nurses in the Northern Province*, Pretoria: Centre for Epidemiological Research in South Africa, Women's Health

SIX | Approaches to the study of non-consensual sex

19 | Pitfalls in the study of sexual coercion: what are we measuring and why?

CICELY MARSTON

Definitions of sexual health increasingly include non-medical factors, and key among these is freedom from sexual coercion (Population Reference Bureau 1997; WHO 2002). Improving sexual health, then, implies reducing or eliminating coercion, but what exactly is sexual coercion? How can we measure levels of coercion in a population in order to assess the extent of the problem?

Coercion implies a mismatch in intentions/desires: one person desires sex, while the potential partner does not. Coerced sex is sex that occurs despite the mismatch, the reluctant partner having been pressured into the act either by physical force or by verbal pressure, blackmail, deception or trickery (Heise 1995; Holland et al. 1992; Rivers et al. 1998; Wood et al. 1998). The crucial distinction (as in English law; Allen 1999) is that the victim submits, rather than consents, to the sexual activity.

Negative sexual experiences, including coerced sex, can be seen from at least two perspectives: internal and external. The internal perspective, which is that of the victim, includes negative feelings of loss of control, fear and deception that would cause the victim to define the event as coercive. The external perspective (for example, that of the researcher) is based on the interpretation of reports of one individual pressuring another into a sexual act, resulting in the event being defined as coercive. It would be expected that these two perspectives would be linked in a given negative event: the external perspective would identify pressure, while the internal perspective would correspondingly include negative responses. As will be seen, however, the two perspectives do not always correspond in reality. Inconsistencies exist, not only where instances of coercion identified by an external observer are not necessarily defined as such by the purported victim, but also when comparing men's and women's experiences of coercion.

Sexual experiences cannot usually be observed directly, and to study coercion, or other sexual experiences, we rely on reports from the individuals involved. Any form of reporting adds an extra social dimension, however. For instance, the person reporting may choose to omit details, may misremember, misunderstand or report in a way calculated to put him or her in a good light (Baruch 1981; Riessman 1990; Wallis and Bruce 1983). Reports about experiences can be collected using standard methods, for example surveys (using direct questions such as 'Have you ever been pressured into having sex?'), in-depth interviews or diaries, and in order to measure coercion effectively it is necessary to establish the most appropriate methodological approach.

Reports of sexual violence and coercion tend to be collected from women and not men (Du Guerny and Sjöberg 1993; Jewkes 2003; Maman et al. 2000). In many cultures, men experience disproportionate social pressure to use physical violence compared with women (Heise 1995; Seidler 1996). It has consistently been found that women are in a relatively weak position with respect to negotiating when and how they engage in sexual activity (Ingham and van Zessen 1997). Nevertheless, men also experience sexual coercion (see reviews in Cáceres et al. 1997; García-Moreno and Watts 2000), although they appear to be fewer in number. Studies show that young people in some settings expect sex to involve men pressuring women, or consider it normal (ACOG 1999; Ajuwon et al. 2001; Wood et al. 1998). This may reflect common behaviours in these settings; whether or not the behaviours are common, however, a problem arises if masculine and feminine behaviours come to be perceived as pressuring and resisting, respectively (Muehlenhard and McCoy 1991), and consequently coercion itself is seen as 'men pressuring women' rather than either partner pressuring the other. Such perceptions mean that we can be left without a way of expressing the range of negative sexual experiences that happen to men. Indeed, the notion that men always coerce and women are universal victims – what has been identified as a discourse of 'sexuality as victimization' (Fine 1988) – is relatively common in the research literature (see, for example, Marston 2004). Concentrating solely on women as victims and men as perpetrators of sexual coercion, however, may provide an incomplete analysis of the broader social structures that also disadvantage men and may further contribute to building unhelpful stereotypes of masculine and feminine behaviours.

In Mexico, the typical discourse surrounding 'machismo' presents men as dominant and aggressive, and women as subservient and passive. Virginity is socially valued for women (Amuchástegui 1998), and the act of heterosexual, vaginal intercourse is valued for men (Szasz 1998). As in many cultures, young men are stereotypically expected to work towards sexual access and young women are expected to resist – a process researchers have termed a 'war of attrition' (Holland et al. 1998).

This chapter examines reports and interpretations of pressured sex obtained in interviews drawn from a qualitative study conducted in Mexico City and explores both young men's and women's heterosexual experiences. Using examples from the study, some of the problems of defining sexual coercion are outlined. For example, definitions of coercion are not stable and, crucially, experiences of pressure to have sex are not always interpreted negatively. In the second section the further problems of measurement of sexual coercion are explored, including the complex relationship between reports of coercion and their interpretation.

Methodology

The study under review is part of a larger project examining sexuality among young people in low-income areas of Mexico City. Qualitative research was carried out over fifteen months in the main study site, San Lorenzo, Iztapalapa, a low-income area in the east of the capital. During the course of the study, 152 unmarried young people (eighty-six women and sixty-six men) aged sixteen to twenty-four were recruited from schools, community groups and through friendship networks in the city. Deliberate screening of participants ensured that the majority (114 participants – sixty-one women and fifty-three men) were sexually experienced.

Study participants gave accounts of their life histories and were probed about their families, friendships, sexual experiences and knowledge in semi-structured interviews lasting one to four hours. Respondents were assured that the information gathered would be treated as confidential, procedures to maintain confidentiality were explained in detail and consent obtained. To ensure confidentiality, interviews were held in locations where participants could not be overheard, and the names of all the participants have been changed for presentation here. At the end of the interview referrals to appropriate services were provided if necessary, and written material used to help answer respondents' questions.

Male and female interviewers were recruited locally and were from similar social backgrounds as the respondents, although the interviewers were slightly older (age range twenty to twenty-seven). Interviews were taped and transcribed. The narratives presented here either emerged spontaneously during reports about particular events, for example sexual initiation, or in response to the question: 'Have you ever been pressured into having sex?' The sexual experiences discussed here are confined to those that occurred when the respondents were aged thirteen to twenty-two.

Findings

Defining sexual coercion: a fundamental problem In the study, although very few young people identified themselves as having been sexually coerced (two women reported having been raped), several indirectly reported having experienced pressure to have sexual intercourse. As mentioned earlier, however, interpreting these reports is not always straightforward. A detailed discussion of the theoretical approach to understanding narratives about coercion, also based on this study, is published elsewhere (Marston 2005). This section summarizes that discussion and places it in the context of measurement of coercive experiences.

In this study, both men and women reported sexual activity, including sexual intercourse that appears to have been coerced, in that it involved either verbal or physical pressure. Rather than identifying themselves as victims of coercion in their narratives, however, most respondents constructed the experience to conform to the socially accepted norm: for men, the social norm is to be in control and enjoying the sexual activity, while for women it is to be in a loving and lasting relationship (Marston 2001). The narratives reflected these social expectations.

Women's experiences Women specifically reporting coercion (i.e. those who explicitly stated that they had been pressured into sex) exclusively reported incidents with men with whom they did not have a romantic relationship. With boyfriends, however high the apparent degree of pressure, they did not report the experience as one of coercion.

This is illustrated in Xochitl's story. Her boyfriend of long standing invited her to come round when he knew his family would be out. She reports that she agreed to have sex with him, but her own account suggests otherwise: 'Yes, it was more willingly, I think it was more willing than forced ... I think that it was all about ... that I didn't know how to say no in time ... To tell you the truth, I didn't know even what it was to have sexual relations ... I even said to him: no, no I don't want to, I don't want to, and he didn't want to let go of me at that point' (woman aged twenty-two; female interviewer aged twenty-six). Xochitl's story suggests that she was pressured into having sex (she says she told him 'no, no I don't want to'), but she does not define herself as being coerced and emphasizes that she was a willing partner ('more willing than forced'). An external observer noting her first comments about her resistance, however, might disagree with this assertion.

In their narratives, some women went even farther and constructed what appeared to be extremely coercive events as positive. This is illustrated in Blanca's narrative of her first coitus. An older, sexually experienced man approached her at school and asked her to go on a date with him. They arranged to go to La Villa de Guadalupe, a religious site in another part of Mexico City, but he took her instead to a hotel, where they had sexual intercourse, apparently under pressure from him. This scenario, in which the incident occurred on a first date, the woman is a virgin and her partner is nearly twice her age, was not common among the respondents.

In her narrative, Blanca laughs at herself for her nervousness and unwillingness to comply with her partner's wishes once she is in the hotel room, where she knew 'what [she was] there for'. Blanca, like the other women who reported 'positive coercion', went on to have a long-term relationship with this man:

BLANCA: He says to me: shall we go to La Villa? I say: let's go. But instead of La Villa he took me to a hotel and that's where it happened (laughs).

INTERVIEWER: And you, how would you describe what happened?

BLANCA: Well, look, I didn't want to, you know? I'll tell you a funny story. I didn't want to. He says to me: shall I go and wash? I say to him: yes. And after that, I crawled under the bed because I knew what I was there for, you know? I crawled under the bed. He was looking for me, he says: what are you doing under the bed? I say: oh, it's because I dropped a peso. He says to me: go and wash. I say: yes, and I go and wash and he comes into the bathroom to wash at the same time. I say: no, no, what are you doing here? – just think! – I cover myself with the towel, everything [*is*] getting soaked. He says to me: I like being with you, I've come to admire you. No, I say to him, get out of here! He says: no, you've got to understand me, I mean, even the first time I saw you I loved you, I found you attractive, I'd already seen you a few times but I'd never introduced myself. OK, I say, and that was when the lesson began, and that's how it ended. But, just imagine, how funny – crawling under the bed!

INTERVIEWER: How old was he?

BLANCA: Him? He was twenty-eight

INTERVIEWER: And you?

BLANCA: Guess!

INTERVIEWER: You said fifteen, right? (woman aged nineteen; female interviewer aged twenty-four)

As can be seen from Blanca's narrative, the construction of an event as positive requires the story to be told in a particular way, with reference to over-arching concepts of appropriate norms of sexual behaviour for women. In her story, for example, Blanca reports her partner saying 'the first time I saw you I loved you', thus implying that the relationship was a loving one, despite their having only just met. It is likely that had their relationship not continued, Blanca would have constructed this experience more negatively: 'he locked me in a hotel room and forced me to have sex with him'. Indeed, in all the narratives of 'positive coercion' in this study, the key to whether or not the event is reported as positive appears to be related to how closely it approximates to the socially approved model. Women who go on to have loving and long-term relationships with that partner may be more inclined to interpret their initial coercive experience in the light of positive outcomes and report accordingly.

Men's experiences Men also reported pressure to have sex, but described these incidents differently. All the men who reported pressure told the story in a light-hearted, jocular tone.

Germán's description of his experience is illustrative:

Almost straight away she started, and she said to me ... No, well, on purpose, she just turned around and went past, almost rubbing against my legs. She says: ooh! What a big one you've got (laughs) ... and me: my God! Shut up! Shut up! Shut up! You know? She says to me: don't tell me you're afraid – no, well, actually yes. She says: what of? Of pregnancy – well, it'll only be stroking ... And me: oh, what's happening. And she says: go on! And she says: just look. And she starts to take her blouse off. Ah! I didn't want to look! I didn't ... I say to her: no! Get away! You know? I say to her: if you're going to get naked, go somewhere else! She says to me: what are you, a *puñal* [homosexual] or what? I say, no ... I say no, come off it! She says: well then? And I'm like: no, no, no! No – I'd better bring you your posters, and then you should go, you know? She says: no (singing). You are a *puñal*, you are a *puñal*! And I'm like: Shut up! She says: let's see, try to ... let's see. If you're not a *puñal*, let's see you do something to me. And I'm here: oh! You want to see? Well, that was enough. I said: no, well, if this girl wants it, well, you can't exactly deny her it, can you? Well, you know, he who's hungry asks for bread ... (man aged sixteen, female interviewer aged twenty-four)

In Germán's telling of the story, the woman uses a number of methods to exert pressure, including undressing, touching him and commenting on his penis. Although he initially resists, he gives in when she begins to taunt him. When describing how he gives in to her pressure, however, he constructs the woman not as a sexual aggressor, which might make him appear less masculine, but as 'hungry'.

Men sometimes reported negative emotional outcomes following their first coitus, even when they did not specifically report pressure. All their partners were older, sexually experienced women. Their negative responses appeared to be linked to the fact that their experiences of sexual initiation did not fit the stereotype of masculine behaviour as sexually controlling and dominant (Marston 2005), as seen in Mauricio's narrative.

MAURICIO: The first time was ... in the Cerro de la Estrella [a hill in Mexico City] when I was at secondary school. A few of us went, and, well, I saw that everyone left, and they left me with some girl in some cave* up there, you know? And that's where we started. I didn't know how to kiss very well, and supposedly she taught me. And we started, and everything came off, I took everything off, and me shaking, really no one had seen my body before, and I wasn't sure what it was all about. And she said: no, look, we're going to do this and this. But the thing is that I don't know ... No, but you have to put your penis in here, and over here and like this. Then I just put it in like four times and pulled it out, and pulled up my trousers, and said: no, I'm scared. In that moment, I knew that people could get pregnant like that. My fear was, I said: she mustn't get pregnant and so no, better not. I still didn't know much about AIDS, about condoms and all that. That was the first time.

INTERVIEWER: How did you feel after that happened?

MAURICIO: Normal ... I said what an idiot I am. I don't know. I should know this, but no, no. It wasn't a case of thinking about it as such. No, it happened, you know? That's what it was.

INTERVIEWER: How would you rate that experience?

MAURICIO: It was stupid.

INTERVIEWER: How did you feel emotionally and physically?

MAURICIO: Normal. I'm just saying that ... it was just the thing of saying: I was an idiot. Because in the films it happens so easily and simply, and I couldn't do it. (man aged nineteen; female interviewer aged twenty-four)

*Translation note: He says '*con una chavilla en una cuevilla de ahí*'. Both *chava* (slang for 'girl') and *cueva* ('cave') have been made into diminutives: a way of sounding dismissive of both.

Mauricio's narrative suggests that he had ample reason to stop the sexual encounter. When he describes his state of mind at the time, he uses negative words ('my fear', 'shaking', 'scared'), suggesting that the experience was unpleasant. Yet he does not mention his own desire to stop the encounter from this point of view; rather, he mentions his fear of pregnancy as the reason for cutting short his first sexual coitus and another reason – lack of knowledge of AIDS/condoms – that he says he did not even know about at the time. His negativity about the event, however, seems related more to the fact that he has to endure the indignity of his partner telling him what to do as well as his humiliation because of his inability to 'do it'. He says twice that his own emotional state was 'normal'; he also calls himself an 'idiot' (*pendejo*) twice.

A woman who is experienced clearly 'knows' what sex should be like. She is able to compare her partner with previous partners. A man who has sex with a non-virgin therefore invites comparison between himself and other men. As in Mauricio's case, where he compares himself to actors in films, possibly pornographic films ('in the films it happens so easily and simply'), the concern is not the woman's pleasure, but whether his performance matches up to that of other men: whether he is also able to 'do it'.

Fernando, in his narrative (not presented here), also reported a negative experience when his friends put pressure on him to have sex with a woman at a party. As in the case of Germán's woman partner above, Fernando's friends taunted him, saying that he must be homosexual, until he acquiesced.

As we have seen, both men and women describe experiencing pressure to have sex rather than sexual coercion per se. Their narratives and interpretation of these experiences, however, differ systematically, in a gender-defined way.

In this study, the only coercive experiences that men defined as such were perpetrated by other men. Where they were pressured by women, the men acknowledged the pressure but tended to recount the story in a way that was in keeping with the gender stereotype of male control (as in Germán's narrative). The only examples where men directly reported coercive behaviour perpetrated by women were in cases where the woman pressured the man, but the episode did not end in sexual intercourse. Paco, for instance, described resisting pressure to have sexual intercourse:

> I didn't like the sexual insinuations that she made towards me. I didn't like them at all. I felt like the only thing she wanted from me was sex. She was twenty-two when I was sixteen. She was six years older than me, and that was exactly why it made me ... that was exactly why things didn't work. Because she, in the moment when I told her that I didn't want to have sex with her, three days later, she dumped me. She got really angry with me. She stopped talking to me, and apart from that, she went around saying that I was immature ... It made me scared that that was the only thing that she was looking for and that as soon as I, I mean I was going to commit myself emotionally to her, and as soon as I didn't fit with what she wanted sexually, or emotionally, she was going to get rid of me. (man aged eighteen; female interviewer aged twenty-four)

It seems that in general reports reflect not just the sexual event itself, but also prior expectations and social consequences of that event. Narratives of sexual experiences are informed by social expectations of masculine/feminine behaviour and identity (see also Marston 2004, 2005). They also help construct the person's masculine or feminine identity: for example, a man's experience of coercion by a woman may be narrated with a particular emphasis to reduce any appearance of unmanliness. Consequently, negative and positive accounts of experiences are not necessarily related directly to the event itself.

Both men and women reported experiences as negative when stereotypical gender roles were not fulfilled. The presence or absence of pressure was not the crucial factor in whether or not reports were positive or negative.

Women sometimes seemed to reinterpret their pressured experiences in retrospect when their subsequent relationship with the same man was loving and lasting. As in the case of Blanca, they made light of the pressure in their accounts, or even joked about it afterwards.

Men were sometimes directly pressured by their partners (as in the case of Germán) or others in their social group (as for Fernando). In both cases, pressure consisted of playing on social expectations that a man must prove his masculinity by engaging in heterosexual vaginal intercourse. Individuals' expectations of sexual events based on gender stereotypes play a key role in determining negative and positive accounts. This helps to explain why some men, who do not, at first sight, appear to have been coerced (as in the case of Mauricio) nevertheless report negative experiences. Clearly, pressure to have sex and pressure to 'perform' have important social dimensions, and it is over-simplistic to view pressure as something that exclusively comes from the partner.

Measuring coercion using reports

Key concepts in measuring coercion The fact that defining coercion is problematic is not the only difficulty in measuring the relationship between coercion and reports of coercion. There are other problems that are inherent in the nature

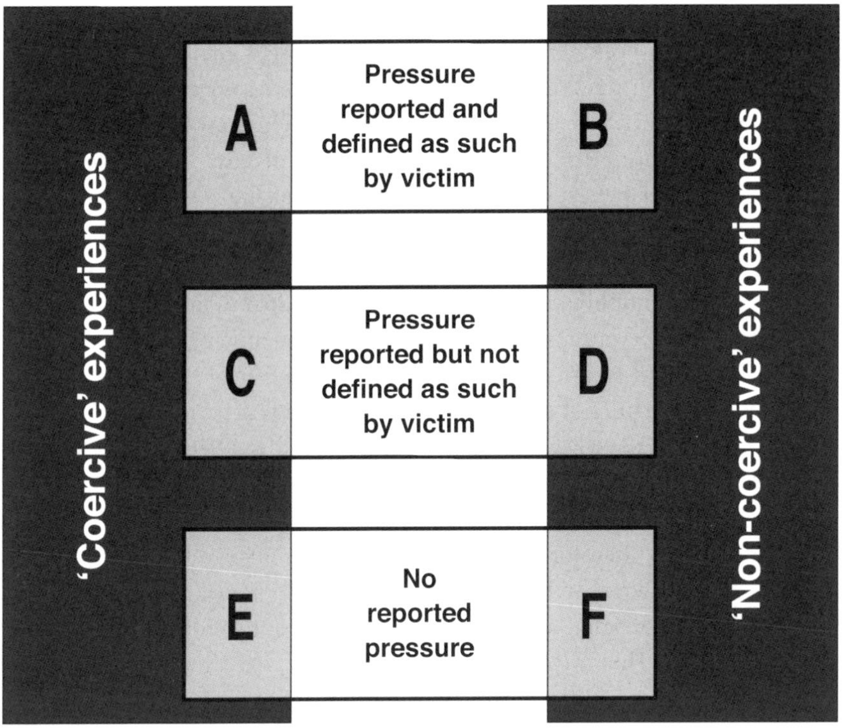

Figure 19.1 Measuring coercion with interviews: six key components

of reports of coercive events. To illustrate this, let us assume for the moment that it is possible for researchers to provide an external definition of coercion based on accounts in interviews (for example, 'reports verbal and/or physical pressure to have sex'). Such a definition is necessary if, for instance, we are to measure the prevalence of coercion in a survey. The formulation of a definition would make it possible to categorize experiences as 'coercive' or 'non-coercive' with reference to their reported characteristics.

Types of reports can theoretically be categorized into three broad groups. First, reports of coercion where the interviewee defines the event as coercive (for example, 'I was pressured into having sex'). Second, reports of pressure where the respondent does not define the event as coercive, but reports apparent pressure (as in Blanca's narrative). Third, reports specifically stating that there was no pressure, or where pressure is not mentioned.

Figure 19.1 breaks down reports of coercion and their classification by the researcher as 'coercive' or 'non-coercive' into six categories. All three groups of reports described above could refer to coercive or non-coercive experiences as defined by the researcher.

Category A covers respondents' reports of coercion that are also defined as coercive by the researcher. Most reports of coercion are likely to fall into this category. It is, however, possible that some reports of coercion might not be judged coercive by the researcher. Such reports fall into category B and are likely to be far more rare. Examples might include a man reporting coercion to a researcher who refuses to believe it possible for a man to be coerced, or where a researcher believes, rightly or wrongly, that the respondent is simply not telling the truth.

Cases such as that of Blanca, described earlier, where a respondent reports pressure but does not himself or herself see it as coercion, fall into categories C and D. Category C covers cases where the researcher defines the event as coercive based on the report, and D covers cases where the researcher agrees with the respondent that it was not coercive. It must be emphasized that the distinction between C and D can only be made by the researcher and depends on his or her ideas about what coercion is and how it can be recognized.

Finally, there are cases where no pressure is reported. Generally the researcher will also infer that therefore there was no coercion (category F). It is possible, however, that if the researcher has information from another source, he or she may define the experience as coercive even if the respondent reported no pressure (category E). This might occur if, for instance, each member of a couple was interviewed consecutively and information from one interview influenced interpretation of the other.

Coercion is multi-faceted and changing As illustrated in Figure 19.1 and as discussed earlier in the chapter, there are at least two versions of 'coercion' in the study of the phenomenon – the researcher's and the respondent's. In reality there are likely to be many more. The different versions are socially defined, and can change over time. They may also differ with changing cultural norms and perceptions of gender roles.

For instance, in the USA, changes are occurring in what is perceived as 'coercion': 'Acts that would have been cited as the girl's fault or ascribed to "bad manners" on the part of the boy are increasingly being labelled "date rape" ... The dominant definition [of acceptable behaviour] that holds sway at any one time ... has nothing to do with whether coercion actually occurred. This is a subjective reality that can only be determined by the woman' (Heise et al. 1995: 20).

While this quotation takes into account changing norms, it fails to mention another important influence on each individual's 'subjective' view of what occurred: his or her experiences before and after the event. The quotation also raises an interesting question about the nature of coercion: the authors assert that it is the coerced partner who 'determines' whether or not coercion has occurred. The quote alludes to circumstances (in this case the time before the notion of date rape was popularized) when women in extreme situations find their experiences painful and traumatic but, for cultural reasons, do not recognize them as 'rape' in the way that researchers might. Interpreting reports of coercion, however, is complicated by the fact that pressure can also come indirectly from sources that are difficult to pinpoint, such as a feeling that one 'has to' have sex under particular circumstances, whether or not there is explicit pressure from the partner (as in the case of Fernando mentioned above; see also, e.g., Vicary et al. 1995).

Researchers must decide whether to define experiences as coercive even if those reporting such experiences themselves do not, or whether to follow the respondent's own definitions. Heise et al. (1995) explicitly use their own definition of whether a woman was raped or not after noting that the women themselves redefined their experiences as 'rape' when they entered a new social environment with different expectations of behaviour (see also Heise 1995).

The difficulties of reporting and defining coercion are exacerbated by gender stereotypes: for example, the idea that men cannot be coerced by women. This means that the distribution of men among the categories in Figure 19.1 is likely to be different to that of women. If the popular view is that women cannot coerce men, or if it is seen as 'unmanly' to complain about being pressured into sex, men will tend not to report pressure. This would make men more likely than women to fall into category E. In any case, even if men report pressure, researchers may not see their experiences as coercive. Men may also tend not to define themselves as having been coerced. This implies that they are also more likely to fall into categories B or D. Admittedly, we do not know how much gender stereotyping distorts research on coercion. Nevertheless, the way in which gender stereotyping influences researchers' findings must be borne in mind.

Conclusions

Findings of the study show that men and women report and probably experience pressure in different ways. Individuals' responses to sexual experiences seem to be related more to how closely they match socially accepted norms than to whether or not pressure is actually involved. As mentioned earlier, women identified themselves as having been coerced only if the man concerned was not someone with whom they were romantically involved (similar to findings in the UK; see Holland et al. 1992). Indeed, in many cases women reporting pressure reconstructed the event as positive.

Researchers studying coercion have their own ideas about what constitutes pressure. The definition of coercion given in the introduction to this chapter does not mention social pressure, such as the idea that to be 'manly' it is necessary to engage in vaginal intercourse, yet from this study there appears to be a case for considering this as a type of pressure alongside 'verbal and physical' pressure.

We must define coercion carefully in order to measure it. Using researchers', rather than respondents', definitions of coercion may enable us to capture some of men's experiences that would otherwise be missed, because the men would not be required to define their own experiences as coercive. There are a number of problems with rigidly applying an external definition, however. First, we risk ignoring social norms that require 'good' women to resist sexual advances – a factor relevant in the context of this study (Marston 2001; see also Muehlenhard and McCoy 1991). Our external definition, therefore, does not allow us to differentiate between 'real' and 'token' resistance in reports, even if such a differentiation were possible, which is questionable given possible subsequent reassessment of the event by those concerned. Second, the emphasis is entirely on the sexual act itself, and not on prior and subsequent events, reducing the meaning of the act to what 'really' happened at the moment of the event. If a woman, after being 'coerced', is entirely positive about the event, or a man after having not been 'coerced', is negative, perhaps a single-point reference for the definition of coercion is too limited to enable us to understand its complexities.

Coercion, then, is socially defined and variable. Not only are definitions unstable, but gendered differences in reporting and in interpreting sexual experiences mean that we risk ignoring experiences which occur that do not to fit into current definitions of coercion. Figure 19.1 illustrates a methodology of making explicit some of the preconceptions and limitations involved in the measurement of coercion. It is inevitable that researchers will decide what constitutes coercion in any given study, but because 'coercion' can mean a number of different things, it is crucial that we report and acknowledge the assumptions we make. Rather than simply ignoring problematic examples, we should note how well or how poorly they fit with the overall concepts and definitions used in a particular study, and make overt decisions to include or exclude specific cases as examples of coercion.

It may also be that the researcher is working with an implicit hierarchy of coercion. He or she may presume, for example, that physical pressure is always worse than other forms of coercion. Such implicit hierarchies should be made explicit so that the underlying assumptions can be assessed.

Clearly all research on coercion is influenced by the social background and beliefs of the researcher. For example, men may be excluded from studies of coercion, implying that researchers feel men's experiences are less important than women's. Or a researcher may conclude that a woman has been coerced even though she may not see the event she reported in this way.

By adopting a systematic approach to identifying the assumptions that underpin the study of such a complex phenomenon, we can begin to compare analyses of different settings by different researchers. Judgements about what is and is not coercion are inevitable in this area of research, but at the very least the assumptions that lead to such judgements should be discussed openly and justified.

Note

This study was funded by grants from the UK Economic and Social Research Council. Additional fieldwork costs were met by grants from the Simon Population Trust, the Population Investigation Committee and the University of London Central Research Fund. Field support was provided by the Fundación Mexicana para la Planeación Familiar (Mexfam). I am indebted to Fatima Juarez, who provided support and guidance throughout. I thank John Cleland and Judy Green for their comments on earlier drafts of this chapter, and Alicia Caballero, Israel Balderas García, José Fonseca, Virginia Fonseca, Flavio Hernández Hernández, Edith Lara Herrera and Luz María Velasco Reyero, who conducted the majority of the interviews. I particularly thank Alicia Caballero and Flavio Hernández for their invaluable contributions to all aspects of the fieldwork.

References

ACOG (American College of Obstetricians and Gynecologists) (1999) 'Adolescent victims of sexual assault', *International Journal of Gynecology and Obstetrics*, 64(2): 195–9

Ajuwon, A. J., I. Akin-Jimoh, B. O. Olley et al. (2001) 'Perceptions of sexual coercion: learning from young people in Ibadan, Nigeria', *Reproductive Health Matters*, 9(17): 128–36

Allen, M. J. (1999) *Textbook on Criminal Law*, London: Blackstone Press

Amuchástegui, A. M. G. (1998) 'Virginity and sexual initiation in Mexico: the dialogic negotiation of meaning', Doctoral thesis, Goldsmiths College, University of London

Baruch, G. (1981) 'Moral tales: parents' stories of encounters with the health professions', *Sociology of Health and Illness*, 3(3): 275–93

Cáceres, C. F., B. V. Marín, E. S. Hudes et al. (1997) 'Young people and the structure of sexual risks in Lima', *AIDS*, 11(1): S67–S77

Du Guerny, J. and E. Sjöberg (1993) 'Inter-relationship between gender relations and the HIV/AIDS epidemic: some possible considerations for policies and programmes', *AIDS*, 7: 1027–34

Fine, M. (1988) 'Sexuality, schooling, and adolescent females: the missing discourse of desire', *Harvard Educational Review*, 58(1): 29–53

García-Moreno, C. and C. Watts (2000) 'Violence against women: its importance for HIV/AIDS', *AIDS*, 14(suppl. 3): S253–S265

Heise, L. H. (1995) 'Violence, sexuality, and women's lives', in R. G. Parker and J. H. Gagnon (eds), *Conceiving Sexuality: Approaches to Sex Research in a Postmodern World*, New York: Routledge, pp. 109–34

Heise, L., K. Moore and N. Toubia (1995) *Sexual Coercion and Reproductive Health: A Focus on Research*, New York: Population Council

Holland, J., C. Ramazanoglu, S. Sharpe et al. (1992) 'Pleasure, pressure and power: some contradictions of gendered sexuality', *Sociological Review*, 40(4): 645–74

— (1998) *The Male in the Head: Young People, Heterosexuality and Power*, London: Tufnell Press

Ingham, R. and G. van Zessen (1997) 'From individual properties to interactional processes', in L. Van Campenhoudt, M. Cohen, G. Guizzardi et al. (eds), *Sexual Interactions and HIV Risk*, London: Taylor and Francis

Jewkes, R. (2003) 'Gender inequalities, intimate partner violence and hiv preventive practices: findings of a South African cross-sectional study', *Social Science and Medicine*, 56(1): 125–34

Maman, S., J. Campbell, M. D. Sweat et al. (2000) 'The intersections of HIV and violence: directions for future research and interventions', *Social Science and Medicine*, 50(4): 459–78

Marston, C. A. (2001) '"A man gets as far as a woman wants him to"? Sexual behaviour change among young people in Mexico', Doctoral thesis, London School of Hygiene and Tropical Medicine, University of London

— (2004) 'Gendered communication among young people in Mexico: implications for sexual health interventions', *Social Science and Medicine*, 59(3): 445–56

— (2005) 'What is heterosexual coercion? Interpreting narratives from young people in Mexico City', *Sociology of Health and Illness*, 27(1): 68–91

Muehlenhard, C. L. and M. L. McCoy (1991) 'Double standard/double bind: the sexual double standard and women's communication about sex', *Psychology of Women Quarterly*, 15: 447–61

Population Reference Bureau (1997) *Improving Reproductive Health in Developing Countries: A Summary of Findings from the National Research Council of the US National Academy of Sciences*, Washington, DC: Population Reference Bureau

Riessman, C. K (1990) 'Strategic uses of narrative in the presentation of self and illness: a research note', *Social Science and Medicine*, 30(11): 1195–200

Rivers, K., P. Aggleton, J. Elizondo et al. (1998) 'Gender relations, sexual communication, and the female condom', *Critical Public Health*, 8(4): 273–90

Seidler, V. (1996) 'Masculinity and violence', in L. May, R. Strikwerda and P. D. Hopkins (eds), *Rethinking Masculinity: Philosophical Explorations in the Light of Feminism*, London: Rowman and Littlefield, pp. 63–75

Szasz, I. (1998) 'Masculine identity and the meanings of sexuality: a review of research in Mexico', *Reproductive Health Matters*, 6(12): 97–104

Vicary, J. R., L. R. Klingaman and W. L. Harkness (1995) 'Risk factors associated with date rape and sexual assault of adolescent girls', *Journal of Adolescence*, 18(3): 289–306

Wallis, R. and S. Bruce (1983) 'Accounting for action: defending the common sense heresy', *Sociology*, 17(1): 97–111

WHO (World Health Organization) (2002) *Technical Consultation on Sexual Health*, Geneva: World Health Organization

Wood, K., F. Maforah and R. Jewkes (1998) '"He forced me to love him": putting violence on adolescent sexual health agendas', *Social Science and Medicine*, 47(2): 233–42

20 | Research designs for investigating non-consensual sexual experiences among young people

PHILIP GUEST

It is clear from even a cursory review of the meagre literature available on non-consensual sexual experiences, particularly among young people, that there are major gaps in our knowledge (Heise et al. 1995). A recent review of the reproductive and sexual health of young people in Asia and the Pacific (Jejeebhoy and Bott 2003) concludes that although there are several small-scale studies that suggest that many young women and men do experience non-consensual sex, it is difficult to determine with any accuracy the levels of such behaviour or its determinants (see also Gabahju 2002).

These gaps in knowledge range from the quantification of the basic parameters of non-consensual sex, i.e. how often it occurs, and the characteristics of those who experience or perpetrate the behaviour, to the circumstances in which such acts occur, including its determinants at different levels and its consequences, and the evaluation of programmes that address non-consensual sex and its adverse outcomes.

A major reason for the large gaps in our knowledge is that recognition of and interest in this issue have been relatively recent. Spurred by concerns about adolescent fertility, and even more recent concerns over the risk of exposure to HIV/AIDS, studies of young people's sexual behaviour have increased over the last two decades, and awareness of non-consensual sexual experiences of young people, especially young women, has grown. Relatively few studies, however, focus on the issue of non-consensual sexual experiences of young people.

The lack of research on non-consensual sex has been compounded by the conceptual and methodological difficulties faced by researchers concerned with this subject,[1] particularly in the context of young people. The lack of consistency of definitions of non-consensual sex, the sensitivity of the topic and the complexity of causal processes have limited the extent and quality of research that has been undertaken.

This chapter addresses issues of research design in studies of the non-consensual experiences of young people. It is based on the premise that both quantitative and qualitative data are required for a better appreciation of the issues. Both approaches have strengths when applied with methodological rigour and particularly when applied together within the same research design.

This chapter is divided into three sections. The first reviews issues related to the measurement of non-consensual sexual experiences, including operationalizing a definition, representativeness of data, quality of data and ethical issues in research. The second focuses on design issues related to understanding the context, meanings, determinants and outcomes of non-consensual sex. Finally, issues related to the evaluation of programmes are explored.

Measuring non-consensual sex

Any study of non-consensual sex would need to determine the prevalence of such acts in a population if effective interventions are to be planned and for advocacy. While programme implementers argue that the focus of research should be on understanding the process leading to non-consensual sex in order to design effective interventions, at the same time accurate information on the prevalence and correlates of non-consensual sex are necessary for advocacy, planning and to understand the phenomenon of non-consensual sex.

Some of the scepticism over the quantification of non-consensual sex undoubtedly stems from the high level of variation in estimates of such experiences across studies and the resultant belief that it is not possible to obtain accurate estimates of such sensitive behaviour through standard survey techniques. Though such concerns are warranted, there are ways in which the problems of data consistency and quality can be addressed, leading to increased reliability and validity of quantitative data.

Quantification of the prevalence of non-consensual sex requires a clear definition of the term. There is no commonly accepted definition of non-consensual sex, which is perhaps the main reason why there are large variations in the estimates of the prevalence of non-consensual sex, even within the same society. The problem is compounded by the fact that in many published studies researchers have not defined how they have used this term.

Most societies have legal definitions of what constitute the most violent forms of non-consensual sex. It is not feasible, however, to utilize crime statistics as a source of data on the prevalence of non-consensual sex owing to under-reporting of such events and because legal definitions typically include only a limited range of non-consensual sexual experiences.

Surveys using structured questionnaires are the standard method of obtaining estimates of the prevalence of non-consensual sex. Before questions on non-consensual sex can be included in a questionnaire, however, there needs to be a clear definition of what constitutes non-consensual sex. Heise et al. (1995) provide a comprehensive definition of coercive sex which includes all forms of sexual behaviour that are engaged in through force, deception, cultural expectation, economic circumstances, and so on, and which the person was forced to perform against his or her will. This definition focuses on the lack of choice in engaging in the sexual act.

Although a range of behaviours can be viewed as being non-consensual, most studies have focused on the most extreme form – forced penetrative sex. The most common way to operationalize this concept of non-consensual sex has been to ask people whether they have been forced to have penetrative sex. Several surveys have asked, for example, whether sex, especially the first sexual experience, was voluntary (see Mensch et al. 1998; Rwenge 2000).[2] The advantage of operationalizing non-consensual sex in terms of the first sexual act is that it focuses on one act and hence facilitates analysis and comparison.

The operationalization of a wider definition of non-consensual sex is more difficult as it assumes that there is a common definition of what constitutes non-consensual sex and the conditions under which people believe that a choice may be exercised. The notion of 'coercion'/'non-consensual' or 'non-voluntary' sexual experiences may vary within and across populations, however. For example, some young persons may not define engaging in sexual behaviour owing to economic circumstances as non-consensual sex. Forms of non-contact behaviour, such as verbal harassment, may also not be defined as non-consensual sex. As discussed later, young people themselves define non-consensual experiences in different ways, and these also need to be considered (Ajuwon et al. 2001; Hulton et al. 2000; Rajani and Kudrati 1996).

Two approaches are generally adopted to operationalize the definition of non-consensual sex. One is to provide respondents with the opportunity to define non-consensual sex in their own terms. For example, have they experienced a non-consensual sexual encounter? The second approach is to clearly define the circumstances/context of what the researcher views as non-consensual sex and to ask questions that correspond to the researcher's definition. Ideally, surveys that attempt to measure the prevalence of a range of non-consensual sex should use both approaches. Questions should be asked about different sexual situations, whether the respondent had experienced sexual behaviours and whether they perceived the behaviour in that situation as voluntary or non-consensual.

Whatever the definition of sexual behaviour used, it is particularly important that the operational definition is discussed in detail in publications. To enable comparison, prevalence data should be reported for a range of behaviours defined as non-consensual.

Representativeness of the sample To fully understand the determinants of non-consensual sex in any study situation, it is important to explore circumstances where non-consensual sex occurred as well as where it did not occur.[3] Although important information can be obtained by focusing only on persons who have experienced non-consensual sex, it is difficult to evaluate the determinants of non-consensual sexual behaviour without comparing those who have been coerced with those who have not experienced coercion. Hence, for example, studies that are based on special groups, such as persons who report non-consensual sexual experiences at facilities, run the risk of linking the experience of non-consensual sex with common characteristics of the respondents, while these characteristics may be just as common among persons who did not experience non-consensual sex. Or it may be possible that the common characteristics are related to the probability of reporting non-consensual sex. Even when a study focuses on a more general population, and therefore potentially includes both those who have and those who have not experienced non-consensual sex, the manner in which study participants are selected may limit the ability of the researcher to draw representative conclusions. For example, most studies focus only on certain segments of the population, such as students and apprentices, high-school students or factory workers (Ajuwon et al. 2001; Brown et al. 2001; Kim 1998). While these studies can provide important information on the levels and correlates of non-consensual sex within the populations they study, there is a need for studies that are representative of more diverse populations.

By comparing levels of non-consensual sex among population groups, it is possible to gain an understanding of the factors, especially the structural factors, contributing to such experiences. Although there has been a move to include questions on non-consensual sex in national-level Demographic and Health Surveys (DHS), the number of questions asked are limited and do not include non-consensual sex that occurs outside the context of sexual intercourse.[4] There is also evidence that questions asked on sexual violence/non-consensual sex in general surveys, such as the DHS, may result in under-reporting of prevalence (see Ellsberg and Heise 2002).

Community-based surveys are required that are representative of a diverse population, that can measure a range of non-consensual sexual experiences, and which focus on issues related to non-consensual sex. The World Health Organization (WHO)-supported multi-country study on women's health and domestic violence provides an example of how prevalence estimates can be obtained from representative samples of a population (Heise 2001). This study also provides a good example of procedures to improve data quality. Qualitative research was employed to refine the questionnaire used in the survey, the survey instrument was extensively pre-tested, interviewers participated in a long training course (three weeks), and special attention was paid to ensuring that women could provide their responses in a private and supportive setting (ibid.).

Although the data in this study are invaluable for describing domestic violence against women in their target population, however – i.e. women between the ages of fifteen and forty-nine years – the sample sizes for young women may be too small to provide accurate estimates of prevalence for that population. For example, the Thailand component of the study had a total sample of 2,815 women, of whom only 702 were between fifteen and twenty-four. Of the 2,078 women who had ever had a partner, and hence who were asked questions about intimate partner violence, only 239 were between fifteen and twenty-four (Im-em et al. 2003). Similarly, the 1998 South Africa DHS covered a sample of 11,735 women aged fifteen to forty-nine, and although there were significant differences by age in the reporting of rape in the sample (Jewkes et al. 2002), the relatively small numbers within age groups contributed to large confidence intervals around estimates. In contrast, in developed countries there are numerous examples of representative surveys targeting young people. Some of these surveys include questions on sexual coercion/non-consensual sex. For example, the 1995/96 National Longitudinal Study of Adolescent Health conducted in the USA had a sample of more than 14,000 adolescents. Using this sample, researchers have been able to focus on particular sub-populations of interest. Ryan et al. (2003) have analysed the context of adolescents' first sexual intercourse for those who had first sex in the twelve months preceding the survey (1,909 adolescents) and found that physical and/or verbal violence was reported by 26 per cent.

There is thus a need for studies in developing countries that focus on young people, which can adapt approaches and data collection methods to suit this group, and which draw representative samples that are of sufficient size to obtain accurate prevalence estimates. At present only a few such studies have been undertaken (see Jejeebhoy and Bott 2003 for a listing).

Quality of data A valid criticism of attempts to quantify the levels of non-consensual sex is that such experiences are so sensitive for many people that there will always be substantial under-reporting of these incidents in quantitative studies. While acknowledging the problems in attempting to obtain quantitative estimates of levels of non-consensual sex, several efforts have been made to reduce the extent of measurement error in recording sensitive behaviour by adapting data collection techniques to increase the confidence of respondents that their responses will be anonymous and confidential.[5] Methods include the use of self-administered questionnaires, audio computer-assisted self-interviewing techniques (ACASI) and mail surveys in place of face-to-face interviews. Another strategy has been to combine methods such as face-to-face interviews with a self-administered questionnaire (placed in a sealed envelope) during the interview.

There is evidence from both developed and developing countries that the use of ACASI increases reporting of sensitive sexual behaviours (Rumakom et al. 2003; Turner et al. 1998). As the computer skills of youth and the portability of computers increase, and the cost of ACASI decreases, ACASI could become a viable method of survey data collection for sensitive behaviour. This method has rarely been used, however, for collecting data on non-consensual sex, and there is a need for further studies to assess its accuracy in reporting sensitive behaviours.[6]

Mensch et al. (2003) provide, perhaps, the only comparative study on the probability of reporting non-consensual sex through the use of different data collection methods. In a study undertaken in two districts of Kenya, data were collected on the sexual behaviour of adolescent boys and girls using three methods: face-to-face interviews, self-administered questionnaires and ACASI. With regard to the question on whether they had ever been tricked/coerced into sex, the odds for boys reporting that they had been coerced were 2.4 for ACASI (the reference category was face-to-face interviews) and the odds for self-administered questionnaires were 2.33. For girls the odds were 3.35 for ACASI and 1.89 for self-administered questionnaires. The predicted percentage of girls who reported sexual coercion was 12.9 for face-to-face interviews, 20.4 for self-administered questionnaires and 31.3 for ACASI. The differentials were particularly pronounced for school students. It must be noted, however, that the authors also reported considerable difficulty in using ACASI in their study sites.

Additional methodological studies are required to examine how question order and content affect the reporting of non-consensual sex. For example, the inclusion of only a single question on non-consensual sex is likely to increase the level of under-reporting compared to the inclusion of a series of questions that commence with milder forms of non-consensual sex and go on to more extreme forms.

Ethical issues in research on non-consensual sex A number of studies published recently have examined ethical issues related to research on non-consensual sexual experiences, including intimate partner violence, and reiterate the need adequately to safeguard the safety, confidentiality and interests of respondents (Artz 2001; Ellsberg and Heise 2002; Ellsberg et al. 2001). Owing to the nature of sexual violence/non-consensual sex and the trauma that can result from discussing the subject, it is advised that referrals for care and support be provided for both respondents and field staff (Ellsberg and Heise 2002). It has also been argued that there is an ethical need to utilize the results of research on non-consensual sex for political and social change (Artz 2001; Ellsberg and Heise 2002).

These issues are also relevant for research that investigates the non-consensual sexual experiences of young persons. There are, however, additional issues related to the ability of young persons to participate in research. While under standard research ethics guidelines young people are required to provide assent for research, the conditions under which parental permission is needed for adolescent children to participate in research remains unclear (Society for Adolescent Medicine 2003). It has been argued that although there are situations where parental permission to talk to their adolescent children can be waived, there is a need to put in place procedures where other trained and knowledgeable adults are involved in the decision on whether the young person is in a position to provide informed consent (Townsend 2003). In many research contexts such a situation may not be practicable and other remedies may be available, including waiver of parental consent, if it can be argued that there are minimal risks associated with the research and that the requirement of parental consent may compromise the research objectives (see Society for Adolescent Medicine 2003). Given the special ethical issues related to studying non-consensual sex among young persons, studies need to focus on this group rather than include them in studies on non-consensual sex that have a wide age range of participants.

Understanding non-consensual sexual experiences of young people

As important as quantifying the levels of non-consensual sex is documenting and understanding the determinants, context and outcomes of such experiences.

Determinants of non-consensual sex Research that is designed to understand the determinants of non-consensual sex can include both quantitative and qualitative methods, or a combination of both. The particular method, or combination of methods, employed would depend on the objectives of the research.

The first step in understanding the determinants of non-consensual sex is to explore what young people mean by non-consensual sex. The categories employed by young people to describe non-consensual sex can be fairly detailed, and may not necessarily be the same categories that researchers would use when collecting information. For example, young street children in Mwanza, Tanzania, categorize non-consensual anal sex in different ways depending on the circumstances surrounding the act (Rajani and Kudrati 1996). Similarly, focus group discussions among young men and women in Uganda show that women categorized non-consensual sex in a variety of ways (Hulton et al. 2000). Likewise, in Ibadan a free listing revealed that young people perceived non-consensual sex in different ways, and the coercive behaviours identified varied between young men and women as well as between different groups of young men and women (Ajuwon et al. 2001). Thus, before any research is undertaken to explore the correlates of non-consensual sex, qualitative research is required to understand how young people perceive non-consensual sex.

Documenting the voices of those who experienced non-consensual sex and those who perpetrated non-consensual sex can be particularly useful in exploring the complexity of such behaviours, although studies of perpetrators are rare (see Cáceres et al. 1997). Documentation can be undertaken through case studies of one or several persons or a larger group (see Wood et al. 1998). As the sample of these studies tends to be focused, participants are often drawn from facilities.

Interpretive studies that aim to understand how people who suffer or perpetuate non-consensual sex perceive such experiences are also useful in understanding how local value systems influence the meanings attached to non-consensual sex. For example, Balmer et al. (1997) report how young men differentiated between types of sexual assault based on the actions of the women whom they assaulted rather than the form of their behaviour. Similarly, culturally accepted exchanges such as a boy or man spending money to take a girl out may affect perceptions of entitlement to force sex (Eggleston et al. 1999; Rajani and Kudrati 1996).

A range of qualitative methods can be used to obtain the data necessary to explore the determinants of non-consensual sex. These include a variety of participatory research techniques, which are useful in providing young people with the opportunity to explore and understand issues of non-consensual sex (see Ajuwon et al. 2001), in-depth interviews used to document the experiences of non-consensual sex , and focus group discussions, which can be used to explore community attitudes and values related to non-consensual sex.

Males, either as perpetrators or victims of non-consensual sex, are generally ignored in studies on sexual coercion.[7] There is evidence that young males and females view non-consensual sex in different ways (Wood 2001). Research designs, both quantitative and qualitative, that include both young men and women are required. Although it would be difficult, and perhaps even unethical, to probe issues of non-consensual sex among couples, research on sexual negotiation and the meaning of non-consensual sex among intimate partners would add valuable knowledge on how sexual negotiation is related to the construction of non-consensual sex.

Although lacking the depth of qualitative research, well-designed quantitative research can provide valuable information on the risk factors involved in non-consensual sex. An advantage of quantitative data is that they allow the researcher to use well-established probability theory to assess whether observed relationships in the sample can be expected to be observed at the population level. Techniques of multi-variate analysis also allow researchers to tease out the net effects of variables, after controlling for the effects of confounding variables. Where there are well-defined conceptual frameworks for understanding non-consensual sex,[8] quantitative studies that involve the testing of hypotheses related to the determinants of non-consensual sex can be undertaken.

Contextual factors The context in which non-consensual sex takes place is an important determinant of the definition, extent, forms and outcomes of such acts. Clearly sexual behaviour is socially and culturally defined and there is a need to examine how social processes shape and perpetuate meanings related to non-consensual sex. These processes vary across and within societies, and are best studied through ethnographic research and other qualitative methodologies.

As the nature of qualitative research is intensive, such methods can be effectively applied in small population groups. Research that is undertaken to understand how non-consensual sex is a part of the social life of young people is facilitated by the close and ongoing contact that ethnographic research can provide. For example, a study of the sexual experiences, including non-consensual sexual experiences, of street children in Mwanza, Tanzania, shows how non-consensual sex among young boys is often based on unequal power relations and reflects positions within the social hierarchy of the streets. For girls living on the street, experiences of non-consensual sex were often related to economic need (Rajani and Kudrati 1996).

An indication that quantitative research on non-consensual sexual experiences of young people is at an early stage of development is its failure to move beyond individual-level correlates of non-consensual sexual experiences and incorporate contextual factors. Research in the USA, for example, has demonstrated the large impact of neighbourhood characteristics on explaining variation in sexual behaviour between black and white adolescent girls (Brewster 1994). In so far as structural/contextual factors operating at the community and/or peer group level[9] influence non-consensual sex, it is important to measure and model these impacts. This is particularly important for programme development, as many interventions are best implemented at the community level rather than at the individual level.

Contextual factors do not operate only at the level of communities or peer groups but may also operate on other levels, for example at the level of the family or school. Mensch and Lloyd (1998), in a study of the schooling experiences of adolescents in Kenya, document the high levels of sexual harassment and abuse that female adolescents suffer at the hands of both fellow students and teachers. In other research where they examine the effects of school context on various aspects of adolescent sexual behaviour, they suggest that where schools are supportive of girls this may empower girls and reduce the extent to which they suffer harassment (Mensch et. al. 2001).

Although there are no examples of multi-level modelling of non-consensual sex, smaller-scale studies often attempt to incorporate structural factors by making comparisons of different contexts, for example, studies of students and apprentices in Ibadan, adolescents in a slum community and a resettlement community in Delhi, India, and students, apprentices and an 'unaffiliated' group of adolescents in Ghana (Ajuwon et al. 2001; Glover et al. 2003; Mehra et al. 2002).

In addition to small-scale quantitative studies and qualitative studies that incorporate contextual factors by making comparisons between communities or groups, or ethnographic studies that highlight structural factors that impact upon non-consensual sexual behaviour in the communities they study, there is a need for large-scale studies that measure different aspects of communities and examine how these affect non-consensual sexual experiences.

Outcomes of non-consensual sex A variety of adverse psychological outcomes have been documented among persons who experienced non-consensual sex during their childhood and adolescence, including anxiety, guilt and suicidal ideation (Heise et al. 1995). The experience of non-consensual sex can also have negative health outcomes, such as exposure to the risk of contracting sexually transmitted infection (STI) and HIV. There are also negative social consequences, including loss of self-esteem and avoiding places such as schools where incidents of non-consensual sex may occur. Fears of the perpetration of non-consensual sex may, moreover, lead parents to place restrictions on the mobility of their daughters. A study of adolescents in two communities in Delhi, for example, shows that daughters, likewise, accepted these restrictions on their behaviour and movement, perceiving that this would protect them from unwelcome advances from young males (Mehra et al. 2002).

The research designs used to study the outcomes of non-consensual sex will vary according to the outcome being investigated. Facility-based studies of adverse reproductive health outcomes of young women who report experiences of non-consensual sex need carefully to consider the possibility of selectivity bias in their samples. For example, while documenting the proportion of young women reporting with an STI who experienced non-consensual sex is a valuable and important exercise, for a better understanding of the consequences it may be more important to determine the proportion of women who have experienced non-consensual sex who also experience an STI. If we were able to document a statistically significant difference in the proportion of women who have and who have not experienced non-consensual sex contracting an STI, then the evidence of a link between the two events would be much stronger than if all we are able to say is that a high proportion of women who experienced a reproductive tract infection had also experienced non-consensual sex.

To fully understand how non-consensual sexual experiences of young people affect their lives, both in the short and the long term, community-based studies are required that compare persons who have and who have not experienced non-consensual sex on a range of individual, social and health outcome variables. Qualitative research can help us understand the more subtle ways in which experiences of non-consensual sex can affect lives. As in the example cited above (ibid.), the fear of experiencing non-consensual sex can lead to restrictions in behaviours and the mobility of young women. Qualitative research in India has also been used to explore the complex long-term outcomes associated with incest (Gupta and Ailawadi 2003).

Assessing causality and long-term consequences Whatever the levels at which determinants are operating, the consequences of non-consensual sex are likely to occur over a period of time. For example, Heise et al. (1995), in a review of the literature, report that children who had experienced sexual abuse were more likely than other children to have had consensual sex at an earlier age, and to have had unprotected sex and sex with multiple partners later in life. These results have been found in both developing- and developed-country settings (Handwerker 1993; Moore et al. 1989). The study designs that have been used to examine the determinants and outcomes of non-consensual sex, however, are typically cross-sectional.

To identify individual correlates, the strategy used to assess influences that occur over a period of time has been to ask respondents for retrospective information. In surveys this is undertaken through questions that ask for information at some point in the past. In qualitative research, case histories explicitly attempt to link biography to outcomes related to non-consensual sex. The use of retrospective techniques both in cross-sectional surveys and in qualitative research becomes increasingly difficult when we need to obtain information on contextual factors in the past which may influence current behaviour. For many contextual factors that we might want to incorporate into our models, there exist no records of the past situation and our respondents, typically individuals, are unlikely to be aware of contextual characteristics from the past. For example, if we would like to incorporate measures of family dynamics at childhood ages in models examining the experience of non-consensual sex during adolescence, it is unlikely that we could obtain good measures of family dynamics at the time when adolescents were young children.

Longitudinal research designs are clearly the most appropriate for measuring the determinants underlying non-consensual sexual experiences. These designs would be valuable in investigating the long-term consequences of non-consensual sexual experiences. As studies in the USA suggest (Stock et al. 1997; Valois et. al. 1999), the impact of non-consensual sexual experiences in childhood and adolescence is sometimes not apparent for many years. Longitudinal studies could help us understand the processes that lead to these long-term consequences.

A number of panel longitudinal studies on adolescents and young persons are currently being implemented. For example, the Birth to Twenty study in South Africa is following a cohort of children born in Johannesburg over a decade ago. This cohort is now entering adolescence (see <www.wits.ac.za>). Efforts should be made to incorporate measures and outcomes of non-consensual sexual experiences into these studies. These studies typically have a wealth of information collected over time at both the individual and contextual levels and, if information on non-consensual sex were available, would be a valuable source of data for studies of the determinants and outcomes of non-consensual sex.

Evaluation of programmes

There appear to be few programmes that explicitly address the non-consensual sexual experiences of young people and even fewer evaluations of such programmes with subsequent wide-scale dissemination of the results. The impact of programmes should be documented and disseminated so that successful practices can be adopted and unsuccessful practices avoided. Evaluation undertaken within the framework of strong research designs provides the most compelling evidence of the impact of interventions.

There are, however, a few evaluations that appear in the literature of programmes that address non-consensual sex among young people as one of several targeted outcomes. Some, for example, address a range of behaviours among young people, with decline in non-consensual sexual experiences being just one of the targeted outcomes. Others focus on non-consensual sexual experiences of women, with young women being just one of the age groups covered.

An evaluation that sheds light on the impact of an intervention on the sexual behaviour of young people is by Kim et al. (2001). The evaluation assessed an intervention in Zimbabwe that aimed at promoting sexual responsibility among young people and improving their access to reproductive health services. The evaluation employed a quasi-experimental design with pre- and post-tests with intervention and comparison groups. Structured interview surveys were used to collect data. Two of the indicators used to measure aspects of non-consensual sex were 'saying no to sex' and 'avoiding sugar daddies'. The study found that, compared to the comparison group, young persons exposed to the intervention were significantly more likely to say no to sex and to avoid sugar daddies. The effects were more pronounced for young women than for young men, and the findings suggest that the intervention enabled young women to resist the pressure placed on them by boyfriends and older men to have sex.

Most evaluations do not incorporate the same methodological rigour as described in the above example.[10] This does not mean that such evaluations/documentations of experiences are not valuable. Qualitative assessments of the impact of interventions can be especially compelling when using the voices of young people attesting to the impact of the interventions on their own lives.[11] Qualitative assessments also provide a valuable alternative when there are difficulties in obtaining quantitative measures of outcome indicators. Central to the quantitative evaluation of programmes designed to impact upon non-consensual sex or the processes leading to non-consensual sex is the ability reliably to measure the outcome variables of interest. As noted earlier, much work remains to be undertaken in order to obtain accurate information on levels of non-consensual sex.

Qualitative research can also play a major role in evaluation research in helping to understand why an intervention worked or, more frequently, why it did not work. Although quantitative evaluation designs should attempt to measure the intervening processes that are thought to result in change in outcome variables, qualitative methods have the advantage of flexibility and can be used to diagnose why problems occur. The main disadvantages of qualitative research designs are that they fail adequately to control the alternative explanations of change and they are not able to provide measures of how much change has occurred.

Ideally, evaluation research designs should incorporate both quantitative and qualitative components. Quantitative evaluation designs should typically involve the use of quasi-experimental designs. Qualitative research methods should be employed in flexible ways in order to obtain an understanding of how key actors assess the interventions and how they perceive that the intervention affects their experience of non-consensual sex.[12]

Conclusions

We are only just beginning to learn about the non-coercive sexual experiences of young people. We know that non-consensual sex occurs and we know that such experiences are part of the sexual lives of many young people. Even among those who have not experienced coercion, fears of experiencing non-consensual sex on the one hand, and a perceived entitlement to force sex on the other, may influence their behaviour. Programmes are being developed to reduce the incidence and lessen the impact of non-consensual sex.

The information that we have on non-consensual sex is scanty and based on a variety of definitions. Evidence often comes from only segments of the population, and therefore may not be representative. There is a need for greater attention to the development of appropriate definitions that measure the full range of non-consensual sexual behaviours. There is also a need to design and field more community-based representative surveys that focus on non-consensual sex. Owing to the complexity of the issues surrounding non-consensual sex, and the differences between non-consensual sex experienced by young people and that experienced by adults, studies need to focus on such experiences among young people rather than including the study of non-consensual sexual experiences of young people within broader studies. In quantitative research there is a need to pay more attention to the quality of data and to explore how young people can be made more comfortable reporting non-consensual sexual experiences.

Understanding the determinants of non-consensual sex requires a range of research designs. The effect of context on non-consensual sex needs to be addressed through focused ethnographic studies and through quantitative studies that collect information at a variety of levels. Longitudinal research designs should be promoted in order better to understand the temporal ordering of processes related to non-consensual sex. Qualitative methods that explore the meanings that young people attach to non-consensual sex are required to help us understand how such experiences affect their lives. Without information on the risk and protective factors that are related to non-consensual sex, development of programmes will remain largely based on semi-informed guesswork.

Although few programmes are directed towards non-consensual sex among young people, interventions are being implemented in several settings. An evaluation of the impact of the interventions is required both for advocacy purposes and to inform the development of other interventions. To the extent possible, such evaluations should employ both quantitative and qualitative methodologies. In most situations in public health, quasi-experimental research designs are feasible and, in the absence of true experimental designs, provide the strongest evidence of the impact of interventions. Qualitative methodologies used in conjunction with quantitative methods provide us with an understanding of how interventions do or do not work, and also provide an opportunity to examine in greater depth the ways in which the interventions impact upon different people.

Notes

1 There are also important ethical issues involved in researching non-consensual sex. These include the protection of confidentiality, the provision of support to those who have experienced non-consensual sex and the reporting of criminal behaviour.

2 Several Demographic and Health Surveys (DHS) (e.g. Colombia, Nicaragua, South Africa [see Ellsberg et al. 2001; Jewkes et al. 2002]) have included questions on sexual violence.

3 Studies of the outcomes of non-consensual sex focus on those who have experienced such incidents and hence tend to be facility-based. The main limitation of such studies is selectivity bias in attendance at facilities among those who experienced non-consensual sex. To overcome this potential bias, studies of the outcomes of non-consensual sex should also be population-based. A similar selectivity bias can be expected from studies of non-consensual sex that draw information from police or court records. Persons who report the experience of non-consensual sex to the police are likely to be different from those who experience non-consensual sex but do not report the incident. For example, boys may be less likely than girls to report such incidents.

4 There are exceptions. For example, the 1998/99 Nicaragua DHS included a wide range of questions on domestic violence, although the questions were only asked of ever-married women (Ellsberg et al. 2001).

5 There has also been research in other areas, such as question order and the use of supplementary questions (see Dykema and Schaeffer 2000), designed to reduce reporting error in surveys.

6 Hewitt (2002), based on research in the USA, reports that some minority populations prefer face-to-face interviewing techniques to ACASI when reporting on sensitive sexual behaviours.

7 Evidence from the few studies that have investigated males as victims of non-consensual sex suggests that a substantial proportion of young men are sexually coerced. For example, based on a probability sample of youth drawn from a city in Cameroon, Rwenge (2000) reports that first sex was not voluntary for 29.9 per cent of males and 37.3 per cent of females.

8 Such conceptual frameworks are not yet well developed in the area of experiences of non-consensual sex among young people and there is a need for more formative quantitative and qualitative research before studies focused on hypothesis testing take place.

9 Structural factors at this level are different from measures of the position of an individual within the social structure. An example of the latter would be the socio-economic status of an individual. While the latter can be measured at the individual level, structural factors must be measured at the level of social structure. For example, Brewster (1994) shows that the socio-economic status of the community has an effect on young people's sexual behaviour, which is independent of the socio-economic status of the families of young persons.

10 There are other examples of evaluations of sexual health interventions targeting young people which employ quasi-experimental designs, but most do not include measures of non-consensual sex (see Agha 2002).

11 See, for example, the documentation of a 'self-aware sex education' programme in Venezuela designed, in part, to reduce experiences of non-consensual sex among young people (Munoz 2001).

12 Roth and Mehta (2002) argue for research that incorporates both positivist and interpretive perspectives. This approach is also applicable to evaluation research in areas such as non-consensual sex. Such an approach does not just entail the use of quantitative and qualitative methodologies – qualitative data can be interpreted in a positivistic fashion – but rather demands that interpretations of events be understood within local cultural frames of reference. That is, that there is no one truth and we need to investigate and understand the multiple interpretations of experiences that are available from key actors.

References

Agha, S. (2002) 'An assessment of the impact of four adolescent sexual health interventions in sub-Saharan Africa', *International Family Planning Perspectives*, 28(2): 67–70, 113–18

Ajuwon, A., I. Akin-Jimah, B. Oladapo et al. (2001) 'Perceptions of sexual coercion: learning from young people in Ibadan, Nigeria', *Reproductive Health Matters*, 9(17): 128–36

Artz, L. (2001) 'The politics of sexual violence research: feminist methods and ethical responsibilities', in Proceedings of the Fourth Meeting of the International Research Network on Violence against Women, Medical Research Council, Pretoria, 17–24 January, pp. 22–4

Balmer, D., E. Gikundi, M. Billingsley et al. (1997) 'Adolescent knowledge, values, and coping strategies: implications for health in sub-Saharan Africa', *Journal of Adolescent Health*, 21: 33–8

Brewster, K. (1994) 'Race differences in sexual activity among adolescent women: the role of neighborhood characteristics', *American Sociological Review*, 59(3): 408–24

Brown, A., S. Jejeebhoy, I. Shah et al. (2001) *Sexual Relations among Young People in Developing Countries: Evidence from WHO Case Studies*, Geneva: Department of Reproductive Health and Research, World Health Organization

Cáceres, C., B. Marin, E. Hudes et al. (1997) 'Young people and the structure of sexual risks in Lima', *AIDS*, 11(suppl. 1): 567–77

Dykema, J. and N. Schaeffer (2000) 'Events, instruments, and reporting errors', *American Sociological Review*, 65(4): 619–29

Eggleston, E., J. Jackson and K. Hardee (1999) 'Sexual attitudes and behaviour among young adolescents in Jamaica', *International Family Planning Perspectives*, 25(2): 78–84, 91

Ellsberg, M. and L. Heise (2002) 'Bearing witness: ethics in domestic violence research', *Lancet*, 359: 1599–604

Ellsberg, M., L. Heise, R. Pena et al. (2001) 'Researching domestic violence against women: methodological and ethical considerations', *Studies in Family Planning*, 32(1): 1–16

Gabahju, B. (2002) 'Adolescent reproductive health', *Asia-Pacific Population Journal*, 17(4): 97–119

Glover, E., A. Bannerman, B. Pence et al. (2003) 'Sexual health experiences of adolescents in three Ghanian towns', *International Family Planning Perspectives*, 29(1): 32–40

Gupta, A. and A. Ailawadi (2003) 'Incest in Indian families: learnings from a support centre for women survivors', Paper presented at a Consultative Meeting on Non-consensual Sexual Experiences of Young People in Developing Countries, New Delhi, 22–25 September

Handwerker, W. (1993) 'Gender power differences between parents and high-risk sexual behavior by their children: AIDS/STD risk factors extend to prior generation', *Journal of Women's Health*, 2(3): 301–36

Heise, L. L. (2001) 'WHO multi-country study of women's health and domestic violence against women', Proceedings of the Fourth Meeting of the International Research Network on Violence against Women, Pretoria: Medical Research Council, 22–24 January

Heise, L. L., K. Moore and N. Toubia (1995) *Sexual Coercion and Reproductive Health: A Focus on Research*, New York: Population Council

Hewitt, M. (2002) 'Attitudes towards interview mode and comparability of reporting sexual behavior by personal interview and audio computer-assisted self-interviewing', *Sociological Methods and Research*, 31(1): 3–26

Hulton, L., R. Cullen and S. Khalokho (2000) 'Perceptions of the risks of sexual activity and their consequences among ugandan adolescents', *Studies in Family Planning*, 31(1): 35–46

Im-em, W., C. Kanchanachitra and K. Archvanitkul (2003) 'Sexual coercion among women in Thailand: results from the WHO multi-country study on women's health and life experiences', Paper presented at a Consultative Meeting on Non-consensual Sexual Experiences of Young People in Developing Countries, New Delhi, 22–25 September

Jejeebhoy, S. and S. Bott (2003) 'Sexual and reproductive health of young people in the Asia-Pacific region', Fifth Asian and Pacific Population Conference: Selected Papers, Asian Population Studies Series no. 158, New York: United Nations, pp. 275–308

Jewkes, R., J. Levin and N. Mbananga (2002) 'Rape of girls in South Africa', *Lancet*, 359(26): 319–20

Kim, S. (1998) 'High school girls' knowledge and behaviour on sex', *People and Development Challenges*, 5(9): 17–18

Kim, Y., A. Kols, R. Nyakauru et al. (2001) 'Promoting sexual responsibility among young people in Zimbabwe', *International Family Planning Perspectives*, 27(1): 11–19

Mehra, S., R. Savithri and L. Coutinho (2002) 'Sexual behaviour among unmarried adolescents in Delhi, India: opportunities despite parental control', Paper presented at IUSSP Regional Population Conference: Southeast Asia's Population in a Changing Asian Context, Bangkok, 10–13 June

Mensch, B. and C. Lloyd (1998) 'Gender differences in the schooling experiences of adolescents in low-income countries: the case of Kenya', *Studies in Family Planning*, 29(2): 167–84

Mensch, B., J. Bruce and M. Greene (1998) *The Uncharted Passage: Girls' Adolescence in the Developing World*, New York: Population Council

Mensch, B., W. Clark, C. Lloyd et al. (2001) 'Premarital sex, schoolgirl pregnancy, and school quality in rural Kenya', *Studies in Family Planning*, 32(4): 285–301

Mensch, B., P. Hewett and A. Erulkar (2003) 'The reporting of sensitive behaviors by adolescents', *Demography*, 40(2): 247–68

Moore, K., C. Nord and J. Petersen (1989) 'Non-voluntary sexual activity among adolescents', *Family Planning Perspectives*, 21(3): 110–14

Munoz, M. (2001) 'Self-aware sex education: a theoretical and practical approach in Venezuela', *Reproductive Health Matters*, 9(17): 146–52

Rajani, R. and M. Kudrati (1996) 'The varieties of sexual experiences of the street children of Mwanza, Tanzania', in S. Zeidenstein and K. Moore (eds), *Learning about Sexuality*, New York: Population Council, pp. 301–23

Roth, W. and J. Mehta (2002) 'The Rashomon effect: combining positivist and interpretivist approaches in the analysis of contested events', *Sociological Methods and Research*, 31(2): 131–73

Rumakom, P., P. Guest, W. Chinvorasopak et al. (2003) 'Obtaining responses to sensitive questions: a comparison of two data collection techniques', Paper presented at a Consultative Meeting on Non-consensual Sexual Experiences of Young People in Developing Countries, New Delhi, 22–25 September

Rwenge, M. (2000) 'Sexual risk behaviors among young people in Bamenda, Cameroon', *International Family Planning Perspectives*, 26(3): 118–23

Ryan, S., J. Manlove and K. Franzetta (2003) 'The first time: characteristics of teens' first sexual relationships', Child Trends Research Brief, 16, Washington, DC: Child Trends

Society for Adolescent Medicine (2003) 'Guidelines for adolescent health research', *Journal of Adolescent Health*, 33: 396–409

Stock, J., M. Bell, D. Boyer et al. (1997) 'Adolescent pregnancy and sexual risk-taking among sexually abused girls', *Family Planning Perspectives*, 29(5): 200–203, 227

Townsend, J. (2003) 'Ethical issues in research on sexual coercion among youth', Presentation at a Consultative Meeting on Non-consensual Sexual Experiences of Young People in Developing Countries, New Delhi, 22–25 September

Turner, C., L. Ku, S. Rogers et al. (1998) 'Adolescent sexual behavior, drug use and violence: increased reporting with computer survey technology', *Science*, 280: 867–73

Valois, R., R. Oeltmann, J. Waller et al. (1999) 'Relationship between number of sexual intercourse partners and selected health risk behaviors among public high school adolescents', *Journal of Adolescent Health*, 25: 328–35

Wood, K. (2001) 'Defining "forced sex", "stream-line" and gang-rape: notes from a South African township', Proceedings of the Fourth Meeting of the International Research Network on Violence against Women, Pretoria: Medical Research Council, 22–24 January

Wood, K., F. Maforah and R. Jewkes (1998) '"He forced me to love him": putting violence on adolescent sexual health agendas', *Social Science and Medicine*, 47(2): 233–42

21 | Obtaining accurate responses to sensitive questions among Thai students: a comparison of two data collection techniques

PATCHARA RUMAKOM, PHILIP GUEST, WARANUCH CHINVARASOPAK, WATIT UTARMAT AND JIRAPORN SONTANAKANIT

An enduring problem of research on sexual behaviour and other sensitive topics is that the validity and reliability of the data collected depend on the accuracy of answers provided by respondents who, for a variety of reasons, may not wish to disclose personal information. Indeed, there exists well-documented literature on the problems of reliability and validity of data on sexual behaviour collected through standard surveys (Dare and Cleland 1994; Konings et al. 1995; Schopper et al. 1993). There has been increasing recognition, for example, that the interview situation itself places stress on respondents asked to report on potentially sensitive behaviours, and that even if changes are made in relation to the quality and structure of the interview, face-to-face interviews may not always provide accurate information.

Alternatives to the face-to-face interview have been applied in a variety of studies in developing countries. The most commonly used is the self-administered questionnaire (SAQ) method, increasingly promoted among literate populations to whom sensitive questions are posed. The limitations of this method are, however, recognized. For one, concern has been expressed regarding the lack of confidentiality of responses obtained in SAQs and the consequent reluctance to respond accurately to sensitive questions. There has also been a concern that poorly educated respondents may not fully understand the questions posed in SAQs.

In the USA, these concerns have prompted a shift towards various forms of computer-based interviewing.[1] Evaluations of responses concerning sensitive behaviours elicited by these, compared to other methods, have yielded encouraging results. For example, Tourangeau and Smith (1996) compared responses to questions on illegal drug use and number of sexual partners posed through interviewer-administered questionnaires, SAQs and audio-computer-assisted structured interviews (ACASIs). Significantly larger proportions of respondents admitted the experience of these sensitive behaviours in ACASIs than in other methods; and significantly larger proportions admitted these behaviours in SAQs than in interviewer-administered questionnaires. A study by Turner et al. (1998) that compared responses to questions on sexual behaviour and drug use from ACASI and SAQ methods among a sample of adolescent males in the USA found that for particularly sensitive behaviours, for example male-to-male sex and drug use, levels of reported behaviour were considerably higher among students responding through the ACASI compared to the SAQ method. A study in the USA found that reported levels of abortion were significantly higher among women who responded through the ACASI method than those who responded in a face-to-face interview (Moser et al. 1994).[2] Another study in the USA has also highlighted the significantly higher levels of reporting of sensitive behaviours among respondents completing an ACASI-based questionnaire compared to those using other methods (Des Jarlais et al. 1999).

Results from developed countries cannot, however, be generalized to developing countries. Differences may well exist in levels of exposure to surveys and to computer technology, and may result in different patterns of responses to SAQs and ACASIs among respondents from developing and developed countries. Indeed, there are only a few studies from developing countries that compare responses to interviewer-administered questionnaires, SAQs and ACASIs. One study undertaken in Zimbabwe, for example, compared women's responses to sensitive questions related to drug use and sexual behaviour in ACASIs and face-to-face interviews (Van de Wijert et al. 1998).[3] Although the authors report that the level of agreement in responses between the two methods was high, they recommend the use of ACASIs partly because respondents generally reported a preference for this method compared to the interview. They do, however, caution that the ACASI method is best used only among respondents with a secondary or higher level of education. The authors also suggest that the ACASI method may be preferable to SAQs because SAQs require relatively well-developed reading and writing skills and the ability to understand skip patterns, which are not required in the ACASI method.

While similar comparisons are not available for Thailand, and particularly not with regard to reporting of sensitive behaviours among young people, there is some evidence to suggest that the ACASI may be a promising method. For example, a study in Thailand that compared reported responses on sexual behaviours through ACASIs with laboratory findings on HIV, sexually transmitted infections (STI) and drug use revealed a considerable consistency in responses: for instance, the presence of methamphetamine in urine samples was highly correlated with the reported frequency of its use (Sattah et al. 2002). Another study concluded that ACASIs led to increased but not necessarily to complete reporting of drug use behaviour compared to other data collection methods (van Griensven et al. 2001).

Few methodological studies have explored the reliability of responses on forced sexual experiences using different data collection methods. A study conducted in 2003 compared SAQs with face-to-face interviews and concluded that in settings in Brazil, Peru and Japan higher levels of prevalence of sexual abuse were reported in SAQs than in face-to-face interviews (García-Moreno 2003). In settings in Thailand, in comparison, responses on reporting of child sexual abuse through face-to-face interviews and SAQs yielded virtually identical prevalence (Im-em et al. 2003).

Clearly, further methodological research is required in developing-country settings in order to determine whether the ACASI method does indeed offer significant advantages over other more traditional forms of survey data collection. In addition, research is required to identify challenges in the administration of ACASIs and to test how different interfaces in ACASIs might affect responses.

The objective of this chapter is to explore the differences in responses of young people to sensitive questions related to sexual behaviour using different data collection methods. It aims to assess the feasibility of administering these methods, notably the SAQ and ACASI, and to evaluate the validity and reliability of the data gathered as well as the acceptability of different methods to young people. The chapter draws on the findings of a study of college-going adolescents in Thailand that explored such sensitive behaviours as premarital sex and drug use. The study did not include face-to-face interviews as previous studies have clearly shown that this method results in a high level of under-reporting of sensitive behaviours and, as mentioned earlier, may place stress on the respondents (Des Jarlais et al. 1999; Konings et al. 1995; Turner et al. 1998).

Data collection methods

Data for this chapter are drawn from a study designed to test the acceptability and response patterns associated with different methods of investigation. A questionnaire was constructed that aimed to measure several sensitive behaviours including sexual experiences and drug use. The questionnaire was adapted to fit each of three formats – SAQ, ACASI/no photos and ACASI/photos.

Every effort was made in the design of the SAQ to make it as attractive to the respondents as possible; for example, the questionnaire was printed in colour and ample spacing left between questions. ACASI/no photos used a commercially available ACASI programme. ACASI/photos was an ACASI programme specifically developed for the study by Thai computer programmers. Both ACASI versions used the same audio track for reading the instructions, questions and response choices. A young Thai woman was selected to read the instructions, questions and responses, based on the clarity of her voice.

The *Rajabat*[4] chosen for the study is located in a province approximately one hour from Bangkok. All second-year students were eligible for selection in the study. Sample selection and administration of the questionnaire were based on the class; from each class, a pre-determined number of male and female students were randomly selected and randomly assigned to each of the three study arms. A total of 293 male students and 372 female second-year students were thus selected.

Students assigned to the ACASI method completed their interviews in a computer lab. Seventeen computers were assigned to the ACASI/photos arm and sixteen to the ACASI/no photos arm. Seating arrangements ensured that respondents undertaking the same form of ACASI did not sit next to each other. The SAQ was administered in a room close to the computer lab. The responses of students to the ACASIs were entered directly into a database, and consequently the data were ready to use immediately after data collection. In contrast, the data obtained from SAQs were edited and entered into the computer. Owing to problems of limited access to the computer lab, data collection for both the ACASIs and SAQs took two and a half weeks. In addition to the collection of quantitative data, six focus group discussions were held, three with females and three with males. These focus group discussions were held immediately after the collection of the quantitative data was completed. For each sex, one focus group discussion was held with respondents who had completed the SAQ and two focus group discussions were held with those who completed the ACASI. A total of thirty-one students participated in the focus group discussions.

Results

On average, male respondents were aged twenty-one years and females were aged twenty. Over three-quarters of both male and female students were residing at home, either with parents or relatives.

Findings suggest that the ACASI methods elicited a higher response rate and provided greater consistency of responses to sensitive questions than the SAQ method. This was largely the result of the fact that both the ACASI methods required respondents to answer each question before allowing them to proceed to the next, and both used automated 'skip' patterns. In contrast, among students responding to SAQs, 9 per cent (eleven cases) of females and 5 per cent (five cases) of males did not answer questions on masturbation. Considerable inconsistency was observed in the reporting of sexual experiences through SAQs: for example, three students provided information on their last sexual partner but did not respond to questions on whether they had ever experienced sexual relations, the last time they had sexual relations and whether they had used a condom.

Findings, described below, consistently underscore the potential of the ACASI method in enabling young respondents to report sensitive behaviours, including consensual and non-consensual sex, number of sexual partners and masturbation, and sources of information on sex. Also underscoring its potential is young people's own assessment of the ACASI method in terms of simplicity of use, ensuring confidentiality, level of discomfort and motivation to respond.

Sources of information about sex In Thai society, issues related to sex and sexuality are generally not discussed. Females in particular are not encouraged to show an interest in such topics and are kept uninformed about sexual matters

(Ford and Kittisuksathit 1994). In the questionnaire, young people were asked a number of questions about their main sources of information about sex (see Table 21.1).

Clearly, questions on sources of information about sex are far less sensitive than questions on sexual activity. Correspondingly, differences in responses are not large or consistent, especially among males. Among females, however, some differences are worth noting. For one, female students who completed the ACASIs were 15 percentage points more likely than respondents in the SAQ group to report that friends were a major source of information about sex. Second, women in the SAQ arm were between 13 and 19 percentage points more likely than those in the ACASI arms to state that college courses were a major source of information. Differences were statistically significant.

These differences clearly suggest that the ACASI methods may have offered young women an opportunity to give actual rather than normative responses. As mentioned earlier, young single females in Thailand are not expected to discuss issues related to sex, and if they do, this should be in a classroom situation in which basic sex education is imparted and not in discussions with peers. We believe therefore that the pattern of responses reported above does indeed reflect respondents' perceptions about the confidentiality of responses reported under different data collection methods. Respondents in the group using the method perceived to provide limited confidentiality of responses – the SAQ[5] – are more likely than those reporting in ACASIs to provide normative responses, for example with regard to college courses as the main source of information or peers as a relatively minor source of information. In contrast, among young men, for whom discussion of sex is widely accepted, differences in responses are insignificant across the three arms.

Sexual behaviour Table 21.2 reports responses to questions related to sexual behaviour and experiences. For males, there were relatively small differences among the three study arms on the majority of questions. For example, differences in reporting of lifetime sexual experience were marginal, although those responding to the ACASIs were more likely to report a recent (within the last week) sexual experience than those responding to the SAQ: 32 per cent and 47 per cent compared to 21 per cent respectively. Statistically significant differences are observed in responses concerning the number of recent sexual partners: sexually experienced men who undertook the SAQ reported significantly fewer recent sexual partners than did men who completed the ACASI arms of the study. The main reason for these differences is that large proportions of men (37 per cent) in the SAQ arm reported a lifetime but not a recent sexual experience. It is not clear why differences appear in the reporting of recent but not lifetime sexual experience among males; we hypothesize that there may be some sensitivity to reporting oneself as currently sexually active. Finally, considerably

TABLE 21.1 Sources of information about sex by type of data collection method used (%)

Source of information about sex	Male			Female		
	ACASI/ photos	ACASI/ no photos	SAQ	ACASI/ photos	ACASI/ no photos	SAQ
Parents	14.6	14.6	15.8	29.8	28.7	29.5
Friends	84.4	82.3	82.2	76.9	77.0	61.2**
Girlfriend/boyfriend	39.6	29.2	26.7	17.4	18.0	14.0
Teachers	59.4	47.9	58.4	71.9	68.9	66.7
Books	76.0	66.7	63.4	78.5	76.2	69.0
Pornographic magazines	37.5	54.2	36.6*	5.8	5.7	3.9
Movies/television	82.3	72.9	76.2	66.9	65.6	55.8
College courses	67.7	64.6	74.0	52.9	58.2	71.3**
N	96	96	100†	121	122	129

Notes: *Chi square $p<.05$; **$p<.01$. †N differs from total because of non-response.

TABLE 21.2 Respondents' sexual behaviour by type of data collection method used (%)

Sexual behaviour	Male			Female		
	ACASI/ photos	ACASI/ no photos	SAQ	ACASI/ photos	ACASI/ no photos	SAQ
Ever had sexual relations	49.0	58.3	58.4	19.8	14.8	13.3
N	96	96	101	121	122	$128^{\dagger}$
Ever been forced to have sexual contact	2.1	3.1	3.0	15.7	9.0	8.6
N	96	96	101	121	122	$128^{\dagger}$
Ever masturbated	86.5	88.5	83.3	18.2	16.4	6.8*
N	96	96	$96^{\dagger}$	121	122	$117^{\dagger}$
Last time respondent had sexual relations						
Last 24 hours	10.6	8.9	6.6	12.5	(5.6)	(6.3)
> 24 hours, less than 1 week	21.3	37.5	14.8	37.5	(27.8)	(25.0)
> than 1 week, less than 1 month	25.5	26.8	29.5	12.5	(22.2)	(25.0)
> 1 month, less than 3 months	14.9	8.9	9.8	20.8	(11.1)	(12.5)
> 3 months	27.7	17.9	39.3	16.7	(33.3)	(31.3)
N (all sexually experienced respondents)	47	56	59	24	18	16
Condom used at last sex	38.3	30.4	42.4	33.3	(22.2)	(6.7)
N (all sexually experienced respondents)	47	56	59	24	18	$15^{\dagger}$
Mean no. of sexual partners in the last 3 months	1.31	1.40	0.78**	0.83	(0.93)	(0.75)
N (all sexually experienced respondents)	47	$43^{\dagger}$	$58^{\dagger}$	24	$15^{\dagger}$	16
Mean no. of sexual partners in the last month	0.70	0.88	0.57*	0.79	(0.71)	(0.71)
N (all sexually experienced respondents)	47	$49^{\dagger}$	$58^{\dagger}$	24	$14^{\dagger}$	$14^{\dagger}$
Ever taken an HIV test	18.8	24.0	12.1	5.8	11.5	5.6
N	96	96	$99^{\dagger}$	121	122	$125^{\dagger}$

Notes: *Chi square $p<.05$ **$p<.01$. †Ns differ from totals because of non-response. ( ) based on 20 or fewer respondents.

larger percentages of young males who completed the ACASI arms of the study admitted having undergone HIV testing.

For females, the reported differences among the three study arms are generally wider than for males, although for only two questions were these differences statistically significant. With regard to reporting lifetime sexual experience, although women who completed ACASIs (20 and 15 per cent) were more likely to report an experience than those reporting through SAQs (13 per cent), the difference was not statistically significant.

There are few previous studies of sexual experiences conducted among similar populations with which to compare findings from this study. An exception is a recent study of Thai youth aged fifteen to twenty-four, in which 13.4 per cent of urban females and 6.3 per cent of rural females reported ever having had premarital sex in face-to-face interviews (Podhisita and Pattaravanich 1995).[6] Given that the study under review was undertaken in a peri-urban setting, in which sexual activity is likely to be lower, we conclude that levels of lifetime sexual experience as reported from the ACASI arms (and to a lesser extent the SAQs as well) are likely to be higher than those reported in face-to-face interviews.

Reporting of masturbation was significantly different among those reporting through ACASIs and SAQs. The percentage of female students reporting masturbation was over twice as high among those who completed ACASIs as among those who completed the SAQ. Although masturbation is indeed a sensitive behaviour for Thai females to admit, it is not clear why differences in reporting are so much wider for masturbation than for sexual experience. Finally, although differences were not statistically significant, reporting of a forced sexual experience is considerably higher among the ACASI/photos respondents (16 per cent) than the other two groups (9 per cent each).

In general, findings confirm that sexual activity is indeed more likely to be reported in ACASIs than in the SAQs arm, and suggest that ACASIs are perceived to be more likely than SAQs to protect confidentiality.[7]

Respondents' assessment of data collection instruments The study also explored young people's own assessment of the method to which they were assigned, particularly in terms of levels of discomfort in responding to sensitive questions, perceived confidentiality, user-friendliness and level of motivation. Results, shown in Table 21.3, suggest clear differences between the pattern of responses for the SAQ and the two ACASI methods. Differences were always in the expected direction, but were more likely to be significant for female than male students.

Findings suggest, for example, that the ACASI method is associated with less discomfort in responding to questions on sensitive behaviours and greater perceived confidentiality than the SAQ method. While differences in the level of discomfort for males were unclear, among females approximately one-half

TABLE 21.3 Respondents' assessment of the data collection instrument by type of data collection method used

Assessment of data collection instrument	Male			Female		
	ACASI/ photos	ACASI/ no photos	SAQ	ACASI/ photos	ACASI/ no photos	SAQ
How embarrassed were you about answering questions on sexual behaviour?						
Very embarrassed	10.0	1.0	1.9	5.0	2.5	7.8*
Somewhat embarrassed	4.2	4.2	3.0	16.5	17.2	20.3
A little embarrassed	25.0	26.0	36.4	28.9	26.2	37.5
Not embarrassed	60.8	68.8	59.6	49.6	54.1	34.4
N	96	96	99†	121	122	128†
How confident are you in the confidentiality of data?						
Very confident	31.3	33.3	19.4	26.4	30.3	11.7***
Somewhat confident	52.1	42.7	56.1	55.4	48.4	53.1
A little confident	12.5	17.7	21.4	17.4	16.4	27.3
Not at all confident	4.2	6.3	3.1	0.8	4.9	7.8
N	96	96	98†	121	122	128†

How easy was it to complete the questionnaire?						
Very easy	68.8	58.3	40.4**	55.4	48.4	28.1***
Somewhat easy	29.2	41.7	45.5	42.1	45.9	54.7
A little easy	1.0	12.6	14.1	2.5	5.7	14.1
Not easy at all	1.0	0.9				3.1
N	96	96	99†	121	122	128†
To what extent did the method motivate you to answer questions?						
Very much	28.1	30.2	17.2	20.7	18.0	7.8***
Somewhat	65.6	58.3	67.7	66.1	63.1	53.1
A little	6.3	11.5	14.1	12.4	17.2	33.6
Not at all			(1.0)	0.8	1.6	5.5
N	96	96	99†	121	122	128†
Do you think your classmates will answer accurately?						
Yes	74.0	83.3	67.7*	66.9	76.2	58.6*
N	96	96	99†	121	122	128†

Note: *Chi square $p<.05$ **$p<.01$ ***$p<=.001$. † Ns differ from totals because of non-response.

of those in the ACASI arm, compared to slightly over one-third of those in the SAQ arm, reported no embarrassment in responding to questions on sexual experience. These differences in levels of embarrassment may well be related to differences in perceived confidentiality of data collected through the two methods. Differences here are quite striking. Among males, for example, while about one-third of those responding to ACASIs reported confidence in the confidentiality of their responses, only 19 per cent of SAQ respondents reported this perception. Among females, the difference is statistically significant: 26 and 30 per cent of those participating in the two ACASI arms, respectively, perceived that their responses would remain confidential, compared to only 12 per cent of those who responded to SAQs.

The importance of confidentiality in facilitating truthful answers and the differing perceptions of confidentiality of data collected through the ACASIs and SAQs became clear in focus group discussions. Almost all the students argued that the ACASI methods would be more likely than the SAQ to ensure confidentiality of data. Reasons provided included: (a) fewer people could access computerized data; (b) the handwriting of the respondent could be revealed in SAQs and friends might be able to identify the respondent from the handwriting; (c) the ACASI interface shows only one question at a time, and this question disappears from the screen once a response is selected, therefore it is more difficult for friends to look over and see responses. As one student noted, 'my friends can't look. The paper [questionnaire page on SAQ] contains several questions but the computer only shows one question'; and (d) because of the way that the method was applied, with successive rounds of students using the same computers, students who undertook the ACASI felt that it would be hard to remember which computer was used by which student.

With regard to user-friendliness of the format, again, students in the ACASI arms of the study were significantly more likely to agree that the questionnaire was easy to complete than were students in the SAQ arm. For females, for example, 55 per cent of ACASI/photos, 48 per cent of ACASI/no photos and only 28 per cent of SAQ respondents reported that it was easy to complete the questionnaire. This is indeed a significant finding given that students tend to be familiar with SAQs, and several had limited computer skills and had to be taught basic operations, such as using the mouse before responding to the questionnaire. In focus group discussions, students reported that for the estimated 80 per cent of second-year students who have medium to high levels of computer experience, ACASI was particularly easy. Observations by researchers noted, moreover, that many students who completed the SAQ appeared bored, made basic errors and did not appear to play close attention to the instructions or questions. Findings show, for example, that approximately 10 per cent of respondents completing the SAQ filled in the current date when asked to report their date of birth.

The ACASI method was also more likely to engage the interest of students than was the SAQ method. For example, among males almost one-third of ACASI respondents, compared to 17 per cent of SAQ respondents, described the method as motivating them to answer questions. Among females, the difference was wider and statistically significant: 21 and 18 per cent of the two ACASI arm respondents compared to 8 per cent of SAQ respondents. Indeed, in the course of focus group discussions, three of twelve SAQ respondents reported that they had skipped introductory sections whereas in focus group discussions with ACASI respondents all but two participants agreed that they had both read and listened to the introductions and questions.

Results from the focus group discussions also suggest that the interface of the ACASI method contributed to the interest respondents displayed in answering questions. For example, in discussions with SAQ respondents nine of twelve students complained that the SAQ was boring and involved too much reading. In contrast, feedback from ACASI respondents in discussions was far more positive. Frequently highlighted were such features as the sound and pictures associated with the ACASI method. The audio, which used a young woman's voice, gave the questionnaire the appearance of 'a conversation among friends ... I felt relaxed answering', according to one participant.

Insights into students' assessment of the two ACASI methods were also sought in the course of focus group discussions. Discussion participants who were in the ACASI/photos arm agreed that the audio and pictures made the session enjoyable and even relaxing; they looked forward to the next question and picture and this facilitated a careful reading of questions. As one female focus group discussion participant reported: 'The pictures attracted me. I felt more relaxed and was encouraged to follow and read the questions and to answer the questions ... The pictures helped me have a better understanding of what the question was asking.'

Summary and conclusions

Findings of this study indicate that the ACASI method is preferable to the SAQ method for data collection, at least among college students in Thailand. Students who responded in ACASIs were, for one, more likely than those who responded in SAQs to read and respond to every question and perceive that the method offered confidentiality with regard to responses. They were also less likely to report embarrassment in answering sensitive questions. In addition, ACASIs also appear to reduce random measurement error. Students responding through ACASIs reported an interest in and motivation to answer questions posed, as a result of the interesting format. Consequently, the ACASI method was less likely to generate missing responses and the automated 'skip' patterns ensured measurement error was kept to a minimum.

Findings also suggest that the ACASI method may have reduced under-reporting of some sensitive behaviours, but small sample sizes generally preclude identification of statistical significance. Findings have shown, however, that on several items there were differences in patterns of responses, and where this occurred results were generally in the expected direction, with students responding through ACASIs more likely to report the experience of sensitive behaviours or negatively valued attitudes than those reporting through SAQs. Also of interest were the relatively modest differences in reporting between students responding to the two ACASI methods. As expected, because of the greater sensitivity of questions related to sex and sexuality for females than for males, the differences between responses to ACASIs and SAQs were larger among females than among males.

In general, then, findings of this study suggest that the use of ACASI is a feasible and acceptable method of collecting data on sensitive behaviours in Thailand among college students and others who can use, or be easily taught to use, a computer. Data collected through the ACASI method are likely to be more valid and reliable, with a reduction in both systematic and random measurement error than data collected using other methods. In short, the use of the ACASI method will result in quantitative data that are of significantly higher quality than those obtained through other data collection methods.

Balanced against the apparent reduction in systematic and random measurement error that can be obtained through the use of ACASI is the greater difficulty in its administration as compared to SAQs. Even among what might be considered a computer-literate population, a significant amount of time was required to explain to students how to use the computer. A substantial minority of students did not know how to use a mouse or perform simple operations including double-clicking. The ACASI method clearly requires a much more intensive use of resources, both computer and human, than does the SAQ. It must be borne in mind, however, that, unlike the SAQ method, the ACASI method does not require extensive data editing and entry.

Findings suggest, then, that while the use of the ACASI method may be feasible in school/college settings, the extent to which it can be used more generally in community surveys cannot be assumed from this study (see, for example, van Griensven et al. 2001; Mensch et al. 2003). Clearly, a pilot study is required that assesses computer literacy and attitudes towards the use of computer-assisted methods, and also assesses such practical issues as the cost of implementing the ACASI method and the longer period of time required in collecting data through ACASIs compared to SAQs. Finally, while this study was not undertaken with the objective of measuring sexual coercion among young people, its findings do suggest that the ACASI method is likely to reduce under-reporting of this highly sensitive experience. ACASI has a demonstrated advantage over face-to-face interviews and SAQs when collecting data on drug use, sexual experiences and risk behaviour, and lessons learned from this study suggest that it is a promising approach to eliciting information on forced sexual relations among young people as well. What is needed now are studies that compare the validity and reliability of various data collection methods with specific reference to non-consensual sexual experiences in developing-country settings, while at the same time assessing perceptions concerning the use of computers compared to face-to-face interviews and anonymous self-administered reports.

Notes

1 See Weiss (1996) for a review of the different types of computer-assisted interviewing methods available.

2 An interesting and challenging ethical aspect of the study findings is that a monetary incentive ($20) was as effective as the ACASI method in obtaining response rates significantly higher than in an interview situation. In fact, the highest response rates were obtained through the combined use of the ACASI method and a monetary incentive.

3 In this study the same women were exposed to both forms of data collection. In order to test that biases did not arise owing to the ordering of the methods, women were randomly assigned to two conditions – one where the interview followed the ACASI method and the other where the reverse order was applied. Among the better-educated groups, the ordering of the methods appeared to have an effect on responses, with agreement between the methods being lower where the ACASI followed the use of the interview method.

4 A *Rajabat* is a government college-level institution. Although formerly *Rajabats* primarily trained teachers, they now offer degree and non-degree training in a range of professional areas.

5 Findings reported in Table 21.3 confirm this claim.

6 The study used trained interviewers to collect data.

7 It should be noted, however, that for women overall there is an inverse relationship between reported confidence in the confidentiality of the data and the likelihood of reporting that they had ever had sex. This could be interpreted to mean that women who reported a sensitive behaviour were more concerned about the confidentiality of the data than those who had not reported such a behaviour. This interpretation is consistent with the interpretation that using a method that is more likely to be perceived as aiding confidentiality encourages more accurate responses.

References

Dare, O. and J. Cleland (1994) 'Reliability and validity of survey data on sexual behaviour', *Health Transition Review*, 4(suppl.): 93–110

Des Jarlais, D., D. Paone, J. Miliken et al. (1999) 'Audio-computer interviewing to measure risk behaviour for HIV among injecting drug users: a quasi-randomised trial', *Lancet*, 353: 1657–62

Ford, N. and S. Kittisuksathit (1994) 'Destinations unknown: the gender construction and changing nature of the sexual expression of Thai youth', *AIDS Care*, 6(5): 517–31

García-Moreno, C. (2003) 'Relationship violence experiences of young people: an overview and some findings from the WHO VAW study', Presentation at a Consultative Meeting on Non-consensual Sexual Experience of Young People in Developing Countries, New Delhi, 22–25 September

Im-em, W., C. Kanchanachitra and K. Archvanitkul (2003) 'Sexual coercion among women in Thailand: results from the WHO multi-country study on women's health and life experiences', Presentation at a Consultative Meeting on Non-consensual Sexual Experience of Young People in Developing Countries, New Delhi, 22–25 September

Konings, E., G. Bantebya, M. Carael et al. (1995) 'Validating population surveys for the measurement of HIV/STD prevention indicators', *AIDS*, 9: 375–82

Mensch, B., P. Hewett and A. Erulkar (2003) 'The reporting of sensitive behaviour by adolescents: a methodological experiment in Kenya', *Demography*, 40(2): 247–68

Moser, C., W. Pratt and A. Duffer (1994) 'CAPI, event histories, and incentives in the NSFG Cycle 5 pretest', Proceedings on the Section of Survey Research Methods, American Statistical Association, Toronto

Podhisita, C. and U. Pattaravanich (1995) *Youth in Contemporary Thailand*, IPSR Publication no. 197, Bangkok: Institute for Population and Social Research, Mahidol University

Sattah, M., S. Supawitkul, T. Dondero et al. (2002) 'Prevalence of risk factors for methamphetamine use in northern Thailand youth: results of an audio-computer assisted self-interviewing survey with urine testing', *Addiction*, 97: 801–08

Schopper, D., S. Doussantousse and J. Orav (1993) 'Sexual behaviours relevant to HIV transmission in a rural African population: how much can a KAP survey tell us?', *Social Science and Medicine*, 37(3): 401–11

Tourangeau, R. and T. Smith (1996) 'Asking sensitive questions: the impact of data collection mode, question format and question content', *Public Opinion Quarterly*, Summer: 275–304

Turner, C., L. Ku, S. Rogers et al. (1998) 'Adolescent sexual behavior, drug use, and violence: increased reporting with computer survey technology', *Science*, 280: 867–71

Van de Wijert, J., N. Padian, S. Shiboki et al. (1998) 'Is audio computer-assisted self-interviewing a feasible method of surveying sensitive behaviours in Zimbabwe?', Unpublished paper

Van Griensven, F., S. Supawitkul, P. Kilmarx et al. (2001) 'Rapid assessment of sexual behaviour, drug use, Human Immunodeficiency Virus, and sexually transmitted disease in northern Thai youth using audio-computer-assisted self-interviewing and non-invasive specimen collection', *Pediatrics*, 108(1): E13, July

Weiss, S. (1996) 'Recent studies reveal important differences between computer interviewing techniques', Chicago Software News, <www.chisoft.com/articles/>

22 | Ethical issues in research on sexual coercion among youth

JOHN W. TOWNSEND

The complex nature of the available guidance poses a serious challenge in ensuring ethical practice in studies on the experiences of sexual coercion among youth. Diverse rights perspectives are defined in conventions and international declarations as well as in local statutes and regulations. Litigation plays a role in disputes about the violations of rights and sets precedents about how statutes and regulations are interpreted by the courts. Local customs and traditions are often followed in the absence of formal codes, such as for age of consent. In addition, the context of research is critical in that efforts required to protect the welfare of participants may depend on how issues are studied, the nature of the episode of coercion (for example, child abuse, transactional sex or rape within marriage) and the potential consequences for participants.

The legal and moral basis for voluntary consent to participate in medical or scientific experiments was formally articulated in the International Covenant on Civil and Political Rights (UN 1966). More recently, the Declaration of Helsinki adopted by the World Medical Association (WMA 2000) asserted that the well-being of subjects in research must take precedence over the interests of science and society. Currently there is a range of sources for guidance, including international and national guidelines (for example, CIOMS 2002), training programmes (for example, FHI 2001), academic reviews (for example, Cook et al. 2004) and ethical review committees.

The ethical principles that guide research involving humans are respect for persons, beneficence and justice. Respect for persons implies respect for their autonomy, privacy and self-determination, including protecting confidentiality and their right to choose whether or not to participate in the research. The principle of beneficence demands that both the researcher and the participant have the opportunity to weigh the risks and benefits of the research, but the researcher has the additional responsibility of ensuring that no harm is done. This includes not harming the interests of participants, for example avoidance of stigma as well as transgressing their rights. The principle of justice demands that there is an equitable distribution of the burden and benefits of research and that youth, as a particularly vulnerable group, does not have to bear an unfair or disproportionate burden of risk.

These principles are generally communicated with researchers during formal training on ethics in research and orientation to best practices, often through the use of case studies and discussion of how the principles apply to practical research situations. The organization sponsoring the research is ultimately responsible for ensuring compliance with accepted practices to protect the welfare of participants. Of particular concern in protection and consent are those whom society considers most vulnerable, including children and those for whom autonomous decision-making is legally constrained, such as individuals for whom the state is directly responsible, for example orphans or youth offenders in public facilities. As a consequence, there are several special issues in the context of research on coerced sex among youth. Some of these issues are discussed below.

Informed consent

Informed consent requires that participants know the goals and purpose of the research, understand its potential risks and benefits and the procedures they may need to undergo, and are aware that they have the capacity to exercise a choice in providing consent. In many countries, minors may not actually provide consent from a legal perspective, merely assent or agreement, and their parents or guardians must provide consent. The capacity for consent is a function of maturity, however, rather than of age. Sufficient maturity to provide consent for an interview is often judged by whether the young respondent understands the informed-consent language and whether they exhibit mature behaviour in other spheres of their lives – for example, do they live independently, do they have a job, do they have responsibilities that ordinarily would not be given to a minor. The Society for Adolescent Medicine, for example, provides guidance in the area of consent among youth (SAM 1999). In minimum-risk situations, parental permission may be waived when privacy and confidentiality are ensured, more mature or emancipated youths may provide informed consent, or when parental knowledge may place the youth at risk of questioning or even intimidation by their parents. Minimum risk is often defined as a situation in which the risk of participating in the research is no greater than that experienced in routine life activities. The risk of any research activity is increased by the invasive nature of questions, the experience of the respondent and their living arrangements – for example, if they are residing with a perpetrator or if abuse is evident, and if physical examinations not ordinarily required for medical care are part of the protocol.

When conducting research on issues of sexual coercion, it is important to establish confidential assistance procedures for protection before initiating the research. Selected best practices in the area of informed consent include using interviewers trained to competency in the management of the informed-consent process, using simple, non-contractual language that is understandable for respondents, and providing a copy of any informed-consent documents to the respondents, containing contact information for the principal investigator.

The decision on whether or not to provide a copy of any informed-consent documents to young respondents must be made in coordination with the young respondent by weighing the risks and benefits in a given context. For example, in some settings researchers may withhold documents from young people for fear that these documents may be revealed inadvertently to parents or the perpetrator and place the respondent at risk. On the other hand, where parents or other trusted adults and friends are supportive, young respondents may want to share documents with them, or refer to the documents if they have doubts.

It is often suggested that the interviewers make explicit efforts to ensure that young respondents understand the purposes of the research and procedures they will undergo. The more sensitive the topic, the more important it is to provide time for the respondents to gain confidence in the interviewer and the process of dialogue. Conducting the interviews over several sessions both allows respondents the opportunity to decide whether they want to continue, and interviewers the insight they need to probe for greater understanding, increasing the potential benefits of the research. Paying interviewers for completing a fixed number of interviews per day on sensitive topics is a disincentive for a careful informed-consent process.

When the research offers potential benefits for youth, but greater than minimal risk, the researcher should support the youth's capacity for consent. In clinical settings, this implies seeking the advice of a professional unconnected to the research who could assess their capacity to exercise consent. In community settings, the young respondent may identify a trusted adult, for example a teacher, religious leader or member of a local NGO, who may assist in determining whether the respondent has the capacity for consent. The younger the child, the more important adult participation becomes. Regardless of their status, all youths have the right to withdraw from a study whenever they desire, without sanctions or prejudice.

Participation of the community

The participation of the community in addressing and intervening in the prevention of coercive sex is critical. It is helpful to seek the advice and support of members of the community to gain an insight into local norms and access to networks, as well as to debrief the community on issues that need attention, thereby helping to ensure follow-up. The traditions in communities and families play a key role in defining and implementing ethical practice, and local service providers, advocates and youths could all make valuable contributions to understanding this process. The participants and the larger community should share in the benefits of the research – that is, eventual access to helpful information as well as effective services and social support. The relative roles of the community and the family in defining ethical practice and as gatekeepers for care are heavily debated in many countries. In cultures with strong community as opposed to individualistic value structures, for example patriarchal societies and tribal communities, it is important to acknowledge the role of community leaders in granting permission to conduct a study in the village, but individual respondents should still be given the responsibility for providing consent.

Legal context

The role of the ethical review committee is to ensure that the rights and welfare of participants are protected, and to oversee compliance with local ethical guidelines. In some countries, both the institutions and individual researchers are legally liable if they do not make explicit efforts to follow best practices in the protection of respondents. There are other practical roles for the local ethical review committee, however. For example, they can play a key role in obtaining permission from the government to conduct the research and can give confidence to political leaders so that the research process is taken seriously.

In the research protocol, details such as the type of respondents (for example, younger versus older youths), residence patterns, relationship of the participant to the perpetrator and the site of data collection (for example, home, clinic, jail) should be explicitly stated. All participants, perpetrators as well as victims, have rights as informants, but each group may have a different voice and particular issues that are salient to them. There may be legal requirements for reporting cases of abuse, implications of knowledge of impending harm or increased risk of abuse, or special circumstances that may affect the benefit–risk ratio for researchers and participants. Sources of funding and potential conflicts of interest, which may bias the research, should also be made explicit. All participants should be aware of the limits of the investigator to safeguard the confidentiality of data from informants, and the consequences of breaches of confidentiality, either during data management or as a result of law enforcement.

Ensuring the safety of respondents and interviewers

Ensuring the physical safety of respondents and interviewers from retaliatory violence by perpetrators is critical (WHO 1999). Protecting the confidentiality of informants is one key to ensuring safety, but alone it is no guarantee. Generally, interviews should be conducted in a private setting with only one respondent per household. Every effort should be made to reduce the potential distress caused to participants by the research, including the potential for stigma and discrimination as a result of their participation in a study on coerced sex. The stress associated with collecting data on violence should not be underestimated. Best practice suggests that research projects should ensure that interviewers learn about the potential risks of their jobs and have resources such as group debriefing, flexible time and individual counselling available to them as needed.

Logistics planning and budgeting should consider the well-being and safety of both respondents and interviewers. For example, interviewers and their supervisors should have a clear plan for locating respondents and interviewers during data collection, for example by having maps of the community and intended sample sites. They might also identify safe and acceptable locations for conducting the interviews, and interviewers might be provided with mobile phones to alert supervisors if they encounter difficulties. The completed research forms and logs should be kept in a secure place, and identifiers such as names and addresses of respondents should be removed from the completed forms to ensure that the identity of respondents and interviewers is protected.

Ensuring benefits for individuals

Ensuring benefits for individuals implies that the research has a sound methodology, is ethically justifiable, conforms to accepted scientific principles and demonstrates adequate knowledge of the relevant literature on youth, coercion and sexual violence. The principle of distributive justice implies that benefits of the research should be available, to the degree possible, to the respondents. For example, at the conclusion of data collection the interviewer may provide respondents with a pamphlet about sexual coercion or information about the availability of services for persons who have been subjected to such behaviour. Proactive referral of cases of coercion to responsible services and sources of support, where they might receive care, if required, is a minimum ethical response to the detection of coercion. Being proactive implies that the receiving service centre is made aware of the study and is prepared to provide appropriate care to respondents who will be referred. Where these services are not available, the research team may have to arrange for short-term support to be provided by the sponsoring organization.

The use of findings in the public interest

While much of the discussion on ethics is focused on individual study participants, there are also larger social issues. The importance of the knowledge that may be reasonably expected to result from the research must be greater than the risks of the research. It is in the public interest to suspend the research if more than minimal harm is done to a participant, or if the intervention being studied is clearly superior to the current standard of care. This requires that researchers meet periodically during data collection to review the experience of interviewers and respondents and that preliminary data analysis be conducted to determine whether the expected benefits still outweigh the risks for participants.

Moreover, the research should contribute to policy development, advocacy and new intervention models to benefit the community. At a minimum, participants should be informed of the findings of the research, and individuals should be informed of any findings that relate to their health status. This may involve briefings with community leaders, and a formal mechanism for sharing findings with affected individuals. Assistance in the use of the data by the public and the media is also recommended to improve the accuracy of reporting results and to foster a responsible social reaction.

Research organizations have the moral responsibility and legal obligation to follow the principles of respect for persons, beneficence and justice. For individual researchers, learning about best practices in ethics requires special effort, for example explicit training, and a review of specialized journals and professional materials on ethical issues, since most journal articles do not devote sufficient space to elaborate on the detailed procedures used. Poor practices are also likely to be hidden or glossed over unless explicit oversight mechanisms (for example, field visits by supervisors and discussions with interviewers on compliance with informed consent procedures) and responsibilities to identify breaches are developed and followed.

The challenges for ethical practice include, but are not limited to, strengthening training and ensuring research capacity on ethics; the identification of mechanisms for enhancing safety for informants and researchers as well as ensuring care and support for those experiencing sexual coercion; sustaining links with community organizations for collaboration and follow-up on the recommendations of the research; and the sharing of data while preserving the confidentiality and rights of respondents. Research on sexual coercion of youth is difficult and may provide little benefit to individuals or society, and even represent a considerable risk, if it is not conducted in a fashion that respects the principles of ethical practice.

References

CIOMS (Council for International Organizations of Medical Sciences) (2002) *International Ethical Guidelines for Biomedical Research Involving Human Subjects*, Geneva: CIOMS and WHO

Cook, R. J., B. M. Dickens and M. F. Fathalla (2004) *Reproductive Health and Human Rights: Integrating Medicine, Ethics and Law*, Oxford: Clarendon Press

FHI (Family Health International) (2001) 'The role of the ethical review committee is to ensure that the rights and welfare of participants are protected, and to oversee compliance with local ethical guidelines', Research Ethics Training Curriculum (V.2), Chapel Hill, NC: FHI

SAM (Society for Adolescent Medicine) (1999) 'Code of research ethics: position paper of the Society for Adolescent Medicine', *Journal of Adolescent Health*, 24: 277–82

UN (United Nations) (1966) International Covenant on Civil and Political Rights, New York: United Nations General Assembly

WHO (World Health Organization) (1999) 'Putting women's safety first: ethical and safety recommendations for research on domestic violence against women', WHO/EIP/GPE/99.2, Geneva: WHO

WMA (World Medical Association) (2000) 'Ethical principles for medical research involving human subjects, Declaration of Helsinki', Helsinki: WMA

SEVEN | Moving forward

23 | Non-consensual sex and young people: looking ahead

SHIREEN J. JEJEEBHOY, IQBAL H. SHAH AND SHYAM THAPA

Preceding chapters have shown that non-consensual sex is experienced by significant percentages of young people in developing countries, and that these experiences have major adverse health and social consequences. These chapters also highlight the fact that programmes and policies have rarely taken into consideration the extent to which such experiences may contribute to the compromised sexual and reproductive health of adolescents and youths.

The subject of non-consensual sex is indeed sensitive and thus far few researchers have explored its prevalence, correlates or consequences. In view of the dearth of precedent, chapters in this volume are pioneering, and have assembled a rare profile of what is known about non-consensual sexual experiences of young people in developing countries. Findings presented in this volume come from a variety of studies: intensive explorations of small and sometimes unrepresentative samples, as well as from large surveys based on more representative samples of youth. These studies have adopted varying definitions of non-consensual sexual experiences, ranging from a narrow focus on rape or incest to a broader perspective that includes, for example, sex through deception and threats, and unwanted sexual touch. The sensitivity of the issue also makes the reliability of responses, particularly from surveys, difficult to assess. The findings discussed here may reflect no more than the tip of the iceberg in terms of the magnitude of experiences and the extent to which coercive behaviour is normatively accepted in many settings.

Chapters in this volume contain reviews of different aspects of non-consensual sex, and evidence derived from quantitative and/or qualitative studies. They address the situation in a number of countries of Asia, Latin America and sub-Saharan Africa. While all the studies acknowledge that non-consensual sexual experiences comprise a continuum of behaviours ranging from unwanted touch to deception and threats to rape, not all studies have focused on the entire spectrum of behaviours. Several focus on forced intercourse, but those that also include unwanted touch and attempted forced sex note that when these are included there is a marked increase in the magnitude of non-consensual experiences.

Population sub-groups covered in the studies are also diverse: school-going youths, working youths, youths attending health facilities, as well as representative samples of youth drawn from population-based studies. Age groups covered in these studies also vary: indeed, few studies have covered the entire age range defined to constitute adolescents and youth (ten to twenty-four). While most focus on young people themselves, a few have included adults and obtained retrospective evidence on their experiences in adolescence. Some have focused on females, others have included males as well. Some studies describe the situation of youth as gleaned from studies covering a larger age range, which enables comparisons of the current situation of youths and adults. A few have explored the perspectives of providers, some have addressed the perspectives of perpetrators, and a few have provided insights into the perceptions of parents.

Despite the heterogeneity of sociocultural settings, study populations, study designs and operational definitions of non-consensual sex, several consistent findings are evident. For example:

- All young people are at risk of experiencing non-consensual sex, irrespective of sex or marital status. While young females – unmarried and married – are most at risk, the evidence suggests that young males too are vulnerable to such experiences.
- Young people's own interpretation of an incident as non-consensual or consensual is conditioned by many factors. Young people who submit under pressure to a partner's demands for sex as an expression of commitment may not describe the incident as non-consensual; so also those who continue to be in a relationship with the perpetrator and those in a relationship based on material transfers. And in the case of young males, coercion is far more likely to be perceived if the perpetrator was male rather than female.
- While early marital experiences are characterized by forced sex among large numbers of married young women in settings in which marriage is arranged and early, subsequent experiences vary from passive acceptance of continued force, to the adoption of strategies to avoid sex, to greater intimacy and enjoyment of marital sexual relations.
- Perpetrators are overwhelmingly individuals with whom the young victim is acquainted – a boy- or girlfriend, a peer or an authority figure for the most part. Indeed, evidence suggests that the home is not a haven: forced sex perpetrated by family members is reported in a number of studies.
- Evidence also suggests that schools are unsafe: teachers are observed to perpetrate non-consensual sex on students, both directly through the exchange of grades for sex or indirectly by neglecting to intervene in cases in which students perpetrate non-consensual sex on other students.
- Gang rape of young females by young men is increasingly observed in diverse settings, and is perceived as a form of male bonding on the one hand, and a display of masculinity and power on the other.

The outcomes of non-consensual sex for the victim are wide ranging: they may be short- or long-term, and physical, psychological or social. The experience of non-consensual sex in adolescence is associated with a range of risky subsequent behaviours in consensual relationships: unprotected sex, multiple partners, drug and alcohol abuse, and in extreme cases prostitution. A close association is observed between non-consensual first intercourse and early consensual sexual activity. The experience of non-consensual sex can also lead to health problems such as unintended pregnancy and induced abortion among young females, and sexually transmitted infections (STIs), including HIV/AIDS among both females and males. It is associated with the risks of both experiencing sexual and/or physical abuse subsequently in consensual relationships as well as, among young males, perpetrating it. Mental health consequences are also observed, ranging from feelings of worthlessness to depression and suicidal tendencies. Finally, the social consequences of experiencing non-consensual sex are significant, ranging from poor educational achievement to withdrawal from school, to inability to build adult partnerships, to loss of marriage prospects, as well as rejection by family or friends who react negatively to disclosure of the incident.

Underlying the perpetuation of non-consensual sex among young people are a host of structural, normative and systemic factors. Risk factors work at the individual, family, community and systemic levels. Key among these are gender double standards and power imbalances, which perpetuate a sense of entitlement among young men to force sex and support a widespread perception reported in many regions that men's sexual needs are beyond their control and thus demand immediate satisfaction. These same norms tend to hold the victim (woman) responsible for 'inviting' or provoking the coercive incident. Notions of masculinity and the need to prove manliness (particularly if thwarted or humiliated by a female) can, likewise, motivate the perpetration of non-consensual sex. Gang rape is an extreme manifestation of these notions of entitlement and masculinity. And in many settings these norms are translated into fear, expectation or even acceptance among communities – including young married and unmarried women – that men will try to pressure women by force and a general acceptance of violence among women for fear that if sex were refused, the partner would lose interest or abandon them.

Linked to these unequal gender norms are inadequate negotiating skills, especially among young women. Communication on sexual matters is frequently limited. Young females report considerable difficulty in refusing unwanted sex or negotiating a wanted outcome, and, for reasons highlighted above, report that attempts at negotiation often fail.

Other significant obstacles have also been noted. Lack of awareness of rights and opportunities for recourse clearly enables the perpetuation of unequal gender norms described above. At the same time, there remains a huge schism between youths and their parents and other trusted adults which inhibits discussion of sexual health matters in a supportive environment. Help-seeking is further compromised by the lack of institutional response. Institutional indifference – at the community, school, legal and health sector levels – inhibits help-seeking both among victims and others who may wish to seek counselling on how to confront a potentially threatening situation. Teachers, law enforcement agents and health service providers tend to espouse attitudes that resemble those of the wider society and pose a significant challenge to efforts to prevent non-consensual sex or provide care and counselling to young people exposed to such incidents.

Programme recommendations

Neither programmes addressing young people's sexual and reproductive health needs nor those addressing concerns about gender-based violence have adequately addressed the issue of non-consensual sexual experiences of young people. Chapters in this volume show that sexual and reproductive health programmes for youth have tended to skirt around the reality that young people are at risk of experiencing or have experienced non-consensual sex. Messages that advocate 'Abstinence, the need to Be faithful and Condom use' (ABC) implicitly assume that sexual relations among young people are always consensual and unaffected by gender power imbalances; these messages are clearly inadequate and irrelevant to those who face a non-consensual sexual encounter. In contrast, programmes that address non-consensual sex tend to be narrowly focused on rape (the few rape cases that are actually reported to the police) and apprehending and sentencing perpetrators, rather than efforts at prevention, concerns about the psycho-social repercussions faced by young victims, or the need of young victims (for many of whom the incident marks sexual initiation) for confidentiality and support. What is clearly required are programmes that focus on prevention and care for victims of such experiences, and that encompass the multiplicity of concerns – for example, sexual and reproductive health, physical and sexual violence, social and health outcomes and gender power imbalances – required to address the very real phenomenon of non-consensual sex among young people.

The evidence assembled in this volume points to a number of factors that appear to compound young people's vulnerability to non-consensual sex, and describes a number of promising practices and strategies that are of relevance for programmatic actions at the individual, family, community and facility levels.

Raising public awareness against norms that justify the perpetration of non-consensual sex Norms that perceive men as entitled to sex even if at a cost to women, which hold young victims responsible for 'provoking' a coercive incident and which equate masculinity with force have been shown in study after study to be deeply rooted among adult and youth populations, and to be a key factor underlying the persistence of non-consensual sex among young people. The public perception of non-consensual sex must change. Media campaigns and public health programmes must counter norms that condone the perpetration of non-consensual sex and build public sensitivity about the circumstances in which such incidents occur. It is equally important to build respect for the sexual rights of young people in general and of victims in particular. At the same time, commitment from community and political leaders is essential.

Countering traditional gender stereotypes and building communication and negotiation skills Evidence suggests that young people perceive experiences of non-consensual sex as inevitable, and options to prevent or seek help for such incidents are largely unavailable. The findings presented in this volume provide a strong argument for life skills and sexuality education programmes that counter these misperceptions, reverse norms of gender double standards, power imbalances and male entitlement to sex, and build the negotiation skills necessary to enable young people to protect themselves from unwanted sexual advances and to take appropriate action should such incidents occur. Multiple strategies that recognize the different needs and perspectives of females and males are clearly required.

Gender-sensitive interventions are needed for both females and males that enable them to develop a better understanding of human rights, particularly women's rights, to communicate on intimate matters including sex, and to question prevailing unequal gender norms. Traditional interpretations of forced sex and even gang rape as expressions of masculinity, male bonding and male entitlement to sex need to be reversed. So, too, perceptions that victims of forced sex are somehow responsible for having provoked the incident need to be countered. Indeed, alternative interpretations of masculinity are urgently needed.

At the same time, efforts are needed that build agency among young females, including decision-making authority, self-esteem and self-assertiveness, which may enable them to avoid relationships that are potentially risky. In settings in which sexual relationships involve some form of material transfer, programmes must raise awareness among youths, especially young female (and male) recipients, of the risks they face of experiencing non-consensual sex and build their negotiation or bargaining powers in sexual relationships. Livelihood skill-building and opportunities provide a promising means of strengthening negotiation skills and at the same time increasing access to material resources.

Recognizing the rights of women within marriage Existing programmes implicitly assume that sexual relations within marriage are consensual and that married women exercise choice in sexual and reproductive decisions – indeed, findings underscore the need for programmes to appreciate the non-consensual nature of marital sexual relations, especially among young women at the early stages of their married life. Programmes for marriage preparation and reproductive health must build mutual respect, communication skills and opportunities for social interaction among newly-weds, break down gender stereotypes and attitudes that reinforce the husband's entitlement and wife's submissiveness to forced sex, and equip married young women with information on sexual matters, the ability to communicate about sexual matters with the family and future partners, and the skills to negotiate wanted sexual outcomes. At the same time, programmes must sensitize parents to the adverse consequences of both marrying daughters at an early age and withholding information on sex from them, and advocate for delayed marriage and opportunities to develop a better acquaintance with the husband-to-be prior to marriage. Supportive options for a sexually coercive and violent partnership must also be made available. Finally, legal systems must be sensitized about the particular needs and vulnerabilities of married young women who suffer non-consensual sexual relations.

Sensitizing parents to provide a supportive environment This volume has stressed the critical role that parents can play in perpetuating non-consensual sex among young people on the one hand, and preventing non-consensual sex and providing support for victims of non-consensual sex on the other. In some instances, parents are themselves the perpetrators of non-consensual sex on their children. Often they foster an environment that offers sexual freedom to and even condones the perpetration of non-consensual sex by their sons, that inhibits discussion of sexual matters with their children in general, or which blames the victim – even the daughter – for provoking the incident. At the same time, evidence suggests that a close relationship with parents can enable youths better to negotiate sexual relations in general, and can enable victims in particular to disclose a non-consensual sexual incident and avoid serious psycho-social consequences.

Programmes are needed therefore that break down parental inhibitions about communicating about sexual matters with their children, enable them to socialize children from an early age to distinguish between good and bad touch, and raise their awareness about the adverse consequences of patterns of socialization that reinforce gender double standards. More specifically, parents must be sensitized to the reality of non-consensual sex experienced by young people, be acquainted with options available and enabled to provide a supportive environment to young victims.

Making educational institutions and teachers more alert about prevention of and support to victims of non-consensual sex Like parents, teachers too are observed both to perpetrate non-consensual or transactional sex on young students and to be judgemental and unsupportive of young victims. Teacher training must work on making gender norms more egalitarian, enabling teachers and other school staff to recognize signs of abuse and fostering non-threatening responses to victims. Shortcomings in school infrastructure – lack of safe toilet facilities for girls, and remote locations requiring girls to traverse unsafe roads – inattentiveness to teasing in the school premises and so on must also be addressed. So, too, school curricula must emphasize sexuality education and life skills development, and must include in these attention to preventing sexual violence and building egalitarian gender attitudes within the school setting and among young people in the formative years of their lives.

Strengthening the response of the health sector Several chapters have noted that healthcare providers often tend to have negative attitudes towards those who experience non-consensual sex, are ill prepared to recognize or screen young victims and are unable to provide them with sensitive counselling, appropriate services and safe options. Health services need to be reoriented and providers must be trained to recognize and enquire sensitively about non-consensual sex, acknowledging that victims may be unable or unwilling to disclose the incident or to directly seek help. Providers must be sensitized to respect and ensure the privacy and confidentiality of young victims and trained to provide appropriate care. In particular they must be made aware of the physical and mental health consequences of non-consensual sex, as well as its links to subsequent risky sexual behaviours, and must be trained to deal with such incidents, counsel youths to prevent further incidents, provide emergency contraception and/or induced abortion and/or referrals, if needed, and support them in engaging the services of related agencies (including the police). Findings in this volume highlight the importance of integrating the issue of non-consensual sex within reproductive health programmes more generally.

Strengthening the response of the legal system Findings have articulated the extent to which narrow legal definitions of rape and the lack of sensitivity of the law to the special vulnerability of adolescents in situations of sexual violence have prevented many young victims from obtaining or even seeking justice. What is needed now is the adoption of a more comprehensive definition and understanding of non-consensual sex, the incorporation of universal human rights values into national legislation, and a more sensitive and confidential means of addressing the non-consensual sexual experiences of young people within the legal system. At the same time, procedural barriers and biases that undermine the law's ability to deter violence and protect young victims of non-consensual sex should be recognized and addressed, and the sexual rights of both the unmarried and the married should be respected in law. Finally, it is critical that legal issues and options be made available in a language that is comprehensible to different sub-groups such as young people, adults and healthcare providers.

Integrating key messages in reproductive health, HIV and youth-related programmes As mentioned earlier, most programmes relating to sexual and reproductive health or even youth implicitly assume that sexual relations among youths are always consensual, and advocate such measures as condom or contraceptive use, single-partner relations or abstinence which essentially assume that individuals exercise choice in these matters. Several chapters in this volume have described the close association between early non-consensual sexual experiences and STI, subsequent consensual risky sexual behaviours and adverse mental health consequences. Programmes urgently need to recognize the extent to which non-consensual sexual relations exist and deny victims the ability to exercise choice. Programme messages must promote safe and wanted sex on the one hand, and provide information about where to go and what to do in case of experiences of non-consensual sex on the other. Services must be put in place that provide post-rape counselling and care, emergency contraception and links to the police and legal systems. Programmes must ensure the delivery of caring and non-threatening services to youths – both those seeking sexual health information in general and those presenting with a non-consensual sexual experience in particular.

Research recommendations

Research has also overlooked the issue of non-consensual sex among young people. What is known comes from studies addressing young people's sexual and reproductive behaviours or those addressing gender-based violence; as the focus of these studies has been on consensual partnerships and intimate partner violence respectively, however, they have not successfully addressed the range of non-consensual sexual experiences that young people may face, the ways in which they define non-consensual sex or the kinds of partnerships in which they have these experiences. Research, moreover, has tended to be limited in scope, consisting largely of case studies and disproportionately focused on certain settings, notably South Africa. Although the research presented in this volume has significantly advanced what we know about the non-consensual sexual experiences of young people, authors have noted a number of limitations of available evidence and have outlined an ambitious research agenda and recommendations for approaches to research.

Definitions and measures of the continuum of non-consensual sexual behaviours Chapters in this volume have noted the lack of a uniform definition of non-consensual sexual experiences of young people. They have also acknowledged the range of behaviours that constitute non-consensual sex, including unwanted touch, use of deception and threats to obtain sex, and sex in exchange for material transfers. They have pointed out that young people and researchers may conceptualize non-consensual sex differently, and that young people themselves may perceive an incident as consensual or non-consensual depending on the context in which they find themselves when the question is posed. What is very clear is that neither researchers nor youths themselves would confine their definitions of non-consensual sexual experiences to violent rape alone. A wider definition of non-consensual sexual experiences needs to be included in studies with adequate clarity so as to enable the development of appropriate programmatic and policy responses. Methodologies need to be evolved and questions framed that capture the heterogeneity of experiences and yet elicit responses that enable a standard and consistent interpretation. These methodologies and approaches should offer complete confidentiality to the respondent; and formats need to be developed that both provide this level of confidentiality and are suitable for poorly educated or semi-literate populations.

Findings have suggested that young people may under- or, less frequently, over-report a non-consensual sexual experience, depending on the circumstances in which it occurred and the circumstances of the relationship at the time of investigation. For example, young females may under-report any sexual activity, including non-consensual sex, because of the huge stigma that disclosure would attract; at the same time, they may over-report incidents of non-consensual sex in order to cover a consensual experience. Young males may be more likely to report a non-consensual sexual incident as consensual if the perpetrator was female rather than male. And young females may be more likely to overlook the coercive nature of sex with a partner if the relationship is ongoing than if it had been discontinued. Questions need to be framed, therefore, that attempt to capture the context in which the incident occurred as well as construct the sequence of events that may have preceded and followed it.

Context of non-consensual sexual relations and initiation among young females

Young females – unmarried, in union and married – continue to bear the brunt of non-consensual sex. Findings reported in this volume point to a range of perpetrators – partners and husbands, peers, fathers and brothers, trusted adult gatekeepers, and so on; homes, schools and health facilities are not necessarily safe places. Evidence thus far comes from small and in-depth case studies; large surveys of youth have focused for the most part on consensual sexual behaviours and have included at best one or two questions on non-consensual sexual experiences. Studies are needed that explore the continuum of non-consensual sexual behaviours experienced by young females in different cultural settings; which reveal not only prevalence but also information on the context in which the act occurred, including the sequence of events, motives expressed for the coercive act, help sought, individual and community reactions, and health and social consequences.

Research is especially lacking on the patterns and dynamics of forced sex within marriage in settings where early and/or forced marriages are common. Given the indications that forced sex within marriage among young women is quite widespread and opportunities for recourse limited, research is required that explores the factors that place young married women at risk of or protect them from such experiences.

Young males as victims and perpetrators Little is known about the situation of young males as victims and even less about young males as perpetrators of non-consensual sex. A number of chapters in this volume have shed light on both types of experiences but argue that far more research attention is required to understand the experiences and perceptions of young males as victims and perpetrators. For example, we note that in several studies young males report being coerced by their female peers or girlfriends; how this differs from the situation of young female victims and how young males distinguish between experiences of non-consensual sex perpetrated by a female as compared to a male need far more exploration. There is a suggestion that the latter is perceived far less seriously than the former, but research is needed that investigates the experiences of young male victims and the ambiguity in their responses depending on the context of the non-consensual incident.

Information on young males as perpetrators is even more rare, and what we know comes largely from the perspectives of female victims. In this volume, chapters have begun to break this silence: they have described young males' sense of entitlement to sex, particularly if material transfers have been made, about community norms that condone non-consensual sex, and, more specifically, the experiences of young male perpetrators, both singly and in situations of gang rape. Research is needed that investigates these experiences, the factors underlying the perpetration of non-consensual sex and the consequences if any in terms of police action, community reaction or regret or remorse at the individual level.

Gender norms and double standards Several studies have explored in depth the norms endorsed by young people with regard to sexual relations and the circumstances in which non-consensual sex is seen to be acceptable. Chapters in this volume have highlighted how notions of masculinity and male entitlement to sex, and attitudes that blame victims for provoking the coercive incident, are commonly espoused to justify the perpetration of non-consensual sex. At the same time, it is evident that significant numbers of young people do espouse egalitarian gender norms. Research is needed that probes gender norms, double standards and notions of masculinity held by youth in different settings. Of particular importance is research that explores the attitudes held by positive deviants, i.e. those who believe in egalitarian norms, display alternative notions of masculinity and are better aware of their rights

Power in sexual relationships Several chapters in this volume have noted that unequal power relationships are a key factor underlying non-consensual sex.

While age-based unequal power relationships have resulted in non-consensual sexual actions perpetrated on young girls and boys, gender-based power differentials clearly underlie much of the non-consensual sex perpetrated on young females. Research is needed that focuses on issues of power in young people's relationships: how do young females and males perceive their roles in general as well as within relationships? What are the different communication, negotiation and assertiveness skills that females and males display in navigating wanted outcomes, both in general and in terms of sexual and reproductive matters? Is there a link between the use of these skills and the exercise of sexual and reproductive rights, notably protection from non-consensual sex? What are the characteristics of young females and males who report egalitarian partnerships?

How safe is the home? In exploring factors underlying young people's vulnerability to non-consensual sexual encounters, studies have pointed to the role of the family in several contexts. For one, incidents of non-consensual sex among young people do take place within the extended family and numerous studies have identified fathers, brothers and other male relatives as perpetrators. As we have seen, there is often a lack of communication with parents on sexual matters and a perceived lack of parental support in the case of a non-consensual sexual experience. Parental support to married daughters who suffer non-consensual sex is also shown to be limited. And indeed, at least one study has noted that a supportive parental environment can powerfully diminish the deleterious mental health and social outcomes of a non-consensual sexual experience. Studies are needed that assess the barriers to supportive parent–adolescent relationships, and explore the links between community-level acceptance of non-consensual sex among youths and parental attitudes and reactions to such experiences. Also needed are studies that explore parents' perceptions of and attitudes to the socialization of their daughters and sons, and to premarital sexual partnerships of daughters and sons. Also of interest is research that sheds light on the difficulties parents face in communicating with their children on sexual matters, and the kinds of reactions or actions made or taken by parents in response to reports of non-consensual sex suffered by their daughters or sons.

How safe is the school? Studies have also noted that the school may not protect young people from non-consensual sex. Evidence, largely gathered from settings in sub-Saharan Africa, suggests that teachers themselves are observed to force sex on students, compel students to engage in sex in exchange for grades, and turn a blind eye to sexual harassment of students by other students. Evidence from parts of South Asia notes that fears of sexual abuse within and on the way to school are frequently cited as reasons for school discontinuation among girls. Research is needed in diverse regional settings that explores these different experiences of school-going girls and boys. Also of interest are documentations and evaluations of ongoing programmes for students (for example, sexuality or life skills education, leadership training, teacher training) and the extent to which participation in these programmes succeeds in making the school a safer place.

Help-seeking behaviours The available evidence suggests that by and large young people who experience non-consensual sex – whether verbal intimidation, unwanted touch or rape – perceive few help-seeking options in practice. Most stay silent and do not seek help, whether from family, friends, healthcare providers or the police. Research is needed that explores young people's – both young females' and young males' – awareness of available service options, to whom young victims turn for counsel, whether a sequence of help-seeking options is pursued, the quality of available counselling or services, and the extent to which they rate their help-seeking experiences positively. Young people's perceptions and accounts of the role of schools, health facilities, police, families and communities in responding to victims of non-consensual sex also need to be investigated. Studies have suggested that help-seeking options for young female and male victims may differ, and more research is needed that traces the different pathways taken by young males and females in coping with and managing the consequences of non-consensual experiences.

Causality between non-consensual sex and health outcomes Most studies that present evidence of a link between non-consensual sexual experiences and adverse physical or mental health outcomes are based on cross-sectional data that cannot unambiguously determine causality. What is needed is prospective data (for example, those collected in surveillance exercises) that might link a non-consensual sexual experience at one round with health outcomes at subsequent rounds; also needed is further qualitative and quantitative research that can better describe the pathways through which non-consensual sex and adverse health outcomes are associated.

Evidence of promising practices Chapters in this volume have described a number of interventions – life skills programmes, school system-level activities and health sector modifications, for example – that have promise in terms of enhancing young people's negotiation skills or changing provider attitudes. Yet, for the most part, assessments of ongoing programmes are rare and most are not based on sound methodologies. What is needed is rigorously defined quasi-experimental studies that clearly describe programmes that are effective and, equally important, those that do not have promise. As far as possible, these studies should include both quantitative and qualitative methodologies. Findings are urgently needed both for advocacy purposes and to inform the design and scaling up of interventions.

Methodologies and ethical issues Research on the non-consensual sexual experiences of young people is difficult for many reasons. It is an extremely sensitive subject and young people may not wish to disclose their experiences, resulting in severe under-reporting of a relatively common event. Methodologies need to be refined that enable confidentiality and can be employed for uneducated as well as educated respondents, which enable rapport between the research team and the respondent, and which employ non-threatening but acceptable ways of posing questions on non-consensual sexual experiences.

Ethical practices are also of particular relevance here: how do researchers minimize potential anxiety among respondents? How do they ensure appropriate referral mechanisms and that young respondents will avail themselves of these? How should researchers handle issues relating to parental consent? How do researchers balance the promise of confidentiality with the need to report sexual abuse of minors to health facilities or counselling centres? And what measures are necessary to support the interviewer to whom young people may report traumatic experiences? It would be useful to document best as well as promising practices in conducting such research along with examples of lessons learned and the reality of field conditions.

Conclusions

Evidence presented in this volume has convincingly dispelled the myth that sexual relations among adolescents and youths are largely wanted. Indeed, it points out that not only do significant percentages of young females and to a lesser extent males experience forms of non-consensual sex, but also that these experiences remain poorly understood in research and poorly addressed in programmes for youth and sexual and reproductive health in developing countries. Findings highlight the fact that non-consensual sexual experiences may be a key factor underlying the compromised sexual and reproductive health of, and the spread of HIV experienced by, young people in developing countries. Design of evidence-based interventions that reduce young people's vulnerability to non-consensual sex is urgently needed and requires a concerted and multisectoral response. Interventions are clearly both long- and short-term. Some, such as changing prevailing gender norms at the level of young people, families and communities more generally, for example, require sustained and long-term input. Others, such as orienting and sensitizing providers and teachers and making appropriate adjustments at the health service and school levels, for example, can be achieved in the shorter term. This volume offers a detailed but ambitious programme and research agenda to break the silence on this critical infringement of young people's rights.

Notes on contributors

Ashwini Ailawadi, BA, is the co-founder of RAHI Foundation, New Delhi, and is currently in charge of its social communications and programming divisions. He is a trainer, writer and counsellor, focusing largely on substance abuse. He has a background in journalism and has worked extensively at the community level with alcoholics and their families. He has edited *The House I Grew Up In*, a collection of personal testimonies of women survivors of incest.

Ademola J. Ajuwon, MPH, PhD, is a Senior Lecturer at the Department of Health Promotion and Education, College of Medicine, University of Ibadan, Nigeria. His areas of research interest are adolescent reproductive health, gender-based violence, HIV/AIDS prevention and research ethics. He has participated in many local and international training programmes, including the Visiting Scholar Program of the Center for AIDS Prevention Studies, University of California, San Francisco, and the African Bioethics Training Fellowship of the Johns Hopkins School of Public Health, Baltimore, USA.

Gracy Andrew, MA, is a clinical psychologist and the Chairperson of Sangath, an NGO based in Goa, India, where she has been working since its inception. She also heads Sangath's Adolescent and Family Programme and has been involved in several research projects. Her interests lie in the field of adolescent health and she has conducted several training programmes in qualitative research in Goa and at the Institute of Mental Health, Singapore. She has also co-authored several publications including a report on adolescent health needs and a manual on counselling in settings in which facilities are not available.

Kritaya Archavanitkul, PhD, is an Associate Professor at the Institute for Population and Social Research, Mahidol University, Thailand. She has been actively involved in the women's movement in Thailand for the past two decades. She has co-authored *Sexuality and Body Politics in the Thai Women's Movement* (in Thai, and a short version in English) with Kanokwan Tharawan. Her main areas of interest are women's reproductive rights and undocumented migration in Thailand.

Ian Askew, PhD, is Senior Programme Associate and Council Representative, Population Council, Nairobi. He is also the Regional Associate Director for the Population Council's Frontiers in Reproductive Health Programme, which supports operations research to strengthen reproductive health services globally. He has published widely on a range of reproductive health issues including adolescent reproductive health, female genital cutting, community-based services, quality of care and service integration.

Luke Samuel Bearup is a sociologist and community development practitioner, involved in several studies on youth gangs, adolescent and sexual reproductive health and gender-based violence. In addition to supervising several studies, he has published a major work entitled *Paupers and Princelings: Youth Attitudes towards Drugs, Sex, Violence and Youth Gangs*. He has spent the past three years researching youth issues, and most recently working with CARE International on a peer education programme for young males, Playing Safe, to promote safer sexual behaviour and reduce violence against women.

Sarah Bott, MA, MPH, is a freelance consultant based in Los Angeles, California. Previously she was a Technical Officer at the World Health Organization and an Evaluation Officer at the International Planned Parenthood Federation, New York. Her work has involved research and evaluation of international sexual and reproductive health matters, with a particular focus on adolescent reproductive health and violence against women. She has written and edited a number of publications, including *Towards Adulthood: Exploring the Sexual and Reproductive Health of Adolescents in South Asia* (co-edited with S. Jejeebhoy, I. Shah and C. Puri) and *Improving the Health Sector Response to Gender-based Violence: A Resource Manual for Health Care Professionals in Developing Countries* (co-authored with A. Guedes, M. C. Claramunt and A. Guezmes).

Carlos F. Cáceres, MD, PhD, is a Professor of Public Health at Cayetano Heredia University, Lima, Peru, where he coordinates a masters programme in Gender, Sexuality and Reproductive Health and a project on Sexualities, Health and Human Rights in Latin America. A physician and epidemiologist, he has been involved in epidemiological and social science research on sexual health, HIV/AIDS and sexuality for the past fifteen years. He has also focused on social policy and the interconnections between research and practice. He has co-edited *AIDS and Sex between Men in Latin America: Vulnerabilities, Strengths and Proposed Actions* (with M. Pecheny and V. Terto), *La Salud como derecho ciudadaña* (with M. Cueto, M. Ramos and S. Vallenas) and *Ciudadana Sexual en América Latina: abriendo el debate* (with T. Frasca, M. Pecheny and V. Terto).

Jane Chege, PhD, is the Africa Regional HIV/AIDS Monitoring, Evaluation, and Research Advisor for World Vision International, providing leadership in monitoring, evaluation, and research in 25 African countries. At the time of this study she was a Programme Associate for the Population Council's Frontiers in Reproductive Health Programme, Johannesburg. Her work focuses on the integration of services for family planning and STIs, adolescent reproductive health, the behavioural and cultural context of HIV/AIDS, maternal health, gender-based violence and female genital mutilation. Additional interests include gender relations, male involvement in reproductive health/HIV and social science research methodology. Prior to joining the Council, she worked for Kenyatta University, Nairobi, and the Teachers' Service Commission. She has written and lectured widely and is a founder member of Women Educational Researchers of Kenya (WERK), an organization committed to building the research capacity of young people and conducting research on the role of women in history.

Waranuch Chinvarasopak, MA, Senior Programme Officer, PATH Mekong, has thirteen years' experience working on sexual and reproductive health and HIV/AIDS in the Mekong region. Her strengths include the design, management and implementation of capacity-building programmes on sexuality education, adolescent health, behaviour change communication and reproductive health.

Mary C. Ellsberg, PhD, is a senior adviser on Gender, Violence, and Human Rights at PATH, based in Washington, DC. She is an epidemiologist with extensive international research and programme experience in gender and development, with an emphasis on gender equity, domestic violence and sexual and reproductive health. She currently serves as an adviser to the World Health Organization for the design and implementation of a multi-country study on domestic violence and women's health. She has also published a number of articles on the prevalence of domestic violence and its impact on the health of women and children in Nicaragua, Ethiopia and Indonesia, as well as ethical and methodological aspects of research on violence.

Alan J. Flisher, MSc, MB, ChB, MMed, MPhil, PhD, FCPsych (SA), DCH, is a subspecialist in child and adolescent psychiatry. He is currently Professor of Psychiatry and Mental Health at the University of Cape Town (UCT), Director of the Adolescent Health Research Institute at UCT, head of the Division of Child and Adolescent Psychiatry at UCT and Red Cross War Memorial Children's Hospital, Cape Town, and Honorary Senior Research Fellow at the Health Systems Research Unit at the Medical Research Council, Cape Town, and has held visiting appointments at Columbia University, New York, and the University of Oslo. His principal research interests are adolescent health and mental health services. He has authored over one hundred scientific papers and book chapters. He has recently completed a module for the World Health Organization on the development of policies, plans and programmes in child and adolescent mental health.

Ron Gray, MD, is the Robertson Professor of Reproductive Epidemiology at the Johns Hopkins University, School of Public Health, Baltimore. He has conducted several international studies, and for the past fifteen years has been co-principal investigator of the Rakai Programme in Uganda. His areas of research include HIV and STD control, maternal and child health, family planning, cervical cancer screening, determinants of HIV/STD risk, cohort studies and randomized control trials. He has published widely.

Alessandra C. Guedes, MA, MSc, is a freelance consultant based in Brasília. Previously she was a Senior Program Officer at the International Planned Parenthood Federation, Western Hemisphere Region, New York. She has worked for several years in cutting-edge reproductive health issues that are at the nexus of reproductive health and human rights, including adolescent reproductive health, safe abortion, gender-based violence and emergency contraception. She has authored a number of publications, including *Improving the Health Sector Response to Gender-based Violence: A Resource Manual for Health Care Professionals in Developing Countries* (co-authored with S. Bott, M. C. Claramunt and A. Guezmes).

Philip Guest, PhD, Senior Programme Associate and Country Director of the Population Council, Bangkok, coordinates a range of programme research activities dealing with reproductive health, operations research, expansion of contraceptive choice, gender and development research, migration, and institutional strengthening in Thailand, Cambodia, China, Mongolia, Myanmar and the Lao PDR. Over the past five years he has been involved in operations research in HIV/AIDS prevention for migrant workers in Vietnam and private sector involvement in HIV/AIDS programmes in Thailand. He has also undertaken research on marriage patterns in South-East Asia and the relationship between migration and health.

Ana Guezmes, MPH, MD, is a researcher, activist and lecturer on gender, health sector reform and violence against women, and consults for international organizations such as the World Health Organization, UNFPA, PAHO, DFID and the Spanish Cooperation. Currently she is the coordinator of the Observatory of the Right to Health of the Consortium of Economic and Social Research (CIES), a member of the coordinating committee of the gender studies programme at the Universidad Nacional Mayor de San Marcos, Lima, and an associate of the Centre for Peruvian Women, Flora Tristan, Lima. She has authored and edited several publications on violence against women, including *Sexual and Physical Violence against Women in Peru: The WHO Multi-country Study on Domestic Violence and Women's Health* (co-authored with N. Palomino and M. Ramos).

Anuja Gupta, BEd, founder and Executive Director of RAHI Foundation, New Delhi, is a trainer, educator and counsellor in the area of incest/child sexual abuse. Her work involves individual and group counselling with adult women survivors. She lectures and trains on the subject at universities, NGOs and in other forums. She has published *Voices from the Silent Zone*, a research report on incest/child sexual abuse in India. She is currently an Ashoka Fellow and was a fellow of the MacArthur Foundation's leadership development programme in India.

Wassana Im-em, PhD, is an assistant professor at the Institute for Population and Social Research, Mahidol University, Thailand. As a demographer, she has been involved in social science research on various aspects of sexual and reproductive health. Her substantive areas of work have been issues related to HIV/AIDS, gender and sexuality, domestic violence and programme monitoring and evaluation. Her work includes studies on the impact of AIDS on the elderly in Thailand (co-researched with J. Knodel, M. van Landingham and C. Saengtienchai), and an exploration of gender and pleasure in Thailand (co-researched with T. Hull).

Indira Jaising is the founder secretary of the Lawyers Collective, an organization of lawyers and law students. She is currently director of its Women's Rights Initiative, which focuses on the elimination of violence against women and is engaged in drafting a civil law on domestic violence. She was the first woman to be designated a Senior Advocate by the High Court of Bombay in 1986. As founder-editor of *The Lawyers*, a journal published by Law Cooperative, she has attempted to spread awareness of legal rights among women, children and the working classes. She has argued several cases relating to discrimination against women, including equal inheritance rights and sexual harassment of women. She also successfully challenged the discriminatory provisions of the Indian Divorce Act in the High Court of Kerala. She has represented the country at several national and international conferences on women. She has been a fellow at the Institute of Advanced Legal Studies, London, and a visiting scholar at Columbia University, New York. She has been awarded the prestigious Padma Shri for her contribution to public affairs as well as the Rotary Manav Seva Award.

Shireen J. Jejeebhoy, PhD, Senior Programme Associate of the Population Council, New Delhi, is a demographer involved in social science research on various aspects of sexual and reproductive health. Earlier, she was Scientist, Special Programme of Research, Development and Research Training in Human Reproduction, Department of Reproductive Health and Research, World Health Organization, Geneva. Her particular areas of focus have been gender issues and adolescent sexual and reproductive health and development. Her previous work includes *Looking Back, Looking Forward: A Profile of Sexual and Reproductive Health in India* (as editor and contributor); *Towards Adulthood: Exploring the Sexual and Reproductive Health of Adolescents in South Asia* (co-edited with S. Bott, I. Shah and C. Puri); *Research Approaches to the Study of Reproductive Tract Infections and Other Gynaecological Morbidities* (co-edited with M. Koenig and C. Elias); *Women's Reproductive Health in India* (co-edited with R. Ramasubban); and *Women's Education, Autonomy, and Reproductive Behaviour: Experiences from Developing Countries*.

Rachel Jewkes, MBBS, MD, director of the Medical Research Council's Gender and Health Research Unit, Pretoria, is a public health physician involved in research on various aspects of gender-based violence and its intersection with sexual and reproductive health and HIV. She has undertaken both ethnographic and epidemiological research on this issue in South Africa and has to her name over a hundred publications on this and other related research. Her previous work has included community-based research on the prevalence, patterns and risk factors of intimate partner violence, the sociocultural context of child sexual abuse and sexual violence among youths, and the epidemiology of rape and coerced sex, and research on the relationships between gender-based violence, gender inequality and HIV.

Churnrurtai Kanchanachitra, PhD, Associate Professor, Institute for Population and Social Research, Mahidol University, Thailand, is a sociologist involved in research on various aspects of health. Her areas of work include trade and health, HIV/AIDS, gender, poverty, domestic violence and communicating population and health research to policy-makers. Her previous work includes *Women's Health and Life Experience*, a multi-country study supported by the World Health Organization (co-authored with K. Archavanitkul and W. Im-em), *Structural Poverty, Reducing Girls' Vulnerability to HIV/AIDS: The Thai Approach*, and *Trade in Health Service* (co-authored with W. Teokul, V. Tangchareonsathien and C. Patchanee).

Michael A. Koenig, PhD, is an associate professor in the Department of Population and Family Health Sciences at the Johns Hopkins School of Public Health, Baltimore. His areas of research focus include issues related to family planning and reproductive health, unintended pregnancy and domestic violence in developing countries. His previous work includes *Research Approaches to the Study of Reproductive Tract Infections and Other Gynaecological Morbidities* (co-edited with S. Jejeebhoy and C. Elias), *Quality of Care within the India Family Welfare Program* (co-edited with M. E. Khan), and a current volume in preparation entitled *Reproductive Health in India: New Evidence* (co-edited with S. Jejeebhoy, J. Cleland and B. Ganatra).

Nancy Luke, PhD, is Assistant Professor (Research) in the Population Studies and Training Center at Brown University, Providence, Rhode Island, and a research fellow at the Harvard Center for Population and Development Studies, Cambridge, Massachusetts. Her research focuses on the impact of social organization on health and well-being, particularly among women in developing countries. Her current work examines how community institutions, such as marriage, caste and economic exchange, affect individual and couple behaviour, including sexual relations in Kenya and intimate partner violence in India and Vietnam.

Tom Lutalo, MSc (Medical Statistics), is a principal investigator in charge of data management for the Rakai Health Sciences Programme, Uganda Virus Research Institute, Entebbe. His main area of interest is reproductive health and domestic violence and his work focuses on following a community-based cohort under the Rakai Health Sciences Programme in south-west Uganda. He was earlier in charge of the Gates Institute-funded reproductive health programme that also focused on following this cohort.

Cicely Marston, PhD, is a Lecturer in Social Science in the Department of Public Health and Policy at the London School of Hygiene and Tropical Medicine. Her research has focused on sexual and reproductive health and behaviour, and takes an interdisciplinary, multi-method approach.

Judith Mirsky, BA, MSc, is a social scientist involved in research on sexual and reproductive health at St Bartholomew's School of Midwifery, City University, and the London School of Hygiene and Tropical Medicine. She formerly worked with Oxfam and Save the Children, and was the founding director of the Panos Institute Reproductive Health and Gender Programme. Her work includes *Beyond Victims and Villains: Addressing Sexual Violence in the Education Sector*; *Birth Rights: New Approaches to Safe Motherhood*; *No Paradise Yet: The World's Women Face the New Century* (co-edited with M. Radlett) and *Private Decisions, Public Debates: Women, Reproduction and Population* (co-edited with M. Radlett).

Fred Nalugoda, MA, is a co-investigator of the Rakai Health Sciences Progamme and Director of Field Activities, based at Kalisizo, Rakai, Uganda. His previous research work focused on HIV infection in households and families, and the role of domestic violence and coercive sex in the spread of HIV/AIDS. He supervised the STD Control for HIV Prevention study (1994–98), and the community Opinion Leadership (OL) Intervention trial for HIV prevention as part of the Rakai Programme project. His work currently focuses on the effect of anti-retrovirals on the community; marriage, violence and the risk of acquiring HIV infection; and issues related to the cost-effectiveness of research studies. In addition he oversees fieldwork for the Socio Ethnographic Research on Networks (SOCERNET), a Rakai Programme study.

Charles Ngwena, L, LM, Professor of Law at the Department of Constitutional Law, Faculty of Law, University of the Free State, South Africa, has taught, researched and published widely on issues at the intersection between human rights, ethics and healthcare, including HIV/AIDS and reproductive and sexual health. He is on the editorial board of Medical Law International, section editor of *Developing World Bioethics* and chief editor of the *Journal for Juridical Science*. He is co-editor of *Employment Equity Law* (with J. L. Pretorius and M. E. Klink) and has published extensively.

Carolyne Njue is currently completing her doctoral degree on adolescent reproductive health; at the time of this study she was a program officer with the Frontiers in Reproductive Health Programme, Population Council, Nairobi. Carolyne is a medical anthropologist involved in social science research in the field of population and reproductive health. Her particular areas of focus include behavioural and cultural aspects of adolescent reproductive health, HIV/AIDS, female genital cutting, sexuality and gender. Prior to joining the Council, she held research assignments with the Institute of Tropical Medicine (ITM/Antwerp, Kisumu), Centers for Disease Control and Prevention (CDC/KEMRI, Kisumu), Institut de Recherche pour le Développement (IRD, Nairobi) and the French Institute for Research in Africa (IFRA, Nairobi). Her publications include journal articles and technical reports on adolescent reproductive health and HIV/AIDS.

Vikram Patel, PhD, MRCPsych, is a reader in International Mental Health at the London School of Hygiene and Tropical Medicine. He works on service development, advocacy and research at the interface of mental health and other public health priorities, such as child development, reproductive health, adolescent health and STIs. He is the founder of several NGOs (notably Sangath) in Goa, India, and has authored two books, *Where There Is No Psychiatrist* and *Meeting Mental Health Needs in Developing Countries*. He has actively collaborated with researchers in Asia, Africa and Latin America and is engaged in capacity-building programmes for mental health research in developing countries.

Patchara Rumakom, PhD, Strategic Information Specialist (SIS), works at USAID, Regional Development Mission, Asia, based in Bangkok. She has more than ten years of field experience in social science research, targeted/operations research as well as monitoring and evaluation (M&E), particularly on HIV/AIDS in Thailand and other Asian countries. From 1997 to 2003 she worked with the Horizons Project of the Population Council.

K. G. Santhya, PhD, is Senior Programme Officer at the Population Council, New Delhi. Her recent work has focused on designing and testing interventions for married adolescents. She has also worked in other areas, including women's reproductive health and ageing. She has published on a variety of topics including STIs/HIV, abortion, family planning, adolescent reproductive health and couple communication.

Iqbal H. Shah, PhD, currently Team Coordinator for Preventing Unsafe Abortion at the Special Programme of Research, Development and Research Training in Human Reproduction, Department of Reproductive Health and Research, World Health Organization, Geneva, is also responsible for coordinating the department's activities in social science and operations research in reproductive health, including a major research initiative on adolescent sexual and reproductive health. He has to his name a number of publications on issues related to sexual and reproductive health.

Jiraporn Sontanakanit, BSc, works as assistant director of the Education Quality Assurance Department, Faculty of Science and Technology, Rajabhat University,

Rajanagarindra, Chachoengsao Province, Thailand. She was responsible for field management and data collection for a Population Council-assisted school-based project from 1999 to 2003.

Tong Soprach, BA, Project Officer, CARE International, Cambodia, is involved in a sexual health project for young males and is now a recognized public figure advocating against non-consensual sex among young males. His work includes research, training and advocacy, and he has been associated with social research projects and publications on gender and development in Cambodia. He earlier worked as a member of the research unit at the Centre for Population Studies, Phnom Penh, contributing to the analysis of the 1998 census data.

Shyam Thapa, PhD, is a senior scientist with Family Health International (FHI), Virginia. He coordinates and oversees monitoring and evaluation for the FHI-led YouthNet project, which focuses on improving reproductive health and preventing HIV/AIDS among young people in developing countries. He provides technical assistance to YouthNet-supported projects in several countries. He has over twenty years' experience in policy and programme development, knowledge/skills transfer, research and evaluation of youth, maternal and child health, family planning and HIV/AIDS programmes. He has served as technical adviser to the government of Nepal, working with the ministries of health, population and environment, the National Planning Commission and USAID, and as a consultant to other governments, international agencies and NGOs. He has published numerous articles, contributed chapters to books, co-authored monographs, served as co-guest editor of special issues of journals (*Journal of Biosocial Science*, *Contributions to Nepalese Studies*, *Asia-Pacific Population Journal*). He is also an Adjunct Fellow with the Population and Health Studies Program of the East-West Center, Honolulu.

John W. Townsend, PhD, is a Senior Program Associate with the International Programs Division and director of the Frontiers in Reproductive Health Program (FRONTIERS), Population Council, Washington, DC, responsible for the development and implementation of a strategy to promote better reproductive health and family planning programmes worldwide through operations research. He previously served as the Council's regional director for Latin America and the Caribbean in Mexico, the country director for Colombia, and director of the operations research programmes in both Latin America and the Caribbean as well as Asia and the Near East. Before joining the Council, he served for eight years with the Institute of Nutrition for Central America and Panama, in Guatemala. He has published extensively.

Watit Utamarat was, until his untimely death, a lecturer and head of the research unit, Rajabhat University Rajanagarindra and a PhD candidate at the University of Queensland, Australia. His research focused on sexual behaviour among youth, evaluation studies for curriculum development as well as community development studies.

Jennifer Wagman is Staff Associate at Columbia University, Mailman School of Public Health, New York, and head of the Department of Social Sciences at the Rakai Health Sciences Programme in Uganda. She has lived in Uganda since 2000, and has worked on both qualitative and quantitative investigation. Her areas of research focus include issues related to research ethics, HIV and reproductive health, domestic violence and women's reproductive and health rights in Rakai district.

David John Wilkinson, MA, has worked in international health with both government and non-government organizations in Africa, South Asia and South-East Asia. He has conducted social science research and evaluation in various aspects of sexual and reproductive health, largely related to behaviour change communication. Particular areas of focus have been adolescent reproductive health, health-seeking behaviour and gender issues.

Iryna Zablotska, PhD, works primarily in the areas of epidemiology and reproductive health. She has previously worked on reproductive health issues and abortion in the newly independent states; risky sexual behaviours and HIV in developing countries; and the links between alcohol consumption, intimate partner physical violence and sexual coercion, and STI/HIV.

Index